GE STUDIES IN RADICAL HISTORY
ITICS

ors: Thomas Linehan, Brunel University, and
rts, Brunel University

utledge Studies in Radical History and Politics has two areas of
y, this series aims to publish books which focus on the his-
ments of the radical left. 'Movement of the radical left' is
ed in its broadest sense as encompassing those past move-
cal change which operated in the mainstream political arena
al parties, and past movements for change which operated
the mainstream as with millenarian movements, anarchist
an socialist communities, and trade unions. Secondly, this
publish books which focus on more contemporary expres-
l left-wing politics. Recent years have been witness to the
a multitude of new radical movements adept at getting
the public sphere. From those participating in the Arab
Occupy movement, community unionism, social media
endent media outlets, local voluntary organisations cam-
rogressive change, and so on, it seems to be the case that
tworks of radicalism are being constructed in civil society
different public forms.

very much welcomes titles with a British focus, but is not
y particular national context or region. The series will
olars who contribute to this series to draw on perspectives
om other disciplines.
de:

Left Party Family in Western Europe, 1989–2015
tti

amily
kis, Fascism, Espionage and the Cold War

John Green provides a wonderfully rich account of this family of
intellectuals, social activists and fighters against fascism. He also offers
new insights into what it meant to be on the pro-Soviet left during the
twentieth century's 'age of extremes'.

*Matthew Stibbe, Professor of Modern European History,
Sheffield Hallam University, UK*

This captivating account of the Kuczynski is far more than a family
saga. John Green has produced a personalised history of the turbulent
lives of left German Jews from the 1930s till after the Cold War on both
sides of the Iron Curtain. A provoking book that brilliantly challenges
readers to rethink the past.

*Stephan Lieske, Lecturer, English Department,
Humboldt University Berlin, Germany*

This book is the story of a German-Jewish family, the Kuczynskis whose
members, many of whom were remarkable, refused to become victims
of fascist terror, joining the communist movement instead and ded-
icating their lives to fighting fascism and to building a socialist society.
This family biography encapsulates the essence of twentieth century
Europe – war, exile, hope and commitment.

*Mary Davis, Emeritus Professor of Labour History,
Royal Holloway, University of London, UK*

A POLITICAL FA

The Kuczynskis were a Germar
who worked assiduously to cor
during the course of the Second
family of Robert and his wife B
the end of the nineteenth centu
whom became communists and
The parents, and later their childi
comfortable bourgeois heritage an
of privilege and class society. The
was rapidly moving in the opposi

With the rise of German nati
family was confronted with stark (
choices, suffered persecution and
ences shaped their outlook and per
the story of the Kuczynskis for t
and is a fascinating biographical p

John Green is a journalist and au
biographies. His particular area
Germany.

ROUTLED
AND PO

Series edi
John Rob

The series R
interest. Firs
tory of mov
here interpre
ments for rac
as with polit
more outside
groups, utop
series aims t
sions of radi
emergence (
their voices
Spring, the
forums, inde
paigning for
innovative r
that operate
The serie
limited to a
encourage se
and insights
Titles incl

The Radic
Paolo Chiocc

A Political
The Kuczy
John Green

A POLITICAL FAMILY

The Kuczynskis, Fascism, Espionage and the Cold War

John Green

Routledge
Taylor & Francis Group

LONDON AND NEW YORK

First published 2017
by Routledge
2 Park Square, Milton Park, Abingdon, Oxon OX14 4RN

and by Routledge
711 Third Avenue, New York, NY 10017

Routledge is an imprint of the Taylor & Francis Group, an informa business

British Library Cataloguing in Publication Data
A catalogue record for this book is available from the British Library

Library of Congress Cataloging in Publication Data
Library of Congress Cataloging-in-Publication Data
Names: Green, John Christopher, 1941- author.
Title: A political family : the Kuczynskis, fascism, espionage and the Cold War / by John Green.
Description: First edition. | New York, NY : Routledge, [2017] | Series: Routledge studies in radical history and politics | Includes bibliographical references and index.
Identifiers: LCCN 2016047710| ISBN 9781138232310 (hardback) | ISBN 9781138232327 (pbk.) | ISBN 9781315304434 (ebook)
Subjects: LCSH: Kuczynski family. | Jewish families–Germany–Biography. | Holocaust, Jewish (1939-1945)–Germany.
Classification: LCC DS134.4.K83 G74 2017 | DDC 327.470092/3924043–dc23
LC record available at https://lccn.loc.gov/2016047710

ISBN: 978-1-138-23231-0 (hbk)
ISBN: 978-1-138-23232-7 (pbk)
ISBN: 978-1-315-30443-4 (ebk)

Typeset in Bembo
by Taylor & Francis Books

MIX
Paper from
responsible sources
FSC
www.fsc.org   FSC® C013056

Printed and bound in Great Britain by
TJ International Ltd, Padstow, Cornwall

CONTENTS

LIST OF FIGURES

ACKNOWLEDGEMENTS

I wish to express my gratitude to Ludi Simpson for raising the Kuczynski family biography project with me in the first place, and for asking me to write it. He certainly showed a faith in me that I hardly deserved. He has also been extremely helpful in letting me see relevant family documents, making a meticulous criticism of an early draft of the manuscript and putting me in touch with other members of the family.

I am also deeply indebted to Ingrid Kuczynski who kindly agreed to read a later draft of the manuscript. She made useful and perceptive criticisms as well as saving me from including a number of inaccuracies. I am also indebted to other members of the family: Ann Simpson, Neil Taylor, Harriet Loeffler, Jose Nicolson and Mark Long in the UK and Ireland, as well as Thomas Kuczynski, Michael Hamburger and Peter Beurton in Germany. For giving me permission to publish an extract from the unpublished reminiscences of Renate Dorpalen, I am grateful to her son, George Brocksieper. My sincere thanks also go to Anke Spille and her colleagues in the Zentral- und Landesbibliothek Berlin, Diana Weber at the Stadtarchiv Heidelberg, and Judith Meyer at the Universitätsarchiv Heidelberg for readily providing information about Brigitte Kuczynski; to Richard Baxell, Chair of the International Brigades Memorial Trust, for information about Len Beurton's time in

Spain, Matthew Stibbe for permission to quote an extract from his research paper on Jürgen Kuczynski, and to Nicholas Jacobs for his advice on publishers and agents. Thanks are also due to the German Historical Institute, London, for their help in the early stages of my research, to Mark Daniel for reading an early draft and making very helpful comments and to Michal Boncza for his cover design ideas. My deep gratitude also goes to The Society of Authors' Authors' Foundation for awarding me a generous grant to help cover research costs.

I am grateful to my daughters Galina and Franziska for their critical perusal of early drafts, as well as for their encouragement and support and, lastly, but by no means least, to my wife and companion, Bruni de la Motte, for her constant support, critical reading of various drafts and her always apposite, if sometimes acerbic, comments, criticisms and suggestions. And for always being there for me to bounce-off ideas and discuss literary, historical and Germanic issues.

Finally, I would like to thank Craig Fowlie and Richard Skipper at Routledge for their help and support.

This final version of the text, however, is my own and I have to take responsibility for any weaknesses, mistakes or inaccuracies, although I hope there will not be many.

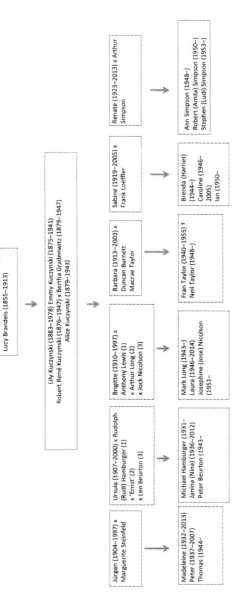

FIGURE 1.1 The Kuczynski family tree

1

INTRODUCTION

Who are the Kuczynskis?

> It is bitter to have to recognise that the imagined world will always be
> better than the one we actually create.
>
> *Ilya Ehrenburg*[1]

The story of the Kuczynski family stands apart from the many other
biographies of German-Jewish families who were caught up in the
turbulence and vicissitudes of the twentieth century. There have been
numerous ones written about the impact of Hitler fascism on Jewish
families and individuals, both novels and biographies; there have been
films, plays and academic studies. The overwhelming majority of these
have been conceived from the point of view of the victims: the discrimination, suffering, displacement and consequent trauma, followed
perhaps by transcendence. Where the Kuczynski family story differs
markedly from such models is that all members of the family, from very
early on, rejected allotted roles as passive extras on the stage of history,
and decided instead to become protagonists in the historical process.
Almost everything they did throughout their lives was dedicated to
changing society and bringing about one with more justice and equality.
In that sense their story as related here runs counter to the mainstream
narratives of Nazi victims.

The first aspect that sets them apart is that they were all active anti-fascists and worked assiduously to combat the rise of Nazism before and during the course of the war. This biographical portrait focuses on the family of Robert and his wife Berta – both born two decades before the end of the nineteenth century – and their six children, five of whom became communists. Jürgen, the eldest, was recruited as a member of the US army during the war and worked alongside the Canadian-born US economist Kenneth Galbraith in the American Strategic Bombing Survey office in London. He also co-operated closely with the Russians, became an economist and statistician of world renown and, after the war, an advisor to East Germany's two leaders. He would become probably the GDR's most celebrated intellectual and a first port of call for any Western journalist looking for unofficial comment from someone close to government. He was a tall and imposing figure with an avuncular disposition but, given his erudition, could appear quite intimidating to lesser mortals.

His sister, Ursula, became one of the most successful secret agents of Soviet military intelligence (GRU), with the codename 'Sonya'. She was active as part of the so-called Red Orchestra counter-intelligence ring and while in Britain became the contact and courier for the atomic spy Klaus Fuchs. Ursula's other four siblings remained in Britain after arriving as refugees in the 1930s; three of them joined the British Communist Party and chose male partners who were also communists.

Ursula's first husband, Rudolf Hamburger, after working as a secret agent for the Russians, spent ten years of his life languishing in the Soviet Union's GULAGs under horrendous conditions, mistakenly accused of being a Western spy, but surviving to return to East Germany in the 1950s where he became a leading architect. All members of the family, during their time in Britain, were kept under continued surveillance by MI5. In the National Archives there are ninety-four large files on the family.

The family history of rebellion, political dissidence and intellectual accomplishment goes back five generations to the eighteenth century. However, it is the twentieth-century generation that encapsulates that aspect most forcefully and lends vibrance to this family saga. This narrative only covers in detail the family of Robert Kuczynski, who was born in 1876. He became a world-renowned demographer, who mixed with Bolshevik leaders as well as leading German revolutionaries and intellectuals of the time, including Albert Einstein who became a close friend. In each generation of the family there have always been members who were forced into political exile because of their rebelliousness and principled attitudes. Members of three generations have experienced terms in prison, labour and concentration camps.

That generation of the Kuczynski family represented in the first instance by Robert and Berta (née Gradenwitz) would reject and rebel against their comfortable bourgeois heritage and devote their lives to the overthrow of privilege and class society. They chose to do this in a Germany that was rapidly moving in the opposite direction. All their children would follow in their footsteps, taking an even more radical stance. Why they chose this route is a fascinating conundrum, and there is no straightforward answer, but in examining their lives I have attempted to offer clues. I have also tried to unravel some of the historical circumstances that have significantly determined individual trajectories. The lives of the Kuczynski family members portrayed here poignantly reflect historical developments in twentieth-century Europe. Overlapping several generations, there were always individual family members who were involved in fighting for a more just society, to defeating fascism and helping build a post-war socialist alternative in East Germany as well as supporting the Communist Party in Britain.

The fact that the family emerges from a long East European Jewish tradition is perhaps also hardly incidental to the trajectories of their subsequent lives and actions. It is not only that they were protagonists in the historical process taking place in several countries or that they attained political and academic prominence or celebrity status, but that they actively engaged with the political and ideological struggles of the era.

Robert would become a leading demographer of his age and pioneered the use of statistics in framing social policy as well as demonstrating the impact of slavery on the development of British colonies. He led campaigns in Germany for better housing, against the powerful Junker class and for peace in Europe. His children – Ursula, Jürgen, Brigitte, Barbara, Sabine and Renate – were exposed to the notions of rebellion and political dissidence early on in life. This is undoubtedly a key to why two of them became world-renowned for delivering highly sensitive information to the Soviet Union during the war. The family's full story has never been told in the English-speaking world, and it can only be properly understood against the background of the politics of the twentieth century.

With the rise of German nationalism and then Hitler fascism, the family was confronted with stark choices and, as a result of making the choices they did, suffered persecution and exile. They lived through and contributed to what Eric Hobsbawm characterised as 'The Age of Extremes'.

The biographer, of course, is always faced with choices in terms of what to select, what is relevant, what best helps explain what happened and why these particular lives took the courses they did. The historian E. H. Carr famously wrote that the status of an event as a historical fact will depend on how it is interpreted by historians, and that the element of interpretation will enter into every fact of history. Choosing which facts to include in a historical narrative, what weight such facts are given and how they are to be interpreted will, in the end, determine how history is written and handed down. These factors are just as relevant when writing about the lives of the Kuczynski family as with any other, broader aspect of history or biography. Here I have made every effort to be scrupulous with the facts and have avoided speculation unless I felt it could aid understanding, but the weighting given to the facts I have chosen to write about and my interpretations of them will differ, often markedly, from those of other writers. That is largely a consequence of my own necessarily subjective understanding of history and of political processes. I hope, though, that this biography will be read as an honest attempt to portray an extraordinary family and that it will be given credence on that basis.

The circumstances that brought about the family's political and social engagement, as well as the historical circumstances that helped determine their life-long commitments are examined. Their motivations are questioned and what they actually achieved – both intellectually and politically – in the context of the struggle against fascism and during the Cold War confrontation, is evaluated.

What is it that makes members of a well-to-do German-Jewish family become committed to social change, to helping the less fortunate and engaging in radical politics during inclement times? There are, of course, rarely, if ever, simple answers to such questions. Why do any of us behave and act as we do? It is, nevertheless, intriguing to try and understand why a whole generation of this family took up the same radical politics as if they were virtually one person. Here, the unique historical circumstances of that period undoubtedly played a central role.

I have attempted to place the pieces of the family's lives into a coherent narrative and also avoid that retrospective 'wisdom' betrayed by a number of historians and writers about this period, who can be patronising about those who threw in their lot with communism, accusing them of not condemning Stalin early enough and of remaining loyal to a discredited ideology. From the luxury of their ivory towers, some writers are only too ready to condemn others who at the time perhaps did allow their idealism and their fears of a fascist Europe to cloud their judgement about Soviet communism.

Anyone who consults the indexes of books dealing with espionage and intelligence work during the twentieth century will invariably come across the name Kuczynski. Many academic papers and books have been written about the family and their involvement in this area, but their lives and achievements represent much more than a link to intelligence work and spying. It is unfortunate that the family is today most widely known in the West for its association with espionage, and emphasis on this aspect has done a disservice to the family's overall achievements and the contribution it has made to our humanistic legacy.

The lives of the Kuczynskis are fascinating for anyone seeking a deeper understanding of the motivations of those who remained active, after the end of the Second World War, at the front, between the opposing forces in the new Cold War. Living in today's Europe does not demand the sort of stark choices, of taking sides, which those living during the 1930s and 1940s faced. At that time, remaining aloof meant abdicating the most basic instincts of human compassion and solidarity.

The Berlin-based Kuczynskis, during the early twentieth century, became a secular Jewish family who threw themselves into the progressive struggles of that time. Several family members became prominent in the business and banking worlds; the new generation would make pioneering contributions in the fields of economics and social statistics. The family felt itself to be thoroughly German, but the turbulence and mayhem of the first half of the twentieth century in Europe – First World War, revolution, inflation, poverty and the rise of fascism – would drive Robert, Berta and their children from their German homeland.

After fleeing Berlin once Hitler had come to power in the 1930s, the family found exile in Britain. Two family members – Ursula and Jürgen – returned to East Germany with their spouses after the war, while the other four sisters married and settled in Britain. Despite their geographical separation, on different sides of the Cold War divide, the family remained largely united and close both on a political as well as on a personal level.

Both the father, Robert, and his son Jürgen, wrote important academic works; the latter was one of the most prolific academics of his generation, authoring over 4,000 books and articles. He completed four volumes of autobiography and a biography of his father. His sister Ursula also wrote her reminiscences, as well as several works of fiction and non-fiction under her pen-name, Ruth Werner. However, most of this literary output has been published in German only, although there have been English translations of Ursula Kuczynski's memoirs (*Sonya's Report*) and a recent biography, *Wall Flower*,[2] by Rita Kuczynski, who was married to Jürgen's son Thomas. The latter is the first quasi-portrait in English of Jürgen's family, albeit an idiosyncratic one.

The family's intriguing development throws a unique light on the history and politics of pre-fascist Germany, the struggle against Hitler and the aftermath of the Second World War. Through the memoirs of Jürgen, who was closely associated with the post-war East German leadership, we are also given a unique insight into how the German Democratic Republic was run; the other siblings provide an equally interesting perspective on post-war life in Britain at the height of the Cold War, through their activities on the ground as British communists. The trajectories of the family members' lives give us new insights into the political upheavals of the period and the struggles between the communist and capitalist worlds.

In writing this biography I am indebted to Jürgen Kuczynski's own memoirs for a substantial amount of information relating to the family, on which I have been able to draw extensively, as well as to his sister

Ursula's reminiscences in *Sonya's Report*, in which she talks about her work as an officer in the Soviet Army's counter-espionage service.

Throughout his life Jürgen kept a detailed diary which provides a unique and contemporaneous insight into the times through which he lived, his own life and that of the extended family. His perceptive understanding of history, culture and politics as well as his wry sense of humour have been invaluable in coming to grips with the narrative of this unusual family. He was, though, a quintessentially rational man, almost monastic in his daily routines, and his memoirs are characterised by being heavily self-centred. He ignored or was largely unaware of emotional factors, being quite parsimonious when dealing with feelings and personal relationships.

When he wrote an epilogue to his own memoirs on the relevance or use of biographies, Jürgen quoted Thomas Carlyle's aphorism that history is the essence of innumerable biographies. He suggests that many (auto)biographies are connected with a need for justification which can lead to conscious or unconscious falsification, and in this sense is very much aware of his own fallible memory. His is a dialectical approach, he maintained, and wrote that his own memoirs are primarily there in order to reveal how he experienced the period through which he lived; he was not writing history, he said, but describing 'the political development of J.K. under the influence of events'. This view is echoed by Ehrenburg, when reflecting on his own experience of that same period.

An early note of warning written around 1947 by Ursula Kuczynski to her brother Jürgen in response to his idea of writing a family history is not exactly an ideal form of encouragement for any would-be biographer, but I decided to see it more as a useful spur than hindrance in my approach:

> Your idea of writing a family history seems completely crazy. But perhaps my views will soften if you can give me some more details. Apart from father and you, we have no one in the family we can boast about. Our grandfather was a rich banker and the other gambled away half his worldly goods. One great-grandfather sold shoe laces from a barrow in Galicia and the other, I suppose, was something of a free-thinker? But perhaps you intend to make it a bit more of a social and historical document?[3]

Each historical epoch is gestated by preceding ones and its genetic makeup laid down in their wombs. In this sense, twentieth-century Germany can only be comprehended by examining the factors that governed its emergence from the nineteenth century.

The latter part of the nineteenth century in Germany was characterised by political instability as well as the country's rapid industrialisation and urbanisation. Heavy industry – especially coal and steel – became an important aspect of manufacturing. These processes led to the creation of a large and powerful class of proletarians, especially in the big cities, that began to challenge traditional social hierarchies and social inequalities. The political expression of this was the associated rise of the Socialist Workers' Party (later known as the Social Democratic Party of Germany or SPD), which was strongly influenced by Marxist ideas, and whose aim was to establish, by peaceful means, a new socialist order through the transformation of existing political and social conditions. During the early part of the twentieth century, in the wake of the calamitous First World War, the Bolshevik Revolution and the attempt to set up Soviets in Germany itself, the country became a volatile cocktail of contradictory forces.

The old Prussian feudal order was crumbling and the burgeoning proletariat was flexing its muscles and demanding social justice. Politically, the traditional nationalist and monarchist forces felt themselves besieged and the left, in the form of a large social democratic party and newly founded Communist Party, was gaining ground.

Artists and intellectuals found themselves involved in a great ferment of ideas and faced challenges that demanded new forms of artistic expression. A clash of class forces and ideologies became unavoidable and those who were at all interested in politics and ideas were obliged to choose sides. The Kuczynskis did too; they chose the side of socialism, later allying themselves with the Communist Party.

The rapid rise of this social democratic movement created fear and panic among the bourgeoisie. In 1878, Bismarck had moved to suppress it by introducing the notorious Anti-Socialist Laws, outlawing the Social Democratic Party (SPD), its assemblies and most of its newspapers. However, when the party was eventually allowed to run candidates, it emerged stronger than ever and by the 1890s it was the largest European socialist party.

Added to this, the always present anti-semitism, often just below the surface, was to erupt in horrendous fashion during the Nazi period of the 1930s and 1940s, and would compound the Kuczynski family's political stance. Like many other German families of Jewish background, its members who grew up in Germany, becoming successful in business, thought of themselves first and foremost as Germans, with Jewish self-identity playing only a minimal role. Although the family had been a secular one for generations, its background was East European Jewish and this heritage was impossible to divest in an increasingly anti-semitic atmosphere.

To understand how a whole generation of this family came to reject their privileged background and commit themselves to socialism, it is instructive to delve back into history for a moment and look at some of the family's antecedents. Wilhelm Kuczynski was born in 1842, and was the first member of the family to move to Berlin from Posen in East Prussia (today *Poznańska* in Poland). He was the son of a merchant, Abraham Kuczynski, and his wife Emilie Cohn. They were among the first of around 3,000 Jews in the district of Posen to receive naturalisation certificates in the wake of the Kaiser's emancipatory edict of 1812.

The family, Jürgen said, can boast 'six generations of intellectuals who have been of the "Left", on the side of the people and of progress, against reaction'.

The first generation to demonstrate such commitment was that of Robert's great-great uncle, Hirschmann Brandeis. Already as a student, he had immersed himself in progressive German philosophy, and become an ardent advocate of Kant's ideas and strong supporter of the enlightenment. It was he, living in Königsberg (today Kaliningrad in Russia) in 1790, who began collecting books which would form the core of the family's famous library, which Robert and then Jürgen would inherit. He was included in every serious encyclopaedia and lexicon of his era, as a famous doctor and medical historian but also Court Counsellor to the Russian Tsar. One of the books contained in his library was a copy of Fichte's *Versuch eine Kritik alle Offenbarung* (An Attempt at a Critique of All Revelation), dated Königsberg 1792. Fichte had to publish it anonymously in order to escape certain opprobrium and persecution.

When Hirschmann Brandeis became seriously ill in 1839 he moved to Paris and began translating Pushkin's *History of the Pugachov Rebellion* into German. While he found fulfilment in translating rebellion, his nephew Samuel Brandeis, grandfather of Robert, became the real rebel. Robert called him the family's first 'white raven', the founder of the family tradition of struggle against reaction and for progress. It was Samuel Brandeis who would also be the greatest political influence on Robert's own son Jürgen. He set the tone of progressive rebellion for all future generations of the family and fought unremittingly against reactionary positions, whether from a Prussian prison or from exile. In 1847 Hirschmann Brandeis provided a vivid picture of his forced exile from Prussia in *Meine Ausweisung aus Preussen* (My Expulsion from Prussia) which was published by Biedermann in Volume 5 of the series *Unsere Gegenwart und Zukunft* (Our Present and Future).

Samuel Brandeis refused to wait until the turbulent year of 1848 in order to become a revolutionary, and was imprisoned by the Prussian state for 'left' political activities already in 1846, and then in 1848 he too was driven into exile to Paris, where, for a few pennies, he bought a copy of the first edition of the *Communist Manifesto* written by two other exiles from the aftermath of the 1848 Revolution – Marx and Engels. It remained in the Kuczynski library until Jürgen's death. After his expulsion from Prussia Samuel Brandeis remained in Paris until he was, ironically, as a nominally Prussian citizen, once again expelled in 1870 at the beginning of the Franco-Prussian War.

Samuel had been a leader of progressive students in Königsberg and fled to France after his imprisonment by the Prussians to escape the tyranny. His grandmother, who was French, moved in the circles of those opposed to the autocracy of Emperor Napoleon III and conspired with prominent German exiles who had fled to France after the collapse of the 1848 Revolution. How far the activities and political views of these ancestors was known to Robert at the time or whether they influenced him in a significant way is difficult to establish, but it seems plausible.

Before his expulsion and while still living in Königsberg, Samuel had been denounced by the prominent editor Gustav Pflugk, with the remark that:

> Student B. is a member of an association, Germania, that holds its meetings in a beer hall in the Polish Prediger Strasse, and whose aim is, through the reading of banned books by its members, to promote a higher political education than would be possible to achieve though a reading of the permitted books ...

Brandeis was president of the association at the time, and was imprisoned before being expelled in 1846 while still a student.

Members of the Germania association read books like Püttmann's *Deutsches Bürgerbuch* which would later be referred to by Engels in a letter to Marx, in which he wrote, 'We will see from Püttmanns *Bürgerbuch* how far we are allowed to go, before we are hounded or arrested.'[4] The formulation of Pflugk's denunciation, writes Jürgen, 'is an exemplary and clear formulation of the anti-democratic and anti-bourgeois character of the Prussian government before the revolution of 1848'.[5] Such banning by the state of the reading of particular books even by bourgeois intellectuals would have more contemporary resonances for later generations, just as the spying on and denunciation of one's peers would.

It was through the family's French connections that Jürgen was introduced to the works of the French utopian socialists alongside the classical works of German socialists. Lucy Brandeis, Samuel's daughter who would become Robert's mother, maintained the family tradition as a progressive thinker. She was born in exile in France, had an excellent education and grew up among French and exiled German intellectuals in Paris. But then, in Jürgen's words, 'for incomprehensible reasons she married Wilhelm Kuczynski, a very average man, but in his specific area, a successful banker', who became very wealthy. He was considered a 'black sheep' of the family, alongside the other 'black sheep', the property developer Adolf Gradenwitz (father of Robert's wife Berta). Those were the ones who did not sit easily on the proud family tree of progressive, left-wing activists.

Lucy Brandeis married Wilhelm in 1873 and in June 1875 their first child, Emmy, was born, followed by Robert in August 1876 and two other daughters, Alice and Lily (Alice and her husband, the gynaecologist Georg Dorpalen, would die in Theresienstadt under the Nazis). Their son Robert became engaged to Berta Gradenwitz in October 1903 and they married on 1 December.[6] She was a lively and intelligent woman, who had learned Latin and Greek at school and was a talented artist. She also had a keen interest in politics and was well informed, which, it can be assumed, was a prerequisite for the marriage she was entering into.

Wealthy Jewish families tended very much to marry within a circle of those from the same ethnicity and a similar class background. The Kuczynskis and Gradenwitzes were no exception, at least until the mid-twentieth century when the mould was very much broken by all of Robert's children.

Robert's father, Wilhelm Kuczynski, was, apart from being a very successful banker, a great believer in charitable activity. He was involved in the *Kinderschutz Verein* (Child Protection Association) and gave generously to other charities, even setting up his own Wilhelm Kuczynski charitable institution. Whether he saw this activity as a means of salving his conscience or did it out of genuine philanthropic motivation is not really relevant here, but this side of his character would have had an impact on the attitudes and outlook of his children.

In Siegmund Kaznelson's collected biographies of Jews in German cultural life (*Biographisches Handbuch zum deutschen Judentum*) Wilhelm was also praised as an 'outstanding member of the board of the Berlin Stock Exchange' of which he became senior president in 1905. He was one of the 'Elders of the Berlin Merchant Federation' and a co-founder of the *Handelshochschule* (College of Business) which represents the beginning of the Kuczynskis' connection with Berlin universities over five generations. In 1938, long after Wilhelm's death, the Kuczynski bank was 'Aryanised' by the Nazis and its Jewish owners ousted.

Wilhelm's son Robert was sent to the French Gymnasium in Berlin where he learned French as well as German. He was apparently an average student, but passed his *Abitur* before going on to university. Despite his relatively privileged background, he would very soon rebel against his father's views and class position in society.

Both the Kuczynski and Gradenwiz families – the antecedents on the paternal and maternal side of the family portrayed here – were bankers and property developers who, in succeeding generations, diversified into textile manufacturing, mechanical engineering, electrical motor production, dental chemistry and other fields. This kind of development was typical of many emancipated, bourgeois Jewish families of the period.

FIGURE 1.2 Portrait of Lucy Kuczynski (née Brandeis) by Ottmar Begas (1905)
Source: Kuczynski family archive.

Paul Kuczynski, the son of banker Louis Kuczynski, came from a side branch of the family on which we focus in the following pages. However, this branch also came from Posen, and made the move to Berlin towards the middle of the nineteenth century. Paul is of interest because he would become a close friend and supporter of Richard Wagner, which is surprising, considering how anti-semitic the latter became. Following his father's wishes, Paul studied economics and jurisprudence, but his chief love was music. His uncle was a violinist in the Royal Opera House orchestra and introduced him to Hans von Bülow, the great conductor and composer, who gave him piano lessons. Through Bülow's then wife, Cosima – Franz Liszt's daughter who would become Wagner's wife – he met Wagner, becoming an ardent admirer. He socialised in both financial and music circles with ease and became a member of Wagner's circle and a patron of the Bayreuth Festival; he was present in 1872 when the foundation stone for the Bayreuth Festival Theatre was laid. He also played a significant role in helping to counter the prevalent anti-Wagner atmosphere within Berlin cultural circles. Paul was, to boot, a competent composer and musician in his own right. He was a representative par excellence of that self perception of many successful German Jews who could be just as proudly nationalist and Teutonic as their non-Jewish compatriots.

Due to the dearth of accurate genealogical records going back far enough, there is a lack of definitive evidence for a relationship between the Paul Kuczynski branch of the family and that of Wilhelm, but I have included him here because his family's common migratory route and involvement in banking would almost certainly have meant that the trajectories of the two branches crossed.[7]

On Berta's side of the family, her uncle, Eduard Gradenwitz, married Rosa Feige, from a well-known Silesian family. Their daughter Else married the textile manufacturer Max Hamburger in 1900. One of Else and Max's three sons, Rudolf, would later marry Robert's daughter, Ursula Kuczynski. The Gradenwitz family was very affluent, but it was also characterised by a mix of commercial and intellectual pursuit. Berta's father Adolph Gradenwitz became a successful property developer and estate agent, and was one of the leading developers of the up-market villa quarter in the suburb of Berlin-Zehlendorf. This area soon became a popular residential area for businessmen, but also for artists and intellectuals.

Robert was of the same generation as Max and Else Hamburger and, after marrying Berta, her cousin Else became known as 'Tante Else' in the Kuczynski household. Else, Berta and Robert had a very amicable relationship and son Jürgen, in his turn, became a close friend of the Hamburger sons Rudolf and Otto.

Robert, in the twentieth century, was the one who would make the first radical break from the family's banking and commercial tradition. He rebelled against his father's banking mentality and his social milieu, deciding instead to enter the world of academia and the struggle for social justice. During the first half of that century he became, alongside Einstein, the only bourgeois German scholar of international repute who allied himself with the working class, and through this association was able to provide working people and society as a whole with a not insignificant service in terms of the advancement of social science. He was an outspoken reformer and political critic who often raised his voice to highlight social problems such as the acute housing or food shortages. He campaigned together with high-profile Social Democrats like Albert Südekum and counted them among his friends who were invited to dinner and became almost part of the family.

The year following Jürgen's birth ushered in Russia's 1905 Revolution, and a wave of mass political and social unrest that spread throughout the Russian Empire. This unrest included workers' strikes, peasant rebellions and military mutinies. It had resonances far beyond Russia's own borders, throughout Europe, and alarmed ruling elites everywhere. In Russia, it led to the establishment of a constitutional monarchy, the setting up of a state Duma and a multi-party political system, culminating in the Bolshevik Revolution of 1917.

Germany was also about to undergo a ferment of political and social change of its own. The November Revolution in 1918, during the end phase of the war, led to the abolition of the monarchy and the establishment of parliamentary democracy. Inspired very much by the Bolshevik Revolution a year earlier and led by the Independent Social Democratic Party (USPD) and the left-wing Spartacist (Marxist) group, it involved soldiers, sailors and workers. In Kiel a revolt in the navy spread rapidly and led to the setting up of Workers and Soldiers

Councils (Soviets) in many big cities, including Munich and Berlin which declared short-lived Soviet republics. The movement also led, on 1 January 1919, to the formation of the German Communist Party (KPD) under the leadership of the Spartacists Rosa Luxemburg and Karl Liebknecht. Only a fortnight later both were to be murdered by right-wing military officers. Surprisingly, though, these cataclysmic events receive hardly a mention in either Robert's or Jürgen's writings, but they must have had a profound impact on the family in terms of developing their ideas and allegiances.

On 10 November 1918 Kaiser Wilhelm II fled to the Netherlands in exile and on the 28th of the same month signed his abdication. Of these momentous events, Hitler wrote later:

> Kaiser Wilhelm II was the first German Kaiser to offer the leaders of Marxism his hand in reconciliation without suspecting that these villains have no honour. While they held the Kaiser's hand in their own, their other hand reached for the dagger – there can be no pact-making with the Jews, but only an either or – that's when I decided to become a politician.[8]

This early pronouncement by Hitler is an ominous pointer to his future career and political ideology and the impact that it would have on the lives of the Kuczynskis, who would be deemed doubly 'culpable' as Jews and communists.

The establishment of the Weimar Republic in 1918, after the unsuccessful revolution of that same year and the writing of a new constitution, ushered in a fifteen-year period of liberal democracy which, however, failed to address the fundamental problems the country was facing, thus helping pave the way for the Nazi takeover in 1933. Robert and Berta were very much involved in that ferment and in the associated political and social struggles.

As historian Ian Kershaw puts it in his book, *To Hell and Back*, Germany during the twentieth century was:

> the pivotal centre of the continent … more crucial than any other country to Europe's destiny. German governments and their foreign policy effectively determined the behaviour and choices, as

well as the lives, or more accurately the deaths, of many of Europe's peoples. At one key juncture after another, its leaders and mobilised people created the conditions to which other countries could only react.[9]

This was the crucible in which the Kuczynski family was forged. Its antecedents emerged during the nineteenth century from a mixture of Eastern, Central European and Jewish cultures, and it established itself firmly in Germany as an integral part of that country's bourgeoisie. Like many others of similar heritage, its members had gradually become secularised and fully integrated into German and then, in exile, into English society, shedding any vestiges of religious belief or Jewish self-identity. Berta and Robert let their nominal membership of Berlin's Jewish religious community lapse in 1920 and 1930 respectively.[10]

Notes

1 Ilya Ehrenburg, *Menschen Jahre Leben. Memoiren*, Volk und Welt, 1990.
2 Rita Kuczynski, *Mauerblume: Ein Leben auf der Grenze*, Claassen 1999; *Wall Flower: A Life on the German Border*, University of Toronto Press, 2015.
3 Ruth Werner, *Sonya's Report*, Chatto & Windus, 1991, p. 284.
4 Karl Marx, *K. Marx und Fr. Engels, Briefwechsel*, Berlin, Band I, 1949, p. 13.
5 Jürgen Kuczynski, *René Kuczynski: Ein fortschrittlicher Wissenschaftler in der ersten Hälfte des 20. Jahrhunhunderts*, Berlin, Aufbau Verlag, 1957, p. 9.
6 Hans Lembke, *Die Schwarzen Schafe bei den Gradenwitz und Kuczynski – zwei Berliner Familien im 19. und 20. Jahrhundert*, Berlin, Trafo Verlagsgruppe, 2008, p. 55.
7 In this connection it is of interest to note that Pedro Pablo Kuczynski, who became president of Peru in 2016, is also, like all the other Kuczynskis mentioned here, descended from a Posen-based Jewish family. His father, Maxime 'Max' Hans, was a pathologist whose family moved from what was then East Prussia to Berlin towards the end of the nineteenth century, and where he later became Professor of Pathology at the city's university. He was forced to flee the Nazis in 1933, and invited to Peru to help set up a public health service there. His son Pedro studied economics and worked for both the World Bank and IMF before becoming prime minister, then president, of Peru. His brother, Miguel Jorge, also an economist, is a fellow of Pembroke College, Cambridge.
   Some years before Jürgen's death Pedro Kuczynski wrote to him suggesting that they were related but Jürgen rejected the suggestion. Perhaps, like Paul Kuczynski, the family was only distantly related.

In the Peruvian newspaper *El País Semanal* of 28 July 2016, the journalist Luis Esteban G. Manrique, in his article, 'Confidencias Audaces: la Gran Familia Kuczynski', gives a portrait of the new president's family. He writes that 'Robert Kuczynski and his three children – Ruth, Brigitte and Jürgen, cousins of Max – where the richest in the German capital and convinced communists'. In this article he also reveals that soon after the end of the First World War, Berlin's Humboldt University sent Max to the Soviet Union to help establish faculties of medicine in Minsk and Omsk … of 'different branches of the family'.

8 Christian Graf von Krockow, *Die Deutschen in Ihrem Jahrhundert 1890–1990*, Rowohlt, 1990.
9 Ian Kershaw, *To Hell and Back: Europe, 1914–1949*, Allen Lane, 2015.
10 Ute Frevert, 'Jewish Hearts and Minds? Feelings of Belonging and Political Choices among East German Intellectuals', *Leo Baeck Institute Year Book*, 2011.

2

ROBERT RENÉ, WORLD PIONEER OF SOCIAL STATISTICS (1876–1933)

Robert René Abraham Kuczynski, born in Berlin on 12 August 1876, would become a radical democrat, and win renown as a pioneering demographer and founder of modern population statistics. He was also a leader of the early twentieth-century campaign for peace and justice in Europe. He completed his *Abitur* at the French Gymnasium in Berlin, then studied economics and law in Freiburg, Strasbourg and Munich under such teachers as Lujo Brentano, Georg Friedrich Knapp and Paul Hensel. He would often spend evenings with Brentano listening to stories about the latter's uncle, Clemens and his aunt, Bettina, who was one of Goethe's close confidantes, as well as anecdotes about other leading personalities of the period. Brentano would have a considerable influence on Robert's thinking and encouraged his humanitarian views. He completed his doctorate under Brentano when only 20 years old in 1897. After a short period as a *voluntär* (what we would today call an 'intern') under Richard Böckh, the Director of Berlin's Statistical Office, he decided, as a 23-year-old, to leave for the United States to work as a research intern in the US Census Office, the world's most significant statistical establishment at the time, and would spend four years in America. After completing this internship he went on to work closely with Colonel Carroll D. Wright in the Central Bureau of

Labor Statistics in Washington, where he would write his second major work on the conditions of labour.

In their book about the conditions of the American working class, Eleanor Marx and Edward Aveling characterised them as being as bad as those in Britain, and they quoted from reports and conversations they had with the same Carroll Wright, then director of the Massachusetts statistical office, the first of its kind in the USA. Aveling and Marx described Wright as not only a significant statistician but, perceptively, as the educator of a whole generation of labour statisticians.

While in the United States and during his time in Europe, Robert certainly did not spend his time stuck behind an office desk, but carried out substantial field research. In the USA he was engaged above all in developing a system of collecting and evaluating labour statistics, which was a new field at the time.

Already at this time, his outlook on life was progressive and he identified very much with the struggles of working people. This led him to make contact with trade union leaders and left-wing political figures. In the USA he cultivated relationships with people like leading socialists and union leaders Eugene Debs and Daniel de Leon, and the union leader Samuel Gompers; and in Europe Marx's son-in-law Charles Longuet as well as the German socialist leaders August Bebel and Karl Liebknecht. Such individuals undoubtedly had considerable influence on his political and social development.

Robert spent four years abroad, both in the USA and travelling in a number of European countries. As becomes clear from his writing, while in the USA he learned a considerable amount about the way monopoly capital functioned. While travelling around the country he also witnessed first hand the crass inequalities that so marked the country, particularly the discrimination against black people. In one of the regular letters he wrote to his mother, in 1902, he describes the appalling way black prisoners were treated in the Southern states.[1] When back in Europe and after travelling through several countries, he wrote two reports about the influence of European trade unions on production for the Bureau in Washington.

Returning to Germany in 1903, he became engaged to, and then in the same year married Berta Gradenwitz on 1 December. The couple decided to take their honeymoon in Italy, but it turned out to be more

FIGURE 2.1 Family portrait. Left to right, back row: Jürgen, Marguerite, Brigitte, Barbara, Rudolf Hamburger and Ursula; left to right, front row: Sabine, Berta, Robert with Renate on his knee
Source: Kuczynski family archive.

of a research expedition for him, than a romantic holiday for her. Berta described it thus:

> First we went to Sicily where René investigated the conditions under which children were working in the sulphur mines. As he could not take me or his cigar into the mines, the two of us had to wait outside and so I became a specialist in mine entrances. When, after a fortnight I asked him when we would be going to Florence, he responded: 'Do we really have to look at the pictures of Giotto the lazy?'

Not an ideal start to a marriage, perhaps, but it would remain a very happy one. Berta was highly educated, artistically talented, and came from a family that contained both intellectuals and bankers. Her uncle Otto Gradenwitz, for instance, was a well-known Egyptologist, and a pupil as well as colleague of the classical historian Theodor Mommsen at Heidelberg University. This background provided her with an intellectual curiosity but also a strong sense of being someone with her own interests, beyond those of her husband.

After their honeymoon Robert and his wife moved to Elberfeld in 1904 where, at the age of 27, he took up his first post as Director of the Statistical Office. It was in Elberfeld that same year, on 17 September, where their eldest and only son, Jürgen, was born. Elberfeld would later merge with Barmen, the birthplace of Friedrich Engels, and it was the town in which he mounted the barricades, joining the revolutionary uprising of 1848. Engels, indirectly, alongside Marx, would have a considerable influence on the Kuczynski family.

In 1906, Robert was very pleased to be offered a similar post with better pay, but this time in the capital. He could now leave the rather provincial and stuffy small town of Elberfeld for the vibrant city of Berlin. His new appointment was as Director of the Statistical Office of Berlin-Schöneberg, and he would be employed there for the following seventeen years. While in Berlin he would embark on a distinguished research career, focusing on financial-political issues, housing and nutritional questions. He became very committed to social progress and was involved in many campaigns for social justice. Together with the women's rights activist Helene Stöcker, he would also play a leading role in the campaign opposing the payment of compensation to the expropriated Prussian Junker class or landed aristocracy, as well as in the German section of the League for Human Rights.

In the wake of Germany's 1918 November Revolution, the question had arisen about what to do with the estates of the landed aristocracy. Their traditional and powerful influence in the country had been broken as a result of the revolution, yet there was a series of court cases in which individual aristocrats challenged the expropriation measures taken by several individual states within the German Reich, but overall their battle was lost. The highpoint of the dispute was the successful referendum in 1926 on expropriation without compensation.

FIGURE 2.2 Robert and Berta in the study of the house on Berlin's
Schlachtensee
Source: Kuczynski family archive.

Robert's post in Berlin represented for him simply a means of earning enough to support the family, but it was not the kind of work he
enjoyed doing or saw as his life's purpose. He was academically inclined
and not keen on languishing in a council office as a small-time civil
servant for the rest of his life. His real life began only when he stepped
outside the office, either at home or with his wide circle of friends from
the political and cultural worlds. He and his wife did not confine their

social life to middle-class circles alone, but as a result of their political activities mixed with a wide range of people.

On his appointment in Berlin the family had moved to Friedenau, a mixed suburb, not far from his office. Jürgen describes their house there as a small villa with a garden, surrounded by large blocks of tenements, backing onto a railway and large park. In 1907 their second child, Ursula, was born, to be followed by Brigitte in 1910, and not long afterwards, in 1913, the family would move into a larger house on the Schlachtensee in the affluent Berlin suburb of Zehlendorf, on land bequeathed them by Berta's father. In this house another three daughters would be born: Barbara (1913), Sabine (1919) and Renate (1923).

While employed in Berlin, Robert was very soon writing papers for publication on unemployment, living conditions and wages which were not directly related to his paid work. His publications over a lifetime would be extensive. His chief concerns were connected with social statistics and exposing what he saw as the ravages of the capitalist system. In 1909 he published *Die Entwicklung der gewerblichen Löhne seit Begründung des Deutschen Reiches* (The Development of Commercial Wages since the Founding of the German Empire), the first such comprehensive study on this subject. In that same year he went to the USA to the Brookings School to carry out further research for his book on wages and working conditions in the USA. There he made an examination of the statistical information available concerning the conditions of working people and his evaluations and analyses were laid out in his large monograph, *Arbeitslohn und Arbeitszeit in Europa und Amerika, 1870–1909* (The Working Wage and Working Time in Europe and America, 1870–1909).

After his return to Germany from the USA, Robert began using his position as an urban statistician to investigate such issues as poor housing and its impact on the lives of the working population. Between 1912 and 1914 he became actively involved in the campaign to improve housing in Berlin and was made chairman of its propaganda committee. Other members of the committee were the artists Max Liebermann and Käthe Kollwitz, the Marxist revolutionary leader Karl Liebknecht, Hans Delbrück, Hermann Muthesius, Friedrich Naumann and Lili du Bois-Reymond.

Kuczynski discovered the basic principle that 'the less income you have, the larger proportion of it you have to pay in rent'. His work led to a broad campaign to solve the housing crisis and he continued to collaborate closely with people like Karl Liebknecht and Käthe Kollwitz.

In 1912, forty years after Engels' pamphlet *The Housing Question* had appeared, a broad campaign began in Berlin to improve the appalling housing conditions. In May the committee produced a powerful poster utilising a lithograph by Kollwitz, which was overwritten with a quote from Kuczynski: 'In Greater Berlin 600,000 people live in flats in which every room is occupied by five or more people.' It was plastered all over Berlin, and led to his first major political clash with the establishment. The Berlin authorities were outraged by the poster showing a poor child with her sister on her arm. Kuczynski responded by pointing out that he had used this same statistic in many official publications, including one published by the Imperial Prussian Home Affairs Ministry, and no one had raised any objection, but now the statistic was publicly displayed on a poster it was arousing anger and outrage. The *Tägliche Rundschau* newspaper described it in detail as:

> that poster, so hostile to the state, has been seen for months now on every hoarding. A ragged suburban child, about 12 years old, looking sick and with rickets, holding her skinny sister on her arm and cuddling her with that remnant of tenderness that can still survive even in deepest misery. The 12 year old, despite her tender age, stares at the world with a rare hopeless expression, one that is normally only seen on the faces of older people when all hope has been extinguished ...

The poster was roundly denounced by the conservative establishment and by Berlin's mayor, Martin Kirschner, who said, 'One does not do this sort of thing; it blackens Berlin's image abroad.' He further declared that the children depicted were too poor and malnourished for Berlin conditions. The poster was then immediately banned by the authorities for 'promoting class war'. Others on the right called it an 'appeal for class struggle'. Such was the power of a single poster to shock bourgeois sensibilities. The whole furore led to the development

FIGURE 2.3 The Better Housing Campaign poster with Käthe Kollwitz's illustration
Source: Käthe Kollwitz Museum, Cologne.

of a closer and warm relationship between Käthe Kollwitz and the Kuczynskis. She gave Robert a signed drawing, 'Mother and Child', and from then on it had pride of place in the Kuczynskis' dining room.

During the war Robert would continue to take a keen interest in the housing situation and at its close publish his study: *Die Wohnungsfrage vor und nach dem Kriege* (The Housing Situation Before and after the War), in which he called for the building of more single-family homes and less office blocks, villas and large blocks of flats. This essay was included in a small booklet series, *Schützengraben-Bücher für das deutsche Volk* (Trench Books for the German People), published by Karl Siegismund. In response to the essay he received many supportive letters from soldiers at the front. At the same time he began to undertake an analysis of the financial problems caused by the war and also continue his ongoing research into wages and working time. He was deeply concerned about developing proper analytic methods and focused on collecting statistics to provide strong evidential backing for those seeking social justice. As a result of this work, over a decade and a half, looking at working conditions in various countries, he established close relationships with a number of leading social democrats and trade unionists. His research became increasingly important for, and informed the struggle and campaigns of, the growing German trade union movement. He refused to let the war distract him from this work.

After his return to Europe Robert became a strong supporter of Germany's Social Democratic Party (SPD) and knew most of its leaders personally. With the looming danger of a European conflict in the lead-up to 1914, he had also became a vehement opponent of war. When it did break out, he did not share the elation of his many contemporaries and large sections of the population who were thrilled at the opportunity of demonstrating Germany's greatness and asserting its power in the world. Within days of the general mobilisation in 1914, he too was called up and enlisted as a non-commissioned officer in the Prussian Guards. When his regiment was due to leave for the front, however, he remained behind. At 38, he was one of the oldest of the non-commissioned officers and deemed surplus to requirements at this early stage of the war.

Already by this time, a number of top military officers and government officials had begun to realise that nutrition and feeding the nation would be central issues during the war, so they readily engaged Robert's skills, commissioning him to carry out the necessary research, and as a result he was excused further military service for the duration of the war.

He joined a group of specialists who began analysing the nutritional and food supply situation in Germany and looking at the impact of war on the lives of ordinary people. In 1915, together with Nathan Zuntz, he wrote a small book, *Unsere bisherige und unsere künftige Ernährung im Kriege* (Our Previous and Our Future Nutritional Needs in War Time) in response to the increasing shortage of basic foodstuffs. In their book the authors write, with perhaps a pinch of irony, that:

> since February or March [1915] there has been a situation, which for hundreds of thousands of over-fed people represents healthy moderation, but for the great majority of the population represents

an uncomfortable and productivity-limiting life experience and, for several million more, a significant undernourishment. If such a situation lasted even for a few months it could have a lasting influence on the people's strength. Long term persistence could signify a great danger.

Further results of their research were published under the title *Die deutsche Volksernährung und der englische Aushungerungsplan* (The Nutrition of the German people and the English Plan of Starvation). Kuczynski also campaigned against the imposition of continuous price rises on food to the benefit of the Prussian landed aristocracy. In this context, his demand for mature pigs to be slaughtered in order to better feed the population provoked invective from that same landed gentry and the right-wing nationalists, who called him a 'Jewish pig slaughterer'. His call led to a widespread campaign by the trade unions and Social Democratic Party against food profiteering. That avaricious attitude of the landed aristocracy would influence his decision years later to lead the national campaign for the expropriation of this class of landowners.

He refused to be cowed by such anti-semitic smears and remained all his life a man who refused to respond to any and all attempts to intimidate, buy him off or bribe him. He was prepared to let his own family endure frugality rather than supplement their rations by buying on the black market or accepting 'charitable gifts' from colleagues. At this time, in 1914, he and his wife already had four children: Jürgen was only 10, Ursula 7, Brigitte 4 and the youngest, Barbara, only 1 year old. It was a very difficult time, even for a middle-class household, to obtain sufficient food and clothing, given the voracious demands made by the war, and they all felt the impact. However, they all survived relatively unscathed.

Robert's income as a civil servant would not have afforded the family a luxurious lifestyle, but did allow them to live in relative comfort. Although Ursula, in her memoirs, says she never felt privileged or wealthy in any way and that the family lived modestly. The lives of the middle classes were in any case cushioned to a certain extent against the ravages of inflation and unemployment. Those like Robert, who was employed as a *Beamter* (civil servant) in the public sector, enjoyed job security and regular salaries which rose largely in step with inflation.

When the guns fell silent at the close of the First World War Germany was a broken country, both materially and psychologically. The nation had enjoyed only forty-three years as a united territory before it embarked on a foolhardy world war under its bellicose Kaiser. Begun in a blaze of nationalist fervour and imperial ambition, the war ended in ignominious defeat and abject capitulation. The country's Kaiser represented a supreme father figure and embodiment of the national spirit. With his resignation in 1918, the German people lost their anchor, their nation was in ruins, and there was no other figurehead, party or organisation to take over the helm of a nation adrift.

For both Berta and Robert the experience of the war and its catastrophic repercussions on German society only served to entrench their radical political and social attitudes. He would lead one of the first delegations from Germany to the Soviet Union in 1927 to attend the 10th anniversary celebrations of the revolution in Moscow. The delegation included the theatre director Erwin Piscator, artist Käthe Kollwitz and poet Johannes R. Becher.

The inter-war years for most Central Europeans were not easy – the mass slaughter of the First World War was followed by political and economic instability, mass unemployment and insecurity. This environment fuelled both ultra-nationalist and right-wing groups as well as strong left-wing parties. The first three decades of the twentieth century for Germany were characterised by an increasing polarisation between strong left- and right-wing forces. It is easy to understand why many were drawn to utopian ideas and the vision of a society of equality, stability and justice and of nations living in peace with their neighbours.

Berlin itself, certainly in the 1920s, became a bustling metropolis with a flourishing artistic, musical and theatrical life, but the city was also characterised by its high density of working-class housing and extremes of wealth and poverty. A common sight on the streets after 1918 were the numerous war-disabled beggars and itinerant sellers of matches, shoe laces and trinkets. The city's raw, sharp-edged, excessive and often decadent Bohemian scene made Berlin during the 1920s a magnet for artists and adventurers from around the world. It is this aspect that is particularly remembered by history through the writings of people like W. H. Auden, Christopher Isherwood, Carl Zuckmayer and Kurt Tucholsky, the brutally honest works of painters Otto Dix and Georg Gross, in films like Walter Ruttmann's *Berlin: Symphony of a Metropolis,* and by the work of the young Bauhaus architects. It was a period characterised by a short, fateful and frenetic hedonism, wedged between the fading horrors of the First World War and the looming world depression of 1929.

There appears to be no particular significant event or experience as such that turned Robert Kuczynski into a left-wing political activist. After all, he had grown up in a wealthy, privileged environment, but consciously chose to disown it. The family home hardly provided the yeast for the fermentation of progressive ideas or an easy identification with the working class. It was probably a gradual process. He certainly had an acute social conscience, good observational and analytical skills, had studied labour conditions in the USA and Europe, associated with leading left-wing political leaders and trade unionists, as well as seen first hand the appalling squalor of Berlin's working-class districts. All these factors would have influenced the development of his thinking. His son Jürgen wrote that he detested the company his father kept – all bank directors and their women folk: 'turkeys garlanded with diamonds and pearls', was how he characterised them. Robert held similar views about his father-in-law, a dealer in urban real estate, who, however, would be the one to bequeath the family the idyllically situated villa on the lakeside in Zehlendorf where they would lead a happy and very satisfying existence before the Nazis drove them into exile.

Robert never became a member of any political party but, after 1920, moved ever closer to the German Communist Party (KPD) with the reasoning that it was 'the least insufferable party'. He had felt close to the Social Democrats, but his experience of the way the parliamentary party avidly supported rising militarism in the run-up to the First World War and then the disappointing experience of the Social Democratic-led post-war government would hardly have convinced him of their radicalism. He worked very closely with the KPD from this time on and remained a strong sympathiser and fellow traveller until the end of his life. All but one of his six children would become active members for all or much of their own lives. Not only did they join the Communist Party, either in Germany or in Britain, but one of them, Ursula, would become a full-time agent, working for Soviet counter-intelligence, and her siblings also contributed to that work or gave her assistance, even if only on a minor level.

It was in the Kuczynski home, where the children were nurtured on a diet of intellectual curiosity, that the seeds of their future interest in culture, social justice and political ideas were sown. The home became a central meeting point in Berlin for progressive artists and intellectuals, among them Albert Einstein, who became a close friend of the family. But alongside the family's political engagement, there was always a strong streak of academic and scholarly endeavour. Robert and his son Jürgen were to become leading demographic and economic statisticians, and their intellectual pursuits have been maintained by succeeding generations.

Robert's wife, Berta, was an accomplished artist, but as was usual at the time in bourgeois circles, she remained at home, taking on the roles of home-maker and mother to his children. This left her little time to devote to what she loved doing. She was a painter of mainly floral motifs and portraits, but most of her surviving works are in the possession of family members. She was a talented student of Karl Hagemeister, a landscape painter who lived and worked in Potsdam. In 1898 he became a founding member of the progressive artistic movement of the Berlin Secession, and in 1914 a professor and a member of the Academy of Art. The family also lived not far from the celebrated painter Max Liebermann, who visited the house not only socially but also to give artistic tips to Berta. Like her husband, though, she was also politically interested and in her diary entries during the time of the Russian Revolution she kept detailed notes of its progress and expressed her hopes that it would spell the end of the war in Europe.

The 'golden' twenties

After the end of the war, Robert was asked to work in an honorary capacity for the Reich's Office for the Economy, assisting in the preparation of evidence to be used in the peace negotiations. He had been asked for an estimate of the damage caused by the Allied blockade of Germany which, it was argued, had been carried out in breach of international law. This work was terminated after only a few weeks with a row. He had estimated the damage to the German economy

FIGURE 2.4 Drawing of Robert Kuczynski by his wife Berta
Source: Zentral- und Landesbibliothek, Berlin.

resulting from the Allied blockade policy as 4 billion Reichsmarks. This figure had been calculated after wide consultations with experts and colleagues and had been accepted by all the relevant government departments. However, the State Secretary responsible refused to sign off the document, and instead charged a minor civil servant with producing an alternative report within 24 hours. In line with instructions from above, this civil servant was able to boost the figure by including the putative damage resulting from a loss of foreign imports of cattle feed. As a result, he came up with the exaggerated sum of 35 billion Reichsmarks. The State Secretary had clearly felt Kuczynski's figure was too low and he was determined to demand much higher compensation. In view of the position taken by the Secretary of State, Kuczynski lost support in the Reich's Office, and was released from his job after only four months on the spurious grounds that 'the burden of work on him was too demanding'.

In 1921, Kuczynski came out forcefully against annexations and the payment by Germany of war reparations, which had been proposed by the victorious Allies. (After the war, France retook Alsace-Lorraine and later, in 1923, occupied the industrial Ruhr area when Germany defaulted on its reparation payments.) Instead he called for the imposition of higher taxes on wealth, war profits and on high earners. His argument was that it would be impossible for Germany to pay the enormous sums demanded by the victors and that such draconian measures would ruin the German economy and plunge its people into poverty. Of course the industrial magnates were not over-worried by the victors' proposals because they would not be the ones footing the bill.

Robert had foreseen Germany's military defeat but, like many others, had been taken completely unawares by the Russian Revolution and the attempts to set up a Soviet republic in Germany itself. His increasing disappointment with the role played by the Social Democrats in legitimising the war, not supporting his call for higher taxation of the rich and letting down working people would, though, lead him to move increasingly to the political left. Little wonder that he was now, for the first time, being called a traitor to his country. He became a supporter of the Communist Party, but in the words of his son, 'remained all his life a citizen and individualist', and would remain a critical friend of the Soviet Union. In his view, the Communist Party was the 'only party that a decent, progressive, thinking person can follow'.

In order to break out of the enforced confinement and censorship of the establishment and to ensure that his work found a wider audience, Robert had set up his own economic discussion journal, *Finanzpolitische Korrespondenz* (Financial Political Bulletin) towards the end of 1919.

Here, as owner, editor and main writer, he had free rein and, during the 1920s, published his studies on living costs. In issue 12 he discussed how one could calculate minimum subsistence levels, and from February 1920 onwards he published a monthly 'subsistence minimum' figure. To begin with the idea was vehemently attacked but soon the figures were awaited with interest by a number of official bodies. These calculations provided an invaluable aid in the fight against the impact of inflation and wage cuts. They were also used extensively by the trade unions in wage negotiations, and furthermore provided an important international comparison. As a result of this and his already enormous body of previous work, he was becoming widely known in the international labour movement as 'the famous statistician Robert Kuczynski', as Stephen Stigler calls him in his book, *The History of Statistics*. He had become one of the world's pioneers in using statistics as the basis for social policy making.

In 1920 he received a telegram from Karl Kautsky, leader of the German Social Democratic Party, inviting him to join a second *Sozialisierungskommission* (Socialisation Commission), and he was pleased to accept. In 1918 the Council of the People's Representatives had set up the first Socialisation Commission of experts to look at ways of socialising – i.e. taking into public ownership or placing under public regulation – sections of German industry. The commission had been set up by the Social Democrats in response to the failed Kapp Putsch in 1920 and demands from the working class for improved social legislation. It came about as a result of an accord between the government, trade unions and other parties. On this second commission Robert sat alongside Walther Rathenau, the wealthy industrialist and founder member of the centrist German Democratic Party, with whom he had strong disagreements as to the implementation of the measures proposed. Rathenau characterised Kuczynski patronisingly as, 'a one man party, in which he occupied the left wing'. (Rathenau became Germany's foreign minister during the Weimar Republic.)

As a member of the Commission, Robert argued for the nationalisation of certain key industries like coal mining; he also opposed reparation payments to the industrial magnates in the Ruhr. Although he still very much believed in democratic reform, he became increasingly frustrated by the timidity of the right-wing leadership of the

Social Democrats. He did not mince his words when criticising the super wealthy and could be very sarcastic. His vociferous advocacy of working-class interests and attacks on greedy employers led Emil Kirdorf, alongside Krupp one of the leading Ruhr industrial magnates, to comment: 'He is not only against us, but is also extremely impudent.'

Robert was well read in French as well as in German literature and because of the family connections with France he felt particularly close to that country. From 1918 onwards, he made a great effort to help reconcile the German and French peoples after the disastrous war. One of his chief aims was to promote a new French–German understanding. He was probably the first German to address a public meeting in Paris on the issue, but not without vocal opposition from French nationalists. Similarly in Germany, when he organised a conference in Potsdam to promote bilateral relations between the two countries, he was vilified by the nationalist and right-wing press as a traitor to his country. This led him, in January 1923, to begin publishing his *Deutsch-Französische Wirtschaftskorrespondenz* (German-French Economic Bulletin), that survived for two years and dealt with German-French economic questions. He wrote most of the copy himself. In one issue he published an open letter from Heinrich Mann to the German Chancellor calling for rapprochement. Both of his journals were widely read and influential in political and economic circles.

He was often in France during those years and became friends with leading French intellectuals like Henri Barbusse, Victor Basch, Paul Langevin, and Madame Ménard-Dorian who hosted one of the last big political salons in France, where leading leftists would meet together. Her home was adorned with Rodin sculptures and paintings by Renoir, Monet and Daumier.

In June 1922 Walther Rathenau, a centrist democrat and German Minister for Foreign Affairs, was assassinated by an ultra-right-wing group only two months after signing the Treaty of Rapallo which renounced German territorial claims from before the First World War. He was shot in the Königsallee as he travelled by car from his home in the Grunewald suburb to the Foreign Office.

Shortly beforehand there had been an extraordinary wave of racial vitriol unleashed. The chant, 'Kill Walther Rathenau, the God-damned Jewish pig', was just one of the slogans that echoed around the country, promoted by the right-wing, nationalist *Freikorps*. A German nationalist member of the Reichstag wrote in that June issue of the *Konservativen Monatschrift* (Conservative Monthly), 'Hardly did the international Jew Rathenau have German honour in his grasp, than there was no more talk of it ... German honour will be atoned. You, though, Herr Rathenau ... will be called to justice by the German people ...'[2] That rhetorical demand was immediately carried out by a group of fanatical ultra-nationalists. Yet what happened after the assassination was a surprise for everyone.

On the Sunday following his murder, from early morning until late afternoon hundreds of thousands marched through the streets of central Berlin in silence, but waving black-red-gold flags – symbol of the Weimar Republic – in mourning for Walther Rathenau. This polarisation between the extreme nationalistic and anti-semitic elements, on the one hand, and the progressive forces of the SPD and Communist Party, on the other, would characterise German society and politics throughout the period that led up to the Nazi dictatorship in the 1930s.

Despite the fact that the Weimar Republic represented Germany's first non-monarchical, democratic government, the country as a whole was by no means democratically minded. Throughout the Weimar period entrenched nationalistic and right-wing ideas were still dominant among civil servants as well as throughout academia. The higher educational institutions also played a key role in future developments; they held the educational monopoly on the training of lawyers, medics and higher civil servants, as well as teachers who would be employed in the country's schools. It would be from these educational institutes, dominated by such forces, that the next generation of civil servants and the professional class would emerge.

Right-wing nationalists were overwhelmingly suspicious or dismissive of the Weimar Republic and of democracy itself, placing their faith in the emergence of a new strong leader to replace the Kaiser. Robert and his now grown-up son Jürgen would have been confronted daily with this reality and, as Jews, albeit secular ones, made to feel very much as outsiders both in the civil service and academia.

One of the biggest popular movements to arise in Germany during the inter-war years was the one opposing the payment of reparations to the Prussian Junkers (the landed aristocracy) – the so-called

Fürstenabfindung. Robert would become an active participant in the movement opposed to such payments.

In November 1925 the communists in the Reichstag tabled a motion proposing the expropriation of the landed aristocracy without compensation. And in 1926 the KPD demanded a referendum. Mass meetings took place throughout Germany, many addressed by Kuczynski himself.

In 1926 Robert Kuczynski was appointed Chair of the *Vorläufige Ausschuss zur Regelung der Fürstenabfindung* (Temporary Commission on the Regulation of Compensation to the Aristocracy), the so-called Kuczynski Commission. The Commission campaigned vociferously for the holding of a referendum on the issue. According to the Constitution, the campaign needed to obtain the support of at least 10 per cent of the electorate for a referendum to be held. The electorate was over 39.5 million but more than 12.5 million signed the petition calling for the referendum – a great victory.

During the nineteenth and into the twentieth century, the landed aristocracy had held considerable power in Germany, particularly in Prussia. Its position had become entrenched through the 'three class suffrage' legislation. This was a rather complicated system of voting in elections to the Prussian parliament during the reign of the Kaiser. Voters were classified into three classes based on how much tax they paid and their votes carried more weight accordingly.

The votes of the aristocrats, who owned enormous tracts of land and were extremely conservative, militaristic and anti-liberal, held considerable sway. They had provided the reactionary backing for the monarchy of the Hohenzollerns and dominated the Prussian state apparatus, while their sons made up the officer class of the military. They had also profited enormously during the war from high food prices.

In order to establish real democracy in Germany, it became essential to break the stranglehold of this landed aristocracy. The referendum itself had been initiated by the German League for Human Rights, in which Robert was a leading activist, alongside Helene Stöcker working for women's rights, and the pacifist Ludwig Quidde. Robert's political independence allowed him to take on a key role in persuading the leaderships of both big working-class parties, the SPD and KPD, to undertake joint action in support of the referendum. It could be said that he was possibly the first and last individual to successfully persuade the SPD and the KPD to work together in a joint campaign. If they could have been persuaded to do the same in the 1930s, Hitler's rise to power could probably have been prevented.

The question about what to do about the big estates had already hung in the air for ten years. In the wake of the November Revolution of 1918, the landed aristocracy was supposed to have been politically neutralised. The proposal for expropriation had led to an ongoing debate with no end in sight. It began during the short period of revolution in 1918, but continued during the following years with judicial proceedings and negotiations between the various aristocratic families and individual states making up the German empire.

The campaign reached its zenith in the early part of 1926 when the referendum took place and was supported by both the Communist Party and the Social Democrats, although the latter were, to begin with, rather tentative.

While Robert was a leading figure in the campaign, his 22-year-old son Jürgen was also active, alongside his eldest daughter Ursula, who was 19, and all lobbied for a 'Yes' vote. Both the Social Democratic Party and the Communist Party were key mobilising forces and campaigned vigorously for a 'Yes' vote. In the referendum over 15.5 million citizens took part, of whom around 14.5 million voted for and just under 600,000 against expropriation without compensation. However, it did not achieve its purpose because 'the necessary majority had not been reached'. Shortly beforehand the government had introduced a new rule that for any referendum to succeed it would need the support of an absolute majority of the legitimate electorate, not a relative one.

Berlin was a late addition to the roster of the world's great cities. First documented in the thirteenth century, it had been built on former marshland, surrounded by numerous lakes and extensive forest. From the eighteenth century onwards it became Prussia's capital. By the late nineteenth century, with increased urbanisation, its central areas were characterised by densely populated tenements, in which most ordinary working people lived – in districts like Wedding, Prenzlauer Berg and Friedrichshain. It was in the leafy suburbs to the west of the city where the wealthy citizens lived, in spacious period villas set back from the wide, tree-lined streets. The boroughs of Grunewald and Zehlendorf were adjacent to lakes and woodland, which were favoured places for Berlin family outings. The Schlachtensee, Krumme Lanke and Wannsee were ideal places for bathing and picnics in summer and for skating in winter. Grunewald developed out of a mansion colony established where the city's prestigious avenue, the Kurfürstendamm, terminated. It also became home to a whole number of successful writers and artists. Schlachtensee, where the Kuczynski family settled in 1913, belonged to the borough of Steglitz-Zehlendorf to the southwest, on the edge of the Grunewald forest.

As in most countries, the capital city hardly represents the reality of the country as a whole. Germany was no exception. In the *Länder* beyond Berlin the attitudes and ideas of the people were very much the polar opposite of those in the vibrant city. Berlin could offer its citizens colour, diversion and excitement as no other in the country.

In 1928, the Kuczynski family would have probably taken one of the first journeys on the new electrified Berlin S-Bahn or city railway and flocked to see the first flight over the city of the enormous airship *Graf Zeppelin*. Robert and Berta would have proudly informed their children that one of their relatives on their mother's side had been involved in the successful launching of the great airship. Richard Gradenwitz, who had died four years earlier, had run a successful company connected with the production of Zeppelin and Parseval airships. He was involved in the launch of the first airships for Zeppelin and personally oversaw the pumping of the gas into the balloons on the Bodensee. The company received lucrative contracts to supply the military with airship equipment. Richard became a member of the board of governors of the Airship Society and president of the Emperor's Aero Club.

When the exotically clad king of Afghanistan, Aman-Ullah, arrived on a state visit that same year, he also brought out the crowds to see his arrival at Berlin's 'red' city hall. A real king from the Orient was something Berliners had never witnessed before.

The colourful and frenetic culture of this vibrant city could also mask the extreme poverty and unemployment under which many of its citizens suffered, as well as an inchoate and gestating fascism, alongside increasingly self-confident and powerful communist and social democratic movements, rooted in the densely populated working-class areas.

By the late 1920s, the theatrical innovator and Bertolt Brecht collaborator Erwin Piscator was developing their ideas of epic theatre. In
1928 audiences were being entertained by Brecht and composer Kurt
Weill's sharply satirical *Threepenny Opera*, which was an apposite meta-
phor for the times, portraying a venal, corrupt and cynical ruling elite
living on the backs of the poor; on the streets people were soon singing
and whistling the songs of Mac the Knife and Tiger Brown from the
opera. There were forty theatres in the city and a whole generation of great
actors trod the boards there and learned their trade – Elisabeth Bergner,
Marlene Dietrich, Fritz Kortner, Werner Krauss and many others.

Late afternoon on the Kurfürstendamm – the Champs-Élysées of
Berlin – with its bars and pubs offering a whole variety of amusements,
luxuriously and exotically dressed men and women promenaded as if
on the catwalk, jazz music throbbed from the bars and the cafes would be
heaving. As night fell and the lights went on, the city became brighter
than day. It was here, in Berlin, that the Nazis saw everything they hated
and could attack: *entartete Kunst* (degenerate art), 'negro' jazz music, and
above all a strong Jewish presence. Almost a third of Germany's Jewish
population had settled in Berlin and the community made an enormous
contribution to the culture of the city.

At the height of its attractiveness before the Nazis tarnished its image
irreversibly, Heinrich Mann wrote that 'What is now being lived in
advance in Berlin, gives one a hint of the future of Germany.' Or as
Carl Zuckmayer put it more bluntly, 'Berlin tasted of the future and
that's why one was prepared to accept all the dirt and the cold.' But it
all turned out to be illusory, a self-deception. And, ominously, in 1926,
Dr Joseph Goebbels chose to move to Berlin and from 1927 began
publishing his hate paper, *Der Angriff* (The Attack).

On Berlin's own Piccadilly Circus – Alexanderplatz – there was
always turbulent activity: crowds of shoppers visiting the large retail
stores of Wertheim, Tietz and Israel, or simply window shopping.
Sightseers jostled past itinerant traders calling out their wares, hurdy-
gurdy men played the latest popular tunes and the war-maimed holding
out their caps for small change. Ice cream or a hot *Bockwurst* from the
Jewish *Wurstmaxe* would be bought for the children. In the early evening garishly made-up prostitutes lingered on the corners of the streets
that led off the big square. Alexanderplatz was Berlin's busiest traffic

intersection, with a dozen different tram lines, yellow double-decker buses, delivery vans and private cars criss-crossing the square, scattering the leisurely pedestrians like frightened chickens. Stern Prussian policemen with waxed moustaches would be standing sentry on the street corners and curious passers-by would study the latest announcements on the ubiquitous *Litfasssäulen* – those cast-iron pillars peculiar to Berlin that look like individual pissoirs and are pasted all over with adverts and political posters. In the courtyards of the cramped working-class housing blocks just beyond the square, men would sit in summer playing the popular game of *Skat*, while their wives cooked or washed in their small cramped flats. The oompah, oompah sound of marching military bands would be heard regularly, bouncing off the walls of the city buildings. The city's rise began at the close of the nineteenth century and reached its apogee during these 'golden twenties'. However, by 1933, it would lose its sheen and attractiveness.

The year 1928 in Germany was characterised by a series of large-scale financial scandals involving tax evasion and fraud, which also played into the hands of the ultra-nationalists and fascists. Already in December 1924 there had been the Kutisker affair. Kutisker ran a large company selling surplus German army equipment. He was convicted of fraudulently acquiring millions in unsecured credit from the Prussian state bank. This involved the bribery of civil servants and leading Social Democrats. At the same time there was the even bigger Barmat affair in which the Amexima company, built up by the two Barmat brothers into a huge company on the back of the rampant inflation of the early 1920s, suddenly collapsed. The Barmats were also supporters of the Social Democratic Party. At its peak the company employed 14,000 and had interests in a wide range of industries. When it went bankrupt it was over-indebted and had large unsecured funds from a number of credit institutes. Many small traders, businessmen and savers were severely hit by the company's collapse. This case, too, involved the bribery of civil servants. The owners of both companies were immigrant Jews from Eastern Europe, and the publicity surrounding their cases undoubtedly helped fuel the incipient anti-semitism in the country. The mainstream newspapers were increasingly blaming the 'Jewish business community' for the ongoing economic crisis, and the right wing, contradictorily, blamed it on the 'Jewish-Bolshevik conspiracy'.

It was usual at the time, in most German institutes of higher education, to hold an annual celebration on the date of the establishment of the German Reich. These would invariably be opened with a speech by an academic with strong nationalist credentials. In Erlangen in 1928, the professor of ancient history, Rudolf Schulten, was given the honour of delivering the oration in which he said: 'The hero is something of wonder, that we will never understand, something godly. That's why, more than ever, we must honour the hero, model ourselves on his achievements and retain hope in the emergence of a new hero ...' because, 'with an enthusiastic people, a hero can achieve everything'. This gives a flavour of the dominant intellectual climate of the time and is a premonition of what was to come. During the Weimar Republic – Germany's first democracy – true democrats in academic and professional circles were still a minority in the country and were invariably marginalised. Up until 1933, even the National Student Federation was dominated by the extreme right-wing National Socialists.

During the early decades of the twentieth century, Germany was also characterised by an increasing concentration of economic power. There had been an unashamed amassing of wealth by those who had profited enormously from the war and immediate post-war situations. Alongside the enrichment of a few at the top, there had been wide-scale bankruptcies of smaller business, together with galloping inflation which hit those at the lower end of the economic scale hardest.

In order to pay the cost of the First World War, Germany had funded it entirely by borrowing. This resulted in a falling exchange rate of the Reichsmark against the US dollar during the war period. The Treaty of Versailles then made matters worse, by imposing stringent reparation payments on the defeated nation.

Although German industry had survived the war virtually intact, the 'London ultimatum' in May 1921 demanded reparation payments in gold or foreign currency to be paid in annual instalments, as well as 26 per cent of the value of Germany's exports. It soon became clear that these demands were impossible for Germany to fulfil, with the result that there was a further rapid devaluation of the currency. Hyperinflation ensued. In January 1923, French and Belgian troops occupied Germany's industrial base in the Ruhr to ensure reparations were paid in goods.

Victor Klemperer, the prominent Jewish philologist who survived the Hitler period in Dresden, and whose book of reminiscences, *I Will Bear Witness*, was widely praised, characterised this whole period thus: 'Idiocy is piled on idiocy, shame on shame, billion banknotes on ten-billion banknotes, and in the stultifying paralysis, poverty and horror grow. To fall asleep during the day is best and waking up the most horrific'.[3]

In the country prices were rising by the day and if you were paid on the Friday you would have to spend it immediately otherwise it would be worth only a fraction of its original value a day or two later. It really was a 'mad, mad world'. In September 1923, the year in which Renate, the youngest of Robert and Berta's children was born, one US dollar had become worth 400 million Reichsmarks.

This whole economic destabilisation and high rates of unemployment undoubtedly helped fuel the so-called 'Beer Hall Putsch' that took place in November 1923, when a young Hitler together with a group of fellow Nazis and *Freikorps* officers tried to storm the Munich parliament building and take over the state of Bavaria. On the other hand, that same year also saw an elected government made up of Social Democrats and Communists in the regional state of Saxony – the first such coalition to be formed in Germany.

It has been argued that the German government had let inflation rise intentionally after its defeat in the First World War, in order to reduce the cost to the country of war reparations, a part of which was to be paid in German currency. Reparations accounted for about one third of the German deficit from 1920 to 1923, and the government cited this as one of the main causes of hyperinflation. Other causes cited included the role of bankers and speculators, particularly foreign ones. Whatever the true causes, inflation in the country had reached its peak by November 1923, but ended when a new currency (the Rentenmark) was introduced. In order to make way for the new currency, banks handed over old Reichsmarks by the ton to junk dealers to be recycled.

The monetary law of August 1924 permitted the exchange of each old paper 1 trillion-mark note for one new Reichsmark, equivalent in value to one Rentenmark. With these measures a gradual stabilisation of the German currency was engineered, and there followed a period of relative stabilisation after 1924. The revolutionary situation that had characterised the short period between 1918 and 1923 had subsided in the wake of the SPD-led government's brutal suppression of the short-lived November Revolution.

Between 1924 and 1932 Robert became very busy in the *Liga für Menschenrechte* (German League for Human Rights), which amongst other things, organised meetings and events against the Nazis. He characterised the League as a 'fighting organisation', campaigning for peace and justice and against tyranny, against an economic system of privilege and against racial harassment. He was also an active member of Willi Münzenberg's *Internationale Arbeiterhilfe* (Workers' International Relief).

For his campaigning work in the League on behalf of Sacco and Vanzetti, the anarchists sentenced to death in the USA, Robert was denounced in a 1927 report by the Reich's Commissioner for the Oversight of Public Order as a 'pace-setter for the further development of ... the proletarian united front movement'. During this time he was intensely active, not only continuing his research and writing but also in addressing numerous meetings in Germany and abroad.

From 1926 to 1932 he would spend half his time working in Germany, but his own free time in the USA, where he carried out research at the Brookings School in Washington D.C. undertaking comparative studies into workers' wages in Europe and the USA. His wife accompanied him on several of his visits to the United States and on one of these she utilised the opportunity to write a half-page letter to the editor of the *New Republic* magazine in New York about the dire situation in Germany. It was published in 1932 under the title 'The Misery of Germany' in which she described the impoverishment of the Berlin middle classes, 'the once wealthy intellectual set'.

Robert had been particularly concerned with the question of reparations and US loans to Germany and the way they had been appropriated and misused. He investigated the impact of US capital export to Germany during the Weimar years and the results were published in his book, *Bankers' Profits from German Loans*, which was completed in the USA in 1932 and first published in Leipzig in January 1933. He demonstrated how US banks had made enormous profits from their loans to Germany, and also how US monopoly capital, which blossomed fully only after the Second World War was, even then, more than embryonic. With this work he once again found himself on 'the wrong side' of the establishment. The book was immediately banned in Germany and destroyed in the infamous book burning rampage in May 1933, alongside other books deemed by the Nazis to be anti-German.

After the Second World War the 'Good Samaritans', as Jürgen ironically called those US banks which lent Germany money, were even more forceful. They pressured other capitalist countries, he writes, to accept US help, then pumped so much medicine in the form of US aid into the war-ravaged body of the weaker capitalist countries with the firm expectation that those countries would thus lose their capacity for independent self-regulation.

By the time the Nazis took power, and before his enforced exile, Robert had built up a considerable body of work and an international reputation. He knew, however, that he was no genius, although the foundations he laid for modern population statistics may have entered the realm of such a status. He characterised himself in the following way: 'I hope I am a first-rate second-class scientist.' An American colleague put it to him this way: 'One is bowled over by the simplicity of your methodology and at the same time by the significance of the results to which it leads.' What raised him way above the great mass of second-class economic statisticians in Germany was his ability of also making known the results of his analyses, particularly when they did not fit into the political landscape of the day. His most significant achievement, though, was as a founder of modern population statistics.

This area of research would occupy him over many years. One day, after reading George Bernard Shaw's *Back to Methuselah*, he surprised his family by suggesting that from the point of view of population growth men were becoming almost superfluous and that immortality itself would not have much effect on population growth if women's fertility continued to sink as it was apparently doing. This idea nudged him to devote time researching this area and to look at the whole ramification of population statistics. His works on this subject since 1928, when he produced his first volume of *The Balance of Births and Deaths*, established the basic methodologies that are used still today. Modern population statistics, including the terminology of gross and net reproduction rates, have been largely based on Kuczynski's work, and within a few years of publishing that 1928 work, most statisticians had adopted this way of working. While much of his work was ignored in Germany during the

1930s and 1940s, it found resonance particularly in England and the USA. His calculations on gross and net rates of reproduction in Western European nations and the USA became known in economic circles as 'Kuczynski rates'. And his books were reprinted even right into the 1980s. Yet his name and works were practically unknown after the war in the Federal Republic, while in the GDR his methodological research on fertility and reproduction, *Fruchtbarkeit und Reproduktion*, was regularly reprinted.

Mainstream newspapers and academic journals published his articles, as did Soviet and pre-war German trade union journals. He was widely seen as an authority on conditions of working-class life, the financial system, nutrition and housing, as well as on more general economic issues. Social Democratic and Communist leaders, as well as Wall Street bankers and mainstream politicians, would regularly ask his advice. It was known that his information would be fact-based and that he was interested in neither office nor status, so could not be bribed.

In 1913, after the family had moved into their new home on the lakeside of Schlachtensee, it became, according to Jürgen, his real *Heimat*. 'It was part of a large estate that grandfather had purchased … and my parents bought a piece of it in 1912 and asked their friend, and prominent architect, Hermann Muthesius, to build a house for them directly on the lakeside.' (This statement contradicts what he wrote earlier in his memoirs, that the land had been given his parents as a gift.) It was a wonderful place in which to experience childhood, and Jürgen says he and his siblings were allowed much free rein, growing up as 'outdoor kids' albeit privileged ones.

Later, in 1919, an extension was built in the garden to house the family library and then, after the death of Robert's father, he and his wife bought a neighbouring piece of land, once also belonging to his father, on which the children could play. Their daughter Sabine was born that same year, and the youngest, Renate in 1923. On the plot Robert had a separate, smaller house built specifically for Jürgen and his young wife Marguerite when they returned from the USA in 1929. This house was designed by the young architect Rudolf Hamburger, who would become Ursula's first husband. It was almost completely destroyed during the Second World War, but on his return to Berlin in 1945 Jürgen had it rebuilt and the family lived there until 1950 when, for political reasons, he was obliged to move to the Eastern sector of

Berlin. Today (2015) it is owned by the grandson of Käthe Kollwitz, and in this way its links to the family and Germany's progressive intellectual tradition have been maintained.

For Robert and Berta's young children the big house on Schlachtensee was an idyllic place in which to grow up. Renate, the youngest, describes it thus:

> There was a huge garden, which was partially devoted to an orchard. No vegetables were grown but we did have chickens … the house was on the edge of the lake. We used to go swimming there in the summer and in winter when it was fully frozen we would skate on it. Imagine just coming out of your house and being able to do those things. We tobogganed down the hill out onto the frozen lake. There was woodland we played in and built tree houses with our friends. The first snows came in November and we would have three months of snow and ice. When the lake was frozen we made holes in the ice to catch fish.

In terms of housing, the Kuczynski family were very lucky, being gifted such a large and beautifully situated mansion. Both Robert's and his wife's parents had made their money in banking and property development and were wealthy enough to bestow such largesse. In this lakeside home, despite the unstable and increasingly threatening situation during the late 1920s and early 1930s, Robert and his wife brought three more children into the world who would enjoy a relatively comfortable and carefree childhood. They were lucky to be situated close to a large area of woodland known as Grunewald, where Robert would often wander for two or three hours with friends or by himself in order to relax.

The family was certainly not poor by any standard but neither were they very wealthy, despite being able to employ a nanny for the children and one or two servants as well as a gardener – the norm for middle-class families at the time. Little did they all realise that the 1930s would bring their serene life there to an abrupt and brutal close.

In Eric Hobsbawm's memoirs, *Interesting Times*, he describes this area and its connections with the Kuczynski family. He mentions several of them, including Jürgen with whom he regularly corresponded, albeit in a rather patronising manner here:

The 'Grunewaldviertel' had been originally developed by a millionaire member of a local Jewish family that prided itself on a long left-wing tradition, going back to an avid book-collecting ancestor converted to revolution in 1848 Paris – he had bought a first edition of Marx and Engels' *Communist Manifesto* there. It was represented in my lifetime by the sons and daughters of R.R. Kuczynski, a distinguished demographer who found refuge after 1933 at the LSE. All of them became lifelong communists, the two best known being Ruth [sic], who, in a long and adventurous career in Soviet intelligence acted, among other things, as contact for Klaus Fuchs in Britain, and the charming and ever-hopeful economic historian Jürgen, an ingenious defender of what he took to be Marx's thesis on the pauperization of the proletariat, who took the gigantic family library back to East Berlin, where he died at the age of ninety-three, the doyen of his subject, having probably written more words than any other scholar of my acquaintance, even without counting the forty-two volumes of History of the Conditions of the Working Class. He simply could not stop himself reading and writing. Since the family still owned the Grunewaldviertel, he is probably the richest citizen of East Berlin, which enables him to extend the library and to offer an annual prize of 100,000 (Eastern) Deutschmarks for promising work by young GDR scholars in economic history which, thanks to his support, flourished in East Germany. He survived the GDR, where he had expressed moderately dissenting opinions, which were tolerated because his ingenuous loyalty was so patent. And he had after all been in the Communist Party longer than the state's rulers.[4]

Hobsbawm's suggestion here that 'the family still owned the Grunewaldviertel' in Berlin, and that Jürgen 'is probably the richest citizen of East Berlin' is somewhat surprising as it was not true.

The rise of the Nazis

> Thinking is easy. Acting is hard, but to act in accordance with one's thinking is the hardest of all.
>
> *Johann Wolfgang von Goethe*

Hitler and the Nazis whipped up the incipient anti-semitism already existing in late 1920s Germany into a veritable racial war. Once Hitler had come to power the fascists' ruling aspirations were defined as a life or death struggle against what they labelled a mighty Jewish conspiracy: democratic and cultural attitudes, pacifism, liberalism, cosmopolitism, advocating human rights, the teachings of 'Marx the Jew' as well as US financial capital and the Bolshevik government in Moscow were all ascribed to this worldwide conspiracy and had to be countered, including biologically, by the German people.

Even well before Hitler came to power it was clear from his own writings, particularly in *Mein Kampf* – his blueprint for power – but also in the vitriolic and racial rhetoric of his party's own journals as well as the violence perpetrated by members of the Nazi Party, that this was no party in the traditional mould. For those who wanted to see what Hitler and the Nazis would be capable of, it was there in front of them. Yet politicians from around the world still spoke and negotiated with him as if he were a mainstream representative of a democratic country. Robert would be among the first, in 1929, to organise a big anti-fascist congress in Berlin to highlight the dangers posed by the far right. He was determined to help promote the much-needed unity on the left in order to create a broad front that could defeat fascism.

Even with the increasing raucousness of the Nazis' anti-semitism, many Jews in Germany still felt it would all blow over. While most working-class Jews would tend towards the SPD or Communist Party politically, the more wealthy ones took a more conservative and even nationalist stance, several even voting for the Nazis, thinking such a demonstration of loyalty would appease the latter and ensure their own safety. Those living in working-class areas like Berlin's Scheunenviertel had little to lose by fighting the Nazis; the well-off middle classes of Wilmersdorf and the leafier suburbs were more concerned about saving their wealth than opposing the Nazis and risking everything they possessed. Like many of their non-Jewish compatriots, they sought a modus vivendi with the new fascist authorities. Few envisaged the 'Final Solution' and genocide.

Although the rising Nazi presence during the late 1920s alarmed those on the left who were politically aware, the fact that the communist and social democratic parties were well organised, with large memberships and were well represented in the Reichstag gave them a false sense of complacency. However, the dizzying acceleration of political developments and the sudden tipping of the balance of power, once Hindenburg and the conservatives, backed by big business, banking and the media, came to the conclusion that only Hitler could defeat the communists and socialists, his supremacy was assured. When, on 30 January 1933, the new Nazi cabinet was sworn in during a brief ceremony in Hindenburg's office and Hitler was appointed Chancellor, most on the political left realised that a new and terrible era was in store for the country, even if most of them felt it would only be a short time before the Nazis were ousted.

Hitler and the Nazi Party first set about smashing the KPD and the SPD – their most fervent opponents – and then went on to destroy the trade unions. Once that had been achieved, they would concentrate on the Jews and other 'undesirables' like gypsies, homosexuals and the mentally disabled. On 9 November 1938, throughout the country, Hitler's Storm Troops moved against Jewish-owned businesses and Jews themselves in the notorious *Kristallnacht* or Night of Broken Glass. At least ninety-one Jews were killed on that night and over 30,000 arrested shortly afterwards and despatched to concentration camps. This was the first co-ordinated and systematic attack on the Jews.

The pogrom against the Jews was also carried out in occupied Austria. Edmund de Waal describes this in his poignant family biography, *The Hare with Amber Eyes*:

> There had been 185,000 Jews in Austria before the Anschluss. Of these only 4,500 returned after the war; 65,459 Austrian Jews had been killed. Nobody was called to account. The new democratic Austrian Republic established after the war gave an amnesty to 90 per cent of members of the Nazi party in 1948, and to the SS and Gestapo by 1957.

The Nazi regime attempted to put its persecution of the Jews onto a quasi-legal footing by introducing legislation. The lawyer Hans Globke (in the post-war period he would become a top advisor to West Germany's first chancellor, Konrad Adenauer) was intimately involved in drafting Hitler's anti-semitic Jewish legislation. He and others from 1933 onwards had been preparing legislation to force Jews living in

Germany to adopt designated 'Jewish' names, like 'Sara' and 'Israel' to be added to their German surnames. The year 1936 was the proposed date for the implementation of this legislation, but it was delayed for two years to avoid any possible tarnishing of the Olympic Games. The Nazi hierarchy felt it would have sent out the wrong signals at that sensitive time.

The Kuczynski family was forced to confront the fact that the Nazis labelled them as Jewish and that this affected the way they were obliged to behave. It also, no doubt, influenced their decision to flee Hitler's Germany. However, their radical politics on top of their Jewish background made them a double irritant for the Nazis and this would have compounded their harassment and persecution.

They, like many other integrated and secular German-Jewish families saw themselves as Germans first and did not define themselves in any way as Jewish. As so often with establishing national or racial identity, such concepts are invariably defined by outsiders, rather than by those addressed by the definitions. The youngest of the children, Renate, recalls that at 10 years old she wasn't even aware that she was Jewish.[5]

When the Gestapo came searching for Robert at the family home on Schlachtensee one evening in the spring of 1933, he was fortunately not at home. He did not hang around to give them a second chance: he left the house later that same night and went into hiding. A family friend, Otto A. Hirschmann, who would later become a well-known economist in the USA, managed to find him temporary shelter in an asylum for the mentally ill. Then, at the beginning of April, his friends felt it was safe enough for him to leave the asylum and make his way over the German–Czech border.

Rudolf Hamburger's parents (Rudolf was Ursula's architect husband) had a holiday cottage on the Czech side, in the mountain village of Grenzbauden (Malá Úpa) which they used regularly, so were well known to the border guards. They took Robert in their car to Czechoslovakia and, as they predicted, were not closely scrutinised at the border. He was now in safety, at least temporarily. At this early stage of Nazi rule, he could be reasonably certain that his family would not come to any harm – it was him the Nazis were after. He would seek a more permanent place of refuge and a job before bringing the family out of Germany to join him. He was convinced it would only be a temporary exile and that he and his family would be returning to Germany within a short time. Little did he realise that neither he nor his wife would see Germany ever again.

Robert had a whole number of friends and colleagues in different countries so he was not short of useful contacts or places to stay. After a short sojourn in Czechoslovakia, he moved on to Paris. His mother had been born in France, he spoke the language and was very familiar with the country. Eventually he ended up in Switzerland and was able to find work for a time with the International Labour Organization. The ILO was quite happy to have him, as the work in which they were involved was very much his field. However, only a short time later, the Director of the London School of Economics turned up there by chance and made him a firm job offer on the spot. He felt very happy with that as it also meant he could settle for a time in England – probably a safer haven, in the longer term, than Switzerland.

After working at the LSE for five years, he would be appointed Reader in Demography – the first such appointment at any British university – taking up the post in October 1938. Later he would become an advisor to the Foreign and Colonial Office. His book, *Living Space and Population Problems*, was published in 1939, while his substantial three-volume *Demographic Survey of the British Colonial Empire* was published posthumously. Although there is no propagandistic commentary or agitational rhetoric in these latter works, the facts themselves provide an indictment of the British colonial system. One example he uses shows how deaths from smallpox in the colonies were closely related to the lack of a proper immunisation programme. He came to be recognised as the major figure in the development of British colonial demography.

Both in Germany and the UK he was seen as an honourable and incorruptible figure, and his lack of allegiance to any specific party or ideology compounded that assessment. His pioneering work in collecting statistical data for social policy making was widely known and respected. Jörn Jannsen, a German-born political economist working in the UK, likens him to Emile Durkheim in France and Charles Booth in Britain in terms of significance. A fellow German exile and, later, lecturer at the LSE was Claus Moser, who also respected his work highly and became a friend of the family. Moser would become a professor of social statistics there during the 1950s and director of the Central Statistical Office in 1967. In 1973 he was made Baron Moser for his services to statistical research.

Both Robert and his wife and children who followed him into exile were fortunate in being able to escape the Nazi holocaust in time, but other members of the extended family were not so lucky. Other close and distant relatives of the family were unable to escape and were murdered in Hitler's concentration camps. Dr Benno-Baruch Gradenwitz was the younger brother of the Hanau Rabbi Hugo Hirsch Gradenwitz and lived with his wife in Berlin's Prenzlauer Berg, where he worked as a GP and paediatrician for many years. After the Nazis withdrew his licence to practice he was only allowed to work as a 'medical orderly for Jews', and his wife, Rosa, assisted him in that work. Both were transported to Auschwitz in March 1943 where they were murdered. Robert's sister Alice and her husband Dr Georg Dorpalen were despatched to Theresienstadt concentration camp in September 1942 and murdered there a few months later. Their daughter, Renate Dorpalen, along with her siblings, managed to escape the Holocaust.

Descendants of the Dorpalen family recently and unexpectedly discovered their parents' wedding ring and other jewellery as exhibits in the Jewish museum in Berlin, where the life of Jews in 1930s Berlin is described. What the museum fails to reveal, though, is the vital role played by the German arm of the big US computer company IBM. The company made a significant contribution in helping the Nazis process the large numbers of Jews destined for the concentration camps using an early form of the computer: punch cards. IBM's subsidiary did not merely supply the Reich with machines, but:

> with the full knowledge of its New York headquarters, enthusiastically custom-designed the complex devices and specialized applications as an official corporate undertaking ... Technicians from Dehomag and other IBM subsidiaries sent mock-ups of punch cards back and forth to Reich offices until the data columns were acceptable, much as any software designer would today.[6]

In his book on the Gradenwitz and Kuczynski families, the German academic Hans Lembke writes about the fate of Robert's sister Alice and her gynaecologist husband Georg Dorpalen:

> A year later, they were forced to flee the country and they died by extermination. They allowed themselves – as many other not yet impoverished Jews did – to be misled by the promises of the Nazis, of being able to purchase a secure place of retirement in Theresienstadt. In September 1942 they were installed in this former garrison town under the known precarious conditions and died there a few months later.[7]

Renate Dorpalen, Robert's niece, wrote in her unpublished reminiscences about the turmoil in her own family that preceded Robert's flight in 1933:

> On the night of Hitler's ascent to power long torch light processions wound noisily through the streets to usher in an era of oppression and terror, political sanction of murder, and general violation of law. It was the beginning of the systematic persecution of the German Jews. Michael [Renate Dorpalen's brother] and I first watched the goings-on from our balcony but were soon chased inside by Mürt (Martha Grams) our housekeeper, with the admonition that we must never set eyes on these evil people and must avoid them at all cost. Of course we were fascinated and drawn to the spectacle. Living on one of the main thoroughfares we had a perfect view. We peeked from behind the drapes, with one of us on the lookout in case one of our parents or Mürt might approach. We trembled with fear, mesmerized by the excitement of the marching bands and fanfare. We envied the children who marched alongside the storm troopers, yet we sensed that something was terribly wrong. During the day my parents were huddled in my father's (Dr. med. Georg Dorpalen) study, whispering and conferring as they were to do at moments of crisis in the years to come. They made calls to my father's brother, Uncle Lutz (Dr. Ludwig Dorpalen), a prominent lawyer in Düsseldorf and to my oldest brother, Andreas, who had just been awarded a doctor of

laws degree from the University of Bonn. He had recently started a promising government career at the district court in Reppen, near Frankfurt-an-der-Oder. Calls were made to other relatives, yes and friends. Later we learned that my mother's brother, Uncle Rene (Dr. Rene Kuczynski) [she is referring here to Robert Kuczynski], had fled to Switzerland.[8]

Lembke relates the fate of the Gradenwitz family business under the Nazis and provides a clear picture of the process of 'Aryanisation' of Jewish property. During the 1930s the banker Paul Hamel was intimately involved in the dubiously 'legal' takeover of the highly successful Gradenwitz motor factory and the 'Aryanisation' of a number of other Jewish-owned banks and companies. Fortunately Hermann Gradenwitz was no longer alive to witness his former industrial park being included in Albert Speer's armaments programme; he died in 1940 of a heart thrombosis. He had been degraded from being a top industrialist to being forced to work as a chiropodist and only saved from a concentration camp because he was married to an 'Aryan'.

Hamel proceeded to take over Jewish-owned Lindener Iron and Steel, which was one of the largest companies in the Reich. He was later appointed to the management board of the big Tobis film studios, where many of Goebbels' propaganda films were made. Eventually he became spokesperson for the Bankers' Federation and in March 1944 Goebbels' personal consultant. After the war, with the collusion of British and US occupying forces, Hamel was able to escape retribution by obtaining references from former colleagues. These references purported to show that by risking his life he had been instrumental in saving people's lives and the town of Potsdam from destruction during the capitulation, and that in his position on the administrative board of the stock exchange he had helped Jews and those who were persecuted for their political beliefs. After 1945, the key role he played in the Nazi economy was rapidly forgotten and he escaped punishment. In the Federal Republic, he was able to establish himself once more as a successful and wealthy businessman. Lembke writes that during the war he had made millions in profit from the armaments industry.

Another member of the Gradenwitz family, Robert, a gynaecologist, committed suicide before the Nazis could arrest him. He was widely known in medical circles as the author of an influential book, *Messungen der spezifischen localanästhetisierenden Kraft einiger Mittel* (Measuring the specific local-anaesthetic effectivity of certain treatments), published in Breslau (today Wrocław) in 1898. Peter Gradenwitz, the son of Felix, Berta's brother, was able to emigrate first to Britain in 1934, then to Palestine where he would settle and became a musicologist of world standing. He wrote the classic book, *The Music of Israel: From the Biblical Era to Modern Times*, and would become a close friend and correspondent of the composer and conductor Leonard Bernstein. His biography of Bernstein was published in 1984. After the war, Jürgen and Peter maintained a regular correspondence.

Even in the post-war Federal Republic, the family was still subject to the after-effects of the Nazi anti-Jewish campaign. Fritz Gradenwitz, the older brother of Else and Robert, was a lawyer, but became a town councillor in Stettin, and in 1912 was elected mayor of the expanding port and shipbuilding city of Kiel with support from the SPD. After losing a subsequent election, he became once again a practising lawyer and notary in the city. Although he had become a Lutheran Christian, his Jewish ancestry meant that he was blacklisted when the Nazis came to power. In the *Kristallnacht* of November 1938 his house was ransacked by the Brownshirts and he was arrested and then interned in Sachsenhausen concentration camp. Being married to a non-Jewish woman, though, afforded him a certain protection, and she was able to obtain his early release. After the war he became a judge working for the *Arbeitsgericht* (Industrial Tribunal). In 1945, the pension he should have received as a former mayor was reduced in accordance with the Nazis' emergency regulations. He mounted a legal challenge in response to this, on the basis that it had been made according to Nazi legislation. The Nazis' emergency legislation had been in fact repealed in 1941 but for 'Aryan' pensioners only, not for Jews. His legal challenge was rejected. The way the German government treated those who had suffered under the Nazis is reminiscent of the treatment of those citizens who had opposed the Nazis and been interned. It was also similar to the way the pension rights of GDR civil servants and those 'close to the government' would be treated post-unification in the 1980s: they received reduced, 'punitive' pensions as a result – a policy that would also affect some Kuczynski family members.

Notes

1   Jürgen Kuczynski, *René Kuczynski: Ein fortschrittlicher Wissenschaftler in der ersten Hälfte des 20. Jahrhunhunderts*, Berlin, Aufbau Verlag, 1957, pp. 25–26.
2   Christian Graf von Krockow, *Die Deutschen in Ihrem Jahrhundert 1890–1990*, Rowohlt, 1990, p. 126.
3   Victor Klemperer, *I Shall Bear Witness: The Diaries of Victor Klemperer 1933–41*, 2009.
4   Eric Hobsbawm, *Interesting Times: A Twentieth-Century Life*, Abacus, 2003.
5   Personal conversation with Ingrid Kuczynski, May 2015.
6   Edwin Black, *IBM and the Holocaust: The Strategic Alliance between Nazi Germany and America's Most Powerful Corporation*, Little, Brown, 2001.
7   Hans H. Lembke, *Die schwarzen Schafe bei den Gradenwitz und Kuczynski: Zwei Berliner Familien im 19. und 20. Jahrhundert*, Berlin, Trafo Verlag, 2008.
8   Renate Dorpalen, *Your Faithfull Mürt*, unpublished manuscript, 2011.

3

JÜRGEN FOLLOWS IN
HIS FATHER'S FOOTSTEPS
(1904–1929)

Jürgen chose to preface the biography he wrote of his father with:

> For Freedom's battle once begun,
> Bequeathed by bleeding sire to son,
> Though baffled oft is ever won.[1]

Choosing these lines by Byron he emphasises that he sees himself as following in his father's footsteps and taking up the torch of struggle. Jürgen Kuczynski was the eldest of Robert and Berta's children, and represented the sixth generation of his family to belong to the intelligentsia. Today that intellectual tradition in the family has been continuing already through eight generations.

He was emotionally closer to his mother than his father, but he was very much influenced in his choice of career and political views by the latter. It was his father who, although never a member of any political party, 'largely determined his path to communism and career as a social scientist'.

Despite growing up in a very left-wing and socially engaged family, Jürgen did not immediately become a member of any party. His sister Ursula, the first of the siblings to join the German Communist Party while still in her teens, continually pressured him to join, but he insisted on doing so in his own time. He followed his father's example and worked in the USA as a young man before returning in the late 1920s to a Germany riven by political extremes, and eventually joined the Communist Party in 1930 on the symbolic day of 14 July, the anniversary of the storming of the Bastille, but not as a direct result of his sister's urgings.[2]

Born in Elberfeld in 1904, he grew up in the Berlin suburb of Friedenau before the family moved to the lakeside villa on Schlachtensee. He experienced a childhood in which he mixed with other children from different classes and knew poverty as well as affluence. He says that this helped him adapt much later during his time in exile when money was often scarce and living accommodation makeshift. In New York, during the late 1930s, when he was collecting money in support of the German Communist Party's secret radio transmitter broadcasting to Nazi Germany, he was at times obliged to seek lodgings in slum areas because he had run out of money, but at the same time had to move in Wall Street banking circles to raise the funds.

Jürgen relates that the family home where he grew up was a meeting place for leading intellectual and political figures as well as the wider family. There would be his grandfather Wilhelm, the bank director, for dinner one evening and the next a leader of the Social Democrats, and then his mother invited fellow artists to the house. He also recalls (from his mother's telling) how one evening, when he was a very small child still in the cradle, the well-known statistician Richard Böckh, who was visiting the family home, gave him advice for his future student life on the basis of his own squandered years and those of his older friends like Heinrich Heine, Felix Mendelssohn and other representatives of the Berlin jeunesse dorée of the time.

His uncle, Otto Gradenwitz, was also a regular visitor. He was a professor in Roman law, an expert papyrologist and interpreter of ancient classical texts. He was also a good friend of Thomas Mann. Jürgen mentions the tale, often told in family circles, about how his uncle humiliated one of his academic rivals who was keen to be introduced to the celebrated author. While strolling along the banks of the River Neckar in Munich with Mann one day, Gradenwitz was approached by his rival Professor Thoma. He grudgingly introduced first the professor's wife and only afterwards the professor himself as 'Frau Thoma's Mann' – the humiliation was complete. On another occasion, in Berlin, Gradenwitz wished to take a taxi to his destination but before getting into the vehicle asked the driver if he was a Catholic. The Berlin cabbie answered gruffly: 'That's none o' your business, mate!' To which Gradenwitz responded, 'Let me explain. I wish to go to Martin Luther Street and if you'd been a Catholic, I would not have wished to oblige you to carry out that unenviable task.' He was well known in academic circles as something of a maverick, noted for his sharp wit and sarcasm. In Heidelberg it brought him great popularity. Otto Gradenwitz was, though, a dyed-in-the-wool nationalist and great admirer of Bismarck. When the latter died Gradenwitz felt Germany was truly lost.

Carl von Ossietzky, the renowned German pacifist and recipient of the 1935 Nobel Peace Prize for his work in exposing Germany's clandestine rearmament programme, was also a family friend and member of the League of Human Rights, in which Jürgen's father played a leading role. Jürgen got to know him well and would write articles for his popular weekly journal *Die Weltbühne*, before 1933. The popular satirist Kurt Tucholsky was also part of that circle. Jürgen would encounter Tucholsky again in Paris in the early 1930s and later in Swedish exile, but by then he had become a broken and bitter man. The French novelist Henri Barbusse was also a regular visitor to the Kuczynski household.[3] In 1932, Barbusse and fellow writer Romain Rolland issued an appeal on behalf of the League for an international congress of 'War against War', following the Japanese invasion of Manchuria.

His own schooling, Jürgen says, was indifferent and his educational performance not exactly outstanding. He was, though, even as a schoolboy, already something of a rebel and *Querdenker* as the Germans succinctly put it. (The literal translation, 'lateral thinker' does not adequately express the term; 'discomfiting thinker' is perhaps more apt.) He loved making calculations and working out mathematical puzzles, which no doubt helped prepare him for his later career as a statistician and economist.

He attended the *Gymnasium* (the German equivalent of the British grammar school) in Zehlendorf where, once again, he didn't excel academically, but was a competent athlete. He gives an interesting example of how he stood out from the other pupils even at this age in terms of his politics and attitude to nationhood. When in June 1919 he declared in school that the Treaty of Versailles was a just treaty because the Germans had been responsible for starting the war and had done so much damage to other nations, his class mates, as one body, gave him a thrashing for his 'outrageous' views. After his beating, bruised and battered, he announced bravely, 'And yet it does move', in a recalcitrant reference to Galileo's sotto voce comment after his public recantation before the Inquisition. The erudite reference was lost on his school mates, but the tone of defiance in which it was uttered did earn their respect. His teachers, he says, like their pupils, were virtually without exception, extremely nationalistic and pro-military.

His class was made up of the sons of reasonably well-off (but not extremely wealthy) minor industrialists, civil servants and intellectuals, several from the lower aristocracy, and one or two from the rising middle class. He writes that he did not profit enormously from his schooling but it did endow him with fluency in Greek and Latin. As a counter-pole, social life in the family home and long conversations with his father provided him with the intellectual stimulation lacking in school. Through the combined influence of school and family he was soon widely read in the classics and mainstream world literature and at the same time moved much more to the left in his political opinions than his fellow pupils. As a 17-year-old he had already read his way through volume I of Marx's *Capital*. What he perhaps lacked in natural ability he made up for in sheer assiduity. Six months later, after his seventeenth birthday, he went to university in Erlangen, a small town in Bavaria, north of Nuremberg, where he lodged with Paul Hensel, a friend of his father's and a professor at the university. Hensel was a 'Neo-Kantian' and friend of Max Weber – the greatest German social scientist of his day.

Like most German university students, Jürgen voluntarily attended lectures in a wide range of subjects, but was particularly drawn to philosophy. He didn't have much contact with other students as 'almost all of them were politically right-wing and the majority anti-semitic', he writes. In 1922, after a semester in Erlangen, Hensel advised him to further his studies at Heidelberg before returning to complete his doctorate. However, his parents recommended instead that he complete them in Berlin, which he tried, but was highly disappointed with the lecturers in the capital city and after a short time he headed off to Heidelberg where he would spend the larger part of his university life.

At the time Heidelberg was the most significant German university for the study of social sciences. There Jürgen joined a group centred around the philosopher and psychiatrist Karl Jaspers. His uncle Otto Gradenwitz was also lecturing there, but would die in 1935 without having to experience the worst horrors of the Hitler period. When Jürgen arrived at Heidelberg in the summer of 1923, Max Weber was no longer alive, but his widow Marianne still brought his old circle of friends together on a regular basis and Jürgen was invited to join them. One of the group, Karl Mannheim, was, like Jürgen, later driven into exile by Hitler and settled in Britain. He would have considerable influence on sociology in Britain, helping to shift it from a largely empirical basis to one which took a stronger interest in theory. Another influential figure was Jakob Marschak, who also spent time in exile in Britain before emigrating to the USA, where he became a co-founder of econometrics.

While still a student Jürgen was already very much politically engaged and unafraid of taking on challenging tasks. On one occasion he was asked to address a group of young workers in a local tobacco factory on the subject of 'wage labour and capital'.[4] That is where he learned to speak off the cuff rather than read his lectures, after he realised that most of his audience, after their day's hard work, were already dropping off before he had finished talking. At the same time he also began writing for the local Communist Party newspaper, although he was not yet a member.

He took great pleasure in the lectures of Lujo Brentano (the nephew of Clemens Brentano, a leading German romanticist, whose sister Bettina von Arnim was one of Goethe's regular correspondents, and Brentano himself had been close to Goethe and other leading romanticists of the era). Lujo, Jürgen says, could keep his listeners fascinated by the wonderful stories and anecdotes he could tell about that era.

The lectures Jürgen attended testify to his breadth of interests: he took aesthetics with Glockner, logic with Herrigel and Russian – the language and history, as well as religious philosophy – with Bobnoff. At the same time he polished up his Italian and was soon reading Dante in the original. In his fifth semester – the third at Heidelberg – he completed the major part of his dissertation, 'Economic Value: An Economic Theoretical, Sociological and Historical-Philosophical Examination'.

At this time, in 1923, he was the only one of his siblings to have left home. Ursula, next in line, was then 16, Brigitte 13, Barbara 10, Sabine, the youngest-but-one of the Kuczynski siblings and called 'Binchen' was just 4 years old, while the youngest, Renate, would be born in November of that same year. Jürgen, as the eldest and only male among the children was, of course, the *Hahn im Korb* (Cock of the Walk). All the girls looked up to and admired their big brother.

He spent a year and half at Heidelberg, where he wrote much of his doctoral thesis with help from Max Quarck, a friend of his father's. Quarck had been sacked from his government post under the notorious *Sozialistengesetz* (Bismark's law banning social democrats and socialists from all public employment). Quarck, who wrote the classic work, *The First German Workers' Movement 1848/49*, was able to tell him many stories concerning his friendship with leading German social democrats like Wilhelm Liebknecht (father of Karl) and August Bebel. He had, said Jürgen, an amazing library containing many leaflets and pamphlets from the German working-class movement, as well as original letters from Engels, Bebel, Liebknecht, Kautsky and others. At around this time Jürgen began work on his own first book, with the rather hubristic title of *Zurück zu Marx* (Back to Marx).

Although at this time he had been concentrating very much on philosophy, he was becoming increasingly disappointed by the 'humbug' of abstract philosophy and began to veer towards the applied sciences which appealed to his more rational personality. He began, as he puts it, 'to see through what we would today call the manipulation of opinion as a trick of the ruling class ... something that takes one further than a mere recognition of the fact that each class has its own ideology'. But it would still take five years before he decided to join a political party. When he eventually did, he wrote, 'there will be no more *la science pour la science*, science as simply a pleasurable exercise in attempting to solve difficult problems, never again for him [Jürgen] will there be a contradiction between life and science and life and politics'. (N.B.: In his memoirs he invariably writes about himself in the third person.)

Encouraged by Professor Hensel to submit his doctoral thesis before the latter retired, Jürgen managed to do so, and at the tender age of only 20, he became Hensel's youngest student to complete a doctorate.

Already at that time, in 1925, there were ominous signs of what was soon to unfold in Germany. He remarks that he didn't eat in the student *mensa* (canteen) any more because 'anti-semitism was on the rise again' and this made it impossible for him to take his food there, so was forced to eat outside the campus, where it was more expensive and taxed his modest income.

In April of that year, for the first time, the German people voted in a nationwide presidential election. The conservative and monarchist forces hoped that their preferred candidate Paul Hindenburg would, on becoming president, destroy Weimar democracy and return the country to its old autocratic system of government. He was duly elected with 14.6 million votes, while the SPD and the German Democratic Party won 13.7 million, and the communists 1.7 million. If the communists had pulled their candidate, Ernst Thälmann, in the second round, then the combined votes of the centre parties together with the communists would have been just enough to defeat Hindenburg.

It was ironic, Jürgen noted at the time, that the city of Erlangen, with its university and long inclusive cultural tradition was now united in one thing only – anti-semitism. This was the city in which his friend and teacher Paul Hensel lived and worked. Hensel was the grandchild of Fanny Mendelsohn-Bartholdy and great nephew of her brother Felix. Hensel's great-great grandfather was the philosopher Moses Mendelssohn, grandfather of Felix and Fanny. Such relationships also demonstrate the strong interconnectedness and long tradition of German-Jewish families and the significant contribution they made to German life and culture.

It is 'virtually impossible to go into a café here without being verbally abused' by anti-semites, he writes to his parents from Erlangen. Particularly in Bavaria, though, it was not only anti-semitism that was waxing, but also a rabid nationalism coupled with the persecution of communists. He writes of seeing a headline in the local newspaper, the *Münchener Neueste Nachricht*, announcing 'A search for communists', followed by a story detailing the arrest of almost all leading local communists. In the following years, during the late 1920s, even the newspaper of the Social Democratic Party was forbidden in Erlangen and there was a general witch-hunt of anyone deemed to be Jewish, socialist or communist. When 'Kamerad' Graf Luckner of the Nazi *Stahlhelm* newspaper spoke in the town 'everyone was there', he says.

Around this time, while still in Erlangen, he became increasingly interested in the nineteenth-century Romantic writers who he viewed as representatives of a fascinating and significant social movement, an assessment that would later, after the war, find him in strong disagreement with his friend Georg Lukács, as well as with the ruling Party hierarchy in the GDR, over the essential significance of the Romantic movement.

At the end of the fifth semester and after completing his doctorate he began reading Marxism in earnest. But he was not sure what to do in terms of a career, as a post in academia was on 'political and racial grounds' hardly possible. His father recommended that he return to Berlin and work in a bank for a time to learn the nuts and bolts of economic practice. At the same time this option would allow him to continue working on the book he had already begun writing. Jürgen was thrilled with the idea and, he notes, 'it goes to show that despite his philosophic studies, he feels he is more of an economist'.

However, before he began work at the bank and on his book, he made a trip to Paris – a present from his parents on completing his doctorate. Arriving there in April 1925, he immediately took part in large and lively communist-led demonstrations through the streets on which the police opened fire. Here, for the first time, he gained personal experience of 'class struggle' in the raw, as bullets whistled past his ear and the demonstrators fled for cover.

In the evenings he visited the opera and socialised with friends and acquaintances like Mme Ménard-Dorian, at whose salon he would meet Leon Blum – a leading socialist and future French prime minister – and Lidia Compolonghi, the daughter of the leader of the left in the Italian Socialist Party with whom he developed a long-term friendship. Mme Ménard had been a muse for artists like Rodin and Manet as well as the writer Anatole France, and she introduced Jürgen to her own fascinating Bohemian and artistic circle.

Since that time he would visit many capital cities but none, he writes, 'has the magic, the vitality of Paris' and none has so excited him.

Through his father's many contacts he was also able to meet a number of leading members of the French section of the League of Human Rights. When his father arrived to join him in May, they both met and dined with the satirist Kurt Tucholsky and his wife who were also sojourning in Paris.

On his return from Paris he again worked earnestly on his book, writing in the library, an ideal little place of retreat, purpose-built next to the family house on the Schlachtensee. In August 1926, when the book was published by Kohlhammer, he was still only a callow 21-year-old.

Up until this time he had been perceived by everyone as the son of his father, but when Robert went as head of a delegation to the Soviet Union in 1927 he was asked if he was related in any way to J. Kuczynski who was apparently already well known for his excellent articles on the economy in the journal *Finanzpolitische Korrespondenz* (*FK*). From then on his reputation could stand up on its own. After that visit to Moscow his father wrote to him recommending that he learn Russian properly, because 'Soviet Russia *is* the future'.

The *FK* was not only read in academic institutions but widely throughout the working-class movement and in the trade unions, and articles were also picked up by the wider press. It had been virtually a one-man publication produced by Jürgen's father and published three or four times a month, and would survive a further eight years, from then on with regular contributions from Jürgen, who wrote on almost any subject from economic reports, social issues, political polemics to book reviews.

He began his internship with the bank of Bett, Simon & Co. in October 1925. It was the same bank where only recently Kurt Tucholsky had been private secretary to its director Hugo Simon. At the bank Jürgen was able to work his way through the various departments, and being an avid learner he soon picked up all the tricks and saw how the real financial world and banking functioned. He also discovered how, just as in other capitalist enterprises, banks do all they can to avoid paying taxes and are not averse to using deviousness and swindles to do so. He quickly made use of what he learned there and was soon able to offer (remunerated) advice to others about where and when to invest. In this way he found he could supplement his meagre income relatively easily and even make financial contributions to the Communist Party, although he was still not a member. 'One shouldn't underestimate', he wrote, 'how useful a Marxist political-economic theoretical grounding, together with practical experience of capitalism, was for the party.' Despite this experience which he could have easily utilised to make himself a very rich man, he chose the stonier path of commitment to the communist cause.

While with the bank Jürgen also began editing the house magazine of the League for Human Rights in which his father was very active and which had widespread support amongst social democrats and middle-class radicals. In this capacity he met and made friends with a number of leading political activists like Willi Münzenberg, the communist organiser and propagandist, Carl Mertens, the former army officer and radical pacifist, Ludwig Quidde, the Nobel Peace Prize winner, as well as Albert Einstein, who were all active in the League. At the same time he became intimate with Soviet academics and politicians who regularly visited his parents' home. At a showing in Berlin of the film *Battleship Potemkin* he met Anatole Lunacharsky, the first Soviet commissar of education, and the political economist Yevgeny Varga, who would become a life-long close friend and a model for him 'of a stalwart comrade and political theorist'.

Paul Fröhlich, the prominent socialist and friend of Rosa Luxemburg and Karl Liebknecht as well as biographer of Marx, was a customer of the Bett and Simon Bank and Jürgen got to know him well. Fröhlich had been appointed trustee of Rosa Luxemburg's papers, and when the Nazis came to power in 1933 Fröhlich left a large parcel for safekeeping with Simon, one of the bank's directors. It contained Luxemburg's own papers, including her manuscript of a planned book on the national economy, as well as letters from Clara Zetkin. When the situation in Germany became no longer tolerable, Simon decided to flee Germany and ordered his chauffeur to burn all his papers. A friend of Jürgen's heard what was happening, rushed over, and was able to save the Luxemburg papers and other documents moments before the flames consumed them. He gave these to Jürgen, who, with the help of the Soviet embassy, managed to get much of the material sent to London, along with his grandfather's copy of the original *Communist Manifesto*, but some items were lost irretrievably.

Alongside his work at the bank Jürgen very soon completed writing his second substantial work – *Lehrbuch der Finanzen* (A Text Book of

Financial Affairs) – published in 1927, when he was already in the USA. He had left Germany in the late summer of 1926 after obtaining a place and a grant as a research student at the Brookings Graduate School (attached to the Brookings Institution – the centrist think-tank founded in 1922 by the millionaire Robert S. Brookings, and one of the oldest in the USA); the school had been set up in 1924. Brookings only catered for around twenty to thirty selected students, so Jürgen had been very lucky to be among those. Now with practical experience of the banking sector on top of his theoretical grounding, he felt much more confident in tackling economic issues in some depth.

He arrived in the United States by boat on 17 September, his birthday, and, together with his parents who accompanied him, travelled to Washington D.C. The very next day at breakfast in the refectory, he met a young woman originally from the Alsace region, Marguerite Steinfeld, who was also studying at Brookings. She would very soon become his wife and life-long partner. She would also join the Communist Party, but not until 1940 in London exile.

Anne Marguerite Madeleine Steinfeld was born in December 1904 in Bischheim, Strasbourg in Alsace. Since 1918 Alsace had been French territory once again after its annexation by Germany in the wake of the Franco–Prussian War of 1870–71. So she grew up steeped in both German and French cultures. She first passed her exams as a teacher of French before winning a government grant in 1921 to study in the USA. First she took an economics degree course at the University of Michigan, Ann Arbor, before going on to Brookings. She supported herself financially by working in the holidays as an assistant professor of French. After completing her degree at Ann Arbor, she took up a postgraduate position at the Brookings School in Washington.

She came from a Protestant middle-class family and although both she and Jürgen saw themselves as secular leftists, his Jewish background was a common point of reference. When she introduced him to her family in 1928, she jokingly presented him as personified Jewish vengeance, alluding to the fact that one of her ancestors had opposed Jewish emancipation during the French Revolution.

Robert Brookings, the founder of the school, invited the Kuczynskis to dine with him when they arrived. Jürgen described him as 'already an old man ... modest, lively and with no airs and graces ... very interested in political and economic affairs'. Brookings had made his money in the household goods branch, but once he had made enough, decided to devote the rest of his life to philanthropy and charitable endeavour. In his home, Jürgen was struck by 'the utmost simplicity of his surroundings: unpretentious rooms but expensively furnished; the food seemed very ordinary and was taken at a small table for four, placed against the wall on which was hung a genuine Ruisdael landscape'.

His parents returned to Germany in April 1927, leaving Jürgen to find his own feet. His father's introductions, however, would be extremely useful to him in his future work. One of those, Daniel de Leon, a leading American socialist, would facilitate his access to trade union and working-class circles in New York. Another contact, Oswald Garrison Villard, the publisher of the progressive weekly, *The Nation*, would introduce him to a completely different circle of left and radical middle-class citizens.

His experience and work during his stay in the USA would lead him to the central focus of his life's work: a historical examination of the conditions under which working people live and work. Two years after his arrival there, on exactly the same date, he and Marguerite would be married. On hearing of his son's intention to marry, Robert commented, 'It's much too early to get married, but at least he's marrying a French woman.' Since the day they met, Jürgen wrote much later, they would see or speak to each other daily, unless travelling separately made it impossible.

Marguerite would become a talented economist in her own right and was, at the time, one of the very few women to gain a scholarship to Brookings. She stayed there until March 1927 before going on to New York, to take up a post as an assistant in the National Bureau of Economic Research, where she stayed until 1929. There, she concentrated specifically on the role of the trade unions and wages in the economic structure of the country. This was also a period of intensive collaboration with Jürgen, and they wrote a number of articles and reports together as well as carrying out joint statistical research into the situation of workers within the US economy.

Their collaboration was characterised on the one hand by Jürgen's continual pressure for them to finish things, and her demand for more time, as she was the more meticulous of the two. She also corrected and edited his writing, as her English was better than his. A number of their collaborative works were published anonymously in the Economic Statistics section of the *American Federationist* (the official magazine of the American Federation of Labor). She also became an active trade unionist and joined the Office Workers' Union in 1927, regularly attending union branch meetings.

When the family returned from their London exile to Berlin after the war she would work in the financial department of Berlin's city administration. From there she went to the Ministry of Foreign Trade and then the Institute of Marxism-Leninism. While working at the latter institute she would discover that a Japanese academic owned Marx's personal copy of *The Poverty of Philosophy*, containing marginal notes made by the author himself. She was able to ensure that a copy of this document was made available to future researchers. Another of her discoveries concerned two leading French economists. While researching the pre-Marxist French economists, she rediscovered the innovative work of Quesnay and Turgot, both of whom Marx had respected highly, particularly for their work on added value. Quesnay became one of the great bourgeois economists in eighteenth-century France and also had considerable influence on Adam Smith. His magnum opus, the *Tableau Économique*, appeared in three editions but the latest of his books containing his own corrections had been lost for a century. Marguerite would manage to track it down and ensure that a new edition, including his corrections, was published.

While at Brookings Jürgen also met and became friends with a number of fellow students who went on to occupy prominent positions in the US government or academia, people like Oliver Wendell Holmes, a future high court judge and friend of Franklin D. Roosevelt. These contacts would be very useful later when he returned to the USA to collect money in support of the secret German Communist Party radio station 29.8 broadcasting, first from Spain and then Strasbourg, to Germany during the Nazi period.

He and Marguerite thoroughly enjoyed their time in the USA. It was not only that they had the opportunity of studying the most prominent capitalist country first hand, but they could relish the vibrancy of the country and the openness and tolerance of North Americans in comparison with the rigidities of early twentieth-century Prussian-dominated German society. They would also savour the country's pioneering spirit and the cosmopolitan cultural mix of the big cities on the East Coast.

Jürgen also took the opportunity of this first short sojourn to immerse himself in American culture, particularly its literature. At the same time his own writings on economics and statistics were finding increasing resonance in the USA. After a visit to Brookings by Margaret Scattergood, a Quaker with links to the American labour movement, he was introduced to the American Federation of Labor (AFL) – the main trade union organisation in the USA. Margaret's friend Florence C. Thorne had been secretary to Samuel Gompers, the legendary first president of the AFL, and now worked for his successor William Green (former president of the United Mine Workers of America), and she recommended Jürgen to him as a researcher and writer for the AFL journal, *American Federationist*.

Green had become a coal miner at the age of 16, in 1879, before his involvement in union affairs. He served as president of the American Federation of Labor from 1924 to 1952. He was a strong supporter of worker–management co-operation and fought for wage and benefit protections. As president of the AFL he continued the development of the Federation away from its foundation as a purely trade union orga-nisation, towards a more politically active social reform movement. He was regarded by his contemporaries as a very mild-mannered man who tended to defer on nearly all matters to his aides. He thought it a great idea to employ a young and competent researcher, so immediately appointed Jürgen. To facilitate his new work Jürgen would need to maintain close relations with the US Commissioner of Labor Statistics, which gave him access to vital government figures. Again, he was fol-lowing in his father's footsteps: Jürgen's father himself had prepared some of his first statistical studies on labour relations towards the end of the nineteenth century for the first US Commissioner of Labor Statistics, Carroll D. Wright, and had also worked for his successor.

During his stay in the USA, Jürgen continued to contribute articles to various publications in Germany but then, after only six months in America, he began writing regularly for the *American Federationist*. In it, he wrote mainly about wages and economic cycles and the statistical relationships between wages and productivity, the cost of living and profits. As this sort of research was quite new – hardly anyone in the past apart from Marx and Engels had been interested in the relationship between wages, productivity and the cost of living – his articles in the journal were often reproduced or quoted elsewhere and also published as one-off pamphlets in their own right as 'official publications' of the AFL.

By the following May, only a few months after beginning work for the AFL, Jürgen managed to persuade the leadership of the organisation that it needed a proper research department. So on 1 July he was duly appointed as the grandly titled Director of the Research Office – in essence a one-man undertaking. As a young foreigner, only 22 years old, he was, amazingly, now given relatively free rein to set up and run the AFL's research programme in precisely the areas that interested and excited him the most, and in which little if any work had previously been undertaken. Little did his employers realise what a left-wing firebrand they had taken to their bosom.

Although his research was of general value and interest, his main goal was to provide the trade unions and the working-class movement with solid factual data to back up their arguments for higher wages. However, he had to be very circumspect in doing so because the AFL, unlike most European trade unions, had no socialist leanings and was in the main anti-socialist and virulently anti-Bolshevik. William Green also had to be particularly careful not to anger individual union leaders within the Federation like the powerful Bill Hutcheson of the United Brotherhood of Carpenters and Joiners of America – a dyed-in-the-wool right-winger who described Roosevelt's presidency as 'a dictatorship' – and John Lewis of the big miners' union, a visceral anti-communist who began as a Roosevelt supporter but soon drifted to become a right-wing Republican, as did Matthew Woll, who had the strongest position in the organisation and was also wildly anti-Bolshevik.

Woll became a confidant of AFL president Samuel Gompers and of William Green, who relied on him for advice and guidance during his presidency of the AFL. Woll also became a mentor to Jay Lovestone, a one-time communist who was expelled from the party only to become a rabid red-baiter and AFL–CIO foreign policy advisor.

Much later, in 1944, with the onset of the Cold War, the AFL–CIO would establish the Free Trade Union Committee (FTUC) in order to facilitate the establishment of trade unions abroad, particularly in Europe, in opposition to, and in competition with, those deemed to be close to the communists. Lovestone became its secretary, reporting to Woll. Lovestone's mission was to ensure the elimination of left-leaning unions and supplant them with those that supported capitalism. The CIA funnelled millions of dollars through FTUC in support of such American foreign policy goals.

Jürgen described the whole AFL organisation and its leadership at the time very succinctly in his memoirs as 'this "upstanding" high bourgeois leadership of the organisation, made up of leading officials from many unions [which] was primitive gangsterism closely associated with the theft of union funds as well as murder'. He had to be very circumspect with his own views and to know just how far he could go without being exposed as a 'scheming red'.

During his work for the AFL he made friends with Solon de Leon, son of the US socialist leader Daniel de Leon, who was the director of the Rand School, a working-class college in Washington D.C., but he kept such friendships hidden from his employer. He was also introduced into liberal circles by Oswald Garrison Villard, a friend of his father's and publisher of the widely respected magazine *The Nation*.

At the AFL annual conference in October 1927, the use of accurate statistical information in the trade unions' struggle for better wages was strongly underlined – a tribute to Jürgen's work. His studies and articles in the *American Federationist* were praised for making use of the statistical relationships between wages, prices and productivity. Here, for the first time, an index of the relationship between these three factors was used, on the basis of statistics going back to 1922. Much later the use of such indexes became common currency for economists, statisticians and governments, but were pioneering at the time. These articles gained international recognition, particularly the one he wrote in August 1928 in the form of a declaration, signed by the Federation's president, on the wage struggle, and based on the statistical evidence Jürgen had gathered on wages and living standards.[5] He saw it as a real coup de main, persuading the AFL president to put his name to a declaration on wage policy with more than a whiff of Marxist thinking in it. It declared that the AFL would in future demand wage increases which would hinder the intensification of exploitation and in fact, over time, reduce it.

At the AFL, Jürgen also introduced the idea of publishing regular unemployment statistics, against much initial resistance from Green, who felt it would only undermine the negotiating power of his organisation. At the time, these unemployment statistics were the only ones available in the USA but soon, Jürgen writes in his memoirs, took on an 'official character' and were eventually adopted by the government's own national statistical department.[6] The results of his research on unemployment were used also by progressive senators in Congress as the basis for a bill to be tabled aimed at introducing measures to deal with the rising numbers of unemployed and structures to alleviate the situation. He also ensured that the US Communist Party and the Comintern also made full use of his work.

As Jürgen himself noted,[7] it is amazing how he alone, with only one 17-year-old secretary, managed to set up and maintain an ongoing statistical methodology for calculating the unemployment statistics in the USA, as well as accomplishing the regular writing of articles, many of which were published under Green's name. He says that this necessity of working effectively with little means and logistical support was good training for his later work for the Communist Party, during his exile from Germany in the 1930s and also in the early years of post-war reconstruction in East Germany. Such an attitude was characteristic of this workaholic.

During the late 1920s both Jürgen and Marguerite, back in Germany and alongside his father, became involved in the worldwide campaign to free the imprisoned anarchist trade unionists Sacco and Vanzetti, including gaining support from the German League for Human Rights. The Sacco and Vanzetti case was one of the key events that mobilised Marguerite's political consciousness. Their trial in 1921 and execution in 1927 provoked mass strikes and demonstrations around the country, but particularly in New York. She took part in some of these and experienced the last convulsions of these shocking events, sending graphic accounts of them to Jürgen, who had remained in Washington throughout 1927.

Nicola Sacco and Bartolomeo Vanzetti were Italian-born anarchists convicted of murdering a guard and a paymaster during the armed robbery of a shoe factory in Braintree, Massachusetts in 1920. They were put on trial, and after a few hours' deliberation the jury found them guilty of first-degree murder. A series of appeals followed, funded largely by a private Sacco and Vanzetti Defense Committee. As details of the trial and the men's apparent innocence were made known, the Sacco and Vanzetti case became one of the biggest cause célèbres of the first half of the twentieth century. In 1927, protests on their behalf were held in every major city in North America and Europe. Celebrated writers, artists and academics pleaded for their pardon or for a new trial. Despite these appeals they were finally executed in the electric chair. In response to this judicial murder, subsequent riots destroyed property in Paris, London and other cities. It is reasonably certain that the two men were convicted largely on the basis of the widespread anti-Italian prejudice and their anarchist political beliefs. The German *Reichskommissar* for Public Order noted in an internal report that, 'Dr. Robert Kuczynski [Jürgen's father] was a leading member of the League for Human Rights' and that he 'supported the communist Sacco propaganda campaign'.

While working full-time for the AFL, which he did until September 1928, Jürgen was also beavering away on yet another book, *Economics for Workmen*. Although it was never published, the exercise was very useful because it forced him to deal with complicated issues in an easily accessible and readable form. His research and writing for the US trade unions, which demanded clarity and simplicity, certainly had an impact on the way the unions approached and conducted negotiations with employers.

The research department he set up still existed forty years later and continued to provide trade unions with valuable statistical information. The statistics he collected on unemployment were used by a wide range of organisations and institutions before the government began collecting its own on a much broader basis.

An amusing anecdote he relates in connection with his work for the AFL concerns an article he drafted for Green in 1928 as a forecast for the following year 1929, in which he warned that a deep economic crisis was about to unfold. This was vehemently rejected by Green as too pessimistic and a more optimistic tone was substituted. That year saw the biggest financial crash of the twentieth century – so much for false optimism.

Before he left the AFL, he also co-authored several books with Marguerite, the first of which was *Der Fabrikarbeiter in der amerikanischen Wirtschaft* (The Factory Worker in the American Economy), published in 1930. It was one of the first critical, historical-statistical analyses of the living and working conditions of workers in the USA. These books were also published in Russia in 1930 and 1931.

During his time in the USA he had also taken the opportunity to make contact with a number of leading black progressives at the District of Columbia and Howard universities, two of the few existing black colleges at the time. Among those he met and with whom he held discussions were Alain Locke, a leading advocate of black culture, the celebrated poets Countee Cullen and Langston Hughes, James Weldon Johnson and Charles H. Wesley, whose book, *Negro Labor in the United States*, had taught him a lot. He noted in his memoir how much he absorbed of US culture and its people during his stay, particularly that of the working class and of the left-wing intellectuals he met. The years spent there were very happy ones, he said, for both himself and his wife. These unique experiences of working in the USA gave each a deep understanding of how capitalism in its most vigorous and pioneering form worked, and it would buttress their socialist ideas with firm knowledge rather than hearsay and supposition.

Throughout his stay he maintained regular and close contact by post with his parents and sisters back home. He also developed close and regular relations with the 'inofficial' diplomatic representative of the Soviet Union in Washington. Jürgen became, in his own words 'a spontaneous, useful source of information about my work and environment. From him [the Soviet diplomat] I learnt about how to observe and analyse my environment in the interests of the Soviet Union.'[8] This relationship cemented an already loose, but friendly relationship with Soviet representatives and would determine his continued close working relationship with the Soviet Union throughout the rest of his life.

The period he and Marguerite spent in the States coincided with a period of enormous economic growth and the development of new luxury items which became accessible to ordinary working-class families, such as the motor car and electrical consumer goods like refrigerators, washing machines and vacuum cleaners. This development was transforming the lives of millions. At the same time agriculture was going through a deep structural crisis with mass migration from the land, so well characterised in John Steinbeck's *Grapes of Wrath*. It was also a hard time for the unions, battling greedy and corrupt bosses, many of whom used the Mafia and private security firms to undermine and smash them.

In the early summer of 1929, as the end of their time in the USA drew near, they undertook a trip around the country by bus, using the opportunity to collect further statistics and visit factories. The economic crash of that same year was the culmination of all the factors they had noted during their stay. However, they would experience the consequent Great Depression of the early 1930s back home in Germany. Their return coincided with the country entering a crucial period of sharpened confrontation between right-wing, nationalist forces on the one hand, and the forces of social democracy and communism on the other. This polarisation would force them to make life-transforming choices.

On 4 July 1929 – national Independence Day in the USA and three years since first arriving there – he and Marguerite left the country on the aptly named SS *Lafayette* for France, eventually arriving in Bischeim near Strasbourg, Marguerite's home town, on Bastille Day, 14 July, France's own national day. As they steamed out of New York harbour, they looked back to see the sun glinting on the verdigris crown of the Statue of Liberty, the unforgettable skyline of Manhattan, still wreathed in early morning mist and the churning wake of the ship creating a curving pathway through the sepia-grey waters of New York Bay. They were a happy couple, looking forward to getting home and settling down to raise a family in Berlin. Little did they realise that they would be returning to a country about to experience a seismic tremor that would have a tumultuous impact on their lives. Jürgen would not return to the USA again until 1938, shortly before the outbreak of the Second World War.

In connection with the books he wrote while in America, he relates in his memoirs that when the proofs of the first one to be translated into Russian came into Stalin's hands, he happened to be busy noting the 'many mistakes' when Karl Radek entered his office. Stalin told Radek to write a foreword in order to highlight the 'mistakes'. The news of Stalin's reaction reached Berlin, and Jürgen was made aware of it. He utilised the opportunity afforded by being invited to join a delegation from Germany to Moscow in 1930 to talk with Radek about the book. In Radek's office, before discussing any details, he was asked which sections he had written and which his wife. Jürgen answered, 'as a gentleman would', telling Radek that 'the good parts were written by Marguerite and the bad bits by me'. 'Ah well', replied Radek, 'then it's clear that you wrote the whole book!' On a brighter note, Béla Kun, the Hungarian Communist Party leader who spent a day with Jürgen in Moscow, told him that the book was very useful with numerous facts in it that he hadn't known. Subsequently, it also received good reviews in the Moscow press.

Notes

1 Lord Byron, *The Giaour* (1813).
2 Jürgen Kuczynski, *Ein Linientreuer Dissident: Memoiren 1945–1989*, Aufbau Taschenbuch Verlag, 1999, p. 28.
3 Jürgen Kuczynski, *Die Erziehung des J.K. zum Kommunisten und Wissenschaftler: Memoiren* (1907–45) vol. 1, p. 91.
4 Ibid., p. 62.
5 Ibid., p. 143.
6 Ibid., p. 162.
7 Ibid., p. 163.
8 Ibid., p. 179.

4

URSULA

The politically precocious child (1907–1935)

Ursula, born three years after Jürgen in 1907, would become the most politically radical of all her siblings. She was to achieve renown or notoriety, depending on one's political viewpoint, as the successful Soviet secret agent, codenamed 'Sonya'.

As a 7-year-old she experienced the outbreak of the First World War. Letters to her parents and her memories of the early post-war years tell of hunger, scarcity and widespread poverty of which she was, even as a child, acutely aware. In 1923, the year her youngest sister Renate was born, and five years after the end of the First World War, she was about to leave school. From a children's holiday camp she wrote in a letter to her mother that:

> prices are so hair-raising that I had to borrow 50,000 Marks. Fortunately we were able to get bread coupons. Whatever you do, don't send me that hat. If you want to send me anything at all, make it sausage. That costs 15,000 Marks for a quarter of a pound here. And if by any chance you do send anything, perhaps some sugar?

Such was the impact of hyperinflation on prices, leading to shortages of even basic food items in the wake of the war and imposition of the punitive measures of the Versailles Treaty.

In all likelihood it was her father who awakened in her an early emotional identification with the poor and oppressed. As a 15-year-old Ursula had become fascinated by the earthy novels of Maxim Gorky and Jack London, borrowed from her father's library. Such books would deeply influence her future thinking and political allegiances. A short time later she progressed to reading Lenin and Rosa Luxemburg and they helped her develop the rational ideas that gave focus to her emotional responses which would lead to political action. Within a year, as a 16-year-old only just out of school, she joined the Communist Youth League, and took part in her first May Day demonstration. Here she experienced police brutality first hand, being hit with a rubber truncheon by a large policeman. From then on politics and the various activities of the Communist Youth League became her life-blood. Three years later she took the plunge and joined the Communist Party itself – the first in her family to do so.

Politically, Berlin, with its densely packed working-class areas, was seen very much as a left-wing stronghold, with the Nazis calling it the reddest city after Moscow. Nazi propagandist Joseph Goebbels became his party's *Gauleiter* for Berlin in the autumn of 1926 and had only been in charge a week before the Nazis organised a march through strongly communist-supporting areas, leading to violent confrontations. The police intervened but, as they invariably did, took the side of the fascists. In February of the following year the Nazis held another rally in the Berlin working-class suburb of 'Red' Wedding, which also turned into a violent brawl. Beer glasses, chairs and tables were used as missiles, and severely injured people were left lying on the floor covered with blood. Goebbels claimed it to be a triumph.

Already in 1924, Ursula had begun an apprenticeship in a Berlin bookshop that specialised in law and political science. Through her membership of the communist movement she had by now become involved with a whole number of new contacts and friends from diverse backgrounds which gave her new insights on life. She was instrumental in setting up the *Marxistische Arbeiterbibliothek* (Workers' Marxist Library) in Berlin and became its director. She also began writing articles for the Party newspaper, *Die Rote Fahne* (The Red Flag). In her memoir, *Sonya's Report*, she relates that she:

> observed the wealth of the small, privileged circles and the poverty in which so many people lived; I saw the unemployed begging on the street corners. I pondered on the injustices of this world and how they might be eliminated. And now I also experienced the grim contrasts between my own home life and work: the anxiety of grown-up people trembling at each month's end for fear they might be handed their cards.

Her friend Marthe, who had also begun work at the same time, became the first victim she knew of such arbitrary sackings. But she discovered a deep satisfaction in being part of the young communist movement. She took part in a celebration of the 'Great October Revolution in Russia', organised agit-prop theatre and choral performances of rousing songs, paraded with her comrades holding fluttering banners – all these activities engendered a jubilant and optimistic atmosphere: a conviction that Germany's own socialist revolution was around the corner. It was undoubtedly the happiest time of her life.

This deep commitment, however, became unsettled by an unexpected romantic attachment. In the meantime a young and progressive architectural student, Rudolf Hamburger, or Rolf as friends called him, had fallen head over heels in love with her. He became fascinated by this young, raven-haired woman with her enormous vitality, intellectual acuity and joie de vivre from the first time he met her. Ursula was not immediately smitten as he was, but they soon found they were enjoying each other's company and spent more and more time together. Although he was not as radical as Ursula, she felt certain she could win him over to her communist ideas.

In her revealing semi-autobiographical novel, *Ein Ungewöhnliches Mädchen* (An Unusual Girl) she describes a short discussion between the protagonist 'Vera' (i.e. herself) with 'Gerd' (i.e. Rolf) in which she badgers him to join the Communist Party. He is reluctant to do so. When she presses him why he won't, he responds: 'There are things with the Party that disturb me. Perhaps I'll get there slowly, if you leave me time.'

'What don't you like?' she asks.

'The exaggerations in the press', he says, 'the primitive tone of some articles, the boring speeches with their sloganising, the arrogance towards those with different viewpoints, the clumsy attitude to intellectuals, who are alienated by this, instead of winning them to communism. The insults flung at the opposition instead of countering their arguments with logic.'

'And you call yourself a sympathiser?' she responds him with sarcasm.

This fictional dialogue mirrors very much the situation she describes in her reminiscences, *Sonya's Report*. Interestingly, Rolf's attitude, as described here, is not dissimilar to that of Robert Kuczynski at the time.

She and Rolf began taking outings to the countryside together and met regularly after work and classes. Rolf was very soon keen to get married, but Ursula was reluctant to settle down before she had even begun to enjoy her freedom as a young and independent adult. She did not feel ready, she needed time and space to consider what she wanted to do. So, in September 1928, while Rolf was completing his studies, she took herself off to the United States where her brother Jürgen was at that time living and working. There she transferred her membership of the German Communist Party to that of the American party. With her experience, she very soon found employment in Prosnit, a small bookshop in uptown New York. As an avid reader, she immediately began to immerse herself in American literature in order to learn more about the country. She also helped out in the Henry Street Settlement at 256 Henry Street, where poor Jews were given refuge. She lived there for a time and instead of paying rent carried out social work duties twice a week.

In his own reminiscences, Rudolf writes movingly about his first meeting with Ursula and his immediately falling in love with her. Although he uses the fictitious names of 'Alex' and 'Toni' he is clearly writing about the two of them.

He sees her first on a sandy beach on the outskirts of Berlin. She is with a group of members of the youth organisations of the Social Democratic and Communist parties, enjoying a summer afternoon swimming and sun bathing. She held out the promise of unpredictable adventure and a seductive rebelliousness. He is immediately taken by her passionate and articulate argumentation, her tomboyish vivacity and her shock of black hair. When he asks her if they could chat for a while, she replies that she has no time as she has to go to a Marxist Workers' class. On asking if they could perhaps meet sometime soon she responded: 'I could consider it!' before running off. A short time later he waylaid her outside the building where the Marxist school was held, and was lucky that she responded more positively this time. It did not take long before they became lovers. At the time she was working in a bookshop and he was still completing his architectural degree. Her passion was politics and the Communist Party, his was architecture. Her work in the bookshop was a means of earning her bread and butter, but the only work that gave her life meaning began after the shop was closed: working for the Party's youth wing, organising agit-prop theatrical performances and other political events. Although he was politically left wing, he could not understand why the two big working-class parties – the SPD and KPD – did not work together. He was more tolerant and questioning than she was and did not have her passionate conviction and sense of certainty, of being right. This difference in attitude was one of the first indications of the ideological differences that would later impair their early married life in China.

Rolf loved his profession above everything else and, along with his fellow young architects, was inspired by the new architectural modernism, the influence of the Bauhaus movement, of architects like Le Corbusier, Gropius, Frank Lloyd Wright and others. They were thrilled with the idea of designing grand projects for the people and keen to find a new formal language in architecture, the equivalent of Cubism, Expressionism and New Realism in art. However, Rolf was realist enough to know that his future clients would be those with money – the bourgeoisie – and that the class for whom he would really like to design buildings would not be giving him any commissions for some time to come. Ironically, one of his first minor commissions came through Ursula's connections and was for the interior design of a new 'Red Bookshop' – everything in red. His payment was a series of art prints of works by Käthe Kollwitz, Paula Modersohn and Otto Dix. But Ursula had no interest in or understanding of his work. She told him that it would be useful after the revolution, but at present the urgent task was to break the power of the capitalists and build a workers' state.

On her return from the USA to Germany in 1929, the same year in which Jürgen and Marguerite returned, Ursula seems to have made up her mind about Rolf. They very quickly decided that they did want to live together, and soon got married with no elaborate ceremony.

Both Rolf and his friend Richard Paulick had studied under the then well-known architect Hans Poelzig. The graduating students were told bluntly by their professor that they would hardly find work in Germany, but would have to look further afield. As a freshly graduated architect in late 1920s Berlin – the time of the depression and not much construction being undertaken – there was indeed little opportunity for men or women, even in his profession, of finding work. It was a depressing prospect. He had now completed his studies and was raring to embark on his architectural career, if only there had been jobs available.

At the same time, on the streets, the conflicts between communists and fascists were growing fiercer and more violent, and the arguments between the SPD and KPD more vehement. He argued with Ursula that the two working-class parties needed to fight fascism together, but she rejected his suggestion, emphasising that it was impossible to work with the SPD because, when it came to the crunch, they gave their support to the ruling class. The experiences of the way the SPD had helped crush the short-lived 1918 revolutions in Germany, followed by its pusillanimity during the years of the Weimar Republic, had left its scars.

As a newly married couple they both now had to look seriously for jobs, but these were not easy to find in late 1920s Berlin. Then, out of the blue a telegram arrived for Rudolf from a good friend of his working in China who told him that the Administration of the Shanghai International Settlement was looking for an architect. Without much deliberation he applied for the job and was accepted. He was excited by this opportunity of working as an architect at long last. Ursula, though, felt that moving there with him would be the equivalent of deserting the front line and leaving her comrades in the lurch, but neither he nor she could realistically refuse this lifeline. In the end they agreed to make a go of it. He was required to take up the post immediately and so in 1930 they packed their few belongings and headed east, both excited by the prospect of living in a new and exotic country. They travelled first to Moscow and then by the Trans-Siberian Express to the eastern border of the Soviet Union, which took a whole week, followed by another week on a Chinese train to Shanghai.

China was a very divided country when they arrived, riven by warring groups and still partially occupied by foreign colonialist nations. In 1927 Chiang Kai-shek had formed his nationalist government – the Kuomintang (KMT) – which finally put an end to the dynastic rule of Chinese imperial clans, but his dictatorial regime was opposed by the rapidly growing Communist Party under its leader Mao Tse-tung.

In 1931, Japan, eager for the vast natural resources to be found in China and seeing the country's obvious weakness, invaded and occupied Manchuria. The invaders proceeded to turn it into a nominally independent state which they called Manchukuo, and the Chinese Emperor who supposedly ruled it was merely their puppet. China appealed to the League of Nations to intervene, but the League merely published a report condemning Japanese aggression and undertook no further action.

The communists made efforts to form an alliance with Chiang Kai-shek to defeat the Japanese aggressor, but he was more frightened of the communists than he was of the Japanese, who were granted free rein in the country. The Japanese invasion of China had evoked widespread outrage on the left, and communists worldwide led campaigns to boycott Japanese goods. In 1938 dockers in Middlesbrough refused to load a Japanese ship, the *Haruna Maru*, with a cargo of pig iron destined for Japan. Apart from several popular uprisings by the Chinese peasantry that were brutally suppressed, the Japanese encountered little resistance from the Nationalists. Civil war between the two main Chinese political forces had already erupted in 1930 and eventually, in 1934, when Chiang Kai-shek was in hot pursuit of the communists, Mao's People's Liberation Army was forced into a strategic retreat which became known as the Long March.

The direct confrontation with the extreme social divide in China came as an enormous shock to them both. But Rolf was immediately given challenging and interesting projects to design: the four-storey high Victoria Nurses Home, still widely considered to be one of the pioneer buildings of the Chinese Modern era; and a large girls' school, as well as a prison. As a young architect you can not afford to be choosy about what you are asked to design. These were unexpected commissions for a 27-year-old with no experience. He was thrilled. On a private basis, he also undertook smaller interior design jobs for private individuals.

China at this time was suffering widespread famine and continuous war as a consequence of its weak central government. Local warlords ruled in the various provinces and fighting between them was common. Ordinary people lived in permanent fear of those wielding arbitrary power, and driven by war and dire poverty many fled to the overcrowded cities from the countryside.

Shanghai, when Ursula and Rolf arrived, was already a booming city with skyscrapers and industry, but a section of it was under foreign jurisdiction as a result of the British victory in the Opium War of 1839–42. This International Concession had been created subsequently out of a merger of the British and American enclaves, operating its own administration, largely British-run; it also had its own police and security. That is where they would live, a place in which the Chinese were treated as lepers in their own country. He and Ursula managed to find a small but comfortable house in the French concessionary quarter.

What hit Ursula most forcefully were the appalling conditions under which most Chinese people lived and worked, as well as the callousness or indifference with which many of them treated the daily misfortunes, injustices and even deaths of their compatriots. She was shocked by the crass social divide she encountered. This whole situation moved her profoundly and she was keen to help those seeking radical change. Because she was an avid and descriptive letter writer, and many of her letters to the family survived the war, they provide us today with a graphic description of life in China at that time.

She and Rolf found themselves in a very contradictory situation, but one very different from that in Berlin. In Shanghai, most European citizens were cocooned in a small privileged ghetto, but once outside there was a crassly different reality. The couple very soon found themselves invited to tea parties, European clubs and social events from which Chinese citizens were excluded. But Ursula was not the sort of woman to settle down amicably and join the other European ladies in their subordinate role of support and adornment for their menfolk, ignoring what was going on in the country as a whole. However,

FIGURE 4.1 Rudi and Ursula with another couple, enjoying a traditional
        Chinese evening
Source: Michael Hamburger.

Rolf's work, if he were to be successful, demanded that he and his wife
socialise with the other Europeans and become part of their petit-
bourgeois milieu. For him that didn't seem to be a problem – he
enjoyed leading a comfortable life, liked socialising and partying – but
Ursula was not one to fit at all easily or happily into such a role, and
this made it difficult for Rolf to keep up appearances.

In Berlin Ursula had been able to live and work as she wished and to
undertake political and agitational work, as well as become involved in
various cultural activities. In China her life was circumscribed. She was
expected to behave like all the other wives of the European men who
lived and worked there, something that went against the grain; she was
not one for dressing up to take afternoon tea, making small talk, joining
the appropriate clubs, visiting the hairdressers regularly, flirting, and
behaving as a colonial master towards the natives. She hated that sort of
society and knew she could never fit in. This made Rolf's life unne-
cessarily difficult. How could he explain his wife's 'odd' behaviour?

During the day, while he was at work, she had little to do, as the servants did all the housework and cooking; the climate was very hot with a high humidity, which only compounded the feeling of lethargy that enveloped her.

Determined not to become just another bored housewife – the seeming fate of almost all the other wives in the European community in China – she began seeking out politically like-minded people with whom she could at least talk and perhaps even work. This task was made difficult, however, with the birth of her first child, Michael (known to friends as Maik), in February 1931 – the year the Japanese invaded Manchuria while the rest of the world simply looked on.

Michael relates that his father was a man with charm, humour, tact and presence, which made him a popular member of the small European community based in Shanghai. He remembers his father from those years as a sportily clad man in knickerbockers of Scottish tweed. The soft brown tones of the pepper-and-salt pattern seemed to reflect his personality the best. He was well-built with broad shoulders. On returning home in the evening from his architectural office he would immediately play with Michael on the lawn behind the house.

At one of the European community's soirées, Ursula heard a conversation between a manager of a respectable English company and a local civil servant. The latter asked rhetorically, what should be done about the thousands of beggars and miserable wretches who crowded the streets and made life difficult for Europeans going about their daily business. To the amusement of the other guests, the Englishman replied, 'I would get a big broom and sweep the lot of them into the Huangpo River.' Ursula found it extremely difficult to bite her tongue, and only in order to save Rolf's reputation did she do so.

They had only been in the country a few months before Ursula was able to establish contact with a number of key left-wing foreigners living there. People like Manfred Stern (who, in 1936, would leave to fight in Spain and become better known as the legendary General Kléber, the 'Hero of Madrid') and the well-known American revolutionary journalist Agnes Smedley,[1] with whom she became close friends. Interestingly, Smedley was also at that time an acquaintance of Roger Hollis (later, in 1956, to become Director General of Britain's MI5) who was then living in China and working for British American

Tobacco. It is not known whether Ursula also met Hollis, but it is highly likely in that small European group; she does not mention him in her memoirs and, many years later when asked about whether she had encountered Hollis at that time, vehemently denied ever having met him.

Once she had established contact with Chinese communists and was able to meet people like Agnes Smedley and the Soviet agent Richard Sorge who enthused her with new political vigour and commitment, her marriage became increasingly strained. The couple's lives were taking two entirely different trajectories.

Agnes Smedley had previously spent some years in Berlin as the common-law wife of the Indian communist and one of the leaders of the Indian liberation struggle, Virendranath Chattopadhyaya. She lived in Germany on and off for eight years until 1929 and her path could quite easily have crossed that of Ursula's but neither mention any meeting at that time. Agnes did, however, know the artist Käthe Kollwitz, who was a close friend of the Kuczynski family. In China, Agnes was as horrified as Ursula by the poverty and injustice. She recounts how, in the fanatical struggle against communism, the homes of students and intellectuals would be raided on a regular basis and if any suspect literature was found the students would be arrested, tortured and then invariably executed in mass beheadings. She felt she had travelled back to the Middle Ages.

Two other German comrades who were in China at this time were Arthur Ewart and his wife Elise, known as Sabo. Arthur, unbeknown to Ursula, was working for Soviet Intelligence at the time and MI6 already had a file on him. He and Elise were sent by Moscow to Brazil where Arthur would be captured and brutally tortured, eventually losing his mind. Elise was deported back to Nazi Germany where she died in Ravensbrück concentration camp. Ursula would much later tell their tragic story in her biography *Olga Benário* (Benário was the wife of the Brazilian revolutionary leader Luis Carlos Prestes). Olga had been born into Bavarian high society, a member of the wealthy Gutmann family, but like Ursula had rejected her privileged background to become a militant communist. It is perhaps also significant that Olga Benário was apparently betrayed by British Intelligence to the Brazilians who then handed her over to the Nazis (sometime beforehand she had been temporarily arrested during a stay in Britain and her political allegiances had been duly noted).[2] In Germany she gave birth to a baby daughter in prison, which was taken from her and given to her Brazilian mother-in-law. From prison she, like Elise, was transferred to Ravensbrück concentration camp and died in the gas chamber.

Not long after arriving in China, Ursula got to know the great Czech journalist Egon Erwin Kisch, the 'racing reporter', who had come to the country with the intention of writing a book about it.[3] She also became close friends with Soong Ching-ling, widow of the much-loved nationalist leader Sun Yat-sen, the founding father of the Republic of China. His nationalist party had formed a loose alliance with the communists, but after his death in 1925 the party split into two factions and co-operation with the communists came to an end. Chiang Kai-shek then became leader of the largest faction. Although he had undertaken military training in Moscow, he became rabidly anti-communist. He preferred collaboration with the Japanese to working with Mao Tse-tung and the communists. On taking command of the nationalist forces he immediately instituted the mass slaughter of thousands of factory workers and hundreds of students and intellectuals in Shanghai alone.

Soong Ching-ling had played a prominent political role in pre-war Chinese revolutionary politics and continued to do so after her husband's death. She would eventually break with her family and give her support to the communists, leading to her complete estrangement from the Kuomintang and Chiang Kai-shek. Although she was largely ostracised by the new nationalist leadership, she maintained close links with friends she had made earlier, including many progressive foreigners.

The individual in China who would change the course of Ursula's life radically, however, was Richard Sorge. He was one of the Comintern's[4] most able agents, working in Asia for GRU, the intelligence section of the Red Army General Staff, although Ursula was not aware of exactly what he was doing at the time they met. Sorge was also German, a handsome, charismatic man and clearly committed to the revolutionary struggle. Shortly before the outbreak of the Second World War he would be sent by Moscow to Japan from where, in 1941, he forewarned Stalin of the imminent attack by Nazi Germany on the Soviet Union. Shortly afterwards he was betrayed and executed by the Japanese.

He very quickly made a deep impression on Ursula and won her confidence. He was soon able to persuade her to let him occasionally use the family home for conspiratorial meetings. To begin with she merely allowed him and his Chinese contacts to use a room in her house, without informing her husband Rolf, who would not have approved; he would have deemed it too risky. On one occasion she came up to the room Sorge and his comrades were using to bring them some tea. On opening the door she was confronted by two men holding revolvers and a suitcase open on the floor full of guns. Sorge and his fellow agent Paul (Karl Rimm) were, she says, irritated that she had barged in and had seen things she was not meant to see. But Ursula was secretly pleased that her comrades were not just transporting leaflets in the suitcase, but were clearly involved in more serious activities. Another of the suitcases that Sorge left in her house for safe-keeping, she learned only fifty years later, had held a radio transmitter. If this had been discovered by the Chinese authorities she and her husband would have been in deep trouble.

Despite his initial irritation with her, Sorge was clearly impressed by her commitment, courage and ability to maintain secrecy. He mentioned her to his colleagues back in Moscow and they encouraged him to try and recruit her.

China at this time was an exceedingly dangerous place for anyone, even foreigners, with strong left-wing views. Both the Japanese colonial power and the Chiang Kai-shek nationalist government used draconian measures to harass and eradicate trade unionists, socialists and communists. In the years between 1927 and 1936 around 350,000–400,000 Chinese communists would be murdered by the Kuomintang and the Japanese combined. Both used utmost brutality and horrendous torture methods as well as summary execution for anyone even suspected of being connected with progressive organisations.

While in China Ursula was determined to immerse herself in Chinese culture and set about learning Chinese, which she managed to do to a reasonable standard, so that by the end of her stay, in 1936, she was capable of holding an intelligible conversation and reading documents. This gave her greater access to Chinese nationals and a deeper understanding of their concerns. Her experience of the extreme poverty and deprivation as well as the brutal oppression carried out by the Japanese occupying army, affected her deeply. In a letter home she wrote: 'And it is not something you can ever get used to. The other day I found a dead baby in the street. Its nappy was still wet ...' There is little doubt that the extreme conditions of deprivation in China and what she witnessed of the Japanese colonial occupation fuelled her determination to devote her energies to help make the world a better place.

News from home was also becoming increasingly more alarming, and having left Germany in 1930 before Hitler became Chancellor, she said, 'it was impossible for me to understand how the German working class could permit the fascists to take power'. She had great anxieties about her family who were still there. Her last letter to them was sent in May 1933. In the summer of that same year she heard that her father had successfully fled to Britain and that her mother was making preparations to join him with her three youngest sisters. Brigitte had been able to escape from Heidelberg, where she had been studying, to Basle in Switzerland. The worsening situation in Germany and the threat the Nazis now posed to Europe as a whole undoubtedly spurred her determination to do all she could to combat that threat. She would also have realised that, at least for the foreseeable future, returning home to Germany would not be an option.

Not long after Richard Sorge's recommendation, GRU (the Soviet Military Intelligence Directorate) in Moscow took up the suggestion and asked her formally if she would be prepared to go to Moscow for an initial training course of at least six months, at the same time telling her that she might not be able to return to Shanghai. If she accepted this it would mean having to leave her now 2-year-old son and husband behind – a very difficult decision. Finally, her strong commitment and sense of mission, and perhaps also her desire for adventure, helped her make up her mind. However, instead of leaving Michael in Shanghai with Rolf, she decided to take him to her in-laws in Czechoslovakia while she undertook her training. What Rolf felt about all this, she does not say in her memoirs, although their relationship had already become strained in China, so perhaps there was also a feeling of respite on both sides. Her enforced and much more passive role as the

FIGURE 4.2 Ursula and Rudi with their young son Michael
Source: Michael Hamburger.

spouse of a European civil servant hardly suited her temperament or her political convictions. Rolf, on the other hand was happy to be working at last as an architect and even being given substantial commissions. He could not understand why she would not accept her lot and make the best of it. He did, though, accept her decision to work for the Soviet Union to better combat the fascist threat, even though he was not at all happy with their separation.

She left that same year, accompanied by her son Michael, on a Norwegian freighter from Shanghai, together with two other comrades, bound for Vladivostok, and then took the train to Moscow. From Moscow she went via Prague to the small cottage owned by Rolf's parents in Czechoslovakia where she left Michael for the duration of her training. Her own mother, Berta, also came to the chalet to meet her. Berta had already been separated for weeks from her husband, who had fled to Britain. Increasing Nazi pressure would also force them to relinquish the family's lovely house on the Schlachtensee where her six children had grown up.

After a difficult leave-taking from her son and mother, Ursula returned to Moscow to begin her intensive training as a full-time agent of GRU and was given the code name 'Sonya'. Although she probably relished the challenge her new career offered and the escape it provided from the claustrophobic housewife's fate, it could not have been easy to leave her small son behind in Czechoslovakia with in-laws she hardly knew.

After completing her training she was sent back to China, not to Shanghai this time, but to Mukden, a small town in Japanese-occupied Manchuria. Mukden was a walled Chinese city in a region dominated by the Japanese. She was sent together with another agent, a former seaman, codenamed 'Ernst', from Hamburg, whose real name was Johannes Patra.

Ursula's new assignment was a very difficult and dangerous one, but by sending her to such an isolated town in Japanese-controlled territory, her senior officers at GRU clearly felt she would be capable of mastering the task. There she was to work closely with Ernst, her fellow agent and superior. At first he had been taken aback when she told him that she would be taking her small son with her and that he would have to accept that, but in the end he acquiesced. Ursula was a very persuasive and determined woman.

The task she and Ernst had been given was to liaise with the Chinese partisans in their struggle against the Japanese occupiers, as well as to secretly transmit reports to Moscow and receive instructions. But the two agents were also given the more onerous and dangerous task of obtaining chemicals for the making of explosives and supplying them to the partisan groups. All this didn't appear to faze her at all. She seems to have relished the new challenge and the freedom it gave her, released from restrictive domestic ties.

Perhaps not altogether surprisingly, not long after their arrival in May 1934, she soon developed more than a pure working relationship with Ernst. Their living together, though, was not unproblematic – they came from very different class and cultural backgrounds; but there was clearly a physical attraction and they both shared the same political outlook. Ursula probably saw their relationship more as a temporary affair, but Ernst appeared to take it more seriously. He was a fully committed communist as she was, whereas her husband Rolf, while sympathetic, had kept a certain distance from the Party and direct involvement in political work. His reticence, though, was also influenced by his vulnerable position as a city architect – a quasi-civil servant, expected to be politically neutral – so he could not easily indulge in radical politics, even if he had the inclination, unless he wished to jeopardise his career very quickly.

After almost a year working diligently and successfully in Mukden, Ursula and Ernst were in danger of being discovered after a close comrade was arrested. They took no chances, and Ursula left immediately for Peking (today's Beijing) and shortly afterwards left China altogether. She went with a heavy heart. After almost five years there, having to leave friends and comrades behind to struggle on under the increasingly dangerous circumstances was not easy. Her departure in 1935 was hurried and she was unable to organise a proper leave-taking from her friends. She was also emotionally in some turmoil because she discovered that she was once again pregnant, but this time with Ernst's child, not her husband's. She and Rolf, while not formally divorced, had sometime beforehand come to an amicable understanding to lead their own separate lives. As she and Ernst did not intend becoming a couple and, as far as Moscow was concerned, were two independent agents, he was allocated another assignment.

Notes

1 Agnes Smedley grew up as one of four children in a poor working-class household, in a mining camp in Colorado. As a teenager she took herself off first to New York, then Europe and eventually to China. In China she found her true home and remained there for much of her life, first supporting the struggle for liberation, then the communist government under Mao. In China she was greatly respected and honoured for her work. Agnes Smedley, *Battle Hymn of China*, Left Book Club, 1943.
2 Sarah Helm, *If This Is a Woman: Inside Ravensbrück, Hitler's Concentration Camp for Women*. Little, Brown, 2015.
3 Although a citizen of Czechoslovakia, Kisch lived primarily in Berlin. He won renown for his books of collected journalism such as *Der rasende Reporter* (The Racing Reporter).
4 The Comintern (1919–1943) – abbreviation for the Communist International, the worldwide co-ordinating body for all communist parties, with headquarters in Moscow.

5

LIFE UNDER FASCISM (1929–1933)

In the meantime, Jürgen and Marguerite had returned from the USA to find Germany on the cusp of a dramatic transformation. Jürgen threw himself immediately into the political struggle although, perhaps surprisingly, he still felt unready or reluctant to become a member of the Communist Party (KPD). But he did become involved in a number of left-wing organisations and with many individuals who were communists. He had always been a rebel and probably felt belonging to any organisation, particularly one demanding strict discipline as the Communist Party did, would clip his wings too much. At this time most of those on the left in Germany still felt the fascists could be defeated by the combined forces of the Social Democrat and Communist parties.

As a social scientist, despite his still relatively young age, Jürgen was already well known in the USA, Germany and the Soviet Union and recognised as an authority in his field. He had found what would become his lifetime niche as an economist and statistician. However, in Germany, as a Jew and a socialist, he would not find it easy to find a suitable form of paid employment in order to survive.

As the Soviet Union was not recognised by the USA at the time he was there, it had no diplomatic representation or accredited journalists, so relied on Jürgen for many of its news reports. On this basis, they knew what he was capable of, so on his return to Germany, the Soviet economic journal *Industralisazia* made him their chief correspondent in Berlin, and he wrote a bi-monthly report for the journal. While the payments for this work were not enough for him and his wife to survive on, they represented a useful contribution to the precarious family finances.

From the beginning, his new activities in Germany stirred up several hornets nests. Based on his research, he began arguing forcefully for radical change to the system. The most recent statistics he had collected gained increased significance during the big financial crash of 1929 and its aftermath, and they highlighted particularly the serious deterioration of conditions for working people. This research of his would also play a key role in the Communist Party's agitation and propaganda work. He also took on much of his father's editorial responsibility for the *Finanzpolitische Korrespondenz* and, during his father's enforced absence from Germany from 1933 onwards, he would become its official publisher, until the end of that year when the journal was forced to cease publication. With the seemingly unstoppable rise of fascism and Hitler's appointment as Chancellor in January 1933, Jürgen's relations with the Soviet trade mission in Berlin, which had always maintained close relations with his father, grew even closer.

During this time he also made several close friends in the Soviet Union, including the respected Soviet economist Yevgeny Varga, who had been a member of the 1919 revolutionary government in Hungary. It was Varga, a friend of Lenin, who told him how much Lenin had valued his father's statistical work on wages. Jürgen was determined not to lag behind in terms of hard work and economic analysis. So, on top of his journalistic and political work, he and Marguerite managed during this period to complete their second book together, on the conditions of workers in Germany, which was published by the Communist Party.

On 7 November 1929, Jürgen and Marguerite were invited to the celebrations marking the October Revolution at the Soviet embassy, and such visits would become a regular occurrence in the following months. In those critical years of the late 1920s, whether in the USA or Germany, he identified more closely with the Soviet Union than with the German Communist Party. However, in the following two decades, work for the German Party would become more central for him.

His sister Ursula had badgered him for some time to join the Party but he had resisted. However, through her, in the spring of 1930, he got to know Erich Kunik – 'a charming, undogmatic and clever friend … selfless and always helpful' – who was in charge of the Party's information office. It was Erich who eventually managed to achieve what his sister Ursula had failed to do: persuade him to join. Kunik soon became a very close friend.

On 14 July 1930, he had his first invitation to attend a branch meeting of the Party and, somewhat delayed, on 16 September received his membership card, one day before he celebrated his twenty-sixth birthday. He wrote that from that day onwards he had taken on no job or function without the agreement, or on the instructions, of the Party unless, he added, the suggestion or instruction came directly from the Soviet Union, 'the mother of my party'. He was, he noted, 'over the years, often at loggerheads or in disagreement with the Party leadership or apparatus, but never with the Party itself. To leave the Party would have seemed to me like leaving life, leaving humanity', he said.

From 1930 onwards his life would be devoted to the Party. He threw himself into political work despite, or perhaps precisely because of, the rise of fascism in Germany and the increasing danger to himself, as well as his family and friends. Carrying the double stigma of being of Jewish background and a communist meant that he would be doubly targeted by the fascists, but this did not deter him.

Soon after joining he undertook his first visit to the Soviet Union, which 'was a great and singular experience that has never left him'. Even before he joined the Party he had worked regularly for Willi Münzenberg's journal *Roter Aufbau* (Red Construction). Münzenberg was for many years the secretary of the *Internationale Arbeiterhilfe* (Workers' International Relief), an organisation nominally independent of the Party but which closely followed the line of the Soviet-led Comintern. It brought together intellectuals and progressives from around the world to support working-class struggles. Münzenberg was, says Jürgen, 'one of the most colourful and exciting figures in the Party during those years'. It was he who invited Jürgen and Marguerite to join a small delegation to the Soviet Union for the annual October celebrations. But in the end Marguerite fell ill and was unable to go. Jürgen was in a group of five, including the composer Hanns Eisler, the playwright Ernst Toller, Paul Friedländer, who worked for Münzen-berg, and the cartoonist Otto Bittner (Bi). Another group was led by Wilhelm Pieck and included Albert Norden. Pieck, after spending his exile years in Moscow during the Hitler period, became the GDR's first president on his return at the end of the war, and Norden became a minister in the new government.

In Moscow Jürgen met Varga once more, other statisticians, and the leader of the Hungarian Communist Party in exile, Béla Kun, who told him everyone had read the book he and Marguerite had written on the US factory worker. On this trip Jürgen would also meet a number of leading Soviet figures, including those who had been close comrades of Lenin, and who only a few years later would be eradicated by Stalin. He describes the Soviet Union of that time as 'reflecting the lustre of the twenties, the wonderful heroic period of struggle, of construction and of great intellectual movement'.

In 1931 the Party gave Jürgen specific work to do: half a day during the week in the *Reichsleitung* (national leadership) of the Revolutionary Trade Union Opposition (RGO) and another half-day at the Party's newspaper *Die Rote Fahne* (The Red Flag). The RGO, he writes, was at the time quite sectarian, above all in its efforts to become an orga-nisation to rival the much stronger, SPD-aligned trade union federation the *Allgemeine Deutsche Gewerkschaftsbund* (ADGB), and it viewed refor-mist trade unionists as little more than 'agents of capital'. This attitude, he remarks, was not in tune with the real situation and certainly contrary to Lenin's dictum that communists should be where the masses are.

Reflecting on that period much later in his life and examining old documents, Jürgen wrote that the situation appeared to be:

> full of hope and expectation, of so much honest commitment to the struggle, but also of so much senseless sectarianism, mixed with self-delusion about the realities, so many reports about great sacri-ficial factory struggles, behind which stood courage and hunger, a high morale as well as bitter suffering …

That description captures the contradictory situation on the left and reflected the prevalent attitudes which may have contributed to the success of the fascists.

The couple's first child, Madeleine, was born on 9 January 1932, not exactly a time of political tranquillity and certainly not one of financial stability for the family. Marguerite was obliged to stay at home to look after their daughter, so was unable to contribute financially to the household. Jürgen's work for the Party was also not well remunerated and payments were often delayed, leaving the family often with hardly anything to live on.

In the 1932 presidential elections Hindenburg, supported by the SPD, defeated Hitler as well as the communist candidate Ernst Thälmann and the other two minor candidates, to become president once again – perhaps a moment of hope, but one that would soon be dashed. In July, new Reichstag elections were called after the right-wing von Papen government collapsed. This time, the SPD won just over 7 million votes, the KPD over 5 million, and the Nazis, the largest party in the Reichstag, increased their representation considerably by winning almost 14 million votes, giving them 230 seats. But in a second round of elections to the Reichstag that same year, on 6 November 1932, the Nazi Party registered considerable losses, gaining only 196 seats, while the SPD and KPD combined won more seats (121 and 100 respectively). If the SPD and KPD had been able to form a coalition, together with one or two of the smaller parties, they would have had a working majority and could have prevented Hitler taking power, but they again failed to collaborate, giving Hindenburg the excuse to make Hitler Chancellor in January 1933. Mutual suspicion and sectarianism undermined all attempts at co-operation and history took its fatal course.

That same year, MI6, which had agents inside Germany, opened a file on Jürgen Kuczynski. To begin with it was a KEOT (Keep an Eye on Them), known as a K file. It is not clear why they did so or whether they opened ones on other communists, but it is likely that they did. How far they showed any interest in fascists is unknown.

What a Nazi regime would signify, particularly for German communists, was spelt out graphically by Hermann Göring in a speech he gave at that time to a rally of the *Sturmabteilung* or SA – the militarised wing of the Nazi Party (the 'Brownshirts' or Stormtroopers). He spoke about his aims in undisguised form:

Volksgenossen, my measures will not be held back by any sort of legalistic considerations. My measures will not be hindered by any kind of bureaucracy. Here I am not carrying out justice, here my aim is to destroy and exterminate, nothing less! ... I will wage such a battle not with political means. That's what a bourgeois state may have done, certainly, I will use the power of the state and police to the full extent in my battle; my gentlemen communists, so that you don't draw the wrong conclusions, it will be a fight to the death – I will put my boot on your neck – and I will wage it with those down there [pointing to his audience]: the Brownshirts.[1]

Many working-class men, even a number of former Communist or Socialist Party supporters, joined Röhm's *Sturmabteilung* out of desperation, following the Great Depression that had begun in 1929. By February 1932 Germany had over 6 million unemployed, over 16 per cent of the whole population – the highest rate in the world. Those who made up the long-term unemployed, living in poverty, with little means of support and despised by those better off, were offered at least one free meal a day once they joined and were provided with a uniform which gave them status and a sense of purpose. Some were also taken in by the avowed aim of socialism, as implied in the party's full name: National Socialist Workers' Party of Germany.

Despite the increasingly fraught situation, Jürgen continued writing articles for the RGO's journal *Betrieb und Gewerkschaft* (Factory and Trade Union) until the final issue, in which he had two articles, appeared in February 1933. All articles were as a matter of course first submitted to the Party leadership for approval, and one of his was returned with a comment by the KPD leader Ernst Thälmann that it included 'too much cyclical crises and not enough broken lavatory seats'. That may not be comprehensible to a reader today, but for Jürgen at the time the message was very clear: less theory and more daily reality.

After six months with the RGO journal, he now began working for another Party paper, the *Nachrichten* (News), which was conceived as an emergency replacement for the *Rote Fahne* should the Nazis ban the latter, which of course they soon did. For this paper, which for a time came out daily, Jürgen wrote a series of articles under the headline 'If the Workers had Power ...' and argued that an alliance between Soviet and German workers under socialist governments would create full employment and produce enough food to feed everyone. It is therefore little wonder that the police immediately issued a ban on that paper too, but the final run of around 80,000 copies had already sold out before the ban came into force.

On 22 January 1933 the Nazis organised a mass demonstration of the SA as a provocation and challenge to the communists. It was given massive police protection on central Berlin's Bülow Platz, directly opposite the Communist Party headquarters in Karl Liebknecht House, today the headquarters of *Die Linke*. This provocative demonstration by the Nazis, and the counter-demonstration, was documented in a graphic eye-witness account by Jürgen's fellow communist, the writer Jan Peterson, in his memoirs of that period, *Unsere Strasse* (Our Street).[2]

Peterson describes the brutality of the militarised Brownshirts, who lashed out at anyone suspected of being a communist or sympathising with them, whether man, woman or young child. Their action was ignored by the police, who provided full protection and a cover for their terror.

In response, the communists organised their own march and, despite a temperature of minus 18°C, there was a massive turnout. It took four hours for it to pass through the centre of Berlin, and marchers were under strict discipline to avoid provocations and violence. In the end it passed off peacefully. That day Ernst Thälmann addressed party members openly for probably the last time before he was forced underground. In his speech he referred to discussions between communists and social democrats, emphasising that they should not always be over-concerned about keeping their shirts whiter than white. Very belatedly, Thälmann and others had realised that the implacable animosity between the two big working-class parties, the SPD and KPD, had allowed Hitler to grab power.

Although the rising Nazi presence during the late 1920s would have alarmed those on the left who were politically aware, the fact that the Communist and Social Democratic parties were well organised, with large memberships, and were well represented in the Reichstag, gave many of their supporters a sense of assurance that the Nazis would never gain power. However, the dizzying acceleration of political developments and the sudden tipping of the balance of power once Hindenburg and the conservatives, backed by big business, banking and the media came to the conclusion that they needed Hitler to defeat the communists and socialists, the die was cast. It was then too late for the SPD and KPD to overcome their differences and work together.

Hitler's accession to the chancellorship on 30 January 1933 ushered in what were to become twelve long years of Nazi terror. Hitler did not hesitate for one moment, but grasped this unique opportunity to begin the systematic destruction of all oppositional organisations. Jürgen's father had already been forced to flee the country and the rest of the family would follow not long after.

Towards the end of February the Reichstag was set on fire and the fascists, who were undoubtedly behind the crime, put the blame on the communists, thus giving them the excuse they needed to clamp down. Mass arrests of anti-fascists quickly followed, among them 10,000 communist officials and elected members of the Reichstag. The president brought in draconian legislation to 'protect the people and state', abolished basic protective legislation contained in the Weimar Constitution and instituted the death penalty for political opponents. All communist demonstrations were forbidden and its party headquarters occupied by the police and later closed, as were the offices of the Communist Party paper; other communist publications, as well as several SPD ones, were banned.

On the morning of 27 February, Jürgen left home to go to the newspaper office – it was the day after the arson attack on the Reichstag. On his way there he met a friend on the street who told him not to enter the office as the whole party headquarters had been occupied by the police. He was saved from arrest and almost certain death by that chance meeting. From that moment on everyone was concerned about saving their friends and comrades from prison, concentration camp, or arbitrary assassination, all of which had become a more common occurrence. A feeling of hopelessness and numb despair became pervasive.

Both he and Marguerite now realised that with the seemingly irresistible rise of fascism life would no longer be straightforward for them and they would have to take vital precautions if they were to survive. Once Hitler outlawed the Communist Party they quickly gathered together any communist or other incriminating literature they had in the house, packed it in a case and buried it against the garden wall. Three years later, in 1936, they would be forced to flee the country, following the rest of the family. Many books in the family library, amassed over six generations, would also be confiscated by the Nazis and, as Jürgen relates, irreplaceable treasures were lost, but luckily he was able to rescue around two-thirds of the 50,000 books and get them out of the country before the Nazis came to take the rest. Any overt opposition to the Nazis in Germany now became virtually impossible; the only way of continuing the struggle was to work clandestinely, and that is what Jürgen and Marguerite did.

Notes

1 Christian Graf von Krockow, *Die Deutschen in Ihrem Jahrhundert 1890–1990*, Rowohlt, 1990, p. 200.
2 Jan Peterson, *Unsere Straße. Eine Chronik. Geschrieben im Herzen des faschistischen Deutschlands 1933/34*, Berlin, Dietz Verlag, 1947.

6

WORKING UNDERGROUND (1933–1936)

Jürgen says of himself, at this time, that his character provided him with ideal prerequisites for working underground: 'an almost blind loyalty in the leadership and a preparedness to accept rigid discipline'. As a corroboration of this character description from another perspective, his wife Marguerite later commented sarcastically, 'If you'd been born 200 years earlier you would have been one of the most loyal sons of the Catholic Church.' He also had the unusual facility of being able to move comfortably and easily between the various social spheres, which afforded him added protection. Marguerite fully supported Jürgen in his illegal work for the KPD. Uncertainty and unrest became part of daily life. There were regular house searches by the Gestapo and, on one occasion, Jürgen was arrested but released after two hours.

On 3 March 1933, Thälmann was captured by the Nazis after being betrayed. The shoemaker with whom he had been lodging at the time had a similar name to the Kuczynskis; so the Nazis soon came knocking on Jürgen's door too, demanding to search the house but could find nothing incriminating. Further house searches followed at short intervals by mixed groups of the SA, Gestapo and police, and at one stage they threatened to requisition the house itself; they left in the end but warned him that further action would be taken. Jürgen remarks that it was at such times quite an advantage to be living in a middle-class residential area, as the Nazis were a little more circumspect in the way they behaved in such locations.

On 5 March new Reichstag elections were held under conditions of fascist terror, but despite this, 12 million votes were still cast for the two working-class parties – SPD and KPD – and another 10 million for the centrist parties, but the Nazis won 17.3 million votes. The election of eighty-one communist representatives was declared invalid and they were all immediately arrested. In addition, there was an increase in attacks on Jewish-owned premises and on individuals. The concept of a Jewish-Bolshevik conspiracy against the German nation became the Nazis' mantra.

On 10 May, Nazi Stormtroopers took the opportunity to go on a rampage of terror and destruction, murder and torture throughout Germany. In Berlin and twenty-one other university cities, bonfires of books by 'Jewish and Marxist' writers were ignited, including works by Heinrich Mann, Lion Feuchtwanger, Erich Kästner, Sigmund Freud, Karl Marx, Egon Erwin Kisch and many others. These book burnings were organised by the *Nationalsozialistischen Deutschen Studentenbund* (National Socialist German Student Association). For Jürgen and Marguerite it meant having to keep their heads down and stay indoors for much of the time or only venturing outside with supreme caution. Within the year a one-party dictatorship had been imposed.

Jürgen's mother had stayed behind at the house on Schlachtensee with her three youngest daughters until, in 1934, she was able to sell it, albeit at a knock-down price. Jewish-owned properties were forcibly purchased or simply commandeered by 'Aryan' Germans. After the sale they immediately left for Britain. Jürgen and Marguerite were now the only family members still remaining and were faced with the question of how to survive, both financially as well as in terms of safety.

Jürgen still had good contact with a wealthy Jewish investor who had also stayed on in Berlin and to whom he regularly passed on investment tips, and this now came in very useful. He advised him to buy shares in small, little-known, armaments manufacturing businesses, realising that these would soon be receiving lucrative government orders. The shares did rise by up to 30 per cent and the benefactor gave him 1,500 Reichsmarks as a thank you, and this helped the family survive for a little while longer. He also received payments for articles he wrote for the Soviet Union and, for a time, he was also stock exchange correspondent for the US *Herald Tribune*, for which Marx had written in his day. Its German representative was an anti-Nazi and sympathetic to those like Jürgen who were working against Hitler.

This short period of working illegally was a very trying and frustrating one. Everyone was obliged to avoid and deny their political friends. When passing comrades in the street, he had to studiously ignore them. To show any sign of acknowledgement could mean their or his own arrest soon after. It was extremely difficult to tolerate such isolation particularly if you were, like Jürgen, a sociable individual. On top of that, his being very Jewish-looking narrowed the scope for his freedom of movement even more. However, his optimism kept him going, believing, as so many on the left even then still did, that the fascists would soon be toppled. He writes that he felt this time was not altogether burdensome. To be able to return home every day, 'to Marguerite and our child, to find letters from good friends from all parts of the world, I felt was a personal gift'. Throughout this time he continued to keep regular contact with the Soviet Union's TASS correspondent and with the embassy. With Party work now made more difficult, he used his free time to visit the city's libraries to carry out the research work he really loved.

As cut-off as he and Marguerite were from the wider movement, they still felt protected by it. Even though they heard regularly about arrests and murders, it brought the comrades who survived closer together. 'Never', he says, 'did German communists feel so isolated and yet so closely connected to each other as at that time, even though those relationships were of necessity very impersonal.'

'One summer day', he wrote in his memoirs:

as I looked out of the window of our office [where the illegal Communist Party paper was produced], more by accident than design because we tried to avoid showing ourselves at the window, I noted a small group gathering outside the front door: SA and police – about 15 of them. Clearly we had been betrayed, or at least discovered. Quickly, I informed the other comrades and within seconds we began chewing and swallowing the results of our morning's labours, including the used carbon paper. We soon heard loud steps coming up the staircase ... but then the footsteps passed by our office and carried on upstairs. It turned out that they were raiding an illegal office of the Social Democrats above us, and of which we had no knowledge. What a narrow escape, but at least we now felt the Gestapo would leave us alone as it was unlikely that there would be two illegal offices in one building ... !

In March 1933 Jürgen began to publish a monthly digest of statistics on food costs, seemingly oblivious to the fact that he was in constant danger of being arrested by the Nazis. He was also able to demonstrate, by using the statistical information he gathered, that the situation for the unemployed at this time was even worse than it had been in the previous year.

In January 1934 he was forced to put an announcement in the then current issue of the *Finanzpolitische Korrespondenz* journal that 'Herr Dr. Jürgen Kuzcynski, a non-Aryan, is no longer able to act as editor of the journal, as a consequence of the *Schriftleitergesetz*' (Law on Editorial Responsibility, passed on 4 October 1933 and enacted on 1 January 1934, regulating the entrance to journalistic careers and the tasks of editors and journalists. This law was a vital instrument in bringing all the media under the control of the Nazis). That would be the last issue of this journal. Interestingly, the US-based agency, Associated Press, signed up readily to the new Nazi law and, as a result, became the only Western news agency to stay open in Hitler's Germany. At around the same time, the RGO office also had to be vacated, but Jürgen kept up his underground work for the Party, from then on working from home.

The year 1934 was significant in other ways too. In the summer the so-called Röhm Affair took place in which Hitler, in a bloody clampdown known as the night of the long knives, smashed the organisation of the Brownshirts (SA), which was seen as a potential rival to his own power base. They had been largely responsible for the violence against Jews, communists and social democrats and for the mayhem – virtually civil war – on the streets. The organisation was made up almost entirely of recruits from the working class and many had dreams of a real 'national socialism'; this was not at all to the liking of the Nazi leadership or its business-class backers. The word 'socialism' had only been included in the party's name to seduce those who would otherwise have been drawn to the communists and social democrats. The SA had, in any case, now done Hitler's dirty work of smashing all opposition and were no longer needed.

Hindenburg died on 2 August 1934 and only a short time later the German Army leadership swore, on its own initiative, an oath of total obedience to Adolf Hitler. Outside Berlin most people appeared to react positively to this declaration by the army, or at least did not oppose it, because Hitler, after all, had supposedly brought *Ruhe und Ordnung* (law and order) to the country, and an end to the petty squabbling of the other political parties. This introduction of 'law and order' through the use of illegal and brute force would have echoes into the future.

The Nazis, though, had also managed to begin reviving the economy, ironically using Keynesian methods before Keynes had developed them. The theories forming the basis of Keynesian economics were first presented in his book *The General Theory of Employment, Interest and Money*, published in 1936, but the Nazis were already putting such ideas into practice, albeit to serve a centrally dictated war machine. They had inherited a large public works programme initiated by the Weimar government, and this was largely continued. The state now became the most significant contractual partner for the steel and armaments industries. In 1936, military spending in Germany exceeded 10 per cent of GNP, at the time higher than any other European country. Military investment also surpassed civilian investment from that year onwards. The demand for uniforms gave a much-needed impetus to the textile industry; infrastructure projects, particularly the development of the autobahn system, led to a boom in the construction industry.

Hitler's coming to power had coincided with a convenient historical moment: the peak of the world economic crisis had passed and economies everywhere were beginning to pick up. In Germany there was a massive increase in jobs, even if it was at the price of an enormously increased state debt and a burgeoning armaments industry. Unemployment fell to only 1.9 per cent by 1938 – a dramatic fall. By 1937, however, following the destruction of the trade unions, real wage levels had only just reached those of 1928/29, and even this had only been achieved on the basis of the average working week increasing from 41.5 to 46.1 hours. In this connection, Jürgen later admitted that at the time he had not appreciated how the cyclical boom after the crash would in actual fact give the fascist economy a new lease of life, in large part due to the impetus from the armaments industry.

During that year of 1934 Jürgen's working relationship with the Soviet Union had become more intimate and he continued writing reports on the current economic and political situation for them. Already beforehand, during the period of legality, he had belonged to a small circle of comrades, including Josef Winternitz, Erich Kunik (who would die in a Soviet GULAG), Christoph Wurm and Richard Löwenthal (after the war to become an anti-communist theoretician in the German SPD), as well as Herbert Wehner, who would also become a leading light in the West German SPD. Jürgen and Herbert Wehner worked together towards the end of 1932 on a book to commemorate the fiftieth anniversary of Marx's death. Sergei Bessonov from the Soviet embassy would also regularly join this circle for theoretical discussions and during the years of working underground he and Jürgen became close friends. He was, Jürgen relates:

> theoretically well grounded, a large man with broad gestures and full of warm friendliness and interested in everything – he could also talk for half an hour seriously and knowledgably with Marguerite about preparing a fish sauce – he seemed to us to be the embodiment of the new man building Soviet society.

He would be later executed in one of Stalin's purges.

Bessenov introduced him to Artur Hirschfeld (known as Stashevsky), the commercial attaché at the embassy who also had responsibility for research and technology. They both began to meet regularly and Jürgen would deliver fortnightly reports of economic analysis which were passed on to Maxim Litvinov, then Foreign Minister of the Soviet Union, who actually read and made use of them. Jürgen said he was amazed that, despite his regular visits to the embassy, he was never stopped nor, apparently, even placed under surveillance by the Nazis. 'With the agreement of his comrades', he also made contact with British and US diplomats and journalists, including the Berlin correspondent of the *Manchester Guardian*, for whom he wrote a report, alongside pieces for the *Herald Tribune* and the *Berliner Börsenzeitung* (Berlin Stock Exchange Journal). As his father had before his enforced departure from Germany, Jürgen also developed a good relationship with the US Consul General, George Messersmith. He was able to capitalise on that relationship and through the Consul General meet a number of other diplomats, who, he says, 'spoke much more openly' about the situation than Messersmith did. The latter was best known in his day for his controversial decision to issue a visa to Albert Einstein so that he could enter the United States, something for which he was strongly criticised by conservative groups and the media in the USA. He also became known for his diplomatic handling of the thorny issue surrounding the dubious political associations of King Edward VIII and Wallis Simpson, later Duke and Duchess of Windsor, in the era leading up to the Second World War. As they were both Nazi sympathisers, he ensured that they were kept under surveillance during their visit to Vienna at the time.

After the Nazis had forced him to relinquish control of the *Finanz-politische Korrespondenz*, within six months Jürgen had founded a new journal, registered in Switzerland: *Konjunkturstatistische Korrespondenz* (Business statistical correspondence), which quite rapidly gained international recognition. He managed to persuade leading economists from a number of countries to write for it, including H. C. B. Mynors, director of the research department of the Bank of England, later to become a deputy governor.

In 1934 he received, via Hirschfeld at the Soviet Consulate, an invitation to visit his friend, the economist Varga, in the Soviet Union. But his German passport was running out and needed renewing. Would he be given a new one, he wondered. And if so, would he be able to keep the old one, as such passports were very useful for underground work. Surprisingly, all went smoothly. With both passports he arrived in Prague on 14 January 1935, before travelling onwards to the Soviet Union, where he spent several days with Varga. During his time in Moscow he was also summoned to meet Walther Ulbricht, the German Communist Party leader who was already in exile there and had replaced the imprisoned Thälmann as general secretary – their first meeting since the Party had been banned. He was asked to give the exiled leaders a detailed report about the situation on the ground in Germany. Jürgen was, at the time, completely unaware, he says, of the huge difference of understanding among the comrades as to the extent of Nazi ideological influence on, and the extent of confusion among, the workers. Because of his ignorance, and unaware that he could be trampling on a number of toes, he felt no constraints about reporting straightforwardly and without pretence. The predominant viewpoint of the Party leadership at the time was that the German working class would very soon come to its senses and recognise fascism for what it was and offer serious opposition, so Jürgen's report, presenting a contrary picture, would not have been music to their ears. He also used the occasion to hand Ulbricht his old passport which he no longer needed.

On this visit he again met Radek, to whom he also had to give an extensive report on the situation in Germany. Radek then asked him, with the express approval of Stalin, he said, whether it would be of help or a hindrance for his work in Germany if he were made a corresponding member of the Soviet Academy of Science. As Jürgen was still only 30 years old, the question took his breath away. He responded mock heroically that he would not become a member before his German compatriots had been able to expel the Nazis from their own Academy. Radek gave him a surprised look – few spurned Stalin's offers – before responding that he would let Stalin know. His final days in Moscow were spent in the ill-fated Hotel Lux where most of the exiled communists from around the world were accommodated. Here he met several of his comrades for the first time since they had left Germany, a number of whom would later be shot or sent to the GULAG as a result of Stalin's political purges. He returned to Berlin in February 1935 still full of hope, 'completely convinced', he said, 'that I would soon be able to welcome my comrades back to Germany'.

This was also the significant year in which Stalin and the Comintern belatedly realised how divisive and self-defeating the 'class against class' policy had been, preventing co-operation between social democrats and communists who, together, could have defeated Hitler. From then onwards, the idea of a 'Popular Front' movement was strenuously promoted in an attempt to unite all progressive forces against the fascists.

Though he was determined to hold out until the fascists were ousted, it nevertheless became increasingly clear to Jürgen how impossible it was becoming to work at all meaningfully. Much of his time was taken up with dodging Nazi spies and avoiding arrest. The number of his friends and comrades being arrested and imprisoned or who were forced to flee was increasing and his scope for manoeuvre became more restricted each day. His mother in England was also putting pressure on him to leave. In June he had a visit from some American friends, the Bradys, who invited him to California, but he was still reluctant to leave Europe at this crucial time. The passing of the Nuremberg race laws on 15 September 1935 only increased the pressure further. These laws permitted full political rights only to those who could prove their Germanic racial purity; marriage between Germans and Jews was a '*Blutschande*' or racial abomination. By January 1936, Jürgen realised it was no longer tenable for him to stay in Germany if he wished to remain free; so he and Marguerite left for Britain. They were the last of the immediate family to leave. Their young daughter Madeleine had been sent on ahead to join Jürgen's parents in London already in 1935.

The day after their arrival in the UK he wrote to Ulbricht in Moscow asking for instructions as to what he should now do. And immediately the next day, he made contact with other German exiles in Britain via his sister Brigitte, who had in the meantime also arrived from Switzerland. On the third day he contacted the British Communist Party. A new period in his life was about to begin, but he felt the recent years in Germany had been a time of maturation for him in so many ways and had helped mould his character. Much later, he would note that he felt he had changed very little since that time. 'The years of illegality made better comrades of us, better fighters for progress – but not more kindly people', he wrote. That period was also, of course, crippling, because it was no longer possible to view life in an unselfconscious way: 'We became suspicious in our daily lives ...' His words echo those of his friend and fellow exile Bertolt Brecht in his seminal poem 'An die Nachgeborenen', dedicated to those who will be born in better times. He reiterates Jürgen's observation that his generation now found it difficult to be friendly, blaming the 'dark' times they were living through.

All members of the Kuczynski family were now together again in Britain, apart from Ursula who was still in China but was about to be recalled to Moscow. Her sister Brigitte, the third eldest of the siblings, had been in Basle working on her doctorate, but on completing it in 1936 she had left immediately for London. She had studied in Heidelberg and joined the Communist Party there, where the Party had asked her to work with a children's group. However, after giving the local leader of the *Deutsches Jungvolk* (the Nazi youth organisation) a clip around the ear in the street in response to insulting anti-semitic remarks he had made about her, she was immediately arrested. She was charged with committing 'a public nuisance, in that she slapped the student Heekmann while exchanging a Hitler salute, and had therewith caused offence'. As a result she was summarily expelled from the university. The university documentation of the time notes that she was among forty-eight other students who were expelled for undertaking activities 'hostile to the state and people'.

The policeman into whose hands she was thrust happened to belong to the Catholic Centre Party and clearly had little sympathy for the Nazis, so he let her go after whispering in her ear that she should get out of Germany post haste.

In 1936, Ursula returned to Moscow for further training, after which they asked her to go to Poland. She travelled there via London to avoid entering the country directly from the Soviet Union which would have aroused suspicions.

In the meantime her estranged husband Rolf had also decided to commit himself to working for the Soviet Union. He witnessed the devastation being caused in China by the invading Japanese forces, and registered with alarm the upsurge of a National Socialist mentality among his German expatriates. In addition, the equivocation of the Western nations towards Hitler and the dire news from Germany itself all helped fuel his fateful decision. In such a dark and threatening situation, his hopes turned towards the Soviet Union – the only country, it seemed at the time, prepared to confront fascism.

After expressing his willingness to work for the Soviets, they left him to decide whether or not to accompany Ursula to Poland – the two were, after all, nominally still a married couple – and in the end, perhaps surprisingly under the circumstances, he decided to do so. Rolf was undoubtedly still very much in love with Ursula and clung to the vain hope that they could be reconciled. This factor would also have played a role in his decision to join her in working for GRU.

Ursula arrived in London accompanied by her infant son Michael. She was overjoyed to see her parents, brother and sisters again after their long separation. They had not seen each other since she had first left Germany for China in 1930, six years beforehand. From that visit she provides us with a thumbnail sketch of her sisters' characteristics: Renate, the youngest was now 12 years old and 'proudly called herself a communist'. Sabine, now 17, she says:

> in contrast to the rest of us [was] a gentle girl … She was the only one to have inherited our mother's beauty. … 'Weepy' [the nickname she gave to her 23-year-old sister Barbara to avoid naming her in her book, *Sonya's Report*] was intelligent, conscientious and ambitious. Brigitte, three years younger than me, had got her doctorate in history in Switzerland and was, as always, full of zeal and enthusiasm for whatever she happened to be engaged in at the time.

Ursula writes that her parents, together with their youngest child Renate, lived in a 'dowdy three-roomed flat in north west London which seemed poky in the extreme' compared with their spacious house in Berlin. The other siblings had taken their own accommodation. Also with the family was 'Ollo' (Olga Muth), their nanny from Berlin who had come to the family after Brigitte was born and accompanied them to London. Although Olga was still very much attached to Renate, she really did not have much to do now that her charge had become a young teenager. She felt her task had been fulfilled, so she begged Ursula to take her along to Poland so that she could look after the soon to be expected baby and Michael. Both Rolf and Ursula agreed to the proposal.

Because of her clandestine work Ursula had been given strict instructions that during her short stay in Britain she was to stay clear of the German League of Culture, other German communists and the British Communist Party, although that must have been difficult as all the other members of the family were very much involved in these areas; both her father and brother were active organisers in the League.

In 1936, Ursula and Rolf, with Olga and Michael in tow, arrived in Poland at a critical and dangerous time. Pilsudski, the autocratic and crypto-fascist leader of Poland since 1926, had died that same year, but little changed under his successors: the government remained virulently anti-Soviet, and the Communist Party was banned or only semi-legal; chauvinism coupled with anti-semitism were endemic in the country and the economic situation was dire. The government had also been attempting, unsuccessfully, to reach an accord with Hitler to jointly attack the Soviet Union.

Their first undertaking in Poland was to obtain residence permits – not an easy task at this internationally tense time – and find work that would legalise their presence in the country, as well as set up their transmitter for radio contact with the Soviet Union. If the couple's clandestine activities were to be discovered, they could expect much worse than a harsh prison sentence – they would have been deported to Germany and if not summarily shot as traitors, incarcerated in a concentration camp. Now the family's initial priority was to search for suitable accommodation in Warsaw, for three adults, a young boy and a baby soon to be born. This was far from being an easy task. An additional stress was that Ursula didn't like Warsaw and found Europe as a whole 'boring' after China.

In April that same year Ursula gave birth to a girl in a Warsaw clinic. Years later, that daughter, Janina, described the situation in her memoir *Die Tochter bin ich* (I'm the daughter):

> Eight hours before my mother delivered her second child into the world, on 27 April 1936, she was sitting next to a shaded lamp at her illegal transmitter, in the late evening, sending a coded report. Later that same night, after returning from the clinic, she continued transmitting. She began her coded message with the sentence 'Please excuse my delay, but I've just given birth to a daughter.'

Janina relates how Ursula was often very tired, obliged to stay awake during the night to transmit her reports or receive messages and at the same time feed and look after a tiny baby. Her mother told her that on 1 May, only three days after giving birth to her in the clinic, a demonstration of Polish workers paraded by the apartment in the street below and were singing the *Internationale*. She picked up her newborn baby and held it up to the window so that it could hear the music. That would probably be the last time Polish workers were able to hold a May Day demonstration.

Given the extreme precariousness of the family's situation, the stresses of obtaining a long-term residence permit – they were obliged to re-apply for one every week – and Rolf's need to find a proper job as cover, plus the dangers involved in making their illegal transmissions to Moscow, life was hardly serene. On top of that, although Rolf and Ursula got on well as colleagues, they found living so intimately together stressful. They had both accepted that the marriage was over, but their situation caused Ursula to become very depressed.

In June 1936, together with the two children and Olga she paid another short visit to London to see her parents. They arrived at Croydon airport from Rotterdam and were issued with a three-month visa. At the same time Rolf had flown to the USA, probably visiting his brother.

On their return to Poland the family would move from Warsaw to the German-governed enclave of Danzig (now Gdansk in Poland), so that they could better monitor German intentions. According to the then constitution, the Polish government had the right to be consulted on any decisions taken with respect to Danzig. However, the Nazis simply went ahead with the city state's Nazification, flying the swastika flag from public buildings and discriminating against Polish public service workers. Despite Poland's vocal complaints about these outrageous violations of the Danzig constitution, nothing was done to counter the Nazis' provocative action. Protests were lodged with the League of Nations, but the latter declared it 'inadvisable to interfere in the internal affairs of Danzig' – yet further evidence of the international community's unwillingness to confront Hitler's imperial ambitions and his flouting of human rights.

In Danzig they quickly found temporary accommodation in a block of flats. But they had hardly settled in before one of her neighbours, who was married to a Nazi but was friendly towards her and liked having a chat, told her they had been experiencing interference on their radio in the evenings and her husband was convinced that someone in the block was illegally transmitting radio signals. She told Ursula that he was organising a security raid on the apartment block to find the culprit. In the nick of time she and Rolf were able to hide their transmitter before the raid took place. They lived day-to-day on tenterhooks.

In June 1937 Ursula travelled again to Moscow for consultations and yet more training, staying there three months, but beforehand made another short trip to London in order to obtain a visa for the Soviet Union, as well as to see her family. (Chapman Pincher, in his book *Treachery*, asks why Ursula didn't obtain a visa from the Soviet embassy in Poland and suggests that her trip to London was for other reasons. But he neglects to point out that there was no Soviet embassy in Poland from 1937 until 1939, as the ambassador had been recalled to Moscow, where he was executed on Stalin's orders.) So Ursula had little option but to go to London. In the meantime, the children, with Olga, were once again sent to Rolf's parents in Czechoslovakia.

This time in Moscow she met her new chief, Hadshi-Omar Mamsurov, an Ossetian who had fought in Spain during the civil war. Alongside its intelligence operations, GRU had also carried out acts of sabotage behind enemy lines during the Spanish Civil War. The men largely responsible for this were Alexander Orlov and Hadshi-Omar. While he was stationed in Spain he had been told by his superior to be co-operative with an American writer, Ernest Hemingway, to whom he had taken a strong dislike. 'He drinks too much', Hadshi had said, but in the end he co-operated fully with Hemingway, providing him with details about partisan campaigns, and explained how they dynamited bridges and derailed trains. Perhaps a number of highly realistic episodes in Hemingway's *For Whom the Bell Tolls* owe a debt to Hadshi. He also taught Ursula how to make explosives from readily available chemicals, and how to construct simple bombs and detonators to blow up railway lines.

With her latest training session completed she returned to Poland, but this time to Zakopane, in the foothills of the Tatra mountains, where the family rented a log house which she liked very much. It was 900 metres above sea level, set in a ravishing landscape with views over the mountains. During the winter spent there she used the opportunity to learn to ski. Why she made this change in location is not explained. Perhaps after the tension of Warsaw and then Danzig, Moscow felt she needed a period of recuperation. While there she was visited by her sister Barbara and they undertook skiing tours together in the mountains. Only a year later, from June 1938, she was to spend another six months in Moscow before being sent to a new country once more, this time Switzerland. But before this she travelled again to Britain and left the children for the summer with Olga in a house on the south coast.

Most full-time agents of the Soviet Red Army were given military ranks, and Ursula had by now been promoted from captain to major – a few years later she enjoyed two more promotions, eventually becoming a colonel, although she said she had no interest in ranks and military hierarchies, but was simply 'proud to be a soldier of the Red Army'. Ursula was the only foreign woman ever to be appointed an honorary colonel.

Once again her work in Switzerland was aimed at Nazi Germany and she was asked to try to infiltrate agents into the country in order to make assessments of the effectiveness of the German armaments industry. The important Dornier aeroplane factory in Friedrichshafen was one of the targets, and I. G. Farben another.

Her travels back and forth to the Soviet Union and through the various European countries necessitated the use of a whole number of passports from different countries. She also had to make the highly dangerous transit through Nazi Germany on two occasions. This must have really tested her resilience. She certainly did not fit the picture of 'Aryan womanhood'; her dark hair and eyes and prominent nose only too readily betrayed her Jewish ethnicity. The consequences if she had been more closely scrutinised or interrogated could have been dire. She needed nerves of steel to complete her assignments. Her residences in several countries, though, had given her a command of languages which came in very useful in all her cross-border travels. She had by then learned Chinese, Russian, English and Polish on top of her native German, and now in Switzerland she would have to learn French.

7

THE EXILE YEARS

England (1936–1945)

The Kuczynski family was one with a deep and long tradition of living and working in Germany. When the family first arrived in Britain, they considered it very much a temporary home, but quickly made contact with a number of British comrades and others in the wider Labour movement. They certainly did not see Britain either as a permanent base or a place in which they would spend more than a short time, until the Nazis had been ousted. The great advantage, though, of belonging to the Communist Party at this time – because of its strong internationalist tradition – was that you could readily find support and friendships in any country where a Communist Party existed.

To be completely uprooted and thrown into an alien environment for an unspecified time was traumatic for all of them. The children, particularly must have felt completely disorientated, as the youngest ones did not even speak the language. Renate and Sabine would have hardly understood what the sudden move was all about; they were at the mercy of nebulous historical processes and necessarily secretive parental decision-making. Ursula was the only one who had not needed to flee – since three years earlier than her parents had been forced to flee Germany she had decided to go with her husband to China and soon afterwards began working for Soviet military intelligence.

For their father, Robert, and his wife Berta the situation was probably not so difficult as both had spent time living in the United States and spoke English fluently. Robert had arrived in Britain in 1933 and had immediately taken up the job offer at the London School of Economics, where he would teach demography and carry out research on behalf of the government. From 1937 onwards he began examining population statistics, particularly of the British colonies, and would make a significant contribution to Britain's statistical research.

In 1936, the year that the remaining members of the Kuczynski family came to Britain, the Olympic Games were held in Germany in triumphant and bombastic style. The Nazis were allowed to turn the occasion into a massive propaganda show of German supremacy and sporting prowess. This was epitomised in the infamous Leni Riefenstahl film glorifying and aestheticising sheer physical power in *Olympia: Fest der Völker* (The Olympics: Festival of the Nations). Those nations taking part, particularly the leading Western ones, willingly participated in Hitler's grandiose pageant, noting only Germany's super efficiency, its organisational panache and national élan. The reverse side of the coin – the persecution and incarceration of Jews and other minorities, the total suppression of democracy, the rapid militarisation of the country and, in the background, the unmistakable drumrolls of war – all went unseen and unheard. Instead, Western newspapers were full of lurid stories of 'communist hordes undermining democracy in Spain, robbing, murdering and rampaging through the country'. Hitler could not have been more pleased.

The large-scale emigration of tens of thousands of its citizens fleeing abroad had no precedent in German history, apart from the large exodus during the nineteenth century in the wake of the 1848 Revolution. After Hitler's rise to power in 1933, the introduction of racist legislation, particularly the infamous Nuremberg Laws of September 1935, increased the trickle of Jewish emigrants to a torrent. The Nuremberg legislation institutionalised many of the racial theories prevalent in Nazi ideology. The laws excluded German Jews from Reich citizenship and prohibited them from marrying or having sexual relations with persons of 'German or related blood'. Jews were also disenfranchised and deprived of most political rights. It is difficult to know exactly how many individuals left Germany as a result of racial or political persecution, but estimates of those from Germany, Austria and the German-speaking regions of Czechoslovakia together range up to 500,000. But this figure excludes the war years for which no figures are available. The number of Jewish emigrants from Germany alone has been estimated at between 270,000 and 300,000, roughly three-fifths of German Jewry.[1] Among the émigrés to Britain, communists were numerically the largest organised political group. The reason for this was probably that the communists were, apart from being the most hated group, widely seen as committed, courageous and as representing the only really effective organised opposition to fascism.

Despite the desperate need to offer refugees fleeing Hitler's Germany a safe haven there was much opposition in Western countries, including Britain, to this sudden influx of foreigners. Laudably, there was also concerted lobbying on behalf of the refugees by prominent figures in the country, among them members of Parliament, like the Labour MPs Philip Noel-Baker and Josiah Wedgwood, but the most forceful of the advocates was the independent Liverpudlian MP Eleanor Rathbone who earned herself the honorary title of 'Minister for Refugees'. The government of the day reluctantly lifted restrictions on immigration after December 1938, largely as a result of that lobbying, but also as a response to the horrors of *Kristallnacht* on 9 November when marauding Nazi Stormtroopers went around the towns and cities of Germany burning synagogues, smashing and robbing Jewish shops, hunting down and killing Jews. There were, however, powerful voices opposed to the influx of refugees, particularly Jewish ones. This opposition came largely from the extreme right-wing and xenophobic sections of the establishment, but there were also those, including from some Jews themselves, who felt that a large new influx from Europe could lead to an increase in anti-semitism.

Jürgen was brave enough to still undertake two short trips back to Germany during 1936 to see friends, visit libraries and the Soviet embassy there. The Party leadership in exile in Paris told him after his second visit to make it his last. On his final journey back from Berlin via Prague he read about the outbreak of the Spanish Civil War, in which many German anti-fascists would take part and a considerable number sacrifice their lives. On that journey he made a detour from Prague via Warsaw to visit his sister Ursula – who was still in Poland at that time – before she moved to Danzig. From there, he travelled via Denmark back to England.

With the new Popular Front policy proclaimed by the Comintern in 1936, relationships with exiled German social democrats, with the Labour Party, as well as with middle-class progressives in Britain, took on a more significant and important role and Jürgen made every effort to promote such links.

He wasted no time in getting down to his new political tasks, and with the help of his new British comrades, began producing anti-fascist leaflets to be distributed to German seamen visiting the UK, as well as to be given to British seamen to smuggle into Germany. His organisation would also send leaflets into Germany by post. The exiles pulled out all the stops to make the world fully aware of Hitler's aims and the real character of German fascism. They organised discussions and public meetings, produced brochures and informational material. There was also educational work to be carried out among the German exile community itself and to encourage all émigrés to become involved in the anti-fascist struggle as well as ensure that the flame of hope of returning to a free Germany in the near future was not extinguished.

Particularly in historically turbulent times the personal does become political, whether the individual consciously chooses a political role or not. Jürgen explains how this impacted on the life of the communist exiles. The demands made on every single comrade were high, as there was so much work to be done and no time to lose. The Party, he wrote, became, of necessity, involved in every comrade's personal life. It tried to ensure that everyone found work, accommodation and had sufficient income to survive. This involved monitoring who was living with whom and discouraging couples from having children under such precarious circumstances. It was a sad occurrence, but also had security implications, when marriages fell apart or when men (it was usually men) changed their partners too often.

Despite this advice given to others and the inauspicious and unstable circumstances both on the political and personal fronts at this time, Marguerite herself gave birth to their second child, a son, at the end of August 1937. He was called Peter. Now with two small children to feed and clothe, she was fully occupied with domestic chores and had to take a back seat while her husband continued his hectic political work.

In 1937 Jürgen published an article in *The Banker*, the magazine for the British financial sector, about spending on armaments in Nazi Germany. The article found considerable resonance and was expanded in later editions and then reprinted as a booklet. This tickled his comrades in the German Communist Party to see one of their own being celebrated by sections of the London City and being able to promote anti-fascism in such key circles. A similar brochure he wrote, under a pseudonym, *Hitler and the Empire*, was also addressed largely to Conservative circles, and had a foreword by Air Commodore L. E. O. Charlton C.B., C.M.G., D.S.O. It sold around 10,000 copies in just a few weeks. In this way Conservative sections of the country were being addressed by those calling for a more radical anti-fascist policy even before this became more acceptable by the spring of 1940, after the appeasers had been defeated: Chamberlain had resigned and Foreign Secretary Halifax was sidelined.

In 1938 his book *Hunger and Work* was published by the British Communist Party. It compared the economic and social situation of workers in a number of leading industries. Trade union leaders found it very useful because it provided them with a basis for their arguments for higher wages and improved working conditions. Apart from the daily organisational work with his fellow émigrés, Jürgen was ceaselessly writing and lecturing. In 1939 the Left Book Club published his *The Condition of the Workers in Great Britain, Germany and the Soviet Union 1932–1938*, and over 50,000 copies were distributed to members of the Club. (Serendipitously, while browsing in my local Oxfam second-hand bookshop in 2015, I came across what must be by now a very rare copy of this book.) Probably as a result of this co-operation with the Left Book Club, he developed very warm relations with its founder and publisher, Victor Gollancz. They not only found common cause in their anti-fascist views but also in their mutual love of detective novels and cigars! Another leading light in the Left Book Club, John Strachey and his wife Celia also became good friends (Strachey would later became an MP and in 1945 Under-Secretary of State for Air under Attlee, then, in 1950, Minister of State for War).

On 11 March 1938 the Austrian Chancellor called a nationwide plebiscite, asking the Austrian people if they wanted *Anschluss* with Germany, i.e. to become part of an enlarged Germany. But before the plebiscite could take place and in the face of threats and German troops massing on the border, he backed down, leaving the Nazis to take over. The rest of the world, once again, simply looked on. Immediately Nazi flags appeared on government buildings, swastikas appeared on the streets and Jews were hounded from their shops, offices and homes. For the exiles in Britain, this was another very depressing event, cementing Hitler's power even more and demonstrating the impotence or unwillingness of other European nations to confront him. The events in Austria increased once more the flow of emigrants from Nazi-occupied territories, and the number of exiles coming to Britain would continue to grow in the period up to 1939 and the outbreak of war. Some came after fighting in Spain and, with the defeat of the Spanish Republican government, internment in France. Greta Wittkowski, who had studied with Brigitte in Basle, came via that route, as did Kurt Hager (who would later become one of the GDR's chief political and cultural ideologists), Hans Kahle and Erich Henschke.

Before the Nazi invasion of France in May 1940, the German Communist Party headquarters in exile had been based in Paris. Jürgen made several visits there from London in order to receive instructions, and during one of these in 1936 was told that he was to take over the political leadership of German émigré communists in Britain. He would remain the leader until 1939 and then take this position again from 1940 to 1941. He felt it was a great responsibility as, faute de mieux, he was very much left to his own devices; communications with the Party leadership were no longer easy, and to meet face-to-face meant a journey of more than a few hours. Two other comrades he met regularly during his visits to Paris, although they had nothing to do with the leadership-in-exile, were the journalist Egon Erwin Kisch and the novelist Anna Seghers with their respective partners. He got to know Kisch after being introduced by his sister Ursula, who knew him from her time in China.

Paul Bertz, who was also based in Paris, had responsibility in the exile-based Party leadership for personnel/membership issues. He was, Jürgen writes, a stalwart individual who refused to be misled or misused in the general climate of suspicion that began to take hold in the Party under the influence of Stalin's purges and by that 'senseless exaggeration of vigilance which often brought about great misfortune' on those often innocently caught up in it, as in the tragic case of Ursula's divorced husband Rolf Hamburger, which is related in Chapter 13.

During this time, on visits to Paris, Jürgen also got to know Gerhart Eisler very well and the two became close friends. Gerhart was the brother of the composer and Brecht collaborator, Hanns. He eventually found refuge in the USA but was expelled at the end of the war as a result of the McCarthy witch-hunts. He then settled in the GDR and became the first director of GDR radio. During the late 1930s Gerhart was based in France with the leadership-in-exile and had responsibility for propaganda and thus for directing and supporting Jürgen's work in Britain. Eisler's sister, Ruth Fischer, once a committed and militant communist, would later become a virulent and vocal opponent of communism.

With Hitler's forces marching through Europe with the efficiency and unstoppability of a robot army, the flow of emigrants to Britain increased once more. Jürgen found himself looking after an increasing Party membership, now scattered throughout the country. Where the density was sufficient, residents' branches were formed, and these would meet usually weekly to discuss political and organisational issues.

The exile Party organisation also played a leading part in attempts to build a People's Front, particularly in France. In March 1939, in Paris, an action committee, German Opposition, was formed with the writer Heinrich Mann as its president. Jürgen persuaded him to become patron of the British People's Front movement as well. Mann promised to try and convince his more famous brother, Thomas, to come on board and put Jürgen in touch with him; but he remained aloof, replying in a friendly tone, but declined on the basis that he was too overworked and needed rest.

While Jürgen was busy organising among the communist exiles, his father was now well established at the LSE and his mother, Berta, was trying to settle down to a new life, one they all hoped would be short-term, but soon realised could go on for several years. Brigitte and Barbara, as the two eldest daughters in London, also had to find work to supplement the family income and schools had to be found for the youngest two. They had arrived with little in the way of possessions and were in a new country; the girls were having to learn a new language and they were all having to adapt to a new culture.

Being forced into exile is invariably a traumatic experience but then to arrive in a country where you were not made welcome and even interned along with some of those from whom you had fled, only compounded the situation. A number of people, who were in exile elsewhere, including some prominent individuals like the writers Kurt Tucholsky, Walter Benjamin, Walter Hasenclever and Stefan Zweig, chose suicide rather than face the uncertainty of exile. The situation was particularly difficult for those whose careers relied on writing or speaking in their own language and who saw themselves reduced to communicating in pidgin. It was a predicament that some, like those mentioned above, were unable to countenance.

The refugees' desire to maintain their cultural traditions led to the setting up of several cultural associations in Britain and these soon became an important element in the life of the émigré community. The most successful event in terms of uniting the German émigrés was the establishment of the *Freie Deutsche Kulturbund* (Free German League of Culture) as a broad and inclusive organisation, in which communists played a leading role. It was set up on 1 March 1939 on the initiative of German communists in the UK, among others, Jürgen Kuczynski. It was constituted as a 'German, anti-National Socialist, anti-fascist, non-party affiliated refugee organisation with the aim of nurturing German culture'. Similar but much smaller cultural organisations were also set up by other groups – there were Zionist and social democratic ones – but it was the communist-organised cultural events that tended to be more successful and effective in terms of audience size and impact. The Free German League of Culture would, in the end, become the largest and most important of the exile cultural organisations in the country.

In 1939 it was given the use of a room by the Church of England in a house at 36 Upper Park Road, Hampstead. It was there that the *Kleine Bühne* (Small Stage) opened in 1940, putting on regular plays and cabarets in the evenings. Marguerite Kuczynski was closely involved in the organisational side of the League and after finding office space for it, she began building a library which could be used by émigrés of all political persuasions. In 1940 the League took over the whole building and was able to establish its own permanent library, a cafe-cum-restaurant and a room for meetings. From its four founding members, it grew to become an organisation of around 1,000. As German refugees were officially forbidden to form political organisations, the League became something of a substitute. Within a very a short time, it had convened five large meetings with an average audience of around 500, organised exhibitions by its participating artists, put on musical performances, lectures, writers' discussion groups and even a cabaret, *The 24 Black Sheep*. British speakers were also invited to address its meetings, among them J. B. Priestley, Hannen Swaffer, Kingsley Martin and Storm Jameson. Among the German speakers were the artist Oskar Kokoschka, the writers Berthold Viertel, Ludwig Renn and Stefan Zweig, and the theatre critic and essayist Alfred Kerr. After leaving Britain for the USA and then Brazil, Zwieg committed suicide after losing all hope.

An MI5 report on the League early on, during the 'phoney' war period, based on information from a regular informer, Karl Otten,[2] expressed surprise that both Robert and Jürgen – the former considered more dangerous than the latter because of his influential position at the LSE, where he was still teaching – 'were being allowed to continue their activities unhampered, since they were spreading defeatism'.[3] It coupled the 'non-aligned' Robert Kuczynski and Alfred Meusel, as being 'the real directing leaders of the anti-war campaign'. The League was an organisation that was kept under continual close scrutiny by MI5 which described it as 'the largest Communist sideshow in London'.[4] This accusation by MI5 of 'spreading defeatism' refers to the period of the phoney war, when, on instructions from the Comintern, communist parties were to describe the war as being one between imperialist powers and not as a genuine war against fascism.

Burke, in his book on the Lawn Road Flats, quotes an MI5 report[5] made during the war which states that 'Professor A. Meusl [sic] ... is the Chief of the Communist Party, a very dangerous man capable of committing every crime'. How such an assessment came about is curious, as Meusel, a friend of the Kuczynskis, was certainly no firebrand, but very much the classic academic, pursuing his historical research assiduously while in exile in Britain. He had been a professor of sociology and political economy at Aachen University from 1930 until 1934. He had been a member of the SPD, but later left and became a KPD sympathiser but did not join the Party until after he came to Britain as a refugee in 1934. Jürgen says that Meusel and his own wife,

Marguerite, were the only two people he knew who were admitted into membership of the Party during the exile years in Britain – there was understandably a great deal of mistrust at this time and only those with a proven track record were accepted. Jürgen describes him and the other comrades who joined the leadership of the Party as being 'upright and loyal, and to the last, clean, honest people who helped make the work a pleasant task'. After the war, he, like Jürgen, settled in the GDR where he played a prominent role in academia and in the *Deutscher Kulturbund* (German Cultural Association).

Among the many other refugees who came to Britain were the journalist Sebastian Haffner, who wrote the anti-Nazi polemic *Germany: Jekyll and Hyde* (1940), the musicologist and composer, Ernst Hermann Meyer, the graphic artist René Graetz and the Austrian poet Erich Fried, to name but a few prominent creative figures. Fried remembered the refugee organisations as 'a basis for our existence, as employment agency, as cheap restaurants where you could have a decent meal, and as cultural organisations …'[6] Britain was a country with a tradition of offering hospitality and refuge to foreigners over the centuries, but this new influx, coinciding as it did with the onset of war, put severe strains on that tradition.

René Graetz was one of those interned and then deported to Canada in 1940, but was able to return to Britain in 1941. He would play a very active role in the League of Culture and designed a number of its posters and backdrops for theatrical performances. He was also a member of the Communist Party, and would later marry the Irish-born artist Elizabeth Shaw. Both would settle in East Germany after the war, where they successfully continued their artistic careers.

Many émigrés, particularly those who arrived in the very last months before the outbreak of war, often found it difficult to obtain work and this often delayed their integration into the British mainstream. Almost all of them were ideologically anti-fascist and thus tended to move in the same cultural and social circles, although tensions were still carried over from the past, as between the Social Democrats and the Communists or between the apolitical and the committed. But Jürgen was never one to have sectarian attitudes or to shun anyone, simply because they had different political opinions. During the war years, he would meet regularly with people like the German aristocrat Prinz Hubertus zu Loewenstein, a rare exiled aristocrat. Although he often visited the Kuczynskis at home and praised their friendship and hospitality, after the war, he would become a leading reactionary and militant anti-communist. Jürgen also had what he called 'a more complicated relationship' with Pastor Wolfgang Büsing who led a circle of Protestants, but he made every effort to be as inclusive in his anti-fascist work as he could.

Another of Jürgen's activities in which he was able to register considerable success was the establishment of a radio station broadcasting to Germany: *Freiheitsender 29.8* (Freedom Radio 29.8). It began as an organ of the KPD but developed into an instrument for the preparation of what would later become the Permanent Committee of the German People's Front. To help promote it, he produced a small brochure: *Freedom Calling: The Story of the Secret German Radio*, published in the UK and which rapidly sold out. He was also able to persuade a number of leading Labour Party MPs, trade union leaders and academics to broadcast on the station.

The German Freedom Radio Station 29.8 began broadcasting from Madrid in January 1937 and continued to do so until March 1939. The impression was deliberately given that it was broadcasting from inside Germany. The content of the broadcasts was determined in Paris where the party leadership in Western exile was based. Its aim was 'to inform the German working class about the true nature of National Socialism and continually called for anti-fascist resistance. Well-known personalities like Einstein, Hemingway, and Thomas and Heinrich Mann wrote scripts for it, and it had a wide audience. The first attempts by the Nazi regime at banning the listening to 'hostile broadcasts' was aimed at silencing Station 29.8.

The financing of the radio station was quite an undertaking and the Party sent Jürgen to the USA in order to raise funds for it. On this six-week trip he was accompanied by Marguerite and their daughter Madeleine. During their time there they were able to catch up with William Dodd,[7] a close friend of President Roosevelt and former US ambassador to Germany during the early Hitler years.

They visited a whole number of cities, utilising the links and contacts made during their previous time in the USA. They went to different places and made contacts separately in order to increase their fundraising potential, managing to return to the UK with substantial funds. During their stay Jürgen also called on Albert Einstein, whom he had met when he was still a schoolboy in Germany, through his father, and with whom he too developed a close friendship. Einstein, his father said, was not only a great physicist but was characterised 'by his sagacious modesty', a comment that particularly impressed Jürgen. One of the latter's friends once remarked sardonically that it was no wonder he was more impressed by this attribute than by Einstein's scientific prowess, as Jürgen was more likely in his life to come up with a more advanced theory of relativity than to achieve 'sagacious modesty'.

Even before Einstein was given refuge in the USA, there had been a concerted campaign to refuse him entry. Both in the USA and worldwide, there were a significant number of individuals who tried to belittle his scientific achievements and sully his reputation. He had many enemies who made great efforts to demolish his Theory of Relativity. There was even an Anti-Einstein 'Academy of Nations' set up by Arvid Reutherdahl, an engineer and Dean of the College of St Thomas in Minnesota, to wage an attack on him and his views. The 'Academy's aim was to promote 'true', 'good' and 'free' science. It ridiculed his ideas, organised disruption of his lectures and published pseudo-scientific and defamatory tracts. Undoubtedly, part of the reason for such animosity towards Einstein were his socialist and progressive views, compounded by his Jewishness.

Even before the end of the war, Einstein would condemn the development and use of nuclear weapons. He openly declared his friendship with the Soviet Union and made no secret of his socialist views. He was also vehemently opposed to the Cold War that would soon unfold, and to the discrimination against black people, so prevalent at the time in the USA.

From Einstein Jürgen received generous support for the radio station and was given contacts to others who would give money. They had long conversations with each other in which they discussed 'everything under the sun, but particularly the contemporary situation'. In a letter Einstein wrote to Jürgen in May 1939, he said: 'I can see from what you indicate that we are in agreement concerning the interpretation of the peculiar position taken by France and England: class interests above state interests.' He was referring here to the 'phoney war' when the

Western powers were unwilling to engage Hitler militarily, hoping he'd march on Russia first. Even well after the end of the war, Einstein was still very much a socialist. In 1949, he would write:

> I am convinced there is only *one* way to eliminate these grave evils [of capitalism], namely through the establishment of a socialist economy, accompanied by an educational system which would be oriented toward social goals.

In his article, he went on to argue that the means of production should be owned by the people and utilised in a planned fashion. He emphasised the role of a proper education which would allow each individual to develop their potential and endow them with a sense of responsibility for their fellow human beings, 'in place of the glorification of power and success in our present society', as he put it.[8]

Given his relationship with Jürgen and openly expressing such thinking, it is perhaps not entirely surprising that Einstein was one of those placed under surveillance by the FBI and included on a list of probable left-wing extremists. In the FBI's Gibarti file[9] visits by Jürgen and his father to Einstein were duly noted, and their correspondence monitored. Louis Gibarti was an FBI informant who also testified against Jürgen.

In political attitudes, Jürgen says, the British people were very different from the Americans because on top of money, the British were prepared to give their political support. One of those who did so was the writer Leo Hamilton Myers who had been Eton and Cambridge educated and was close to the Bloomsbury Circle. He became a good friend and generous supporter of the anti-fascist struggle right up until he took his own life in 1944.

Myers also happened to be married to the daughter of US general William J. Palmer. The Kuczynskis would often spend a day or weekend with the family at one of their country retreats and there made other friends, including the poet Lilian Bowes-Lyon (youngest daughter of the Hon. Francis Bowes-Lyon and first cousin to the late Queen Mother and wife of King George IV). What Lilian Bowes-Lyon made of this young man from Germany, with his easy charm, intellectual acuity and passionate political commitment, is uncertain, but she was clearly impressed enough to support the campaign for his release when he was interned later as an enemy alien. Others with whom he became acquainted were Geoffrey Pyke, the colourful and Bohemian journalist, educationalist and boffin, and the poet Cecil Day Lewis. Jürgen was surprised himself that he appeared to make a whole number of friends in literary circles as he was not known as a literary figure. In addition to those mentioned above, he developed friendships with John and Rosamund Lehmann, Rose Macaulay, Olaf Stapledon, Stephen Spender, Anabel Williams-Ellis, Sylvia Townsend Warner, Randall Swingler and Edgell Rickword – a good selection of some of Britain's most eminent writers of the period. Most of them were, though, committed to the anti-fascist struggle and were keen to give what support they could to the German exiles; so it is perhaps not so surprising that they became acquainted with the Kuzcynskis. Through Leo Myers, he and Marguerite also became close friends with the left-wing physicist J. D. Bernal and his then girlfriend, Margaret Gardiner.

Jürgen maintained good contacts with individuals on the left wing of the Labour Party, particularly those involved in producing the magazine *Tribune*. Leading Labour figures like Aneurin Bevan and his wife Jennie Lee and Ellen Wilkinson also gave much support to the German anti-fascist movement. The trade union leader and friend of Eleanor Marx, Ben Tillett, the left-wing MPs Konni Zilliacus and Tom Driberg, Douglas Jay, editor of the *Daily Herald* and later an MP, as well as John Parker of the Fabian Society, all belonged to his circle. Others that could be added to this list are the Fabians, Sydney and Beatrice Webb, historian Arnold Toynbee, the economist and political theorist G. D. H. Cole, the economist Nicholas Kaldor, the sociologist David Glass and the eminent mathematician Lancelot Hogben. The Kuczynskis' list of friends and acquaintances reads almost like a *Who's Who* of British left-wing political, academic and literary life of the period.

By pure chance, he also made friends with Sylvia Pankhurst. He relates how he was invited to give a talk at the small New Times bookshop and sign copies of his books. It turned out that the shop belonged to Sylvia Pankhurst, who was quite amused at Jürgen's cheek in using the occasion to collect money in support of the German Communist Party. Since that first encounter they met on a number of occasions at anti-fascist events and became good friends. When he visited Addis Abeba in 1966 for a Pugwash conference and met Emperor Haile Selassie there, the latter was fascinated to hear of his friendship with Sylvia Pankhurst as she had been a devoted and tireless supporter of Ethiopia's (then Abyssinia) cause against Italian aggression. Her son, Jürgen relates, had become the emperor's chief economic advisor.

One unusual brochure Jürgen produced in Britain in March 1939 on behalf of the German Party was a fictitious supplement published by the non-existent *Zeitschrift der Deutsch-Englischen Wirtschaftskammer in Grossbritannien* (Journal of the German-English Chamber of Commerce in Great Britain) with articles by Lord Simple-Ton and spoof adverts for the Nazi newspaper, *Der Stürmer*. It was then sent to subscribers in Germany of the genuine chamber of commerce magazine. Those involved in the publication were extremely pleased when the world's press – in the UK, USA, France, Japan and the Soviet Union – reported on this clever send-up. Only after copies of the magazine had already reached their destinations did the Hitler regime get around to officially complaining to the British government about it, and the success of the exercise even prompted an intemperate response from Goebbels. Jürgen had managed to get hold of the address list after he had written to Churchill shortly after his arrival in Britain, requesting support. The latter responded via a foreign editor at the *Financial News*, who was an anti-fascist, and passed on useful information to Jürgen, including this subscription list. The same *Financial News* journalist actually paid the postage for copies sent from Britain and that amounted to 15,000; many were also sent from Paris. Churchill, it should be remembered, was at that time a member of a small Tory cabal of anti-Hitler Tories.

In his role as propagandist, Jürgen also wrote for the *Deutsche Volks-zeitung*, the Party's weekly magazine in Paris, whose editor was Adolf 'Lex' Ende. With the German invasion of France, Ende joined the French resistance and in the last stage of the war fought alongside his French comrades to free Marseilles from the Nazis. He returned to East Germany once the war was over and became chief editor of the Party newspaper *Neues Deutschland* before falling foul of the Stalin-inspired clamp-down on Western exiles, and was demoted to work as an accountant in a steel works.

Apart from this journalistic work, Jürgen still continued with his academic research and wrote a number of reports and political pamphlets for the British Communist Party. The first of these was published in 1936, in booklet form as *Labour Conditions in Europe 1820–1935*, based on the statistical research he was able to carry out during his time working underground in Germany. His second book written in the UK was *New Fashions in Wage Theory*, but leading British Party economists disagreed with a number of his assertions. It found considerable interest, however, particularly because it was intended as a polemic against Keynes from a Marxist perspective, and was reviewed in the *Economist*. One of Keynes' students, Joan Robinson, wrote him a blistering response in defence of Keynes. However, much later, Robinson would change her viewpoint, moving away from Keynes towards a more Marxist position, and became very friendly with Kuczynski. This rapprochement between the two was facilitated by the Cambridge economist Maurice Dobb, who was also a member of the CPGB. Kuczynski's polemic with Keynes, though, had also irritated a number of his comrades in the British Party and he became, in his own words, 'the bête noir of English political economists'.

Jürgen was to visit Dobb again at Trinity College in 1968, long after he had returned permanently to Germany, together with his London-based sister, Renate. Robinson, who was still at Cambridge, had, he writes, by this time taken to 'the Chinese Line' (this was the period of the big rift in the international communist movement between China and the Soviet Union).

Towards the end of his period working underground in Germany, Jürgen had also found time to prepare a manuscript on the French Revolution of 1789, and towards the end of the 'peaceful' years in Britain he completed a manuscript on the English Revolution of 1640, but neither was ever published. With the latter, his interpretation brought him into conflict with the leading British Marxist historian and authority on the English Revolution, Christopher Hill.

He certainly did not let exile in a foreign country and all the associated uncertainties hold him back in his multifarious activities. And in many ways he was more integrated into the life of the British Communist Party than any of the other functionaries among German communist exiles, many of whom preferred working almost exclusively within

exile circles. He played a significant role in helping with the preparation of anti-fascist propaganda and sat on the editorial board of *Labour
Monthly* (from 1936 to 1944), which was edited by the Party's leading
intellectual, Rajani Palme Dutt. He also gave regular lectures on the
situation in Germany and the rise of fascism to a whole number of
British organisations, from Labour Party branches to Co-operative
groups and students. These lecture tours were highly successful and the
meetings well attended. The deterioration of the international situation
and the looming war had politicised many people and encouraged
them to take some form of action, even if it only involved attending
meetings. He calculated that he addressed around 350 meetings altogether during his eight years exile in Britain. His extraordinary energy,
his versatility, sociability and broad knowledge certainly gave him the
opportunity, during his stay, of meeting many people from all areas of
the country and from different class backgrounds, which provided him
with a useful insight into the British way of life during the war.

The political situation in Europe changed remarkably with the signing of the Hitler–Stalin Pact in August 1939. That same month, Jürgen,
with Marguerite and their two children – Madeleine now 7 years old and
Peter almost 2 – were still able to undertake their usual quarter-yearly
visit to France, but it would be the last time.

In August 1939, shortly before war broke out, Marguerite and the
two children accompanied Jürgen to Paris where regular discussions
took place with the Party leadership. Leaving him in Paris, she and the
children travelled on to Switzerland where they visited Ursula. That
same month she wrote to Jürgen from Switzerland expressing her fears
about the imminent threat of war; he was not convinced and still
remained naively optimistic that war could be prevented. Marguerite
left Switzerland earlier than planned because of her fears – in this case
certainly justified: war broke out just three days after their return to
London.

A month later, in September 1939, the United Kingdom declared
war on Germany. At this point, the communist parties, including both
the German and British, despite much disagreement and soul-searching,
toed the Soviet line and characterised the war as an 'inter-imperialist'
one, withholding support for it. This attitude alienated whole swathes
of left and liberal opinion, particularly among Labour Party supporters,

and they distanced themselves from the German communists in exile, making their work from then on very difficult. This situation was compounded by the increasing suspicion of all Germans by the British people and led to many being sacked from their jobs. Tribunals were set up to assess the trustworthiness of German émigrés and travel restrictions were introduced. In France and other European countries, though, the situation had become much worse by this time. In September, Warsaw was subjected to heavy German aerial bombardment with high-explosive and incendiary bombs, which totally destroyed the old centre of the city.

The fallout from the Nazi–Soviet pact caused Jürgen considerable headaches. But what undoubtedly helped to hold the small exile group together was that in Britain they felt secure. They did not face possible expulsion from the country, unlike their comrades in France, because their position as immigrants was officially recognised. Few suffered dire financial strictures or extreme poverty as a result of this crisis and most soon became integrated in the routine daily life of the country once again – at least before the wave of internments began.

A direct repercussion of the declaration of war by the United Kingdom was that on 18 January 1940, Jürgen and Marguerite themselves received notice to appear before one of the tribunals, along with several other comrades, including Kurt Hager. Many Germans were now being interned as a security precaution and not much notice was taken of the political persuasions of the individuals concerned. However, to begin with, Jürgen was the only one of the comrades living in London to be sent to a camp, and the only one from the Party leadership to be interned. On 29 January 1940, he was duly despatched to Warner's Camp in Seaton, Devon. There he met three other comrades from Birmingham, but of the other inmates most were German seamen taken from ships that had been seized by the British, almost all of them Nazis who clung together. The rest were made up of Germans who had been living in Britain for professional reasons, including some Jewish immigrants, of whom several had already spent time in German concentration camps, and one of these remarked that it had not been so cold in the German camp as in the Devon one.

Conditions in these internment camps were quite harsh, especially for those who were no longer young and had been accustomed to relatively comfortable surroundings. The fascist internees were often given more favourable treatment than the anti-fascists because the authorities assumed that if they treated the enemy humanely, then British prisoners of war would be similarly treated by Germany. The Nazis were even allowed to fly the swastika flag and give the Nazi salute in the camps.[10]

The situation in the Devon internment camp, a former holiday camp, was described in even more graphic terms by the national Sunday newspaper *Reynold's News*: 'In this camp about half the men were Nazis, the rest decided friends of our [the anti-fascist] cause. The Nazis were organized by a Gestapo man, and behaved with deliberate arrogance and brutality. They went about singing their blood-thirsty Nazi songs, and occasionally they even beat up Jewish interned ... Life in these conditions was scarcely endurable; there was a daily civil war in the camp.'[11]

Jürgen, because of his position in the Party leadership of the country as a whole, became the de facto leader of the small group of four comrades in the camp. He soon managed to build a 'popular front' to include around eight inmates, who then set up their own educational group which provided language lessons and talks on a variety of subjects. The Nazis, he said, showed no open animosity to them, as the Hitler–Stalin Pact was still in force. As a result, Jürgen found himself once a week lecturing to the whole camp of around 200 inmates. His small group worked well, he writes, and set the tone in the camp and they soon had the most important positions in their hands and were the ones who represented the inmates' interests to the British military camp administration.

Despite his upbeat description of life there he must have missed his family and friends back in London, and was no doubt looking forward to a visit from his wife. However, when Marguerite applied for permission to visit him in the camp she received the following letter from the camp's commandant: 'I regret to inform you that your husband has seen fit to make himself a nuisance in this camp. I have withdrawn all privileges from him and I shall not be able to allow you to visit him on 6 April.' Signed: Colonel X, Commandant Warner's Camp.

This letter was opened by Special Branch, and the copy kept in its files has an internal hand-written note attached to it by an MI5/Special

Branch official which reads: 'please see attached letter to Mrs. K from Colonel Blimp'![12]

In the meantime, the Kuczynskis' friends and comrades on the outside were pulling out all the stops to obtain Jürgen's release. The fact that such a well-known anti-fascist, academic and political activist had been interned had shocked many. Even friends in the USA, like Martha Dodd, daughter of the former US ambassador to Berlin, campaigned for his release and importuned the British ambassador in the USA, Lord Lothian, to help. Harold Laski, the British political theorist and future Chairman of the Labour Party, while cautious not to get too involved with a known communist, also did what he could and intervened privately with President Roosevelt on Kuczynski's behalf. The prominent defence lawyer D. N. Pritt MP also used what legal channels he could to obtain his release. The Queen's cousin, Lilian Bowes-Lyon, was also one of those friends who wrote to the Home Office on Jürgen's behalf. With such figures on board, it is little surprise that the campaign was successful, and he was released on 24 April 1940.

That same month Hitler invaded Denmark and Norway, and then in May, Belgium and France. As a result of this increasing threat to Britain itself, the government and the population at large panicked and now viewed all Germans with renewed suspicion. More German exiles, now including almost all Jürgen's male Party comrades were, in the meantime, interned. The campaign for their release put a great strain on all those not interned. At this time Marguerite, in the early stages of another pregnancy, lost their child and this may have been connected with that additional stress.

MI5 felt its nose put out by Jürgen's release because their opposition to it had been ignored by the Home Office. They considered his release inappropriate, especially in the light of the repeated denunciations of Jürgen that had come their way (largely as a result of his opposition to the 'phoney war'). By July 1940, an MI5 memorandum reported on a plan of Karl Otten's to lay a trap for him, namely to lull him into incriminating himself by uttering 'disloyal' sentiments that could be reported.[13] This plan was either never implemented or it misfired.

Lou Baruch, a young working-class man from Liverpool and a member of the Communist Party, was one of those German-Jewish exiles who was also interned in Seaton Camp. He left a short unpublished memoir in which he talks about life at the camp and meeting Jürgen. But unlike Jürgen who had high-powered friends in the country who were able to successfully secure his release, Baruch was only released three years later. In his memoir, he writes:

There [at Seaton] I first met Jürgen Kuczynski with whom I became friends. This friendship has lasted our whole lives and I have made a point of visiting him over the years from time to time in Berlin. At that time I was unaware that he was the leader of the KPD in the United Kingdom. I only found that out thirty years later from his autobiography.

Warner's Camp was fairly large with good facilities for possibly 300 prisoners who slept in small huts with four bunk beds in each. There were tennis courts, a swimming pool, and space for sport. Hygiene was good and the army personnel tried to be correct, but were completely out of their depth politically, quite incapable of understanding, and ignorant about who their prisoners were, and what the war was about. The physical problems the prisoners faced were two-fold. The first was the unbearable cold in the huts. 1939/40 turned out to be a very cold winter, and secondly the lack of food. I have never been so hungry in my life. It was an outrageous breach of the 1929 Geneva Convention and in spite of continuous protests, the position remained unchanged. It was rumoured that the food destined for the internees was stolen and sold on the black market. This was possible, in view of my later experience of dishonesty in the British army, but impossible to prove.

There were two groups of communists interned in Seaton from the Communist Parties of Germany and Austria. They operated from the very beginning, and did so effectively with membership, meetings, election of offices, and payment of party dues. Organised by the communists in Seaton was also a group of interned trade unionists which operated publicly whilst the Communist Party did not ...This preserved the morale of the anti-fascist majority in the camp, completely isolated a Nazi minority ... The party groups met every day for a formal political discussion and an evaluation of

the political, economic and military position of the United Kingdom and the international situation. Activities were organised such
as discussion circles and public lectures and later on a wall newspaper was published every day which was very popular. The editor
of it was Professor Dr. Jürgen Kuczynski, I was the co-editor and I
typed it. Later this paper was suppressed by the military authorities.

The composition of the inmates of Seaton consisted of a small
group of Jewish refugees, a larger number of political refugees
mostly from the Left, long established German residents in the
United Kingdom, some of whom had already been interned once,
during the First World War, and German seamen captured in
actions at sea, as well as German passengers from various ships. The
number of Nazis was very small, and they kept quiet. There were
also a small number of former members of the International Brigades from the German Thälmann Battalion, mostly captured on
neutral ships escaping mainly from France to Mexico.[14]

There was an odd sequel to Jürgen's internment. Very shortly after his
release his fellow internees from Seaton were despatched to Canada on
the passenger ship *SS Arandora Star*, which would be torpedoed about
150 miles off the Scottish coast. Lou Baruch was one of those on that
ship.

As the ship's officers had made no contingency plans or carried out
any safety drills, chaos ensued after the torpedo struck and there was
considerable loss of life, but many internees, including Baruch, did
manage to survive and were rescued.

During Jürgen's internment, Marguerite had moved out of their old
house, as the rooms were needed for the expanded work of the Cultural League, and had rented a flat with two rooms and a kitchen. On
his release, Jürgen joined her there. Shortly after they had all moved in,
a German bomb landed close by while the whole family – the adults
and the two children – were asleep. The explosion brought a
sudden end to their night, and they awoke to find themselves covered
in splintered glass from the shattered windows and that the door
between their adjoining rooms had been lifted off its hinges. London
and other British cities would from then on experience such raids on a
regular basis.

The situation in France after the Nazi invasion was now dire. Many of the men among the German exiles there had been interned; their partners, wives and/or children had been left to fend for themselves, invariably with no source of income or contact with their men in the camps. Jürgen now found himself having to help these comrades and their families as well as those in Britain itself. Under the prevailing political circumstances and restrictions that were imposed by the government on political activity by German exiles, the Cultural League from then on became the most effective campaigning organisation. Jürgen utilised all his worldwide contacts to drum up support, particularly in the USA, Scandinavia and Moscow, appealing for visas to be issued to those in France who were now in desperate need of them. Many, at least up until June 1941, were able to escape to the USA, including his friends and comrades Gerhart Eisler, Paul Merker, Albert Norden and Alexander Abusch, all of whom would play leading roles in the post-war GDR government. At the same time as all this was happening London was experiencing its first concentrated bombardments by Hitler's war planes and other cities, like Coventry, Liverpool, Plymouth and Birmingham would also be badly hit.

During that very turbulent period, Jürgen found sufficient time and energy to embark on what was to become perhaps his greatest life-long achievement, his mammoth *Lage der Arbeiter unter dem Kapitalismus* (published in Britain under the title *A Short History of Labour Conditions under Industrial Capitalism*). The disruption caused by his internment, German bombing and the added organisational responsibilities clearly hadn't diminished his writing fervour. The 'short' history was a work he was to continue expanding and updating throughout his life. The British version was published in five volumes and the last German edition comprised forty volumes. When he brought the draft of the first volume to the director of the British Communist Party's publishing house, it was rejected on the basis that 'it was too sharp in its judgement of Britain'.

Amazingly, during this very demanding time in his life, he was still able to send reports to Moscow on the political and economic situation in Britain which were delivered by convoy. He maintained warm relations with Anatole Gromov, the Soviet press attaché in London, and Moscow's popular ambassador, Ivan Maiski. They would often visit the Kuczynskis at home, when there would be lively discussions on politics, culture and philosophy. According to Jürgen's account of their meetings, both men told him that they valued his work highly, particularly for its 'ice-cold and bitter logic'.

As Britain was the only Western European nation as yet still beyond the immediate reach of Nazi ground troops, Jürgen found himself acting for all the exiles as the go-between and the one to get things moving or make them happen. Comrades and friends around the world would petition for his help in raising money, writing leaflets or passing on information. Alongside his lectures, publishing activities, the analyses he made and the memoranda he wrote for the Soviet Union, he also continued his economic and statistical research. His brochure *Labour and the Fascist New Economic Order* was particularly popular and went into a second edition. It had a foreword by the British mineworkers' leader Will Lawther, and a cover designed by his friend in exile, John Heartfield, the father of photo-montage.

It was, he emphasised, the intensity of the political process, the historical circumstances and his work for the Party at this time which formed his character and his thinking. He wrote:

> Sometimes one imagines that education through the Party would, in the first instance, be a pedagogic process, like being at school, with the imparting of knowledge, teachers explaining the works of the Marxist classics with guidance on criticism and self-criticism. Of course, it is that too. And, to a great extent perhaps, it has to be like that in a socialist country. In the capitalist world and in J. K's life, though, education through the demands made on one – in which, often, no help could be given – played a decisive role. How often was he thrown in at the deep end and expected to swim …

He argued that this was the best form of education and one he implemented himself as a lecturer and teacher later in the GDR. It is not always the more comfortable route, he noted, but if it is successful, it brings better results and, above all, promotes inner strength and reliability.

In 1940, shortly after the beginning of the war, Marguerite decided to join the KPD, ten years after her husband. Although she had always supported his Party work, she had not felt the urge to join.

With the immediate threat of German bombardment, the government began making plans for the evacuation of women and children from London. When these evacuations took place in April 1940, John Strachey's wife Celia kindly took Madeleine and Peter together with her own children out of London, to Oxford.

As if Jürgen didn't have enough to keep him more than fully occupied at this time, in February 1941 he joined the British Association of Scientific Workers, a professional union body. He became an active member in its Central London branch and developed into such an expert on the arcane rules for conducting union business and the way trade unions in Britain worked, that he was elected as its Chair in 1942. He became so immersed in this work that he and colleagues issued a brochure on the British trade union movement as a study course for researchers and students. He also sat on the London district committee of the union and was a member of its recruitment as well as its national statistical and research committees. Jürgen's wife Marguerite, despite having to look after two small children, played her own not insignificant part in the anti-fascist struggle and in the Cultural League.

On 7 December 1941 the Japanese attacked the US fleet in Pearl Harbor and the US government immediately declared war on Japan. As a result, Hitler then rashly declared war on the USA, giving Roosevelt the argument he needed to persuade a reluctant populace to support a wider war against German fascism in Europe. The entrance of the USA into the conflict would be a decisive factor in the future conduct and outcome of the war. Meanwhile, in Britain the anti-fascist German exiles would continue their organising, mobilising and publicity work undiminished throughout the war years.

In 1942, Marguerite joined the local Hampstead Garden Suburb branch of the Women's Guild and made sure members were aware of what was being done by German exiles in Britain. In 1942 she also wrote an essay, 'German Women against the Swastika', about the lives of women in Hitler's Germany, in a popular brochure produced by the Free German League of Culture in Great Britain, *Women under the Swastika*, and she was secretary of the War Aid Committee for German Women Refugees in Great Britain. The League was originally set up as 'a support organisation for refugees', and with the cultural task of upholding Germany's progressive past. She organised the collecting of money and clothing for the refugees, and set up the League's own library, based largely on donations. It had branches in most of the big cities, like Birmingham, Glasgow, Leeds, Oxford and Manchester, and attempted to involve all those who were anti-fascists and not become an exclusively Communist Party organisation. After the attack on the Soviet Union in 1941, the League's activities became even more politicised. It would only cease activity in June 1946.

The enigma of the Lawn Road Flats – a hub for spies?

Arriving as homeless refugees in Britain, the Kuczynski family was first introduced to Lawn Road by Gertrude Sirnis,[15] who was close to the Communist Party, as was her husband, Alexander Sirnis, who had died in 1918. He had corresponded with Robert Kuczynski. Her daughter, Gerty, had been studying at the London School of Economics where Robert was then working. He told her that his wife and two girls were soon coming over to join him and they desperately needed accommodation. Gerty's mother, who worked for the British Committee for the Relief of the Victims of Fascism, was able to arrange for the Kuczynskis to move into 12 Lawn Road, Hampstead, in northwest London, directly opposite where the Isokon building – Lawn Road Flats – was being constructed at the time. Berta arrived in 1933 on Christmas Eve for a one-month visit, and then on 5 January returned to Berlin to pick up her two youngest daughters. Seven weeks later she came back to London with Sabine, aged 14, and Renate, aged 10, and after a brief stay at 44 Parkhill Road, the family moved into nearby Lawn Road where they were soon joined by Brigitte in September 1935. Residence permits for the UK were eventually granted to all the Kuczynskis, including Jürgen, who arrived, three years later, on 21 January 1936, and to begin with he, Marguerite and their daughter Madeleine lived with his parents.

The Isokon building – or Lawn Road Flats, as it is better known – has, since it was built, become more than an architectural phenomenon. It was, in the 1930s, an iconic and remarkable architectural undertaking, a consummately designed four-storey, gallery-accessed block of thirty-four flats, conceived as an experimental new way of urban living. It was designed by the progressive architect Wells Coates for Molly and

Jack Pritchard, who were innovative interior designers, and it was opened on 9 July 1934. Today it is owned by Notting Hill Housing Group with a small gallery run by the National Trust. It is a modernist block in a road of otherwise traditional large Victorian houses, but has been endowed with a notoriety and engendered an interest certainly unintended by those who conceived it. Jill Pearlman in her essay for the *Journal of the Society of Architectural Historians* describes it thus:

> Outstretched, bright white with a pinkish hue, fearlessly modern and conspicuous, the Lawn Road Flats in Hampstead, London, opened to great fanfare and publicity in the summer of 1934. Thanks to the impressive public relations efforts of both the building's owners, Jack and Molly Pritchard, and its architect, Wells Coates, photographic spreads of the thirty-unit, four-story reinforced concrete block appeared in nearly every British architecture journal, while newspapers from Bournemouth to Belfast trumpeted its opening. With Lawn Road Flats continental modernism made its mark in England on a grand scale, as did a 'revolutionary way of living' in sync with the mobile age ...
>
> The Pritchards lived in the building's penthouse, and staff quarters were located on the ground floor. All flats contained living, sleeping, bathroom, and kitchenette areas ... The units were planned for young middle-class professionals with little time or inclination for domestic chores or household possessions; tenants could move unencumbered into their compact units, for each came equipped with built-in furnishings, the latest appliances, and a staff to clean on a regular basis. According to one writer, the Lawn Road Flats rendered the housewife 'redundant' and household possessions superfluous, while recasting home as a place 'purely incidental to life' rather than at its center.[16]

The aim of Molly and Jack Pritchard had been to create a centre where Bohemian circles, left-wing artists and writers could live in a sort of élite commune. Both Molly and Jack had studied at Cambridge, medicine and engineering respectively. They founded Isokon as a company in 1931, originally to develop the Lawn Road site, but it became better known as a designer and producer of modernist furniture. The name

Isokon arose out of Wells Coates' use of isometric perspective in his drawings, and the flats were designed to be modular, 'isometric units' of construction. In his architectural concept, he had been strongly influenced by Bauhaus architects.

The communal kitchen was converted into the Isobar restaurant in 1937, to a design by Bauhaus-trained Marcel Breuer. The bar and restaurant attracted artists and intellectuals from a wide circle from around Hampstead and beyond. Among those who lived nearby and used the Isobar or visited friends in the flats were people like Roland Penrose, Lee Miller, Oskar Kokoschka, John Heartfield, George Orwell, Barbara Hepworth, Herbert Read, J. D. Bernal, Ernö Goldfinger, Paul Nash and Ben Nicholson. The full list of occupants and visitors reads like a London-based *Who's Who* of British artists and intellectuals.

In the mid-1930s, flat no. 7 was occupied by Arnold Deutsch (codename Otto), one of the Soviet Union's most successful secret agents, who recruited the Cambridge Five spies: Philby, Burgess and Maclean, Blunt and Cairncross. It has been described as a sort of London headquarters for the recruitment of agents for the Soviet intelligence apparatus. Members of the Kuczynski family, including Jürgen, his wife, Marguerite, and Brigitte were also among its one-time residents.

One of those who became a regular visitor to the flats was Andrew Rothstein, whose father had been an intimate friend of Lenin's. Andrew worked for various Soviet publications and press agencies, was a quasi-Soviet consul to Britain, and was also involved in recruiting bright young men and women to work for the Soviet Union's intelligence services. He recruited the eldest daughter of Gertrude Sirnis (neé Stedman), Melitta Norwood, 'the spy who came in from the Co-op'.[17]

Only two full-time employees of the Soviet secret services lived for a time there: the top agent, Arnold Deutsch, and later, for a very short time, Simon Kremer, who was secretary to the Soviet military attaché in London. Most of the other so-called spies who lived there, including the Kuczynskis, were more informal collaborators than agents.

Today, perversely, the Isokon building is more associated with espionage and spies than with architectural innovation, although this was far from the minds of those who designed and built it. It features in most books about twentieth-century spies and espionage as a hub, during the 1930s and 1940s, for KGB operatives to recruit spies for the Soviet Union. A number of writers since the end of the war have indeed attempted to portray Lawn Road Flats as a Soviet spy centre. While this will satisfy those who love conspiracies, it hardly fits the reality. Even though the myths and stories surrounding the flats and the secret agents who lived there are unusual, colourful and exciting, the truth is more banal.

Refugees who came to the country were all in desperate need of immediate accommodation and understandably involved fellow refugees, already based in Britain, to help them. It is little wonder that they – particularly left-wing ones – tended to accumulate around Lawn Road, where there was already a base of like-minded people and where they were made welcome.

This block of flats became transformed not only into an innovative and modernist magnet for artists and intellectuals per se but leftists and communists too, including a whole number of refugees fleeing Nazi Germany. The way the flats were designed and furnished made them ideal as temporary accommodation for refugees, who invariably arrived with only the clothes they stood up in, as well as for those who knew they would only be transient occupiers.

The Pritchards were left wing and enjoyed the company of like-minded intellectuals and artists. Jack himself became involved in helping refugees from Nazi Germany and Austria obtain entry visas for Britain and he offered some of them, including the renowned Bauhaus architect Walter Gropius, refuge in his flats. Jack worked with groups like the German Jewish Aid Committee, the Quakers' Germany Emergency Committee, and the Architects' Czech Refugee Fund, but he also provided direct help to relatives of friends and acquaintances who sought safety in Britain.

Among the flats' sometime occupants were the Austrian-born photographer and Soviet agent Edith Tudor-Hart, Bauhaus émigrés Marcel Breuer and László Moholy-Nagy, the architects Egon Riss and Arthur Korn, Henry Moore and Eva Reckitt and, perhaps surprisingly, crime writer Agatha Christie and British television's first TV cook, Philip Harben.

In David Burke's fascinating, if somewhat imaginative, book *The Lawn Road Flats: Spies, Writers and Artists*, he states that Brigitte had lived with her parents and three of her four sisters at 12 Lawn Road, a large Victorian house converted into apartments … and that she was 'a refugee from Hitler's Germany, a member of the German Communist Party (KPD) *and a talented and prodigious agent working for Stalin's secret service along with her parents and siblings* [my emphasis], two of whom, Jürgen and Ursula would play a critical role in securing Britain's atomic secrets'.[18]

After marrying, in 1936, Brigitte moved into the Isokon building and was from then on known under her married name of Bridget Lewis. When Arnold Deutsch moved into the block, Burke writes, 'his flat was only two doors down from the Soviet agent Brigitte Kuczynski, a German Jew, who lived in Flat 4 with her Scottish husband A.G. Lewis, a member of the CPGB'.

There is little hard evidence of Brigitte/Bridget (she anglicised her name after marriage) being an agent of any secret service, and certainly the adjective 'prodigious' is fictional exaggeration, as is the assertion that Brigitte's parents were agents. This fact was admitted by MI5, when they noted that they declined to interrogate Bridget because sufficient evidence was lacking.[19] The fact that both her father and her brother gave selected results of their economic and statistical research and their assessments of the political and economic situation to their Soviet friends is hardly the same thing as being a spy in the usually accepted sense. Apart from speculative allegations, no one has as yet produced documentation to demonstrate that Brigitte worked for any of the Soviet secret services, apart from some tenuous circumstantial evidence in MI5 files.

Brigitte's MI5 file contains a long, untitled report from 20 April 1944 on her and the whole Kuczynski family. The report recorded that Robert had come to official notice in 'Communist matters', specifically as an official of the Free German Movement. Charmian Brinson, emeritus professor at Imperial College London, and an expert on German and Austrian refugees who came to the UK during the 1930s, notes that:

> A marginal note to a minute in Robert's Home Office file throws
> a little light on the official thinking behind granting him British
> citizenship: 'The father seems to have been singularly detached but

in view of his backing we must agree.' [to grant his request for residency] In other words the British Establishment in the shape of William Beveridge, Alexander Carr-Saunders and others had won the day with the Home Office, even in the face of doubts expressed by the intelligence community.[20]

The security services and the Home Office did not wish to grant Robert citizenship, but his academic standing and political connections worked in his favour.

It is well documented that Arnold Deutsch, an Austrian of Jewish background, worked as an agent for Soviet intelligence. Burke alleges that he worked for OMS and Brigitte for GRU – different Soviet intelligence agencies – but provides no evidence for this assertion about Brigitte's ostensible employer. He writes that '[Arnold] Deutsch and [Teodor Maly] were controlling Philby from 9 Lawn Road' and 'at this time Bridget Lewis was also a Lawn Road resident'. It seems she has been pronounced guilty by association, as she lived in the same block of flats.

In his book on the Lawn Road Flats, Burke describes Jürgen as 'A leading member of the KPD since July 1930, [he] was an influential figure among those members of the German Communist Party exiled in Britain'. He also reveals that as 'A high-ranking communist official, he had met with the leader of the German Communist Party, Walter Ulbricht in 1935, who entrusted him with securing the entire funds of the Communist Party of Germany (KPD)' – 'a very important sum' – instructing him to smuggle them out of Germany and deposit them in the Dutch bank, Rotterdamsche Bankvereeniging. 'Kuczynski', he continues:

> arrived in Britain with his Alsatian-born wife, Marguerite, on 21 January 1936, staying a few days with his parents in Lawn Road before journeying to the continent. His activities were already well known to British intelligence and his movements were closely monitored while he remained in England. MI5 had opened a file on the Kuczynski family already in 1928, based on information from MI6 agents working inside Germany …[21]

The role Jürgen played in securing the German Communist Party's cash is not mentioned in his own memoirs, although it appears to be true if other indications and evidence are taken into account. On Burke's other point, it needs to be asked what exactly Britain's security services were doing monitoring and holding files on German communists as early as 1928 when fascism was on the rise and individuals such as Jürgen hardly posed a threat to Britain. That MI6 had opened a file on Kuczynski that early is also corroborated in Robert Chadwell Williams' book, *Klaus Fuchs, Atom Spy*.

Jürgen came back from Germany to London on 29 July 1936 and again stayed with his parents in Lawn Road before he, Marguerite and Madeleine moved on to nearby Upper Park Road where he began co-ordinating KPD activities in Britain. He was by no means a persona non grata in Britain and would be employed later by the government as an economic statistician, specialising on Germany.

A number of individual communists lived in or passed through the Lawn Road Flats and virtually all have been described automatically as Soviet spies, as Burke does. One does not need to have been involved directly with espionage or the security services to be very sceptical about a serious espionage agency concentrating some of its most important agents and activities in one small place. The fact that Lawn Road Flats was already well known as a hotbed of left-wing Bohemians and intellectuals, including a number of communists, would hardly have escaped the notice of Britain's MI5. So for the Soviet Union to make it the centre of its operations would contravene the most basic rules for any secret agency and risk the easy unmasking of every agent. The fact that two of its temporary residents were at that time full-time employees of the Soviet secret services and that others were involved, at some stage or other, with passing on information to the Soviet Union is almost certainly more a matter of an unusual confluence of circumstances than deliberate planning. Belsize Park, where the flats are situated, is part of Hampstead and close to Muswell Hill, and this whole area became a popular place for refugees to settle. Many communist professionals – artists, intellectuals, lawyers and medics – could be found living around there during and after the war.

Already by the outbreak of war, around 55,000 German and Austrian refugees had been officially granted asylum in the UK and a further

20,000 had been given temporary residents' permits. On 3 September 1939, though, all visas granted to 'enemy nationals' were automatically invalidated and from then on no more were to be admitted. The government and leading establishment figures also made no bones about referring to the dangers of rising anti-semitism if the numbers of Jewish refugees were to increase. Even papers like the *Jewish Chronicle* and the *Manchester Guardian* became increasingly perturbed by the implications of a large influx of Jewish refugees. There was also an increasing anti-refugee mood among the population at large and calls were being made to 'intern the lot'. In response, the government did begin a process of internment. By July 1940, around 27,000 people had been arrested and there was little discrimination between those who were Nazis or their sympathisers, and those who were genuine anti-fascists.

The Red Orchestra in Switzerland (1938–1940)

Before leaving Moscow on her way to Switzerland in 1938, Ursula was awarded the prestigious Order of the Red Banner for her outstanding contribution. Her necessarily circuitous journey allowed her to stop over in London once again and for a few days catch up with her family. GRU headquarters had asked her to travel via London in order to recruit some reliable ex-Spanish Civil War veterans who would be prepared to undertake the dangerous task of working under cover in Germany. They would need to have demonstrated courage and ability in Spain. A former political commissar with the International Brigades, Dave Springhall, who had become secretary of the Communist Party's London district, was able to recommend former International Brigader Alexander Allan Foote to her as a possible candidate.

Foote had arrived in Spain on 26 December 1936, was made a sergeant and was based at Albacete. He was batman to Battalion Commander Fred Copeman and was Jock Cunningham's driver at Jarama. He also acted as a courier between London and the British Battalion in Spain. He returned from Spain in September 1938. In his memoir, *Handbook for Spies*, he says he was recruited by Soviet Intelligence while in Spain, but this seems highly unlikely as he was apparently kicking his heels after his return to Britain, not knowing what to do. Foote would later

FIGURE 7.1 Order of the Red Banner awarded to Ursula by the Soviet Union

Source: Sputnik Images, formerly RIA Novosti.

betray his former comrades and wrote about this work (in collaboration with, and with permission of MI5) in his *Handbook*.[22]

On Copeman and Springhall's recommendation he was told to see Ursula, as there was a job he could do, and he jumped at the opportunity. If he had already been in Soviet employ this rigmarole would hardly have been necessary because they would have liaised directly with him.

Foote was unable to make the planned meeting with Ursula, who had to leave for Switzerland beforehand, but she left behind instructions for Foote to meet her sister Brigitte, then living in London. Ursula doesn't recount this episode in the published version of her own book, *Sonya's Report*, probably to protect her sister. It is reasonably certain, though, that she did leave instructions with Brigitte to interview and vet Foote and, shortly afterwards, another candidate, Len Beurton, before sending them on to Switzerland if she deemed them appropriate for undertaking surveillance activities in Germany. Although Foote, in his reminiscences, writes that he did not know Brigitte's name when he first met her, this is contradicted by his statement given to MI5 when he was interrogated. Whether either of the two recruits knew Brigitte's name at the time or of her relationship to Ursula is unclear.

On 30 September 1938, shortly after Ursula's arrival in Switzerland, Britain and France signed the notorious Munich Agreement with Hitler. This agreement was the last attempt by the Western world to appease Hitler and encourage him to move against the Soviet Union first. It also placed a seal on Germany's annexation of those parts of Czechoslovakia with large German populations. Chamberlain naively thought it would satisfy Hitler's territorial ambitions and help prevent a wider conflict and all-out war but, in fact, it had the opposite effect. Barely six months later, Hitler had occupied Czechoslovakia. Then, on 1 September 1939, despite having previously signed a non-aggression pact with Poland, Germany invaded and occupied that country too. This is what led Britain to declare war on Germany that same month. But even then, with Germany's expansionist aims clearly demonstrated, Western Europe was still very much preoccupied with the 'Soviet threat'. Despite the declaration of war, France's government appeared to be more concerned with confronting its own trade unions at home, suppressing the country's communists and banning the party, rather than preparing to confront the Wehrmacht massing on its own borders.

After a temporary stay in Lausanne, Ursula found a small but comfortable chalet, similar to the one in which she had lived in Zakopane – high in the mountains, in Caux-sur-Montreux, overlooking the town of Montreux and Lake Geneva. It was relatively isolated, and therefore easier for her to monitor any surveillance by Swiss authorities. Once settled in, she very soon made friends with several English people working for the International Labour Organization (ILO) attached to the League of Nations. One of these was David Blelloch, who was married to Sylvia, the daughter of *Manchester Guardian* journalist Robert Dell.[23] The latter was 'an intelligent and principled liberal journalist, alert and lively despite his considerable age', she says, and she much preferred talking to him than with the ILO people.

A short time after she had settled into her new home, Alexander Foote, given the codename 'Jim', arrived in Switzerland after being vetted by Brigitte. He had agreed to take on the secret and dangerous role of working as a clandestine agent in Nazi Germany. Ursula asked him to travel to Munich and if possible establish connections with workers in the Messerschmitt plane factory there.

Foote turned out to be a controversial figure, and would later write his reminiscences, published in 1949. These memoirs cover his time working as a Soviet agent and are, as Ursula and others have noted, self-aggrandising and littered with mistakes or misinformation. They also appear to have been ghost-written, even if not very competently, and milked for their sensational value. The style and language used in the book hardly feels like that of an ordinary working-class man who had received only a basic schooling. How far MI5 were involved in the writing can only be speculated on, but they certainly vetted the text.

The book's opening paragraph provides a flavour of its style:

> It was a perfectly ordinary front door. Its shining brass knocker, its neat but slightly faded green paint, did not distinguish it from thousands of others of its kind. But that door was my entrance to espionage. Beyond that door lay the dim passage-way leading to a twilight labyrinth of international intrigue …

That is how he describes his visit to Brigitte who had been asked by Ursula to vet potential recruits for her. He visited Brigitte – although in his memoir, he says he never knew the name of the woman who interviewed him in London although he did suspect that she was someone known to or related to 'Sonya', who he would meet later, 'on an autumn day in October 1938'. Chapman Pincher in his book, *Treachery*, alleges that under interrogation Foote admitted to MI5 that 'on indications supplied to me by a certain Brigitte Lewis, I kept a conspiratorial rendezvous with "Sonia" [sic] in Geneva'.[24]

From his memoirs, Foote comes across as someone who was unsure of what he wanted to do in life and was looking for excitement, although he was progressively inclined and did have strong anti-fascist convictions. He took himself off to fight on the Republican side in Spain, but on returning to Britain was again at a loose end and with itchy feet.

He says he was sent by Fred Copeman, his former battalion commander, who was now working for the Communist Party, 'to a flat in St John's Wood'. The instructions he received:

> were not illuminating and I learned nothing much more from the respectable housewife with a slight foreign accent who interviewed me. Her name I never knew for certain … I do not suppose I was in the house more than ten minutes. I was dealt with by the lady of the house in as brisk and impersonal a way as she would have used to engage a house-maid.

After accepting the assignment outlined by Brigitte, Foote left immediately for Switzerland. The contact there, he was told, would give him details of what he was expected to do. He was to meet her outside the central post office, next to the railway station, in Geneva. She would be holding an orange in one hand and have a green parcel in her handbag. While waiting, he scanned the crowds milling around and discovered a whole number of people who seemed to have been given oranges for their lunch, but no one looked in his direction. But then, 'I noticed her', he writes:

> Punctuality may be the politeness of princes, but it is certainly a prerequisite of Soviet spies. Slim, with a good figure and even better legs, her black hair demurely dressed, she stood out from the Swiss crowd. In her early thirties, she might have been the wife of a minor French consular official.

Later, he would add that 'she was a pleasant person and an amusing companion'.

She told him he should call her 'Sonia' [sic]. 'I later learnt her name', he writes, 'it was 'Maria Schultz, and [she] had a long career as a Red agent. She and her husband Alfred Schultz had worked for the Red Army in Poland and the far East ...' He also calls Olga, Ursula's nanny, Lisa Brockel for some unknown reason. Where he got these names from is anyone's guess, but he may have used them to protect Ursula and Rolf, or Foote may have been told to use them by his MI5 collaborators who, for their own reasons, did not want the real names made public at the time. His co-recruitee, Len Beurton, who joins him later in Switzerland, he describes as Bill Phillips and his codename as 'Jack'. Len (full name: Leon Charles Beurton) had also been with the International Brigades in Spain and worked as a driver there. He was eventually repatriated towards the end of 1938.

In his imaginative work, Foote describes at one point sitting in a beer cellar in Bavaria when Hitler walked in. This, it turns out, is the Führer's 'local'. It leads him to the idea of hatching a plan to assassinate Hitler there, but the idea is soon ditched. On another occasion, when 'Jack' (i.e. Len) returns from his first assignment and describes the factory where the Zeppelin hot air balloon is being built, he asserts that they both manage to convince Ursula that it would be a good idea to try and blow it up, so they experiment with bomb-making materials, but without success. This is, again, an unlikely story. Both Len and Foote would make several trips into Germany, completing simple assignments, perfecting their German and gathering intelligence, but how useful the information they gathered was is hard to say. Interestingly, Len later told his son Peter the story of being in the Munich beer cellar when Hitler came in, but does not mention Foote. It is hardly possible now to discover which of the two was telling the truth.

An unlikely love match

Len Beurton was 25 years old and like Foote had fought in Spain, where he won a reputation of being absolutely fearless.[25] He was one of the first of the British volunteers to reach Spain and as the British

Battalion had not yet been formed at that time, he enlisted with the German one, only joining the British one later.

When Ursula told him he had been chosen for dangerous work in Germany 'his face lit up', she said. Len was first asked to go to Frankfurt-am-Main and there try to establish contacts in the big chemical company I. G. Farben, that was to gain later notoriety as the manufacturer of Zyklon B, the poison gas used for the extermination of Jews and others in Nazi concentration camps. Len had first joined the Communist Party in Spain when he went out to fight and only joined the British Party on his return. Once in Switzerland, Len and Alexander Foote worked together to begin with, living in a small pension in Montreux, and when necessary would trudge up the hill to Sonya's little chalet for instructions.

In the early summer of 1939 as war grew increasingly certain, it was clear to Ursula that even Switzerland would not necessarily remain a safe haven for opponents of Hitler. She found herself with an out-of-date German passport, now useless for an emigrant, and a hastily issued Honduran one, which didn't offer much security either. If the Swiss authorities decided to expel her, she would be returned to Germany and certain death. Her estranged husband Rolf was already planning to work elsewhere as it was clear there was going to be no marital reconciliation between the two of them and neither was happy with the situation as it was. The Centre in Moscow agreed to Rolf's request to be sent back to China, but before he left Ursula and he agreed to commence divorce proceedings. The journalist and spy historian Chapman Pincher has written that Ursula was ordered by Moscow to enter a sham marriage in order to move to Britain where she would continue working as an agent. This viewpoint is repeated by Burke in his book *The Lawn Road Flats*, where he writes that 'Moscow Centre had sent instructions to "Sonya" to divorce her German husband, Rudolf Hamburger, in order to enter into a pro-forma marriage with an Englishman and obtain a British passport'. Burke's version, while superficially fitting the facts, does not take into account that life itself sometimes trumps the best laid plans.

Once the divorce formalities had been completed, she would be free to remarry and could indeed enter a 'paper marriage' with a British man in order to qualify for a British passport. Both Jim and Len were bachelors, so both were eligible, so to speak. She asked Jim first, and he declared his willingness to go through with the sham marriage, but then got cold feet. So Ursula turned to Len, who was very willing; in fact he was annoyed that Ursula was suggesting only a sham marriage rather than a genuine one and that she promised to divorce him as soon as he requested it. He was a relatively shy young man and found it difficult to express his emotions. But luckily Ursula found him attractive too – she describes him as tall, muscular, good-looking and brave – but for her it was not, she admits, exactly love at first sight.

Len was an orphan; his father, a French-born citizen, probably died in the First World War and his mother, after persuading a railwayman's family to foster him, had disappeared out of his life for good. He became politicised while working in a quarry with a former seaman on the island of Jersey. This man, an Irishman by birth, had been an ardent member of the Industrial Workers of the World (IWW) and told Len many adventurous tales of rebellion, mutiny, and of working-class struggles in which he had been involved. He was to become a decisive influence on Len's future life.

The time was not exactly auspicious for a young couple like Len and Ursula with two small children, needing peace and stability; Hitler had by then already occupied Austria and Czechoslovakia – war appeared imminent, and if it did break out then even Switzerland would be unlikely to remain immune for long.

Then seemingly out of the blue on 23 August 1939, the Soviet Union and Germany signed a non-aggression pact. It came as a complete surprise to almost everyone on both the right and left, but the impact on anti-fascists everywhere was like an atomic explosion: amazement, dismay, anger and bewilderment. For those who had always opposed the Soviet Union, it only served to underline the commonality between the 'two dictatorships' and between communism and fascism. For the left it was a bitter pill to swallow, but was then explained, not without justification, as Stalin's attempt to win time, as the West had been exceedingly unwilling to form an anti-fascist coalition with the Soviet Union and was clearly nudging Hitler to attack the Soviet Union.

Eventually, those like Ursula realised that the Western powers had been trying to push Germany to attack the Soviet Union in the hope that they would both annihilate each other, leaving the West unscathed and victorious without having had to lift a finger. Little did they realise, however, that Stalin would take the pact seriously and not only neglect to adopt all the necessary steps to ensure the Soviet Union's security, but would actually co-operate with the Nazis by deporting a number of communist exiles back to Germany.[26]

At this time Len had already begun working as an agent in Germany, but almost all British residents there had left and he was one of the last to do so. He managed to make it back to Montreux shortly before war was declared between the two countries. On 27 August, the Swiss army had been mobilised and on 1 September, Hitler occupied Danzig. The invasion of Poland followed, with the declaration of war on Germany by the UK on 3 September 1939.

Interestingly, at the time Switzerland was the only neutral European country not to impose a blackout and kept all its street lights on. Because of this British bombers used it for orientation when flying sorties over Germany. As a result, the Germans referred bitterly to Switzerland as 'The Lighthouse'.

Although the Swiss security forces were clearly keeping an eye on Ursula and on one occasion even called her in for questioning, they accepted her made-up story and thereafter left her in peace. She did, though, take the precaution of hiding her transmitter in a secure box under coals in the shed.

Towards the end of 1939 she was asked by the Centre in Moscow whether she could get some money through to Rosa Thälmann, the wife of Ernst, the leader of the German Communist Party who had been imprisoned by the Nazis. He would be murdered shortly before the end of the war after twelve years held in a concentration camp. Ursula persuaded Olga, the nanny, to undertake this onerous task. As a small, grey-haired woman in her late fifties, she would not be conspicuous nor be likely to raise the suspicions of either the Swiss authorities or the Nazis. She carried out her task successfully.

Despite taking the most rigorous precautions, Ursula was still confronted with some unpleasant surprises that could easily have cost her life. She came close to disaster when one of her fellow agents, Hermann, to whom she had given a transmitter, was arrested by the Swiss security forces. The Nazis immediately demanded his extradition – he had already been tried for treason and condemned to death in

Germany – but the Swiss had their own proceedings pending against him, so refused to hand him over. Luckily Hermann divulged no details about other agents associated with him.

Ursula's planned marriage of convenience to Len was already turning into something more romantic than either had perhaps realised. They were getting on increasingly well and found they had much in common, including enjoying walking together in the uplifting Swiss countryside. Len also developed a close and loving relationship with her two children which helped cement their relationship further.

By February 1940, she had, at last, all the documents together that she needed in order to remarry; they decided on the date of 23 February, the anniversary of the establishment of the Red Army. After the modest ceremony, she went straight to the British Consulate to apply for a British passport but found the response 'distinctly cool'. However, only ten weeks later she had one in her hand.

There is an MI5 Memo (KV2/41/6a), reacting to Ursula's passport application, noting that: 'The applicant states that she is the daughter of Professor Kuczynski Polish [sic] reader in demography at the University of London.' The memo also states that 'the local Swiss authorities have refused to extend her residence permit'. (This information strongly indicates that Ursula had little option but to leave Switzerland very quickly and Britain would be an obvious refuge.) In late 1940, in view of Ursula's increasingly precarious situation, Moscow suggested that she and Len move to Britain.

In the spring of 1940, Denmark, Norway, the Netherlands, Belgium and Luxembourg were all rapidly overrun by the Nazis. Each newly occupied country represented a terrible blow to them both and brought the danger of a German takeover of Switzerland much closer. Towards the end of May 1940, she learned about the fiasco of Dunkirk and the evacuation of British troops with the loss of much equipment. The Battle of Dunkirk involved the defence and evacuation of British and allied forces and took place from 26 May until 4 June 1940. This left the Germans free to occupy the whole western coast of mainland France, Holland and Belgium. Later that year the massive German bombing of British cities, including London, began in earnest.

As if this in itself was not stressful enough, another crisis blew up from an unexpected quarter. Olga Muth, the family nanny, suddenly realised that without a British passport herself (and, as a German national with no family connections to Britain, there was little chance of her being granted one), she might be left behind and lose the children, particularly Nina to whom she had become very attached. As a result, she suffered a kind of mental breakdown and became obsessive in her determination to keep Nina with her. With this aim in mind, she went to the British consulate in Montreux and in her broken and garbled English exposed Ursula and Len as secret agents. She also told some of their neighbours a similar story.

At the time, in the febrile atmosphere of war and national uncertainty, rumours and denunciations abounded, so luckily the British consular officials and her neighbours just assumed that Olga was somewhat deranged and gave no credence to her accusations. However, Ursula felt obliged to send the children away quickly to boarding school, out of Olga's clutches. This tense and uncertain predicament left her in a state of despair and depression. However, despite the seemingly dire situation she and Len still managed to recruit other local agents: a radio repair man and his wife, to continue the work after they had gone. The pair would eventually be discovered in October 1943 by the Swiss authorities monitoring illegal transmissions, but they did not betray their fellow agents. Alexander 'Jim' Foote, who had remained in Switzerland, would also be arrested in November, and offer his full co-operation to the Anglo-US secret services. Ursula wrote, in her memoirs, that 'his lurid spy-thriller memoirs ensured his prosperity'. Olga subsequently returned to Germany and found work in a children's home.

By December 1941 Nazi counter-intelligence had managed to detect the whereabouts of a key Red Orchestra 'pianist' (this was the name given to those transmitting secret radio messages to Moscow) in Brussels. The agents were taken by surprise and arrested. They underwent horrendous torture at the hands of the SS before being executed, but the key operatives remained silent. However, the Nazis were able to glean enough information to begin the slow uncovering and dismantling of the Soviet's Red Orchestra network. Ursula was never captured, but if she had been, her fate would have been no different to that of her Belgian comrades.

There are a number of documents in the released MI5 files giving details about Foote's revelations on being interrogated by MI6. In his interrogation on 20 July 1947, he said that he had heard about Rudi [Rudolf] Hamburger from Olga Muth and divulged the information that Ursula had given Olga the task of taking money to the wife of Ernst Thälmann. The interrogator then writes: 'I asked him if he considered this mission to be part of Ursula's normal work for the Russians, he said that he regarded it as an odd job carried out at the time that Ursula was inactive'.

In the same report Foote said 'Moscow considered Ursula and [Len] Beurton to have been compromised by the action of OLGA MUTH, and it was the basis for their decision to return to England'. Foote went on to tell MI6 about Ursula's previous work in Poland and against the Germans from Switzerland. He also revealed that he knew she worked in China … He gave MI6 full details of Sonya's work as a radio operator, transmitting from Switzerland and said that she handed over to him the cipher with which he could continue communicating with Moscow. He also confirmed that Len was involved. The report extract also states that Foote gave his interrogators information purporting to show Ursula's continued connections with Russia after her arrival in England.

In the extract of the report of the interrogation, he said that he had several interviews with a certain Brigitte Lewis [before his departure for Switzerland] and she told him he would need to establish himself in Munich. But no information was given about the tasks involved or for whom he would be working. Foote passed on details of Len to Ursula after she asked him if he knew of other ex-Brigaders who might be willing to undertake similar work. According to the report, Len first went to Frankfurt-am-Main where he made contact with Foote. He was to establish contact with staff there working for the big German chemical conglomerate I. G. Farben. Len and Foote both received instruction and training from 'Sonya' in the construction and operation of short-wave radio transmitters, he says. He also reveals that Ursula had been informed that Rudi Hamburger had been arrested by the Chinese but that he had later been released and was safe in Moscow. In one report, dated 23 July 1947, the interrogator writes: 'F[oote] told me [Len] Beurton hated Rado and was extremely critical of the Russians.'

On 15 July 1947, a memo from MI5's J. H. Marriott noted that, on the basis of Foote's information given to MI6, 'It is I think desirable that we should investigate contacts of the Beurton family …' This would appear not to have happened to any depth, at least there are no records.

The role of agent 'Dora'

In the winter of 1939, the Centre in Moscow asked Ursula to make contact with a new comrade, also working as an agent in Switzerland, and offer him assistance. This turned out to be Sándor Radó (code name 'Dora'), who had been a political commissar in the Hungarian Red Army.[27]

As Radó had already been working as an agent in Switzerland since December 1939, he was perfectly capable of taking on Ursula's tasks once she left a year later.

After the Nazis had taken power in Germany, Radó and his wife Helene fled Germany through Austria to France. In Paris, together with other journalists, including British author Arthur Koestler, he established 'Inpress', an independent anti-fascist news agency. In 1935, while on a visit to Moscow, he was asked if he would be willing to work for Soviet military intelligence with his main task being to obtain information from Nazi Germany. He agreed and began working in France before moving to Belgium, but he failed to obtain a residence permit there, so returned to France. As a propagandist and agent he had become so effective that Hitler called him and his press agency 'public enemy No. 1'.

With the increasing chaos and uncertainty in France and the threat of immediate German invasion, he lost contact with Moscow, but managed, with 'Sonya''s help, to re-establish it while in Switzerland, where he fled in December 1939. He managed to gain resident status in Switzerland and would work there assiduously supplying Moscow with vital military intelligence until he was finally forced to flee in 1943. He had been a Bolshevik of long standing and had even met Lenin. His real profession, though, was that of a geographer and cartographer and he had trained as such in Moscow and Berlin.

In his memoirs, he writes that once he had arrived in Geneva he received a letter telling him that someone would be in touch, 'and a few days later I received a visit from a tall, slender, almost fragile-looking woman in a closely-fitting woollen dress. I put her age at about

35. Her movements were smooth and a trifle languid.' That was his description of 'Sonya'. He knew 'precious little about her', he notes. All the time they worked together, he never knew where she lived, who she worked with or what intelligence she collected.

Under Radó's direction Switzerland would become one of the key centres for supplying Moscow with vital information about Nazi war plans. The Red Orchestra (*Rote Kapelle*) was a collective term used by the Gestapo to lump together all the Soviet secret service agencies carrying out operations against the Nazis. Himmler founded a so-called 'Red Orchestra Detachment' at the Führer's insistence in order to combat the very effective Soviet intelligence network in Europe, but particularly that part of it based in Switzerland.

One of Radó's colleagues and the chief source of his information was Rudolf Roessler, who had excellent links to people in the German high command, some, if not all, of whom would have been part of the Soviet network of secret agents working inside Germany. Roessler, a conservative democrat and central figure of the Lucy spy ring, had become an active anti-Nazi before leaving Germany and settling in Swizerland. The information he collected was sent to Moscow via the Swiss agents, notably Ursula, while she remained stationed there, and then via Sándor Radó.

Tragically, a number of key figures in the German-based network supplying Roessler were caught and executed in 1942 and 1943, among them Harro Schulze-Boysen, Adam Kukhof and Arvid Harnack. In an act of unusual carelessness, the addresses of these three had been transmitted in coded form from Moscow to an agent in Germany, but unbeknown to the Soviets, the Germans had already cracked the code they were using.

The names of other Wehrmacht officers who passed vital information to him Roessler took to his grave, Radó says. He did beforehand pass these names on to a reliable younger friend, but told him not to divulge them until at least twenty years later, because otherwise the Nazis would exact their revenge on the officers involved. Unfortunately that young man was killed in a car crash before he could pass on the information.

Through Roessler, in 1941, Stalin had been warned a fortnight beforehand of the impending Nazi invasion of the Soviet Union but, as

with other corroborative evidence he was given about this, he dis-
believed it with catastrophic consequences. However, Roessler's subsequent reports, once the Nazis had invaded Soviet territory, were
believed and acted upon, enabling Soviet forces to pre-empt many of
the Nazis' manoeuvres. The only one that went wrong was the massive
tank battle at Kharkov where the information the Soviets had been
given via Roessler appeared to be incorrect; as a result, it cost the
Soviets thousands of soldiers' lives.

Roessler, a German refugee who had moved to Switzerland in 1933,
was the owner of a small publishing company. He worked for both
Swiss intelligence and the Soviets. Throughout the war he provided
very accurate and timely intelligence about German operations and
intentions on the Eastern Front, usually within a day or two of opera-
tional decisions being taken. His information was so good and accurate
that Moscow, to begin with, had doubts about its authenticity.

This vital and invariably reliable intelligence source continued during
almost the whole course of the war until the cover of the Swiss network was blown. Himmler's Red Orchestra Detachment had managed
to pick up agents in France and Belgium and some of them, under
interrogation, had provided sufficient information to lead the Nazis to
the Swiss network.

In late 1943 the Germans persuaded the Swiss authorities to act
against Radó's network. Using mobile radio direction finders, Swiss
police tracked down one of the transmitters operated by Swiss agents
Edgar and Olga Hamel. They were arrested on 14 October 1943, and
several other members of the group, including Foote, were arrested on
20 November. Luckily, as a British citizen Foote was not deported to
Germany but released instead. Radó and his wife managed to go into
hiding before they could be captured and eventually, in 1944, made a
daring escape across the border, by hiding on a milk delivery train that
went daily through a tunnel between Switzerland and France. He and
his wife were then taken into hiding in the Haute Savoie region of
France controlled by the Maquis.

All the agents, including Radó in his absence, were put on trial in
Switzerland between October 1945 and 1947, after the war had ended.
Ten were tried, but only three were present in court, the others having
escaped beforehand. This late prosecution was 'clearly intended as a

sacrifice on the altar of the Cold War, then just beginning'. All the agents were charged with 'having conducted intelligence operations against Germany ...'[28] The court martial passed sentences of between three months and three years prison and fines. As leader of the group, Radó was given three years.

Two years after his arrest, at the end of the war, in 1945, Foote met Sándor Radó again in Paris and they were both able to re-establish contact with Moscow Central. The two agreed to fly to Moscow for further instructions. The plane taking them had to make a stop-over in Cairo where, Foote alleges, Radó defected, leaving him to fly on to Moscow alone. It is quite likely that Radó knew enough about Stalin's treatment of former comrades and agents to fear what would happen to him once he arrived in Moscow.

Apparently, using the stop-over in Cairo, Radó vanished and managed to enter the British embassy under an alias. He applied for political asylum, but this was denied. Based on a false accusation, he was then extradited by the Egyptians to the Soviet Union and in August 1945 was brought to Moscow. In December 1946, he was sentenced, without trial, just like Ursula's first husband Rolf Hamburger, to ten years for the alleged carrying out of espionage against the Soviet Union.

In the last paragraph of his book, Foote wrote: 'Radó is dead, his wife probably still in Paris unless she has been lured back [to the Soviet Union]' In actual fact, following the death of Stalin, Radó was released in November 1954, and allowed to return to Hungary. He was officially rehabilitated in 1956. In Budapest he took up his previous career of geographer and cartographer and went on to win widespread recognition for his pioneering work in this field. In 1955 he was appointed chief of the Hungarian cartographic service, and in 1958 Chair of Cartography at the Budapest Karl Marx University of Economic Sciences. In 1971 he published his memoirs, *Code Name Dora*, in Hungarian, but they have since been translated into several languages. A first uncensored edition, based on the original manuscript, was only published, in Budapest, in 2006. Radó died there in 1981. Almost all his relations, including his mother, had been killed in Auschwitz. His wife died on 1 September in 1958 and is also buried in Budapest. On her gravestone is engraved: 'Founder member of the German Communist Party'.

Foote's exaggerated sense of his own importance is, once again, amply revealed in his book of reminiscences:

> As a result of my call, I was, for three vital years of the war, a member, and to a large extent controller of, the Russian spy net in Switzerland, which was working against Germany. The information I passed to Moscow over my secret transmitter affected the course of the war at one of its crucial stages.

Foote calls himself the 'controller' of the Swiss operation, but contradicts himself later in his own words by correctly naming Radó, known to him as 'Albert', as 'Resident Director' and himself as his 'deputy'. In fact, Foote was merely one of several operators, albeit a very competent one, of a clandestine radio transmitter, and had learned everything he knew from 'Sonya'. Radó writes that Ursula taught 'Jim' (Foote), and 'John' (Radó uses this alias for Len) everything about 'the rules of conspiracy, how to use secret codes and operate a radio, and in fact everything an intelligence agent needed to know'.[29] She would leave Foote behind in Switzerland in the capable hands of the new chief of operations, Sándor Radó, when she left in 1940. He continued transmitting the coded messages to Moscow, using Ursula's old transmitter, so would have been party to their content. He was, Radó said, 'an outstanding radio operator'.

Foote's revelations about his work have led some to suggest that he was a British secret service double agent and one conduit (perhaps even the main one) of intelligence from Britain to the Soviet Union via Rudolf Roessler, who was a naturalised Swiss citizen. This suggestion, though, has little foundation.

Journalist, broadcaster and author Malcolm Muggeridge, himself a wartime MI6 officer, 'got to know Foote after the war' when Foote paid Muggeridge 'regular visits' at his flat near Regent's Park, London. Foote at this time was a clerk in the Ministry of Agriculture and Fisheries but, according to Muggeridge, found the work 'very tedious'. Muggeridge was convinced that the information Foote had sent to Moscow 'could only, in fact, have come from Bletchley'. It has also been suggested that John Cairncross, 'the fifth man' in the Cambridge spy ring, was the one who passed the decoded information, gained from the breaking of the Enigma code at Bletchley, to Roessler via Foote.[30] This version of events is, though, again highly unlikely and Radó calls it rubbish, as Foote never knew Roessler. Radó was the one who passed all information directly from Roessler to 'Jim' (Foote) to transmit to Moscow.

In relation to Foote's book, Radó, in his own memoirs, quotes the Swiss cipher expert, Marc Payout – 'a man no one would describe as harbouring leftist sympathies'. Payout writes: 'Foote's book positively teems with inaccuracies and even untruths.' Others, like the Wehrmacht officer and author Wilhelm von Schramm, say much the same about it: 'His book is a first-person account and not a historical report. He wanted it to sell and so strove for a sensational effect.'[31] But worse than all Foote's sensation-seeking, Radó writes:

> was his political volte-face and his utter repudiation of the work he had done during the war. He sank back into the swamp of petty-bourgeois existence from which, fired by a momentous task, he had been able for a while to free himself. His character was marked by an inner contradiction that his betrayal finally sealed.

Foote was, as a young man, undoubtedly politically idealistic and perhaps naive, but unlike his more famous Cambridge-educated contemporaries, his attraction to communism was not based on a deep study of Marxism. Whether he simply became disillusioned with Soviet-style communism, was simply won over by a persuasive MI5 agent, or a combination of both is an interesting question.

Notes

1 Günter Berghaus, ed., *Theatre and Film in Exile*, Oswald Wolff Books, Berg Publishers, 1989.
2 Karl Otten, German writer and journalist who fled the Nazis, spending his exile in Britain. He worked for the BBC and wrote for English and German language journals. He was given British citizenship in 1947, but moved to Switzerland where he remained until his death.
3 Charmian Brinson, 23 November 1939, The National Archives, KV2/1871, 39a.
4 'Other organisations which should be watched', 30 May 1940, The National Archives, KV2/1872. 92ab. (Quoted in Brinson.)

5 Ibid., p. 137.

6 Ibid., p. 25.

7 Martha Dodd, daughter of William Dodd, US ambassador to Germany during the 1930s, became the lover of a Soviet agent, Vinogradov, and agreed to work for the Soviets. She had a reputation of 'sleeping around' and even had an affair with Colonel General Ernst Udet, at the time second in command to Hermann Goering in the German Luftwaffe. She maintained that this affair was undertaken at the request of her Soviet lover who asked her to get close to leading Nazis. In *Yellow Notebooks* by Alexander Vassiliev, p. 9.

   Her brother William Dodd (Jr) is also listed in KGB files as a Soviet agent (*White Notebook* # 1., p. 107 in document, pp. 58–59 in online version).

8 Albert Einstein, 'Why Socialism?', *Monthly Review*, May 1949.

9 FBI's Gibarti file (61–6629), www.theeinsteinfile.com/portal/alias_einstein/ lang_en-US/tabid_3339/default.aspx.

10 Alan Clarke, *German Refugee Theatre in Internment*, Berghaus edn, p. 191. Oxford/Munich, Berg, 1989.

11 Ibid.

12 MI5 archives, KV2/1871, item 76a.

13 MI5 archives, The National Archives, KV2/1872, 95b on Jürgen Kuczynski; 15 July 1940.

14 Lou Baruch, unpublished memoirs, University of Bradford Library.

15 Gertrude Sirnis, mother of Melitta Norwood, a civil servant, also worked as a Soviet agent.

16 Jill Pearlman, *Journal of the Society of Architectural Historians*, vol. 72, no. 3 (September 2013), p. 284.

17 David Burke, *The Spy Who Came In from the Co-op: Melitta Norwood and the Ending of Cold War Espionage*, Boydell Press, 2008.

18 David Burke, *The Lawn Road Flats: Spies, Writers and Artists*, Boydell Press, 2014, p. 67.

19 MI5 files, Government National Archives.

20 Quoted by Charmian Brinson.

21 Burke, *The Lawn Road Flats*, p. 134.

22 Alexander Allan Foote, *Handbook for Spies*, Coachwhip Publications, 2011.

23 Robert Dell, foreign correspondent for the *Manchester Guardian*, the *Nation* and other newspapers, from 1920 to 1938. From 1932 onwards Dell was based in Geneva.

24 Chapman Pincher, *Treachery: Betrayals, Blunders and Cover-Ups: Six Decades of Espionage,* Mainstream Publishing, 2011, p. 272.

25 MI5 became very interested in Len Beurton after he had gone to Spain to join the International Brigades. There is a record of him leaving Newhaven in January 1937 'believed travelling to Spain with other members of the IB'. His name was kept on file, along with those of the other 292 British ex-members repatriated from Spain at the end of the Civil War.

   According to Somerset House records, Len's father was Leon Beurton, a French-born hotel waiter, and Florence Sophia née Smith. They lived in

London. Len's father went back to France and his mother left for Scotland, after which Len was adopted by the Fenton family. Nothing more was heard of his father.

After his return from Spain he was clearly kept under observation as one of the files notes that, 'from time to time he has purchased various books including a German Grammar and German readers, also some engineering technical works'. This was around the time when he had been recruited by Brigitte to work with Ursula as a clandestine agent in Nazi Germany.

In this connection, there is a request from the Chief Constable, Special Branch, Wood Green 'for any info on Len/ Mr. Fenton who went to Germany in the beginning of July' (dated 30 August 1939).

Once Len had travelled to Switzerland and he and Ursula fell in love, she was keen to find out if she could obtain British citizenship if they were to marry. A personal letter from Ursula to her mother is on file in which she asks her to check if the law is still valid that on marriage you get British citizenship and a passport, as she intends to marry Len – 'I love him', she adds (addressed to: Mrs M. Kuczynski 36 Upper Park Road, London). This information became of critical importance once the Swiss authorities refused to extend her resident's visa. If she were forced to leave in a hurry, and as a German citizen, she would most probably be sent back to Germany. Once she and Len had married, she applied immediately for British citizenship.

26 *Der Spiegel* magazine, 17 July 1989, 'Solche Verräter': 'Around 4,000 Communist Party members, who had come to Moscow either on orders from the German Communist Party or as volunteers to help with the building of socialism, were, after the signing of the Hitler-Stalin Pact, expelled from the Soviet Union and handed back to the Gestapo.' One of the GDR's best-loved actors, Erwin Geschonneck, was one of those.

27 Not to be confused with Sándor Radó the psychoanalyst.

28 Sándor Radó, *Code Name Dora*, London, Aberlard-Schuhmann, 1976, p. 293.

29 Sándor Radó, *Code Name Dora*, p. 33.

30 Malcolm Muggeridge, *Chronicles of Wasted Time Volume II*, Fontana/Collins edn, 1981, pp. 207–208.

31 Wilhelm von Schramm, *Verrat im Zweiten Weltkrieg*, Düsseldorf, Econ-Verlag, 1969, pp. 25, 146.

8

URSULA

A Soviet agent in the
Oxfordshire countryside

Because of German encirclement and the blockade, Ursula could only reach Britain by the most improbable detours, via Spain and Portugal – there was no other way. On 18 December 1940 Ursula and the children set out on their journey, leaving Len behind – as a former member of the International Brigade, he had been banned by Franco from entering Spain and could not risk travelling through the country. On top of that problem, Radó had asked Moscow if he could keep Len in Switzerland as he needed him, given the amount of material that was coming in. Len was prepared to stay on and help Radó if Moscow asked him to, but after a few months they told him to join Ursula in Britain as soon as he could. It would, though, be twenty long months before they would see each other again.

After an arduous and perilous journey in the middle of winter, overland through Spain and Portugal, Ursula and the children eventually arrived in Lisbon. After waiting there another three weeks, the British consulate then informed her that she could travel to the UK by ship. They boarded the SS *Avoceta*, which was to take them in a convoy of twelve other ships from Lisbon to Liverpool. It would be a long and tense zig-zag journey. The cabins had to be blacked out, portholes kept shut and every passenger given a life belt in case of a German torpedo attack. Each day was faced with trepidation and the hours dragged on interminably. After almost three weeks at sea, they arrived at the mouth of the Mersey in the evening. A chill wind was blowing and the skies were grey; the unimpressive Liverpool skyline emerged slowly out of the dusk as the ship chugged sluggishly up the river. The children were cold and tired, but their ordeal was not quite over. Ursula was the only passenger disembarking to be interrogated by immigration officers, but was much relieved when they eventually did let her into the country. It had been seven weeks since they had left Switzerland.

Because of the regular German raids on London, her parents, like a number of other Londoners, had found temporary accommodation near Oxford with friends, so she joined them there at 78 Woodstock Road. But that house was suddenly needed by its owners, so her parents returned to London, leaving her to look around for a place of her own. However, house-hunting in towns that were close to London and relatively safe from bombing was hopeless, she says. Nor would she be able to find anything in those cities that had been bombed, as so many houses had been destroyed. Her other siblings, all based in London, were too preoccupied with their own survival and with earning a living to be able to offer much support. Sabine was working in a factory assembling radio parts during much of the war, but she was also involved in helping other refugees and while doing so met her future husband Frank, who she would marry in 1941. Brigitte was doing clerical work for her father at the LSE and the youngest, Renate, had just begun a degree course there.

Ursula did not wish to look for accommodation in London, feeling she would be more secure and unmolested in the Oxfordshire countryside. Being so close to the other family members would also not be appropriate given their open political allegiances and her own need for secrecy. Unbeknown to her, she was being kept under observation by the security forces from the moment she arrived in the country. As soon as she arrived in Oxford, MI5 asked the local police to keep an eye on her.[1]

Looking for accommodation so near to London was very difficult also because so many better-off families were moving to the countryside to escape the bombing, but in the end she did eventually manage to find somewhere. Her joy, however, was short lived: the new landlady soon asked her to move as she 'couldn't endure my foreign countenance', Ursula related. Then the next landlady did not allow visits by children and told Ursula she would in any case 'prefer a gentleman'. But finally, in April 1941, she was able to find a more amenable landlady and a room in the Glympton Rectory near Woodstock, but only after the vicar's wife had enquired if she was a member of the church, and whether she prayed. She also asked if Ursula agreed with her that Chamberlain was a wonderful man. A few white lies and dissembling were no doubt necessary here, but after passing the examination, she was able to move into the beautiful house with its park-like garden and little brook. She was so lucky to find refuge in Oxfordshire, unlike her parents and siblings in London who had to face regular German bombing raids.

Oddly, two acclaimed books on Soviet espionage, *The Mitrokhin Archive*, by Christopher Andrew and *The Red Orchestra* by V. E. Tarrant, mention Ursula living in Oxfordshire under the pseudonym of Mrs Brewer. This pseudonym is not mentioned in any MI5 file or by other writers, and it seems very unlikely that she would have adopted this name as she entered the country and was registered as Ursula Beurton. If she had begun using a pseudonym it would have immediately aroused suspicion, particularly as her mail was also being monitored by the security services.

After months of constantly moving house and long journeys from place to place, Ursula thought she would now be able to relax at last with the children and, for a short time, enjoy the bucolic bliss – here the war seemed a great distance away, apart from the odd military vehicle trundling past or a plane flying low overhead. She could ride on her ancient bicycle along the Oxfordshire lanes, admiring the honey-coloured, dry stone walls and pretty cottages, take in the rolling hills and quiet woods. How easy it would have been to forget all about undercover work and the war, but Ursula was not that sort of woman.

She had been given instructions already in Switzerland for making contact with her Soviet handler in Britain, but after several unsuccessful attempts to meet, she was on the verge of giving up. She thought she might have got the instructions wrong. First she tried in London's Hyde Park, then another pre-arranged assignation. That latter was in a red light district, and she caused much irritation among the regular girls with her slow pacing up and down the street. This situation not only left her in limbo as far as work was concerned, but she was also very short of money. The family had left Switzerland with only bare essentials and now she needed to buy food, clothing and household goods. Her money was running out and she still had no permanent place to live – none of her siblings could help because they were already living in overcrowded and cramped quarters in London and had their own concerns. She was also worried because she had not heard from Rolf for some time – he always remembered the children's birthdays and had written from China now and again – but she was informed soon afterwards that he had been arrested in China, and she knew this meant his life was in danger. Being unable to do anything for him only increased the worries she already had.

The only consolation from her abortive visits to London every two weeks or so was that these gave her the opportunity to see her parents and sisters. Her father by now – 1941 – had more spare time to spend with his children as he had retired from his job at the LSE on reaching the age of 65. However, he also had minimal financial reserves and was obliged to look for other remunerative work to survive. Despite being world famous in his field and regularly receiving invitations to lecture – he was overwhelmed by government and scientific institutes requesting his advice and help – these requests usually involved no remuneration. On one of Ursula's visits to London he took her to see Chaplin's *The Great Dictator* in a West End cinema, but she found it difficult to understand how Chaplin could make fun of Hitler. She was, though, somewhat reconciled by his moving speech against fascism at the end of the film.

She wrote regular letters to Len in Switzerland, and in the spring of 1941 she told him:

> Tomorrow my parents are coming, I am on particularly good terms with father, but every one of us is … he has practically no financial reserves, which means that he must find some other work. He is much too modest and much too proud to be a good job-hunter. His professional status is beyond all question. He is always receiving honorary invitations. He is world famous in his field. All his life he has worked … now at 65, he does not know whether he will find anything to earn his bread by … it really is a scandal …

In a later passage of this letter she reveals clearly her attitude to those who are, unlike her, not willing to sacrifice for the cause:

> [I] have been reading a biography of Noël Coward. His reactions as a soldier in the First World War are exactly the reactions of a liberal intellectual incapable of disciplining himself, incapable of giving up his individualism, of subordinating himself and of standing up to physical effort. I do not despise him for not enjoying being a soldier, but rather for his reasons for not enjoying it. However, I admire his honesty ...

In another letter though, she writes in a totally different vein: 'I am wearing a new dress; the first that you do not know. Red with little white polka dots on it, white belt and white collar ...' She tells him she is reading a book on China. 'Will I ever lose my longing for that country?' she asks rhetorically. Finishing her letter on an even more melancholic note, she writes, 'It is after midnight. The sirens have begun to wail and in a few minutes people just like us, who are bringing up their children and who enjoy nature, will have had the life blown out of them by bombs.'

In 'accordance with the rules', 'Sonya' kept strictly away from the British Communist Party as well as other exiled German communists outside the family, but through her brother, who was the group's political organiser at the time, she was able to establish contact with a number of reliable individuals. Apart from her father, Jürgen and Brigitte, none of her siblings were fully aware of what she was really doing, although they would have realised that she was undertaking some secret work, maybe for the Party. How could she survive otherwise?

In April 1941 she managed at last to find a furnished bungalow in Kidlington, just north of Oxford, where she could live for several months, but where she would still feel very lonely and isolated, with Len stuck in Geneva. As MI5 files reveal, an immediate order was issued to have her telephone tapped at this new address as soon as she moved in.

In May she tried one more time to make contact with her Soviet handler, and this time it clicked. He impressed upon her that influential right-wing circles in Britain and in the West as a whole, were always ready to come to an understanding with Hitler against the Soviet Union – this had been clearly demonstrated by Chamberlain's attempts to appease Hitler and encourage him to march East. He asked her to try and establish an information network and wanted to know when her transmitter would begin to function. She had already purchased the radio transmitter parts and had worked on them 'between praying and playing cards in the rectory'.

There was not an insignificant number of influential individuals in Britain who were more than sympathetic to Hitler, apart from the well-known Cliveden set. Sidney Larkin (the poet Philip Larkin's father), who was Treasurer of the City of Coventry, used to keep Nazi memorabilia, including a swastika, in his office and had even attended one or two of Hitler's rallies in Nuremberg. Another local worthy, the secretary of the Coventry Employers' Federation said, 'A bit of the Hitler regime would do the Coventry worker good. He's an undisciplined blighter'.[2] But there were also many others in the political establishment like these two. This 'fifth column' factor made Ursula's work in support of the Soviet Union even more vital, she felt, helping ensure that it was kept up to date with political shifts and Britain's level of commitment to the war against fascism. In this area, both her father and brother were very useful in passing on information to her, particularly statistical data and analyses of a political and economic nature. Her father mixed regularly with Labour politicians and leading left-wing economists and many of them had jobs connected with the war effort, so any useful gossip or fragment of information garnered in this way was of value.

What with the depressing news of Hitler's successes in Europe, and with no companion with whom she could talk about these things, and then the considerable responsibility of looking after her two small children, household chores and shopping in an unaccustomed environment, she came close to a serious depression. The German attack on the Soviet Union on 22 June 1941 was shattering, but it also helped shake her out of her stupor. It also signified the end of the Nazi–Soviet Pact and gave the green light for communist parties around the world to support the war, which they had up until then characterised as one between imperialist powers.

The attack had a powerful impact on Britain as a whole and made people more ready to help support the Soviet Union now that it had joined the war. It brought the communists out of their ghetto and back into the mainstream. Once the Nazis had launched their attack, few Western politicians credited the Soviet Union with lasting more than a few weeks; they were unable to believe that a 'worker-run' state would be effective in combatting Hitler's ruthless and well-organised war machine. This attack on Russia also afforded temporary relief for Britain: a threat of imminent invasion was minimised and Nazi aerial bombardment was diminished.

Many in the West had hoped that the Nazis could be persuaded to attack the Soviet Union and that the two nations would fight each other to a standstill, leaving the West to mop up. That scenario failed to materialise. Hanson W. Baldwin, a former military editor of the *New York Times* and Pulitzer Prize winner, reinforces this in his book, *The Crucial Years 1939–41*. 'The German invasion of Russia', he writes:

> offered the United States alternatives short of all out war … It was certainly not – as the post-war decades have shown – in the American interest, or world interest, to help one menace [Nazi Germany] to replace another [the Soviet Union]. The destruction of both … could only have benefited not harmed …

Such calculations were the basis of Western government thinking even up to the outbreak of war.

Once Len had been given permission by Moscow to travel to Britain he was keen to leave as soon as he could, but it was not at all easy to obtain new travel documentation from the British consulate, which was overwhelmed by other British citizens of military age requiring help to return to Britain. Only after Ursula, through her father's contacts, was able to persuade the MP Eleanor Rathbone to raise the issue in Parliament, were things expedited for Len. He was eventually issued with a passport under the name of John William Miller, enabling him to travel through Spain unhindered. On 29 July 1942, twenty long months since Ursula and the two children had left Switzerland, Len arrived in Poole on the south coast by ship from Lisbon. On arrival he gave up his false Bolivian passport in the name of Luis Carlos Bilboa to the

British immigration authorities. He had been able to obtain this pass-port as a back-up but had not needed to use it. He was now keen to sign up for military service and 'do his bit', but it took another year before he was finally called up. This delay was probably as a result of his having fought on the Republican side in Spain. Not long after his arrival back in the UK he was also called in for a 'routine' interrogation by MI5. In one of these interrogations he apparently expressed his frustration at not being able to join up and being turned down by the RAF. (A note to this effect dated 19 December 1942 is attached to one of the files on him held by MI5.) The Military Training Act of 1939 introduced conscription for all men aged between 18 and 41. However, Len had not been called up because he had been placed on a 'suspense register', effectively barring certain individuals, for various reasons, from joining the armed forces. In his case, the reason was clearly political.

He joined his wife and children at 134 Oxford Road, Kidlington. It was a happy reunion for all of them. Then came the official welcome: only three days after arriving home, he received a letter from the Treasury demanding repayment of the money he owed the govern-ment for paying for his transport back from the Spanish border to London after his repatriation as a former member of the International Brigades, four years previously in 1938. Then, on top of it all, and before he even had time to unpack his bags, the owners of the cottage decided to give them notice as they needed it themselves, they said. So the family was obliged, once again, to start looking for a suitable place to live. What a homecoming! Eventually they found a little coachman's house, Avenue Cottage, in the grounds of a large mansion owned by Judge Neville Laski, brother of the prominent Labour Party intellectual and academic Harold Laski. It was ideal for their purposes. There was even a stone wall beside the house in which they found they could remove one of the stones and create a cavity to store their transmitter safe enough, they felt, from prying eyes. In using it, though, they would have to reckon with discovery at any moment, as the use of even amateur transmitters was strictly forbidden during the war. A detective from Oxford police actually visited Mrs Laski, the owner, immediately after the Beurtons had moved in, and made enquiries about them. She told him that they were friendly and she had nothing untoward to say about them. The report to MI5 from Oxford City

Police said that the 'Beurtons live quite isolated but have contacts with the Laskis who live nearby'. The officer also reported that Ursula had introduced Neville Laski to her sister Barbara and her husband [Duncan] who was then serving as an intelligence officer with the RAF in the Middle East and had taken a course on intelligence work. The report also included the information that they 'have a rather large wireless set and recently had a special pole installed in the house ...' This report was followed up by another, later memo (25 January 1943) marked SECRET and addressed to H. Shillitoe from Major Phipps, who said he had been unable to obtain much information about the Beurtons but 'The most interesting point appears to be their possession of a large wireless set, and you may think this is worthy of further enquiry.' This last paragraph is marked in the margin with a double pencil line, i.e. as being of special interest. MI5 clearly had this highly significant information but, surprisingly, took no action on it. There are also MI5 notes to the effect that the Beurtons seemed to be able to survive quite well with no apparent income, but again this does not seem to have been further investigated.

Before Len's arrival, Ursula had been able to make friendly contact with a local RAF officer whose wife and child had been evacuated to Oxford. He was one of the few officers who came from a working-class background – he had been a welder – and he also had progressive political views. Like many on the left, he was also baffled, or rather made angry, by the government's refusal to open up a second front to take some pressure off the Soviet Union. These views made him quite amenable to offer what help he could, including passing on information that would be of use to the Soviets. As a member of a technical branch of the RAF, he was able to give information about weights, dimensions, load-carrying capacities and also blueprints of planes that had not yet been flown. James, as he was known, refused to take any payment and didn't consider himself to be a 'spy', but someone aiding an allied country bearing the heaviest sacrifices in the war against fascism.

It was becoming increasingly urgent for Ursula to open up her own 'second front' and find someone else she could train in radio transmitting to take over should she or Len be arrested – an ever present possibility. With this in mind, she recruited Tom, a fitter in the local Cowley car factory, who would become a reliable and dependent back-up. He, like James, refused to accept any payment for his work. And a chance meeting with an old acquaintance of Len's who had previously shown sympathy for the communist movement turned into a new source of vital information. He was a specialist in sea-borne tank landing, and was able to supply useful information on tank-landing operations and details about a new submarine radar system that was being developed. Ursula writes in her autobiography that right 'up to the end of the war there was no difficulty winning people, because in that period work for the Soviet Union was seen as work for an ally in the war against Hitler'.

On his return to the UK, Len had immediately volunteered for the armed forces but was still waiting to hear when he would be called up. In the meantime he tried to find work in the Oxford area, but that too was made impossible. He would have been unaware that not only was the army not keen to have him, but that he had been effectively blacklisted in the civilian world too. A copy of a letter from the Pressed Steel Company in Cowley to Len, who had applied for a job with them, that was consequently filed by MI5, is testimony to this. The company rejected his application on the ostensible grounds that he was 'unsuitable for present requirements'.[3]

The Klaus Fuchs case

Life, even for a secret agent, can easily become routine and boring. Ursula's seemed to have fallen into that pattern. She met her Soviet contact twice a month in London, sometimes, if deemed necessary, more often, but there was little to report. When in London she would usually lodge with her parents or with one of her siblings. But then, towards the end of 1942, something totally unexpected happened with results that would help shape the course of post-war history.

Klaus Fuchs, one of the most brilliant minds working on the atomic bomb project during the 1940s, would, in 1950, be propelled from relative anonymity into the spotlight after being 'outed' as a Soviet spy. He would enter Ursula Kuczynski's life while she was living in Oxfordshire during the Second World War. The results of their contact and co-operation would send shock waves around the world and propel Ursula into the 'super spy' category. They would both meet again, long after the end of the war, in the German Democratic Republic.

Towards the end of 1941 the news from Germany was dire. The gifted physicist Fuchs had received reports of the imprisonment and persecution of his father, his brother and brother-in-law, and then on top of that the tragic death of his sister. The additionally grim news that Hitler's army had almost reached the gates of Moscow contributed to his momentous decision to offer his help to the embattled Soviet Union. He was no adventurer, maverick or spy – he simply wanted to pursue his work as a physicist in the interests of human progress – but the apocalyptic historical situation forced his hand. In court when he was later put on trial, he expressed it movingly thus: 'From time to time there have to be individuals who deliberately take on the burden of guilt because they see the situation clearer than those who have the power.' Fuchs' justification is not dissimilar to that made by Edward Snowden for his revelations in 2013.

Although the Soviet Union in 1941 was an ally of Britain and the USA, it was clear to Fuchs that the Western allies were deliberately holding back the opening of a second front in Europe and were hoping that the Germans and the Russians would destroy each other so that they could then move in and determine the post-war map of Europe. He had also realised that the Western powers were determined to keep from the Russians all their research into the development of atomic weapons. That's why, he said, he never hesitated to pass on the information he had, at first simply information about work he himself was carrying out, but later this was widened. The whole story of Klaus Fuchs' role in supplying the Soviet Union with vital details in connection with the building of an atomic bomb has been written about extensively elsewhere, so there is no need to repeat that detail here.

After taking the decision to provide the Russians with the results of his own research, Fuchs approached Jürgen Kuczynski, as the leader of the German communist exiles in Britain, requesting him to help set up renewed contact with the Soviet Union, as he was in possession of vital and worthwhile military information which could be valuable to them. Jürgen immediately told Ursula about him, and she in turn asked Moscow whether they were interested: they were indeed. He was first put in contact with Simon Davidovitch Kremer (codename 'Alexander'), secretary to the military attaché at the Soviet embassy, who was also an officer of the Red Army's foreign military intelligence directorate. Fuchs was later teamed up with a courier so that he would not have to find excuses to travel regularly to London and have direct contact with embassy officials. That courier was Ursula.

Fuchs had begun studying physics at Leipzig University, but was forced to leave Germany in 1933. Originally he had been a member of the student branch of the SPD, but was expelled for being too radical, and in 1932 he joined the Communist Party. He went into hiding after the Reichstag fire, and fled to England. In the UK he continued his Ph.D. studies first in Bristol, then at Edinburgh University under Max Born, the German-born physicist and mathematician who has been largely credited with the development of quantum mechanics. At Bristol University one of his research colleagues was Ronald Gurney, a local Communist Party member, and they both worked with Professor Nevill Mott, who was a member of the British–Soviet Friendship Society. Another colleague in the physics department there was Cecil Powell, who was probably also a member of the Party. Both Mott and Powell would go on to win Nobel Prizes and were active in the anti-nuclear Pugwash movement.

While in Bristol, Fuchs needed to renew his residency permit and when he applied to do so MI5 requested a report on him from the German consulate in the city. Based on a Gestapo report, the embassy confirmed that he had been involved in communist activities. MI5 clearly saw no contradiction in asking the representative of a Nazi state for comment on an anti-fascist refugee. In fact MI5 had already opened a file on Fuchs in 1933, when an MI6 agent in Kiel reported on his communist party activities there.[4] One has to wonder how many files on German communists and anti-fascists MI6 collected at this time and, in comparison, how many on fascists.

The early war years interrupted Fuchs' studies and he soon found himself, alongside other emigrés, interned on the Isle of Man as an 'enemy alien'. He was a short time later despatched by ship, along with other internees, to Canada. Fuchs was held in the Canadian internment camp of Sherbrooke in Quebec, where he soon joined a communist discussion group led by Hans Kahle, a KPD member who had fought in the Spanish Civil War. After fleeing to Britain with his family, Kahle had helped Jürgen Kuczynski organise the communist group of refugees in Britain, before himself being despatched to Canada.

In Britain, Fuchs' scientific and political friends soon began a concerted campaign to persuade the government to release him from internment. Fuchs' obvious abilities in the field of theoretical physics had already been noted by those who had worked closely with him, like Max Born who also campaigned actively for his release, and described him as one of the most talented young physicists around. He was eventually released in 1941 and was able to return to the UK.

After his return, he was asked by Professor Rudolf Peierls, who was involved in atomic research and the development of nuclear weapons, to join his team in Birmingham. Peierls, was working on tube alloys in connection with the British atomic bomb project. Only a year later Fuchs would make his first contact with Ursula. Neither she nor Jürgen knew exactly what work he was doing – it was top secret – but Moscow was very interested.

There are too many books on the Fuchs case to list, but some of the better-known ones are Alan Moorhead's *The Traitors* (1952), Rebecca West's *The Meaning of Treason* (1982), Robert Williams' *Klaus Fuchs, Atom Spy* (1987) and the most recent, Mike Rossiter's *The Spy Who Changed the World* (2014). While most of the books are well researched and relatively accurate in what they reveal, they are all written with a more or less Cold War mindset and with a black-and-white concept of the espionage world. None of them attempts to delve beneath appearances and examine Fuchs' or the Kuczynskis' motivation for their actions in the context of the anti-fascist struggle.

When Ursula first met Fuchs in Banbury he was working in Peierls' Birmingham laboratory. He travelled down to Banbury to meet her, but without any indication of her name or who she was. They went for a long walk together and found much to talk about and discuss – nothing to do with the central issue, but about books, films, politics, Germany and exile. He was 'a sensitive and intelligent comrade and scientist', she commented in her autobiographical reminiscences, and 'I noticed that very first time how calm, thoughtful, tactful and cultured he was'. After that first assignation they met regularly in secluded places and arranged secret 'letter boxes'. Ursula would cycle out into the countryside to meet him. They both felt freer there, as they could be reasonably certain of not being followed or overlooked without their noticing it; They used holes in the roots of trees as hiding places for the documents. Neither knew the other's address and Fuchs almost certainly did not even know at the time that she was related to Jürgen.

During the decisive period of atomic weapons development, between the end of 1942 until the summer of 1943, when Fuchs left for the USA, Ursula would meet him at least once a month. The last time she met Fuchs she was already pregnant with Len's child. On this occasion Fuchs gave her a thick book of blueprints – over a hundred pages – and asked her to forward it quickly. This was undoubtedly one of the most important documents he would pass on to the Soviets, as it contained detailed information about how far the atomic bomb project had developed. When Fuchs left for New York, Ursula lost contact with him. As a result of this valuable information that she passed on to the Soviet Union, she was highly praised by Moscow headquarters. Her contact man in Britain, Sergei, told her that the director had said that 'if they only had five "Sonyas" in Britain the war would be over much more quickly'.[5]

On the basis of information passed to MI5 by the FBI, Fuchs had come under increasing suspicion. After being interrogated by William Skardon of MI5, he confessed to what he had done. His trial in 1950 was over in a matter of a couple of hours; there was no hearing of witnesses, no cross-examination and only one witness for the prosecution: William Skardon. He was sentenced to fourteen years imprisonment, but was released in 1959 after serving nine years and four months, and emigrated to the GDR where he continued his work as a scientist and was elected to the Academy of Sciences. He was later appointed deputy director of the Institute for Nuclear Research in Rossendorf, where he served until he retired in 1979. The 1989 GDR film, *Väter der Tausend Sonnen* (Fathers of a Thousand Suns) was a commemoration of his life and work. Fuchs' father also remained in the GDR city of Leipzig where he continued his academic work as a theologian. He always remained fully supportive of his son.

Shortly before his death in 1988, Fuchs reiterated that:

> I never saw myself as a spy. I just couldn't understand why the West was not prepared to share the atom bomb with Moscow. I was of the opinion that something with that immense destructive potential should be made available to the big powers equally ...[6]

Jürgen noted that most Western scientists, like Fuchs, were quite willing to work on the development of the atom bomb during the war, seeing it as a potential and vital antidote to Hitler's worldwide domination. But with the dropping of atomic bombs on Hiroshima and Nagasaki demonstrating the appalling impact of such weaponry and coinciding with the defeat of fascism, such attitudes changed. Once the war was over, more than half of the scientists involved, including Einstein himself, came out against any further development and use of such weaponry.

Ursula met Fuchs again after his release from imprisonment. In 1976, shortly before her reminiscences, *Sonya's Report*, were published, she travelled to his home in Dresden and told him about the book. She was extremely grateful to him that he never betrayed her to the British secret services.

The course of the war changes (1942–1944)

Ursula and Len, like so many others in the country and worldwide, avidly followed the battles on the Eastern Front during the latter years of the war but at the same time there was an underlying fear that Hitler could still be victorious. 'Then, as now', Ursula wrote, 'we would have refuted any suggestion that we, or the comrades working with us, were betraying Britain by our actions. The Soviet Union was, after all, a key ally, even if Western governments viewed it with deep suspicion and, in secret, still thought of it as the "real enemy".'

By August 1942 the Soviet army had begun encircling the Wehrmacht forces at Stalingrad and at last there was a promise of reversing the seemingly inexorable tide of Nazi victories. The Battle of Stalingrad raged between August 1942 and February 1943. In the city Soviet soldiers fought house to house, cellar by cellar, in a city cut off from all food supplies and virtually razed to the ground by German bombardment. The rest of the world listened to reports on the radio and read the daily papers with bated breath. This was the key battle and turning point in the war. Soviet losses in this battle have been calculated at more that 1,129,000. From this point on the Red Army would begin its counter-offensive and start to drive German forces out of the country.

With the war now in its fourth year, the thoughts of German exiles began increasingly to focus on a post-war Germany and what form it could or should take. A festive event held in July 1943 saw the establishment of the *Bewegung Freies Deutschland* (the National Committee for a Free Germany). As an organisation it was intended to prepare the exiles for their return and encourage them to work together to build a new post-war society.

After Robert Kuczynski's pre-war success in managing to bring the main left forces in Germany together in the campaign to expropriate the landed aristocracy, it was thought he would be the ideal person to do the same in exile. He became the organisation's first president. Jürgen, alongside his father, was also actively involved in setting up the organisation and remained a member of its leadership until his place was taken by Kurt Hager in the summer of 1944.

The National Committee for a Free Germany was formed in accordance with the policies of the Comintern and was intended to become a popular front type of movement, bringing together all anti-fascist exiles in the country under one umbrella organisation. However, this time the German Social Democratic leadership in Britain refused to take part without, as they phrased it, a 'discussion on fundamentals' beforehand.

Despite this shaky start, the Committee held its first conference on 25 September 1943 in Trinity Hall, London with the participation of around 400 people, and soon had branches in a number of towns throughout the country. The organisation immediately came under close scrutiny by MI5.

After Stalingrad, everyone felt that the war was entering its final stages, but the Germans would still fight on for almost another two years. On 8 September 1943, the day that Italy signed a ceasefire, Ursula gave birth to a baby boy, also named Peter, like Marguerite and Jürgen's first son. That very same day she also had an appointment with her Soviet handler – the baby had arrived inconveniently two or three weeks early.

Very soon after the birth of his son – hardly an ideal moment – Len was finally called up and offered a basic training with the RAF. Despite receiving the highest A1 grade, his application to go on to train as a pilot was rejected. Still hoping for active service, he then applied to train as a radio operator, but when he was turned down again, asked to be transferred to a fighting unit of the army instead. During this time he was billeted only 25 miles from Oxford, so Ursula could visit him on her bicycle regularly. In this connection, there is a letter in MI5's files (dated 23 November 1943) from a Major Phipps to MI5's H. Shillitoe, stating that Len had 'now been enlisted in the RAF as a training wireless operator ... I am arranging for him to be kept under observation and will let you know if there is any interesting result.' A report from Roger Hollis, dated 10 August 1944, states that 'Mrs. Beurton appears to devote her time to her children and domestic affairs ...' and on Len, that 'her present husband has been the subject of investigation on account of possible Communist activities. He is, however, now serving in the Royal Air Force and our investigations have so far failed to substantiate the suspicions against him.' The Home Office warrant which allowed the security services to open Len's post and to tap his telephone was cancelled by Shillitoe on 19 December 1944.[7] The latter had by 1944, it appears, become reluctant to continue investigations of either Ursula or Len, and said that he would instruct the postmaster 'to lay off for the time being'.

It appeared to be policy that few former International Brigaders, especially if they were working class, were allowed to rise through the ranks of the armed forces, despite their first-hand training and experience of battle, and in this respect Len was no exception.[8] Rather surprisingly for everyone, though, he was eventually posted to the Coldstream Guards, the oldest regiment of the regular army and steeped in tradition; but he would be despatched to the front as a member of the 1st Armoured Battalion only shortly before the end of the war.

With Len gone, Ursula's mother arrived in Oxfordshire to help out, but when she herself fell ill things became too much and Ursula was obliged to pack the children off to boarding school once again.

In 1943, after the Soviet army's victory at Stalingrad, King George VI presented Stalin with a sword of honour; but there was still no second front, and the Soviets had to battle on without that much-needed support from the Western allies. At the meeting in Tehran of the Allied heads of state, Churchill advocated opening a second front in the Balkans, while Stalin insisted on one in France; on this occasion

Roosevelt agreed with Stalin. Finally, on 6 June 1944 – 'D-Day' – only when it had become very clear that the Soviet Union was assured of victory, did the long-promised second front materialise, and for the first time the Germans had to divert a substantial number of men and weaponry from the Russian front. Then, in July 1944 the Nazis launched their new and much-feared '*Wunderwaffe*' – the V2 rocket – against British cities. It was developed under the leadership of the German scientist Werner von Braun who, after the war, would find lucrative employment in the USA helping in that country's own rocket development programme.

Only a few months after the first V2s started falling on London, on 7 November, Ursula's friend and fellow agent from her China days, Richard Sorge, would be executed by the Japanese although she only heard of his death much later. He had been able to forewarn Stalin of the impending Nazi invasion of the Soviet Union in 1941, although Stalin had not believed his intelligence.

Already by February 1944 it was becoming clearer than ever that the war would be over in another year at most. So young couples in the exile community felt it would now be safe to bring children into the world. In that year three other children were born into the small group of German communist exiles in London, including Jürgen and Marguerite's second son (on 12 November), and all named Thomas – but this was sheer coincidence, apparently, and not as a result of Party instructions!

Notes

1 Oxford City Police report to MI5 from 24 February 1941(?). The Chief Constable has made enquires and finds Ursula 'is now living at 97 Kingston Road, Oxford and has rooms there with her sister Mrs. Taylor. I am informed that Mrs. Taylor's husband is now serving in the RAF and is stationed at Blackpool, where he is training as a wireless operator. Previous to joining the RAF he was a school-teacher at Clifton, Bristol, and was later evacuated to Cornwall. ... the only other people to visit her are her father ... Kuczynski, [who] I am informed, holds strong Communist views.' This report was signed off by H. Shillitoe, who then surprisingly adds: 'I do not think it necessary to take any further action with regard to Mrs. Beurton but I should be grateful if you would keep an eye on her.'

2 Frederick Taylor, *Coventry Thursday 14 November 1940*, London, Bloomsbury Press, 2015, pp. 28, 42.

3 MI5 file KV6/41: Job application rejection letter (dated 28.10.43). Followed up by a letter to Major J. C. Phipps from MI5's H. Shillitoe: 'I have now received confirmation that Beurton has been turned down by the Pressed Steel Co. Ltd. on the ostensible grounds that he is "unsuitable for present requirements". ... I should like to know what work he eventually does find.'

4 Robert Williams, *Klaus Fuchs, Atom Spy*, Cambridge MA, Harvard University Press, 1987, p. 22.

5 Ibid., p. 199.

6 Eberhard Panitz, *Treffpunkt Banbury: Oder wie die Atombombe zu den Russen kam: Klaus Fuchs, Ruth Werner und der größte Spionagefall der Geschichte*, Berlin, Das Neue Berlin, 2003, p. 163.

7 MI5 file KV6/41, 1944.

8 This discrimination has been confirmed by several sources, for instance a *Guardian* obituary of the last British commander in Spain, Bill Alexander (14 July 2000), relates that although he managed to attain the rank of captain, 'Many of his comrades from Spain were not so fortunate, and suffered persistent discrimination'.

9

JÜRGEN JOINS THE US ARMY

Under Roosevelt, it was not unusual to find a good number of left-wing 'civilians in uniform' working for the administration. With Roosevelt's more progressive government in the USA and with the Soviet Union an ally, there developed in the country a new, if short-lived, tolerance of left-wing individuals even in leading positions. That situation would change dramatically after the end of the war and, following the death of Roosevelt, culminate in the notorious McCarthy witch-hunts.

The American Joseph (Joe) Gould was one of those with a good progressive track record who joined the army under the Roosevelt administration. He had been a motion picture publicist for United Artists in New York, the film studio then owned by Charlie Chaplin and Douglas Fairbanks. He joined the East Coast chapter of the Screen Publicists Guild, which elected him its first president in 1938, and his leadership proved to be effective. The Guild's first contract with the film studios doubled the weekly pay of its members. During contract renegotiations in 1940, Gould led a picket line of guild members outside the New York theatre premiering Disney's *Fantasia*. A better deal for the screen publicists was signed shortly thereafter. In June 1944 Gould enlisted in the army, and after completing basic training and achieving the rank of lieutenant was assigned to the Office of Strategic Services (OSS) – forerunner of the CIA – joining the staff of the Labor Branch in the London office.

According to a CIA report, Gould was given the task of finding suitable German exiles who would be willing to be parachuted into Germany as special agents. So he roamed London in search of information about the Free Germany Committee in the UK, and with this aim in mind decided to explore local bookstores as likely places to come across such exiles and the best way to find suitable candidates. That hunch yielded results when he encountered Morris Abbey, the friendly owner of a small bookstore on New Bond Street. Abbey took an immediate liking to Gould, and offered him an introduction to one of his regular customers, Dr Jürgen Kuczynski, 'an economist whose father was president of the Free Germany Movement'.

Gould contacted Jürgen straight away and asked him if he felt it would be feasible, using US aircraft, to parachute some reliable Germans into Nazi Germany to carry out secret surveillance work there. Jürgen did indeed have the necessary close contacts and was able to recommend a number of candidates. The go-between for this operation was Erich Henschke, a member of the underground London branch of the German Communist Party. Joe agreed to Erich co-ordinating the recruitment and was happy for the parachutists to be chosen from among the German communists 'as they were the most dependable in the fight against fascism'.

Jürgen informed his sister Ursula about this operation so that she could let the Soviet Union know about it too.[1] Those they were able to recruit underwent two months intensive training including practice parachute jumps and using 'walkie-talkies' – a new and sensational invention at the time and developed specifically for them. This whole exercise is described in detail in *Piercing the Reich* by Joseph E. Persico. The recruits were eventually parachuted successfully into Germany, not only as US agents, but with Ursula's help, as Soviet ones as well – an irony of the time.

The progress of the war and increased US involvement would also have a rather curious but important impact on Jürgen's life. By the summer of 1944 his volume III, part 2 of *Geschichte der Lage der Arbeiter im Kapitalismus* (A History of the Conditions of the Working Class under Capitalism) had been published. This dealt with Germany under fascism, from 1933 to the present. It was a largely theoretical, historical and statistical analysis of the fascist economy. It was a book that was read particularly by advisors to allied governments as well as intelligence officers in the military leaderships. Despite the fact that most of his publications on economics had been published by Communist Party publishing houses, both in the USA and UK as well as in pre-war Germany, this appeared to be no barrier to what happened next.

In September of that same year, probably largely as a result of those economic publications, he unexpectedly received a letter from the Economic Management department of the US embassy in London asking him to come for an interview. As it later became clear, the letter was sent at the request of the United States Strategic Bombing Survey (USSBS) which was keen to obtain his collaboration. He was immediately offered a job on the basis of his knowledge of economic conditions in Germany. He asked for time to think it over before accepting, giving Ursula the opportunity of reporting to Moscow. They gave him the green light, so he accepted the job.

After brief negotiations with the Americans, and after Jürgen had obtained agreement of the Party, he became a member of the United States Armed Forces, with a not insubstantial salary and with the rank of lieutenant colonel. He was appointed despite Roger Hollis (who in 1956 would become Director General of MI5) warning the US authorities that Jürgen was a member of the Communist Party and that 'those who make use of his services should be aware that his conclusions on economic conditions in Germany may be influenced by his political beliefs'.[2]

In this new job with USSBS, he found himself unexpectedly working next door to Joe Gould. Jürgen relates that he and Gould would remain close friends until the latter's death in the early 1990s.[3] In 1989, Gould would visit Berlin and be keen to catch up with some of the parachutists who undertook those dangerous missions, but sadly, as Ursula relates in *Sonya's Report*, none were still alive. This close cooperation with OSS was terminated a few weeks after the end of the war when the Americans demobilised those who had been recruited for clandestine work in Germany.

In the London office of the Survey there were already, apart from Jürgen, a number of progressive economists working. Among them was

Tibor Scitowski who, in the post-war era, would become a leading theoretician of welfare economics in the USA. At this time the US authorities did not seem to care what your politics were as long as you were useful to them. Two other OSS men Jürgen would get to know quite well while working there were Richard Francis Ruggles and 'a Norwegian, called Ohlin'. Ruggles would go on to become a professor of economics at Harvard, best known for developing accounting tools for measuring national income and improving price indexes used in formulating government policy. It was Ruggles who developed the novel idea of noting the motor serial numbers of destroyed German tanks and shot down planes and using this information to estimate production levels. Ohlin had an even simpler idea: he checked the journals of international organisations and discovered that the German administration, being as officious as ever, even during the war, continued to send information on goods trains timetables and the cargoes they carried to a Swiss transport journal. From this the USA was able to glean information about the most important oil transportations.

Jürgen found all this exceedingly instructive, and he was keen to make use of the newly gained knowledge when he eventually returned to Germany, where it would be helpful in planning the desperately needed reconstruction work. At the time, he noted, 'we were at loggerheads with our British colleagues on bombing strategies'. The British were all for a 'carpet bombing strategy', as a means of demoralising the German population. The Survey was of the opinion that pinpoint bombing would be more effective, i.e. the selection of specific key targets. In the end it was agreed to pursue both strategies. The Soviets, he said, adopted neither of these techniques. And, in the end, both strategies proved to be ineffective in halting or even slowing German arms production. Pinpoint bombing involved collaboration with the espionage agencies to ensure the correct targets were chosen, and that is probably why the OSS was quartered in the same building as the Survey people, and maintained cordial relations with each other during this period.

Working conditions in the office were ideal, Jürgen said, so that he and his close colleagues were usually given immediate access to all available information on the economic situation and developments in Germany, even before the intelligence chief or Eisenhower had seen it.

Although Jürgen did not collaborate directly with OSS in his work, he did have access to their information on fascist production figures for tanks, planes, etc. Apart from OSS itself and his department, this information was given only to Roosevelt, Eisenhower, Churchill and Lord Ismay, the latter's chief military advisor. However, Jürgen, via Ursula, ensured that Stalin was also included on the list of recipients.

He soon became accustomed to military discipline and although he understood virtually nothing of military matters, he found a niche where he could develop his own expertise and that was in questions of protocol. Very soon he had managed to push through a change in accepted military protocol: 'civilians in uniform' would no longer have to stand to attention like jumping-jacks every time a general entered the room. Towards the end of his stint with the Survey, he was recommended for the award of a Bronze Star for 'courage and general proficiency', but when he did not get it, his colleagues argued over whether it was as a result of his politics or because of the protocol 'improvements' he had introduced.

In December 1944 Jürgen and his colleague in the Survey office, Richard Ruggles, received orders to fly to Paris. Returning to a liberated Paris after so many years was an indescribably joyous experience. The plan had been to travel on to Germany afterwards, but after the unexpected Ardennes offensive by the Germans in January 1945 he was forced to return to London, where he spent twelve long weeks kicking his heels. On 27 March he was again ordered to fly to Paris, this time with Major Ellis H. Wilner, a textile businessman from new York – 'a thoroughly decent, upright, bourgeois-liberal guy', with whom he got on exceedingly well. From Paris he managed to travel to Strasbourg, where Marguerite's mother lived. He met her at the house just as she was returning from a shopping trip. She told him that the area had been liberated only two days before she was due to be deported to Germany. He was happy to be able to reassure Marguerite in London that her mother was well.

In April he was in Augsburg where a number of prominent Nazis were being held by US forces. He was offered the opportunity of questioning any of them he wished, but was given orders to be 'firm but courteous'. So he declined to talk to Goering, as 'having to be courteous would have been a demand too far'. Instead he spoke to

Walther Funk about the fascist administration of the economy. Funk had been Hitler's Reichsminister for Economic Affairs and President of the Reichsbank. It was Funk who had been directly responsible for the acceleration of Hitler's rearmament programme. Later he would be convicted at Nuremberg as a major war criminal. He was, Jürgen writes, 'obsequiously craven, and maintained that as minister for economic affairs he had really only played the piano, particularly Wagner, and then he asked us for a pair of trousers'. Funk waffled on about having had a 'disinterested attitude' during the Hitler years. Before leaving, Jürgen responded: 'When we capture Hitler I'll ask him if that's true', at which Funk cringed with fear. Jürgen then left for Heidelberg, the old stomping ground of his student years, travelling there via Würzburg which, he writes, had put up a senseless final resistance and had been equally senselessly bombed. The stench of thousands of incinerated bodies hung in the air. Heidelberg, in contrast, had hardly been scratched.

Jürgen knew that Hermann Schmitz, the boss of I. G. Farben, lived nearby and he was determined to arrest him. At the mansion just outside the city a maid opened the door and led him and his companion, sergeant Bob Stern, into the living room where Schmitz greeted them. They began questioning him about his role during the fascist period; but he, like most of the others, denied any real involvement and told them he had made no money out of the war and that his dividends were being given to a charity for war widows. When he saw Jürgen's stern and unbelieving expression, he immediately told them about his wonderful collection of cameras and said they could choose any ones they wanted. They arrested him on the spot and handed him over to the appropriate authority in Heidelberg to be tried as a war criminal.

Later, in 1964, when Jürgen was invited as an expert to the Auschwitz trial in Frankfurt-am-Main, the defence lawyer for the accused Nazis told the court that Schmitz had been arrested in Würzburg. 'It wouldn't surprise me', Jürgen commented, 'if the Americans in Heidelberg hadn't released him and that he had then been re-arrested in Würzburg'.

In Heidelberg he was also able to visit some of his old pre-war acquaintances, like Karl Jaspers – whose wife was Jewish and had been forced to spend weeks living in a cellar to escape being hauled away by the Nazis at the last minute – and Marianne Weber, the widow of sociologist Max Weber, with whom, as a student, he had enjoyed such animated Sunday afternoons with her circle of friends.

His real task while travelling through Germany was to gather statistical material for a report on the effects of the allied bombing strategy, particularly on industrial production, within a framework of the general economic situation. In Saarbrücken or Saarlouis (he could not recall which) they discovered a unique treasure in the form of the library of the chamber of commerce. His companion Major Wilner first wanted to have it searched for booby traps, but it would have taken much valuable time to get hold of a specialist unit to do this, so Jürgen, to avoid delay, decided to enter the library himself and was able to remove dozens of useful document files. Among these were the *Statistical Year Books of the German Reich*, which since 1940 had been classified, first as 'confidential' and later as 'top secret' as they contained a mass of important internal economic data. Because of Jürgen's action, Major Wilner in his report commended him 'for bravery in a dangerous situation' but little did he realise, Jürgen says, 'that for me the opportunity of getting my hands on books, transcended any fears I might have had, and my behaviour had nothing to do with bravery'.

A short time later, in Kiel, northern Germany, he and his unit were taken to an enormous salt cavern in which hundreds of thousands of secret files from the state archives were stored. Among them he noticed one devoted to the leading nineteenth-century Social Democrat, August Bebel. By chance he became involved in high-level discussions about what to do with the library, where the suggestion was put forward that it should be moved to the USA. He was able to argue successfully against this and thus helped ensure that the unique library of the World Economic Institute was kept in place and saved for posterity.

On his travels through Germany Jürgen made efforts to contact as many of his Party comrades as possible. He discovered that many of them at this time, though, were 'strongly sectarian'. 'Only with the passing of time, once more and more comrades emerged from the concentration camps and returned to political work, and when the Party line in the Soviet Zone of Occupation also gained influence in the West, did this sectarianism ebb somewhat', he wrote. Jürgen was probably referring here to the attitude of these communists to working together with the SPD and other broadly democratic organisations and individuals. The pre-war period and the rise of the Nazis had left a legacy of deep resentments, bitterness and suspicion.

While he was in Germany the management personnel of the United States Bombing Survey in London changed. Its new chief was Henry Clay Alexander, who after the war would become a director of the Morgan Trust, together with Paul Nitze, later to become a leading neo-conservative. Nitze would play a significant role in US military and foreign affairs under President Johnson. Others Jürgen worked with were George Ball, who became a leading light in the Department of Foreign Affairs, and Kenneth Galbraith, who became probably the country's leading liberal economist and a friend of President Kennedy. Kuczynski and Galbraith did not take to each other at all to begin with but within a short space of time were nevertheless on friendly terms and maintained amicable relations for the rest of their lives.

Galbraith, Kuczynski and other members of the new team were deployed to Bad Nauheim where they remained stationed until the end of August when the Survey team was broken up and sections of it moved to Japan. Galbraith, in his memoirs, mentions with gratitude how Jürgen once protected him from Eisenhower's ire in connection with the kidnapping by US forces of German professionals from the Soviet Zone in Germany. Both big powers were keen to locate and haul on board any top German scientist, academic or expert who could be useful to them, and to prevent 'the other side' from getting there first.

Galbraith explains:

> One German we needed for work that summer was Dr. Rolf Wagenführ, the senior economist and statistician in the Speer ministry. Exceptionally among the staff of such departments he had remained behind in Berlin. Other German officials brought to Bad Nauheim claimed to have known him as a 'roast beef Nazi' – brown outside, red inside. He was finally located in West Berlin from where he was engaged in rehabilitating the German statistical services for the Soviets in East Berlin ... Although we had the right of summary arrest, I was uneasy as to its use and had specified that for professors, scientists, officials and the like, notice should be

given. On being told of our desire that he go to Bad Nauheim, Wagenführ removed himself to a house in Neukölln in the Russian [sic] sector.[4]

In Galbraith's team was a sergeant named Baran, who was 'one of the most brilliant and, by a wide margin, the most interesting economist I have ever known', he wrote. Baran came from a family of Polish Jews and was, according to Galbraith, a communist, but an undisciplined one. In the US army he represented 'a headache for US security'. In the 1930s he had arrived at Harvard and 'impressed everyone' and then went on 'to serve brilliantly' during the war with the Survey. He went on to become 'an immensely popular professor at Stanford' after the war.

Sergeant Baran led a posse to Wagenführ's home, Galbraith relates:

and, quite literally, lifted him out of bed from beside his wife. He was flown to Bad Nauheim, and the Soviets, very properly were outraged. A strong protest went from Marshal Zhukov and across to General Eisenhower; I was, of course, the person responsible and in line for Ike's anger. The matter was resolved when Jürgen Kuczynski, a German Communist on our staff, advised me that he much wanted to go to Berlin to see if his house and library had survived the war. Were he allowed to go, he could, as a practicing comrade, square things with his fellow Communists. So, a fortnight or so after the kidnapping, as the Soviets called it, and after Wagenführ had given us much useful guidance on the German production statistics, Kuczynski took him back to Berlin. I asked James Barr Ames to go along and keep an eye on the operation. And sure enough, Kuczynski was warmly welcomed by the Soviet officials, our well-rehearsed explanation of our aberration was accepted. Wagenführ was reinstated in the Soviet statistical operations and Ike's fury was averted.[5]

In the meantime Jürgen was able to make several trips back to London or was sent to General Eisenhower's HQ in Paris. The days and weeks the team spent in Bad Nauheim were very relaxed and enjoyable, he recalled, and with no pressing schedule of assignments he and his colleagues undertook a great deal of social activity. Even many years after the war, since when they had had no contact, if he met former members of the team anywhere in the world there was within minutes a renewed intimacy.

At last, in August he was able to visit Berlin for a few days and, as soon as he had the opportunity, went straight to the Party's central committee headquarters 'of course in uniform'. Understandably, no one wanted to let him in until an old comrade recognised him and brought him to see general secretary Walter Ulbricht. Although his visit was unannounced, Ulbricht greeted him warmly and then took him to talk with Wilhelm Pieck. Afterwards Ulbricht drove him in his own car to the border checkpoint to the US sector, and said to him, 'Come back as soon as you can but if possible without the uniform.' What he didn't tell him was that the chief of staff of the Soviet military administration had apparently just appointed Jürgen as president of the central administration of finances in the sector with the assumption that he would accept the post. Jürgen only gathered this, he says, after he had returned to London and heard it announced on Radio Berlin.

End of the war and uncertainty (1945–1956)

In early 1945, with the end of the war in sight, Renate, the youngest of Robert and Berta's children, who had met and fallen in love with Arthur Simpson, a fellow student, felt the time had now come for them to get married. They tied the knot in March of that same year. Two months, later, in May, street parties took place all over Britain to celebrate the end of the war. Mrs Laski organised a celebration in the street where Ursula lived and 'with relief', she wrote:

I shared everyone's joy about the victorious end of the war; I felt the same relief, because the anxiety about relatives at the front had come to an end. Everyone hoped for a better world, but there our visions of the future differed.

In the same month that Renate and Arthur married, Ursula and family were forced to move home yet again as the owner wanted Avenue Cottage back now the war was over. This time they moved to 'The

Firs' in the Oxfordshire village of Great Rollright. Len, however, had to remain in the army for another 21 months before he would be demobbed. He had finally seen action in the closing weeks with the British army in Germany and eventually reached Berlin with his battalion as the war came to an end.

On 2 August 1945 the Potsdam Agreement was signed by Stalin, Truman and Attlee. The agreement laid down the principles for the post-war reconstruction of Germany, its demilitarisation, payment of reparations and the prosecution of war criminals. Shortly after the historic document had been signed, Len read about a new monument to the victorious Soviet forces being erected in the centre of Berlin. On one of his days off, he bought some red dahlias and laid them at the foot of the two tanks that formed the monument, stepped back and saluted. This intrigued some watching Soviet soldiers who took him to their commanding officer who wanted to know why a British soldier had made this gesture. Len told him that he had great respect for the Soviet Army, particularly as he had also fought in Spain alongside Russian volunteers. The Russians were suitably impressed, but his British commanding officers less so. They had also been informed of

FIGURE 9.1 'The Firs', Great Rollright, where Ursula and her family last
lived in Oxfordshire
Source: Kuczynski family archive.

Len's action and as a punishment he was given 28 days arrest. This small incident was a reflection of how attitudes were to change radically and rapidly. The general euphoria everywhere after the end of the war would be tempered by Churchill's 'iron curtain' speech given in March 1946 at Fulton, Missouri. It ushered in the Cold War and defined a new enemy: the Soviet Union.

In the summer of 1946 Moscow Centre broke off all contact with Ursula, but the reason for this was unclear even to Ursula herself. Only much later did she find out that it was down to a silly misunderstanding. In KGB records it was noted:

> Since January 1946 S. has been inactive, and no personal contact with her is maintained. However, from time to time she keeps us informed about her situation using pre-arranged signals, which we passed on to her through her sister, Renata [sic] Simpson, in 1948.[6]

That KGB note is odd in that it appears to contradict what Ursula relates in her own memoirs. She said that her lack of contact at this time left her very short of money. Len was unable to help as he was still in the army and away in Germany. Her daughter describes in her memoir how they were so short of money that Ursula had to take in paying lodgers for a time, cooking and looking after them. By this time Jürgen had already returned to Germany. She did, though, use the opportunity to do more with the children and undertook a day's outing to Stratford-on-Avon – something she had wanted to do for some time.

In the vicinity of their small village was a prisoner of war camp housing German POWs who were working as labourers on the nearby Lonsdale Farm. At this time, over a year after the end of the war, many POWs, if they were just ordinary soldiers, were held, like non-dangerous criminals, in an open prison. Although they had to complete their daily work rota, they could do as they liked with their free time. Ursula's garden was quite large and needed a lot of work doing in it, so she asked two of the young German prisoners if they would help her and they willingly agreed to do so. She used the situation to chat with them using her German for the first time in many years, apart from when meeting family, which was not often. They talked about the situation in Germany and about the future, and she asked tentatively whether they had learned any lessons from the war, but she does not relate what their responses were. Janina taught the young POWs English words as she played with her dolls and watched them digging in the garden. In December, Ursula invited them to join the family for Christmas and celebrated in the German fashion with the main event and exchange of presents taking place on Christmas Eve. It was undoubtedly a very emotional moment for this isolated family in exile as well as for the young POWs far from home and longing to return. Here was a woman from a Jewish family background, a refugee from the regime for which these young soldiers had fought, finding common ground around the Christmas tree. While celebrating, they were visited by eight bell-ringers from the village who also sang carols. They were, she relates, rather surprised to see her German visitors, but Ursula thought 'it right to make a little speech about Christmas, peace on earth and the need to overcome the enmities of war'.

After Len was finally demobbed, in the autumn of 1946, Jürgen's wife Marguerite found him a job in a London factory that had patented a means of spraying patterns onto plastic material. However, this was far from where Ursula and the children were living and meant that he had to find lodgings in London – there was no hope of finding suitable employment in the immediate vicinity of Great Rollright for either of them.

In the extremely cold winter of 1946/47 Ursula found herself once again alone with the children in the village and with little money coming in. The roads were impassable and the snow drifted up against the doors, meaning that they had to dig their way out each morning. Every little task, particularly shopping, became an ordeal. With the war over, and the Soviet Union apparently no longer interested in contacting her, she began to yearn to return to Germany to help with rebuilding a new and, as she hoped, democratic country, and to settle down properly with her family.

In June 1947 her mother died after a short illness and was buried in the beautiful old village churchyard of Great Rollright. Thereafter, her father came to stay with her for a short time to help him recover from the loss. He could not face living alone in his London flat without Berta.

That summer, Len did at last manage to find a job only 13 miles from the village, at the Northern Aluminium Company, in Banbury, which employed around 3,000 workers. But by now both of them were feeling in limbo, with no political tasks to do. Since Ursula no longer had any contact with the Centre in Moscow, they decided to join the British Communist Party, as both wished to remain politically active.

In August or September 1947, Ursula was unexpectedly contacted by an Austrian comrade who informed her that their former colleague, Alexander Foote, from Switzerland days, had appeared out of the blue one day on his doorstep and had told him to pass on a warning to them both to cease any further activities. As luck would have it, by this time their work had already ceased anyway through lack of contact with Moscow. So they didn't need to take any further action, but the news must have disconcerted them. Not long after this warning, on the morning of 13 September 1947, there was a knock on their front door, and three men greeted her politely, but even before they entered the house, one of them said to her sotto voce: 'You were a Russian agent for a long time, until the Finnish War disillusioned you. We know you haven't been active in England and we haven't come to arrest you, but to ask you for your co-operation.' Ursula relates that this 'psychological' attempt to take her by surprise was 'so funny and inept' that she almost burst out laughing rather than being thrown off balance. Luckily she was well prepared for such an eventuality and was able to deal with it in a calm and controlled way. While she invited the men into the house, Len was working out in the garden and her father was reading in a room above.

The three men were William 'Jim' Skardon and Michael Serpell from MI5 and Detective Herbert from the Oxfordshire Police. When they mentioned some incidents in Switzerland it became clear to Ursula that only Foote could have been the source. The men reiterated their belief that she had become disillusioned with communism and asked whether she would consider working for them instead, but she was able to procrastinate. Finally the officers left empty handed. Skardon, the man in charge during this visit would later interrogate Klaus Fuchs shortly before his arrest. After their visit, though, it was clear that neither Ursula nor Len would be able to continue working for Moscow from Britain even if asked to do so. From now on, they could reasonably assume that they would be kept under surveillance, not aware that they had been monitored since their arrival in Britain.

What is surprising about the visit is that MI5 apparently assumed that this 'former Soviet agent' was living isolated in the English countryside simply for the good of her health; or was it meant simply as a veiled warning to her to enable an escape while she could? Either MI5 was incredibly incompetent or, as has often been suggested, someone at the top of the organisation was giving her protection. Before leaving, the agents remarked that they too would like to live in such an idyllic country house, to which she replied that she took in guests and they would be welcome to stay.

The report of that visit, written by William Skardon, MI5's chief investigations officer, read: 'a rather abject failure to make Mrs. Beurton talk'. He went on to note that while he assumed she had previously worked for Russian intelligence:

> the only good that the interview can have done may be to strengthen the resolve of the Beurtons to have nothing more to do with intelligence work. We are reasonably satisfied that they are not at present active, and there is no reason to suppose that they have been for some years.[7]

MI5's behaviour appears to have been even more lax than one could imagine, as already in January 1943 the Oxford City Police had reported the existence of a wireless set and, a few days later, their report formed the subject of an internal MI5 memorandum. Amazingly, especially given that even amateur broadcasting was illegal in wartime Britain, no follow-up enquires took place.[8] According to Peter Wright in his book *Spycatcher*, 'GCHQ denied vehemently that Sonia [sic] could ever have been broadcasting her radio messages from her home near Oxford during the period between 1941 and 1943'. Wright felt that the head of MI5, Richard Hollis, had deliberately buried the information from the Oxford police.

The day after MI5's visit, Ursula's father returned to London and immediately spoke to his daughter Barbara, telling her that he wished to speak to Brigitte urgently. He was clearly alarmed by MI5's visit to Ursula. His calls were intercepted by MI5.

FIGURE 9.2 The gravestone of Robert and Berta Kuczynski in the church-
        yard of Great Rollright, Oxfordshire
Source: Kuczynski family archive.

Robert was undoubtedly worried, too, about whether his own role would be exposed. During his exile and in connection with his statistical work for the government, he had maintained good connections with top government circles, particularly with Stafford Cripps, British ambassador to the Soviet Union from 1940 until 1942. He had been one of the chief sources of statistical and economic information that was passed on to the Soviet Union. Ursula had also been able to supply the Soviets with information from Churchill's war cabinet that he had collected. During the period in which the Soviet Union and the United Kingdom were allies, this could be considered a legitimate, even if unorthodox, sharing of information rather than espionage, but with the onset of the Cold War such exchanges of information took on an altogether different significance.

After alerting his children about MI5's visit Robert returned to Great Rollright, but hardly a month would pass before he died of cancer.

At the end of the war Robert had applied for British naturalisation and his application was supported by a number of eminent figures in the British establishment. It had been granted him in mid-1946, although Jürgen had intended bringing his parents back to Berlin to join him there. At around the same time Robert had been unexpectedly offered a professorship in demographics at Berlin's university in the Eastern sector which he was keen to take up after completing his latest book, but that was not to be. He died in Oxford on 27 November 1947, six months after his wife. Both are buried in the tranquil little churchyard of Great Rollright – the village where his eldest daughter carried out one of her most daring intelligence operations. The gravestone, with the names of the children on it too, is still there.

The Times carried a laudatory obituary, praising his work as a theoretician but also his practical work in drawing up radical plans for censuses to conform with the requirements of modern communities. In 1948, the first volume of Robert's 'magnum opus' – *A Demographic Survey of the British Colonial Empire* – was published, followed by volumes II and III which were published in 1949 by Oxford University Press after being completed by Brigitte. His grandchild Ludi, son of his youngest daughter Renate, would follow closely in his footsteps, becoming a professor of population studies at Manchester University, and also publishing pioneering work on demographic issues and their social implications.

In the meantime, Len was finding his work at the aluminium factory in Banbury pure drudgery, and being chained to this treadmill in order to feed his family was not how he had envisaged his life after the war. He pined for the purposeful action and excitement of Spain. As a former tank driver, he was also suffering from tinnitus as a result of gunfire noise and this, too, made him prone to depression. Ursula's life had also come to a standstill. Her son Michael had now finished school and had won a scholarship to Aberdeen University where he would read philosophy and psychology, and both she and Len felt that they were unable to carry on as before. Ursula then made urgent attempts to see Jürgen in order to discuss their options, but the US military administration for Germany would not grant her permission to travel to Berlin.

By January 1949 they still had no contact with Soviet headquarters, so Ursula decided to travel to Prague and hoped to meet Jürgen there to discuss with him her worries, both personal and political. She was keen to return to Germany. He was, though, very busy, she relates, and could only give her two half-hour meetings. She felt hurt by his rather cool and perfunctory attitude and 'had forgotten that he had never been one for expressing heartfelt emotions'. He told her that she could not think of moving to Germany without the approval of the Soviets, as that would only make life more complicated. So, even though it was out of the ordinary and against all the rules, she decided to go to the Soviet embassy in Prague and deposit a letter there addressed to GRU headquarters.

In the autumn of that same year Len had an accident on his motorbike and had to take time off work. The company used this as an excuse to sack him, which only compounded the family's problems. Their increasingly precarious financial situation gave Ursula a renewed sense of urgency in pursuing her wish to return to Germany, so she applied once again for a visa.

It took until the following year, in January 1950, that she at last received a response from Moscow. Once more, as on many previous occasions, she cycled to the dead letter box under the designated tree near the railway cutting and this time found a letter. It gave her permission to make her way to Berlin. Only after she had returned to

Berlin later did she learn that her Soviet contact in Britain had confused the hiding place, which explained why she had not received their messages nor they hers. This had led Moscow to break off contact. Money and instructions had been deposited in a dead letter box but had not been collected by Ursula because it was hidden under the wrong tree. Her Soviet contact hadn't taken into account a crossroad when counting the trees. Only after they had received her letter from Prague did they realise what had gone wrong. This episode is also corroborated in the KGB's own files:

> 'S' put out the last signal, indicating that 'all was well', in September 1949. We provide S. with mater. assistance without personal contact through a dead letter drop (the money is paid twice a year). For reasons unknown, in August 1949 S. did not remove the money from the dead drop in the agreed upon period of time, and we took the money back. In Sept. 1947, two counterintelligence agents came to see S., told her that they knew about her work for S. intelligence in Switzerland and asked her to tell them about this work. However, S. denied everything and did not give any evidence.[9]

Preparations for the journey back to Germany began immediately: she buried her Party membership card, and the transmitter, which is probably still today rusting away somewhere in the Oxfordshire countryside. They decided that to begin with she would travel without Len, but take the two youngest children with her. It was another enormous uprooting for them as they had become quite settled in their retreat in the tranquil Oxford countryside. Six-year-old Peter 'had become attached to Mrs. Thomas, the vicar's wife, who ran his little school in Chipping Norton, as well as to his teacher, Mrs. Willets', Ursula wrote in her memoirs.

While her plans were going ahead quite smoothly, something then happened to give them added urgency. In February 1950 she and Len read the sensational news in the morning papers that Klaus Fuchs had been arrested. They could not know then what the British or US security services knew about his work and about his contacts or what, if anything, Fuchs had told them, but they could not take the risk of waiting to find out. When they also read reports in the papers that

Fuchs had 'been meeting a foreign woman with black hair in Banbury', Ursula expected her arrest any day. She had to leave immediately, and managed to do so only one day before the trial of Fuchs began on the 27th of that month, flying with the two children via Hamburg to West Berlin. The USA was furious about what it saw, once again, as MI5 incompetence in the whole affair. But was it incompetence or was she indeed being shielded by someone high up in MI5's organisation? That remains one of the imponderables concerning her case. In her autobiography, *Sonya's Report*, she denies having any contact with anyone at MI5 and certainly, she says, had no idea whether or not she was being protected or if she just had a lucky escape.

Although she intended to leave for good, she applied for a permit simply to visit friends abroad, and her application was stamped 'No Objection' by the Home Office. However, as the German refugee specialist, Charmian Brinson, pointed out, 'Strangely, despite the presence of this permit in Ursula's file, MI5 appear to have been the last to know of her departure from Britain – even in May 1950, they were still debating whether to re-interrogate her.'[10]

Burke, in his book on the Lawn Road Flats, writes that Ursula and Jürgen were 'allowed to escape and slip across the border to East Berlin'. The term 'escape', though, is hardly applicable here. They both travelled openly by regular transport back to Germany and no attempt was made to hinder either of them in any way. In any case, back in Germany, Jürgen, to begin with, settled in the US sector of Berlin, so was easily accessible to the intelligence agencies if they had wished to contact him. After moving to the Eastern sector later, he continued to maintain links with friends in West Berlin.[11] Ursula, arriving much later, did settle immediately in the East.

After Fuchs' trial in 1950 the world's press attempted to find explanations for his 'betrayal'. According to various versions, he was schizophrenic or he had been on the point of ending his association with the Soviet Union, and similar fabulations. Ursula found all these allegations implausible. Klaus Fuchs had been a committed communist and his main aim had been to assist the fight to defeat fascism and if passing on atomic know-how to the Soviet Union helped in that struggle, then he was prepared to do so. With the final defeat of Hitler Germany and the prospect of a world living in peace he, like several other scientists who had worked on the bomb, was horrified at its use on Hiroshima and Nagasaki in the final days of the war in the Far East. He was also perturbed by the new aggressive stance taken by the United States towards the Soviet Union. He felt that by sharing the atomic know-how with the Soviet Union, at least a balance would be achieved which would help prevent the bomb being used again.

Already by mid-1945, the ideological constellation of forces in Europe had been shifting profoundly. While acting as film advisor to Britain's Ministry of Information, Sidney Bernstein was collaborating with Alfred Hitchcock on producing a documentary about Nazi atrocities intended to be shown in Germany. However, with the Soviet Union now seen once again by the West as the enemy, Germany had to be wooed to join the emerging anti-Soviet bloc. In this atmosphere, it was felt that showing such films would jeopardise this aim. By July, the Americans had already withdrawn their support and pressure was exerted by the British government on the makers to discontinue the project. The post-war battle for German hearts and minds was now crucial in what were the early stages of the Cold War.

By late 1945, the Nuremberg war crime trials had begun. Lawyers and advisors from the Soviet Union, France, the United Kingdom and the USA were working together to ensure that leading Nazis were dealt with appropriately. At the same time, Western leaders were already moving to isolate the Soviet Union and project it as the new enemy. Churchill began making overtures to the USA about setting up a new military alliance to confront the Soviet Union. The past was already in the process of being forgotten and future hostilities planned for. The fact that the Soviet Union had lost 20 million of its people as a result of the war and faced rebuilding a country largely laid waste by the Nazis did not appear to figure in Western thinking. The survivors in the Soviet Union were sick of war and the country was hardly in a position to even envisage waging another one in the short term, even if the leadership had desired it.

Notes

1 CIA Library – 'The OSS and the London "Free Germans"', in Jonathan S. Gould, *Strange Bedfellows*.

2 Charmian Brinson, '"Very Much a Family Affair": The Kuczynski Family and British Intelligence', in *Voices from Exile: Essays in Memory of Hamish Ritchie*, ed. Ian Wallace, Leiden/Boston MA, Brill Rodolpi, 2015, p. 9.
3 *Freunde und Gute Bekannte: Gespräche mit Thomas Grimm*, Schwarzkopf & Schwarzkopf, 1997; and https://www.cia.gov/library/center-for-the-study-of-intelligence/csi-publications/csi-studies/studies/vol46no1/article03.html.
4 John Kenneth Galbraith, *A Life in Our Times*, Andre Deutsch, 1981.
5 Ibid., pp. 222–223.
6 Alexander Vassiliev, *Yellow Notebook #1*, Washington DC, The Wilson Center Digital Archive, 2009, p. 128 (p. 86 in online document).
7 MI5 files, 15 September 1947, The National Archives KV2/1568 111b, marked secret. In his report, J. S. Skardon writes that 'She preserved a Slav-like indifference to the kind of arguments he used' (i.e. that non-co-operation could have repercussions on her family).
8 Brinson, '"Very Much a Family Affair"', p. 12.
9 Vassiliev, *Yellow Notebook #1*.
10 Brinson, '"Very Much a Family Affair"'.
11 Ibid., p. 159.

10

BACK IN GERMANY AT LAST

In November 1945 Jürgen had finally been allowed to travel back to Berlin, 'for good and without interruption, to help with the rebuilding. Life and the Party had well prepared him, and as a social scientist he was fully matured … to become a lecturer and director of a research institution', he wrote.

He had been allowed to leave Britain for Germany despite official British determination to keep 'potentially disruptive' German political exiles in Britain, at least until 1946. Even strong protests from, among others, Lord Vansittart, a former Foreign Office minister, arguing that he should not be allowed to leave Britain, failed to hinder his return.[1] British secret services also wanted to keep him in the UK so that they could maintain tabs on him; the last thing they wanted was a very capable academic and communist leaving to help the Soviets in post-war Germany.

Jürgen's and Ursula's dreams of building a new and democratic post-war Germany on the ashes of the old were immediately confronted by the sobering realities. Not only was East Germany in ruins after the bitter resistance the Nazis had mounted to the Soviet advance, but the onset of the Cold War and, after 1949, a divided Germany meant that a new source of tension in Europe emerged seamlessly from the old.

Where former leading Nazis were relentlessly weeded out in the East, in the West many soon had their old jobs back and were more than prepared to take revenge on the 'communist' victors.

Beneath the level of big power confrontation, life for ordinary citizens was a continuous struggle for survival in those early years. In Germany as a whole there were many shortages, but in the East the situation was much harsher; shortages of food, housing, energy and basic material goods were the norm. As leading anti-fascists, both Ursula and Jürgen were given priority in terms of housing and secure jobs, but even for them life was no rose garden.

Berlin in the immediate aftermath of the war was hardly a tranquil or relaxing haven, as much of the city still lay in ruins and the infrastructure was ramshackle, but its inhabitants tried to make the best of it and set about rebuilding their lives. All that the Soviet Union had gone through – the devastation, misery and hunger – and the revelations about the concentration camp horrors, made it very difficult for those like Ursula and Jürgen to observe with equanimity how so many of its citizens appeared to be unaware of, or indifferent about, what their country had inflicted on Europe. To see young people in Berlin, particularly young men, promenading among the ruins seeking pleasure was an affront to their sensibilities. As Ursula's friend and colleague Markus Wolf put it:

> it was as if they hadn't understood what they and their country had done to the world. There was no sense of guilt. One was cautious, suspicious of everyone who hadn't been in the resistance movement, not knowing their recent history.[2]

But at the time those like Ursula, Len, Jürgen and their fellow anti-fascists were making strenuous efforts to analyse the roots of Nazism and trying to ensure it could never happen again. They were very aware that these same people had to be won over, educated and rehabilitated if a new and better society were to arise from the ruins.

On his return to Germany, Jürgen had initially hoped to be made the first Minister for Economics in the Soviet Occupied Zone, but was not given the job. Instead, he was appointed President of the *Zentralverwaltung für Finanzen* (Central Administration of Finances). In 1946 he was also appointed Director of the *Institut für Wirtschaftsgeschichte* (Institute of Economic History) at Berlin's Humboldt University, where he would remain until 1956.

To begin with he settled in the American sector, moving into the house of his old friend Hans Gaffron, who had emigrated to the USA. The house, in Zehlendorf, was not far from his own pre-war residence, but that had been too badly damaged by bombing to be occupied. It was not until March 1947 that he would be joined by Marguerite and the children in Gaffron's house. Madeleine, then 15 years old, and in London still at school, was very upset about having to leave and had no desire to return to Germany. Shortly after Marguerite and the children had arrived, they were all able to move back into their pre-war house which had by then been restored, and they would live there until 1950.

During these early years back in Germany Marguerite was largely preoccupied with looking after the children and organising home life in the difficult post-war circumstances, while Jürgen worked at the university in East Berlin. However, she did remain politically active. At this time Peter was 10 years old and Thomas was 3. When Madeleine, on her sixteenth birthday, joined the SED, her mother had become the party secretary of her local branch.

The creation of the German Democratic Republic (1945–1949)

The Soviet Occupied Zone of Germany to which Jürgen would eventually return was a place of devastation, tension and uncertainty. It would, in 1949, become the German Democratic Republic. In 1950 Ursula left Britain in a hurry and would settle in this new state. The challenges for individuals who had spent the years of the war in exile would be enormous.

Within weeks of the end of the war, the Soviet occupation forces had encouraged the re-establishment of trade unions, cultural organisations and political parties in their zone of occupation. Already by July 1945 a *Kulturbund* (Cultural League for Democratic renewal in Germany) was set up in the Soviet sector to assist with the reopening of theatres, music venues and cinemas in order to promote Germany's democratic cultural legacy as an antidote to Hitler's fascist de-culturalisation and xenophobia. It took another three months before the formation of political parties and trade unions were permitted in the US sector, which also actively hindered the setting up of cultural organisations, fearing that they would rapidly become dominated by communists and leftist forces.

Hitler's former chief security officer on the Eastern Front, Major General Reinhard Gehlen, was recruited in 1946 by the USA largely because of his detailed knowledge of the Soviet Union and of communist organisation. Gehlen offered the USA his intelligence archives and his network of contacts in return for his freedom and that of his colleagues. He went on to head West Germany's intelligence organisation, the BND, until 1968. The BND had a clear anti-communist focus right from the start, and the organisation was populated by many former Nazis. In response the Soviet Union felt obliged to set up its own security organisation in East Germany, which morphed into the GDR's Ministry of State Security in 1950.

The Western occupying powers had mooted the idea of a separate West German state already in 1948 when they introduced a new currency in the Western sectors. This became a reality a year later, with the establishment of a de facto West German state in May of that same year, when a new constitution was inaugurated. The establishment of the GDR was announced on 7 October 1949, four months after the setting up of the FRG. But even after its establishment, there still remained a leaky border with the Federal Republic, particularly through the 'open' city of Berlin, which provided ample opportunity for spies to operate and acts of sabotage to be carried out. Until the Wall was built in 1961, the divided city was a powder keg waiting to explode. US tanks faced Soviet ones across the open border and armed guards tensely faced each other only metres apart.

A separate state in the East came about almost as a historical accident. The Soviet zone of occupation was, in terms of area, only a third of German territory, and it was this third that eventually became the GDR. The Soviet Union saw the creation of this separate state as a temporary measure, with eventual reunification still the logical outcome of a post-war settlement. It actually put forward proposals for reunification in 1952, but these were peremptorily rejected by the West German Chancellor Konrad Adenauer.

As soon as it was created, the GDR faced an implacable enemy in the form of the Federal Republic, which, in its founding constitution, claimed to represent all Germans and was determined, with US support, to eliminate the East German state as soon as possible, but in the meantime to make its continued survival as difficult as possible. It refused to recognise GDR sovereignty in any area, nor did it recognise GDR citizenship or travel documents. On the other hand, the young GDR was firmly under the control and domination of its big brother to the east, the Soviet Union, and had its hands largely tied. Until Stalin died in 1953, a quasi-dictatorial control was imposed by the Soviet Union on the GDR.

Many of the leaders of the post-war East German, later GDR, government had a track record of active opposition to the Nazi regime; many had spent years in concentration camps, prison and exile, either in the Soviet Union or in Western countries like France, Britain, Mexico or the USA, and a number of them were Jewish. They were idealists, full of hope, determined to build a democratic, anti-fascist Germany – that was the intention at least, and even if those goals were not achieved, fascism would be eradicated and an attempt made, under the most inauspicious circumstances, to build an alternative society to that which had led inexorably to the emergence of fascism.

The workers' and socialist movements within Germany had been effectively destroyed by Hitler and many of the leaders had been murdered in concentration camps, and as a result there was a limited number of experienced cadres. The inclusion of prominent figures from Jewish backgrounds in the first and subsequent East German governments and in leading positions of the state undermines the more recent accusations that the GDR was anti-semitic. In West Germany there were no Jews in top government positions and few who had actively opposed the Nazis.

There are a whole number of reasons why East Germany began life at a great disadvantage when compared with West Germany. In 1945 when the Soviet Army arrived, the German population was still infected by a visceral hatred and fear of the 'Bolshevik beast' – represented in Nazi posters, films and articles as an uncultured Asiatic horde, whereas there was little hatred for the USA, Britain or France, despite their also belonging to the former enemy. There was certainly no racial animosity towards the Western allies either, as they 'belonged to the Aryan race, unlike the Slavs in the East'. So when the Russians occupied the eastern third of Germany, many citizens had already fled westwards, but even those who remained were still imbued with fear and often hatred. Before one could begin to build a new Germany, those attitudes had to be neutralised and overcome – an almost insurmountable task. When the Soviet Zone of Occupation became the GDR and proclaimed its aim as the building of socialism, its enemies predicted it would only survive a few months before collapsing, and did everything they could to assist that process. Throughout its existence the GDR found itself in a permanent state of siege and subject to an economic war not unlike that endured in more recent times by Cuba.

The East was also considerably poorer than its much larger Western counterpart, having little heavy industry and few mineral resources apart from lignite, potash and uranium, so was reliant on imports. Without raw materials the establishment of a manufacturing industry and economic development was impossible. And at the end of the war it was a territory in ruins. Cities and villages had been devastated even more during the last-ditch efforts by the Nazis to halt the advance of the Red Army; tens of thousands were homeless with little available housing and, in addition, the authorities had to cope with the thousands of refugees from the territories further east which had since come under Polish or Czech jurisdiction. Most factories had also been bombed and badly damaged.

The country was unable to offer the more comfortable life and material goods that West Germany could, helped by a large influx of US Marshall Aid. But an authoritarian government with its hands tied by the Soviet Union also militated against the creation of free and democratic social structures in the East. With its open border in Berlin up until 1961, GDR citizens could leave whenever they wished and many did, leading to a serious labour and brain-drain and compounding an already difficult situation.

The Soviet Union, in the early years, not only invested little in the economy of its zone, it actually removed significant sections of the remaining enterprises and infrastructure as reparation for the devastation caused by the Nazis in the Soviet Union.[3]

In 1949 Jürgen was elected as a member of the *Volkskammer* (the GDR's parliament) and would remain one until 1958. Members of parliament were elected from the officially recognised political parties as well as from the so-called 'mass social organisations' like the German–Soviet Friendship Society (DFS), which elected Jürgen. Alongside these political responsibilities, he continued writing and publishing prodigiously, as well as lecturing. In 1949, the *Deutsche Wirtschaftsinstitut* (German Economic Institute) was founded in East Berlin and out of this emerged the *Institut für Internationale Politik und Wirtschaft* (Institute of International Politics and Economics), and Jürgen became its first director. The institute was structured very much as he wanted it.

As a member of parliament, representing Rostock, he was in that city on the fateful day in May 1950, when Marguerite was sitting at her desk alone in the Berlin house when a stone came crashing through the window. Luckily no one was injured, but it reminded them of the pre-war period. From that moment on, the family no longer felt safe and decided to move to East Berlin. Their move had to take place in secret as, under Allied regulations, such moves required prior official sanction. They transported their belongings by horse-drawn cart, which took several days. By moving to the East, Jürgen lost the right to visit West Berlin at any future date.

It would be in the East where both Jürgen and, later, Ursula with their families chose to settle permanently and continue the struggle to fulfil their dreams. Jürgen had been obliged to renounce his British citizenship already in 1947, the year his father died, as neither German state at the time recognised dual citizenship. In 1950 the family moved to the suburb of Weissensee in East Berlin, where they would live for the rest of their lives.

Already well known as an outstanding political economist and statistician before he returned to Germany after the end of the War, he would go on to play a prominent role in the GDR as political activist, academic, researcher, writer and lecturer. He would devote himself to economic theory and the promotion of communism and the ideas of Marx, Engels, Lenin (and, until Krushchev's revelations, Stalin). He would always remain a loyal, if critical supporter of the GDR (as he put it himself, *'ein linientreuer Dissident'* – a loyal dissident). He would outlive the state to which he had devoted so much of his life and remain an optimistic socialist to the end, despite all the setbacks. In that he was not very different from his friend Bertolt Brecht.

In June 1947 he was invited to a meeting with Sergei Ivanovitch Tulpanov (then a colonel and later general) of the Soviet occupation forces. Tulpanov asked Jürgen to become Chair of the newly founded *Gesellschaft zum Studium der Kultur der Sowjetunion* (Society for the Study of the Culture of the Soviet Union), which was the forerunner of the *Gesellschaft für Deutsch–Sowjetische Freundschaft* or DSF (Society for German–Soviet Friendship). This society's role was very important in helping to overcome hatred and animosity in the country towards the Soviet Union. Jürgen was initially reluctant to take on this role for various reasons but, in the end, it became clear that this was almost like an order and he agreed to do it. He threw himself wholeheartedly into the work – not easy with the still prevalent anti-Russian feelings in Germany and widespread mistrust of the 'Big Bear'.

Within five years, since the end of the war and under his presidency, the German–Soviet Friendship Association had carried out a great deal of effective educational work. Numerous lectures were given, cultural events organised and the society grew to around 1 million members. He was justly proud of these achievements, but then, in 1953, came a big shock. Already, 'By 1948, in the Soviet Union under Stalin and Beria anti-semitism had grown rapidly and there was a terrible persecution of Jews', he noted in his memoirs. Vladimir Semyonov, the Soviet ambassador to the GDR, followed the line. 'Both my friend Hans Mark, who had been among those storming the Winter Palace in St. Petersburg [in 1917] and was general secretary of the Association, and I were forced to resign because of our "Jewish lineage"', he wrote. 'I have never seen Wilhelm Pieck and Walter Ulbricht – both of whom were far from being anti-Semitic – so embarrassed as when they gave me the news of my dismissal', he continued. 'The real reason for it was told me later by Tulpanov.' But Semyonov, he said, 'was not satisfied with my sacking alone, but wanted to have me, politically at least, dead'. Semyonov had asked the management committee of the Association to find suitable material that could be used as evidence against him, but nothing was forthcoming. Jürgen says in his memoir[4] that the German Party had been relatively spared the extremes of Stalinism, but it still tended to be sectarian and was obliged to follow the Soviet line to the letter. What he does not relate was how close he must have come to end up as another of Stalin's victims.[5]

The trial of Laszlo Raik in Hungary in 1949, then that of Rudolf Slánský, General Secretary of the KSČ, and others in Czechoslovakia in 1952, were followed by purges in the Soviet Union itself. Tensions, fears and suspicions were running rife throughout Eastern Europe and the GDR was not spared. It also came under increasing pressure from Stalinist forces in the Soviet Union to carry out its own purge. It was the height of the Cold War and Stalin's paranoia had reached fever pitch. Anyone who could be associated with the West, and that included all those refugees from Hitler fascism who had not chosen exile in the Soviet Union, was suspected of being a Western agent. The purges were associated with an insidious strand of anti-semitism, always just beneath the surface in the countries of Eastern Europe, but often masked as anti-Zionism.[6]

But it is a tribute to the GDR's Party leaders that they refused to go down the road of the other Eastern Bloc countries and stage witch-hunts and show trials against loyal party members, even though the pressure from the Soviet Union to do so was intense. This pressure was eased a short time later by the death of Stalin on 5 March 1953 and the removal of his henchman Beria.

In the SED archives opened up after reunification, historian Matthew Stibbe discovered interesting material about Jürgen Kuczynski and the impact of Soviet-imposed measures to remove Jews, particularly those who had been in Western exile during the war, from important positions within government and state organs. Stibbe found that Jürgen had been questioned intensively at this time by the GDR's Central Party Control Commission (ZPKK). He had been denounced by one of his former comrades in British exile, Wilhelm Koenen. Stibbe writes:

> In January 1953 two important letters were sent regarding the wartime activities of the East German communist Jürgen Kuczynski, who had been a leading figure in the London group of the Communist Party of Germany (KPD) (also known as the 'English emigration') from 1936 to 1944. The first, dated 13 January 1953, was written by Wilhelm Koenen, himself a veteran KPD member and fellow London exile with Kuczynski, and was addressed to Hermann Matern, Politburo member and chairman of the Central Party Control Commission. In it Koenen denounced Kuczynski as

an imperialist agent who had worked in London for the American military and for the 'Jewish-Trotskyist' newspaper *Left News*, owned by the 'anti-Soviet propagandist' Victor Gollancz. The second, dated 23 January, was from a senior figure in the Security Service (MI5) in London to his counterpart in the Secret Intelligence Service (MI6) in West Berlin. As the recipient was informed, the British security services believed that the East German regime was about to embark on a major purge of Jewish communists, some of whom might be tempted to defect. The individuals of greatest interest were Kuczynski himself, his sister Ursula, also known as Ruth Werner or 'Sonya', her husband Leon Beurton, and another former member of the KPD in Britain, Johanna Klopstech. All four had been involved in Soviet military espionage during the war and were associated in particular with the famous atom spy Klaus Fuchs, who had been arrested in London in February 1950.[7]

However, Jürgen makes no mention of this in his own memoirs. He undoubtedly found the episode an embarrassing one, not only for himself but for the Party too and preferred to omit it.

In those memoirs, Jürgen acknowledged that he had taken up a position with the United States Bombing Survey, but with the agreement of the Soviets, and had worked closely with OSS, the forerunner of the CIA. But, he says, 'because I understood nothing about military matters, I was unable to pass on any information about the United States armed forces, but could pass on very useful material to Moscow about the German war economy'. Alexander ('Jim') Foote had also confirmed Jürgen's regular contacts with the Soviet embassy in London to MI5. According to him Jürgen had written economic reports for the Soviet Union which he took personally to the embassy and had, apparently, never been followed or stopped.[8]

June 1950 also saw the outbreak of the Korean War, which not only heightened tensions even more between the Soviet Union and the USA, but also, before it ended in 1953, threatened to escalate into an all-out nuclear war. It was not a time conducive to tolerance, understanding or optimism. The war's repercussions were felt particularly in Berlin, where the superpowers confronted each other daily across an open border.

In 1950, as part of his battle against the GDR and communist influence, West German Chancellor Konrad Adenauer banned all communists from public service, and in 1956 outlawed the Communist Party of Germany (KPD), the Free German Youth organisation (FDJ), the Federation of Victims of Fascism (VVN) and the German–Soviet Friendship Society (DSFS), while at the same time protecting and reinstating former Nazis.

The new GDR state, as well as the policies it pursued, were determined by a special combination of circumstances. First, throughout its existence, its policies could not be separated from those of its 'protector' the USSR; and second, the fact that it was geographically situated on the front line of the Cold War.

In June 1953 there was a popular uprising in East Berlin, in response to the government's arbitrarily imposed new productivity norms for industrial workers. It was suppressed only with the help of Soviet tanks. This was an early warning sign that top-down decision-making was not the best way of winning over a still sceptical population. Partially in response to this unrest, the Soviet Union began to return the East German factories it had taken in reparations and to provide vital economic support, not least in the form of cheap raw materials, including oil. It was realised that the goodwill of the people had to be won if the GDR were to be successful.

It was a country of only 16 million people, but in time it became a developed, industrialised nation that was virtually self-sufficient. In industry alone, 3 million were employed, almost a third of those in the machine tool sector. In addition there were precision engineering, shipbuilding, chemical and electrical engineering sectors, to name just the largest. On the world market the GDR was recognised as a leading industrial nation (for example the name Carl Zeiss of Jena was world renowned) and, above all, it was known for its exports of machinery and tool-making equipment, printing presses, furniture, and musical instruments such as the highly regarded Blüthner pianos. By 1988 it was exporting 39 per cent of its total industrial output; most of this (69 per cent) went to Eastern Europe, but a not insignificant amount to Western countries.[9]

East Germany's economy became one of the most successful and most stable of the socialist bloc. In 1987 the UN published a development programme in which it listed the per capita GDP of the world's leading 130 states, according to which 110 of those states had a lower GDP than the GDR. The country had become one of the world's twenty leading industrialised countries.

As we know, however, despite these genuine achievements, there was a serious deficit in terms of political and individual freedoms. An oppressive security apparatus, increasing frustration and dissatisfaction, particularly during the 1980s, led to a large exodus of young people, and eventually came mass demonstrations on the streets which would bring about the fall of the government.

Notes

1 Charmian Brinson, '"Very Much a Family Affair": The Kuczynski Family and British Intelligence', in *Voices from Exile: Essays in Memory of Hamish Ritchie*, ed. Ian Wallace, Leiden/Boston MA, Brill Rodolpi, 2015.
2 Markus Wolf, *In eigenem Auftrag*, Schneekluth, 1991, p. 278.
3 Bruni de la Motte and John Green, *Stasi State or Socialist Paradise*, Artery Publications, 2015.
4 Jürgen Kuczynski, *Ein Linientreue Dissident* (memoirs 1945–1989), p. 41.
5 Matthew Stibbe, 'Jürgen Kuczynski and the Search for a (Non-Existent) Western Spy Ring in the East German Communist Party in 1953', *Contemporary European History*, vol. 20, no. 1 (January 2011), pp. 61–79.
6 Ibid.
7 Ibid.
8 MI5 files, The National Archives, 11 March 1950, KV2/1879, 521b.
9 Ibid.

11

URSULA'S RETURN TO THE GERMAN DEMOCRATIC REPUBLIC (1950)

Ursula, in her memoirs, relates that after her return to Germany she was keen to rejoin the German Communist Party (which had, in 1946, become the Socialist Unity Party after amalgamation of the East German sections of the Social Democratic and Communist Parties in the Soviet Occupied Zone). However, as she was nominally still a serving officer in the Soviet military she couldn't do this without Moscow's permission. As anyone with knowledge of the intelligence world will know, agents anywhere cannot simply take independent action without informing their employer. When she eventually met a Soviet contact in Berlin, she told him that after twenty years working for Soviet intelligence she had had enough: her 'nerves and powers of concentration were no longer what they used to be' and she would prefer to bow out of intelligence work. Moscow agreed to her request.

Her new life in what began as the Soviet sector of war-ravaged Germany, now the separate state of the GDR, could not have been more different from the pastoral atmosphere of Great Rollright. In the summer of 1950 she began her first 'normal' job in many years, in Berlin, as section head in the GDR government's Office of Information. She was made editor-in-chief of its fortnightly publication, the *Bulletin against American Imperialism*, and later was responsible for daily government press releases.

Her son Peter, then six and a half years old, began a new school and had to learn a new language. His first words in German to his mother on returning home from school one day were, 'Hello, you old sow'. His new schoolmates had clearly taken advantage of his lack of German to teach him a few earthy Berlin expressions. He was not at all happy at leaving his school, his friends and Oxfordshire village life behind him. Before Ursula and the two children left for Germany, for security reasons, she told them that they were only going for a short holiday. It was a deep shock for him to belatedly realise the move was for good, and he became quite homesick. Apart from realising he and the family would not be returning, he had been forced to leave his beloved cat 'Penny' behind, as well as his Dinky cars and his 'Smarties'. He found learning German difficult – possibly his inner reluctance to leave his Englishness behind played a role here – but, as children invariably do, he soon settled down to his new routine. Even so, when he reached 13 years of age, he said that the realisation came to him that 'I had now lived longer in Germany than in England and that saddened me deeply'.[1] Before arriving in Berlin he only knew vaguely that his mother had a German background, nothing more. At home they had always spoken English.

Nina at fourteen found it somewhat easier to adapt and 'soon forgot her collection of photographs of the British Royal family and became a keen member of the Free German Youth'. After completing his degree in Aberdeen, Ursula's oldest son Michael would follow her to the GDR in 1951. He had, for a short time, deliberated whether to go to Israel and work on a Kibbutz, but in the end decided, completely independently, to settle, at least for a time, in the GDR.

In the meantime, Moscow had also agreed that Len could emigrate to the GDR. He joined Ursula that same year, only a few weeks after receiving the green light and soon found work with the GDR's ADN news agency. So the family was again reunited and enjoyed a regular income. From this point on Ursula and Len did indeed cease working for the Soviet Union and had no further contact with GRU headquarters.

Returning to the country of her birth, but one devastated by the war and a population that had been steeped in Nazi ideology for a decade and a half, was not easy. Life was austere, but Ursula felt up to the

FIGURE 11.1 Janina, Peter, Ursula and Michael, shortly after their return to the GDR

Source: Peter Beurton.

struggle. In a letter to her sisters in Britain in the spring of 1950 she wrote cautiously: 'My daily life here is of course quite different from the beautiful but insulated little world of Great Rollright. I am drinking it all in – theatres, cinemas, problems, progress, the negative and the positive people ...'

Like so many of her comrades, though, she very soon had run-ins with the controlling Party apparatus over minor political issues. The year 1953 saw an uprising of GDR workers against newly imposed productivity demands and increased work norms. In that same year Ursula began having her own difficulties with the new director of her department, and when she once forgot to lock a safe, she was accused of 'insufficient vigilance' (even though no confidential papers or other valuable items were held in it) and was told she should resign. She was also accused of 'petty bourgeois tendencies' – a favoured accusation against those who were deemed to be trouble-makers. She was discharged from her job, but immediately found another with the Chamber of Foreign Trade. There she became head of the press section and began writing topical pamphlets which elicited favourable and encouraging responses from those who read them. She enjoyed writing and felt she had found her true niche, and so in 1956 gave up full-time work in order to pursue her long-held ambition to write as her main occupation. In this work she found refuge from the petty conflicts and frustrations, both personal and ideological, of working in large organisations. She went on to publish a series of novels for children, several non-fiction books and an excellent biography of Olga Benário, who had been born into an upper middle-class Bavarian family but became a revolutionary. Ursula's life became divided between writing and giving talks, readings and addressing meetings up and down the country about the anti-fascist struggle.

Renate's daughter, Ann, told me that on visiting Ursula many years later, after German reunification, how depressed she became on seeing young neo-Nazis on the streets of East German cities. Had the efforts of Ursula and all those other anti-fascists, attempting to re-educate the German people and warn the new generation, been in vain, she asked herself.

Ernst: a ghost from the past

Ursula's daughter Janina was born in Poland as a result of Ursula's short affair with her fellow agent 'Ernst' (real name Johannes Patra). Janina had never met or known of him and had assumed Rolf (Rudolf) Hamburger to be her real father. Ursula did not know what had happened since she had last heard from Patra when he was still in China. He had remained there after she left in 1935 and, during the war, they were not able to communicate, given the nature of their secret work.

But while still in Britain, in 1946 she had received a letter from him saying that he was in a bad way and he requested her help in his quest to return to Germany. A German emigrant organisation in China needed confirmation that Patra had indeed been forced to flee Nazi Germany. She was able to provide the evidence he needed, and used Marguerite's address to write to the German émigré organisation on his behalf. His doctor, he told her, had calculated that he had survived the previous 30 months on only 400 calories a day; he was merely skin and bone and only just about alive. Since that time, she had heard nothing more from him.

Then, out of the blue, he contacted her again. It transpired that, despite her help, he had been denied a visa and so had emigrated to Argentina instead. Now, in 1955, twenty years since they had last seen each other, he wrote once more and told her that he was keen to meet up. When they did so, in Berlin, she was horrified by the state of his health and of his nerves. He told her that after Rolf's arrest in China, his own contact with the Soviet Union had broken down, but he could find no work in China, and after the country's liberation in 1949 all foreigners were ordered to leave the country. In Argentina he had earned his bread and butter as a mechanic and had even married an Argentinian woman. He now felt he could perhaps settle and work in the GDR, he told her, and bring his wife over later. But in their conversation Ursula and Len both realised that he was a very intransigent character, and had also become a devoted follower of Mao Tse-tung and the Chinese political line (at that time the Soviet Union and China were at ideological loggerheads and the GDR followed the Soviet line). Given his political stance and stubbornness, it would hardly have been possible for him to settle in the GDR without encountering serious problems, so they discouraged him. In the end he decided to return and work for the revolution in Latin America, saying that one could not expect anything from the European working class and even the GDR was petit-bourgeois. Since then nothing more was heard from him. He became just one more on a long list of tragic victims of the political battles of that period.

Note

1 Personal conversation between the author and Peter Beurton, 8 May 2016.

12

LIFE FOR JÜRGEN AND MARGUERITE IN THE GDR

Jürgen had always been the most active of the siblings in the political as well as the academic field, and he maintained that activity after settling in the GDR. For most of his life there he was the Director of the Institute for Economic History in Berlin and ran it much as he wished with little interference from above; it enjoyed virtual autonomy among the GDR's academic institutes. As Director, he became an outstanding example of original and courageous thinking for several generations of students. His main purpose when working with doctoral students, he said, was to encourage their learning how to think. He would famously ask each of his new students to bring him a brief outline of their proposed doctoral thesis. After reading the outline he then told them: 'Alright, now I can see that you can think', before proceeding to screw up the paper and throw it in the bin, telling the student to now forget it and go off to carry out the necessary research to test the validity of their ideas.

The 20th Soviet Communist Party Congress in 1956 represented a radical change of weather in the communist world, and appeared to offer an opening for neo-Marxist thinking. Jürgen immediately grasped the opportunity to challenge some of the Stalinist dogmas. He argued for an opening-up of the GDR's own historical research vis-à-vis bourgeois-humanistic ideas, and called for a broader inclusion from the historical legacy, even of those who were 'anti-working class'. In the following year he published several articles and a book, *Der Ausbruch des Ersten Weltkrieges und die deutsche Sozialdemokratie* (The Outbreak of the First World War and German Social Democracy). He also published an essay in the Moscow journal *Voprosy filosofii* with the title 'Sociological Laws', in which he attempted to rescue sociology from its imposed quarantine and argued that there were specific sociological-historical laws that are relatively independent from the general historical laws of historical materialism. Although both Lenin and Bucharin had used the term sociology, the subject had been seen by the Soviet Union from the 1930s onwards as a bourgeois pseudo-science. This attitude had also been adopted by the other East European states after the war, and it was some time before the subject became accepted. However, Jürgen's article did eventually stimulate the belated development of sociology in the GDR and the taking of sociological questions seriously. For his efforts at the time, though, he earned severe censure by the Party leadership.

He had been, very early on, appreciated widely for his political-economic analysis of the approaching world economic crisis towards the end of the 1920s. By 1960 he had already published the first volume of his life-long project – *Geschichte der Lage der Arbeiter im Kapitalismus* (A History of Labour Conditions under Capitalism). In this and his other writings, though, he never concentrated solely on the economic situation of the working class, but included the whole social sphere and also considered the impact of international economic relations. As virtually no other academic did, he also investigated how economic phenomena were reflected in literature and art. In this connection he wrote a number of essays on literary and cultural history. By 1968, he had completed five volumes on the history of English, American and French literature (after long discussions with the relevant GDR authorities, only two were eventually published). In this respect he was very much a broad thinker, not a narrow specialist.

He fought vehemently at all levels in the GDR for the maintenance of academic standards and the promotion of genuinely creative thinking rather than the parroting of so-called Marxist principles. He was a man who loved contradictions and paradoxes, seeing them as a stimulus to

Jürgen Kuczynski

FIGURE 12.1 Caricature of Jürgen drawn by the GDR cartoonist Harald
  Kretzchsmar
Source: Neues Deutschland and Harald Kretzchsmar.

creative thought. But the Institute's relative autonomy and its atmosphere of independent and radical thought were not to the liking of many in the leadership of the Party. These forces later tried to use the alibi of proposed academic reforms in the GDR to remove the semi-autonomy of his institute and integrate it within the *Zentralinstitut für Geschichte* (Central Institute for Historical Research). He fought this strenuously and took the fight to Erich Honecker, General Secretary of the Party, managing to get the proposal rescinded. The Institute was thus saved and its unique intellectual atmosphere maintained until the end of the GDR in 1990. Jürgen's nephew Peter Beurton said that he very cleverly upheld a tight Party discipline at the Institute to avoid any accusations of fostering political dissidence.[1]

Jürgen was, though, not concerned simply with the fate of his own institute, but with the general standards of academic work and research in the country as a whole. Throughout his life he was preoccupied with the treatment of the humanities in the institutes of learning, and was strongly critical of the dominating influence of the state's ideological organs – press, television and journals – and their negative impact on original, independent thinking and the way they tended to discourage the raising of new and important questions. During the last decade of the GDR, he argued, perhaps rather sweepingly, that 'in general the scientific standards [in the GDR] were low and *that was because the striving for truth has atrophied*'. In other words, 'this striving for truth ... was a great scarcity in the intellectual sphere of our Republic' (emphasis in the original). Throughout his life Jürgen had always emphasised the importance of conflict and contradiction in debate and in the development of ideas. This, he felt, was fundamental to Marxism. The Party leadership, however, argued that under socialism there were no longer any contradictions, or at most minor ones.

In 1964 Jürgen was invited to act as a consultant for the Accessory Prosecutor at the first Frankfurt Auschwitz trial. This trial, nineteen years after the end of the war, came about largely as a result of the assiduous work carried out by the West German, Jewish-born jurist Fritz Bauer, who played a key role in getting the Frankfurt Auschwitz trials off the ground. He fought a battle of attrition to obtain justice and compensation for victims of the Nazi regime. He was also instrumental in the later capture and trial of Adolf Eichmann. Pressure by the GDR, on the basis of documentation it had collected on former top Nazis, and which it had made publicly available, also played a key role in the trial.

In his historical evaluation, Jürgen had analysed the 'interconnected-ness between the security apparatus and business interests during the building of the Auschwitz concentration camp', i.e. between I. G. Farben and the SS. He demonstrated that the I. G. Farben company, that had been operating in Auschwitz–Monowitz since 1941 and had built the largest artificial rubber and power plants in Europe, had helped the SS commandant's office financially and supplied it with building materials for the concentration camp. As a quid pro quo, the company had been allocated a contingent of prisoners from the camp for the factory's construction. His evaluation was not accepted at the time, with the argument that 'he was a paid professor from the Soviet zone of occu-pation' and operated within the 'guidelines of the communist SED', and therefore for the Federal Republic of Germany his methodology was suspect.

While he remained a member of the Party, he had continual run-ins with the powers that be, was severely criticised at various times by the Party leadership and was often close to despair over the narrow-mindedness and dogmatism he encountered. He, like his sister Ursula and many other intellectuals of that generation in the GDR, remained loyal and disciplined party members most of their lives, but they did so with gritted teeth. The daily confrontations with dogmatism, bureau-cracy and sometimes injustice tested their loyalties to the full. However, with all their criticisms and reservations about the GDR, the capitalist world was never seen as an alternative for them. Their frustration and anger only reached tipping point shortly before the final collapse of the GDR in 1989 when, with the flood of young people leaving the GDR and demonstrations beginning on the streets, they realised they had to speak out.

Jürgen's book, *Dialog mit meinem Urenkel* (Dialogue with My Great-Grandchild), completed in 1977, but only published in 1983, was one of the most controversial books published in the GDR and became extremely popular. In the form of invented questions from his great-grandson, the book questioned historical developments and the role played by 'the grandfather', i.e. Kuczynski himself. It included a critical assessment of certain aspects of the state and the Party in the GDR. As a consequence of the book's publication, he received yet another party disciplinary censure. There was much controversy in the Party leadership about whether to publish the book at all, but after Honecker's daughter read it and recommended it to her father, it was given the go-ahead. This book was followed by a sequel in 1996, *Fortgesetzter Dialog mit meinem Urenkel* (Continued Dialogue with My Great-Grandchild). Peter Beurton says of the first book:

> It functioned as a safety valve or that's the way it affected us younger GDR citizens. It was mildly critical of the GDR leadership and polemical, but it was only published in the eighties when the GDR was already in its end phase.

For some in the GDR he had been seen as a source of hope for change, and functioned as the country's confessor, receiving numerous letters requesting help, advice and information; for others, though, he was someone who kept silent about so much injustice when he could have been more influential by speaking out.

Jürgen's love of crime novels and of cigars was legendary and he shared these indulgences with his friend Bertolt Brecht. He had been friends with Brecht and his wife Helene Weigel since 1929. The two of them developed a mutually beneficial barter when they were living in the same Berlin suburb of Weissensee during the 1950s. Brecht had the better connections when it came to procuring good cigars from Western sources and Jürgen for detective novels. 'And thus he would come twice a week, ring the doorbell, holding a cigar in one hand and a detective story he was returning in the other', Jürgen relates, 'I would give him a new book and he would give me the cigar'.[2] Jürgen consumed at least one book a week. That unique relationship ended with Brecht's death in 1956.

As a leading academic and close comrade of a number of government leaders, Jürgen enjoyed certain privileges. He was, for instance, allowed to import books from Western countries that were not accessible to ordinary GDR citizens. Such dispensations were given to a number of academics so that they could carry out their work more effectively. However, Jürgen used his dispensation to also obtain a number of his beloved crime novels. On one occasion he received a message from the GDR customs office to say that 'the following books sent from the USA have been impounded': *For Your Eyes Only, Diamonds are Forever, On Her Majesty's Secret Service*, all by Ian Fleming, and three others by different crime writers. When he wrote protesting, the customs '*Oberkommissar*' responded that 'according to the laws of the GDR only literature that in terms of its content does not contravene the interest of our socialist state and its citizens' is accorded dispensation. And, these books 'do not conform to that requirement'! That must have stymied him, as he could hardly argue that Ian Fleming was a pro-communist author or that James Bond's antics were in the interests of the GDR.[3]

While Jürgen did travel abroad, it was very difficult in the early years before the GDR was more widely recognised, to travel to Western countries. He and Marguerite were even denied entry visas to France in 1948 to attend the funeral of her mother. They were also denied entry to the USA. Even his son Thomas, who would fly to the USA in 1988 to attend a conference of historians, was only granted a visa after a representation to the State Department by a leading American academic, an hour and half before he was due to depart. The whole family was clearly still viewed with suspicion.

Jürgen was always one of those figures to whom Western academics and journalists particularly turned when they wished to have a commentary on what was happening in the GDR. They would beat a path to his door. He was not only one of the few leading individuals with fluent English and French, but he was prepared to speak off-the-cuff and not simply spout the Party line.

Once officially retired and as Professor Emeritus, Jürgen could, during the 1980s, behave with relative impunity as a 'maverick and happy Marxist' and was popular particularly among the younger generation of critical thinkers. His public lectures were always packed out and, as a consequence of his revolutionary credentials and old age, he enjoyed a sort of fool's freedom from Party control. After the demise of the GDR in 1990 he became very active as a journalist, writing for the left-wing daily papers *Neues Deutschland* and *Junge Welt* on world economic issues. Alongside Ursula, and Markus Wolf, he became an active member of the Elders' Council (modelled on the ancient Spartan *gerousia*, which provided an advisory function to city administrators) of the Party of Democratic Socialism (PDS – the successor party to the SED and later to become *Die Linke* – The Left Party).

He had always been a complex character, highly intelligent and innovative in his professional work and not subservient or easily cowed, yet he submitted willingly to the strict discipline of the Party, which he deemed necessary at the time. With the constant attacks on both the GDR and the SED by West Germany throughout the GDR's short life, any signs of disagreement or dissidence within the SED would have been, and indeed were, fully exploited by the West. This discouraged most Party members from expressing publicly any disagreements they may have had with the leadership.

Jürgen was, though, certainly in the earlier years, a very sociable and tolerant individual, mixing with a wide variety of people from all walks of life and disciplines; his erudition, dry sense of humour and charm endeared him to many. But he was also a vain man – very aware of his own worth and ability – and expected recognition, not in terms of material reward or honours, but in social status. But he was quite capable of mocking himself: he was fond of saying that he knew he was not in the premier league of political economists but he was one of the best in the second division.

He had always been a workaholic, and in the GDR during his life as an academic he would rise at 7 every morning. He liked to complete his own academic work before attending to his duties at the Institute. He lived to a strict routine and demanded peace and quiet when at work. His son Peter said of his father's dominant role in the family, 'truly he wasn't easy'. Family life revolved around the workplace sanctum. Thomas mentions that there was often incredible pressure on the family because of his father's unrelenting productivity.

He is not remembered for undertaking any physical activity with his children, although he would play a game of chess with them on some days. Jürgen worked in his sanctum every weekday until midday, even into his sunset years, and after lunch would receive visitors – friends and colleagues – or hold meetings. Weekends, though, were reserved for the family and there was a more relaxed atmosphere. The whole family would eat a meal together, cooked by Marguerite, followed invariably by a political debate. On Sunday afternoons the males in the household would often play a few rounds of Skat (a more complicated German version of whist) together. For relaxation, before going to bed punctually at 8.30 every evening, he would read detective novels, wreathed in cigar smoke.

He and Marguerite went to the theatre and concerts but not on a regular basis. Important galleries were visited as a matter of course when the two of them were in large cities, but Jürgen was not really interested in the visual arts and he hardly ever went to the cinema. Nevertheless, Thomas recalled one occasion when he took one of his grandchildren to watch the film *Der verkaufte Grossvater* (The Grandfather Who Was Sold). It was made in 1962 in West Germany, and is a comedy with a moral that he doubtlessly approved. It was based on a German folk comedy, written by Franz Streicher, and was often played in the theatre. A rich peasant learns that the grandfather of a poor peasant owns two houses and tries to buy the grandfather from the poor peasant. The grandfather, though, is cleverer than the inheritance vulture and so everything has a happy end for the poor peasant, whose son then gets to marry the daughter of the rich peasant.

Although the family had a television in the house they didn't watch very much. Jürgen, though, would religiously every evening watch the *Tagesschau* (the West German news broadcast), but rarely, if ever, the GDR's own turgid *Aktuelle Kamera*. The *Tagesschau*, Thomas said, in the weeks before Christmas was preceded by a five-minute religious slot in which a children's choir would sing a carol. Jürgen 'would always watch this with glistening eyes'. After watching the *Tagesschau* at 8 o'clock he would retire to bed.

Despite the ideological ups and downs and U-turns that characterised Party life in the post-war period, Jürgen remained on amicable terms with the GDR's first leader, Walter Ulbricht and with his successor Erich Honecker, to whom he became an unofficial economic advisor. But he had regular run-ins with a number of the Party's ideologues, particularly his old comrade in arms from British exile years, Kurt Hager, with whom he was often at loggerheads.

Although he was rarely, if ever, a blind follower of Party diktats, a straightforward opportunist or careerist, it could be argued that someone of his international prominence and considerable standing in his own country could have been more forceful in his critique of a failing and very flawed system. Although many in the GDR saw him as a welcome critical voice, many also were suspicious of his close links with the ruling elite. When it was suggested to him later by critics in the reunited Germany that he could have done more, his response was always that if he had been more openly critical or more forceful in attacking flagrant transgressions of democratic norms, he would have been ostracised and rendered powerless to do any good at all. As it was, he says he was able to help a number of those who fell foul of the Party hierarchy's demands and had been plunged into disgrace.

Throughout his life he also kept channels open to Western politicians and academics, but he only met and got to know Willy Brandt – one of those who had a considerable influence on post-war German politics – in the last year of the GDR's existence. In December 1989 he had a lengthy conversation with Brandt at the 80th birthday celebration for Gräfin Marion Dönhoff, publisher of the weekly *Die Zeit*. At that event Brandt told Jürgen that he was opposed to the reunification of the two German states but in favour of a confederation and that he would be speaking at the forthcoming party conference of the SPD in that vein. Then early in 1990, the Evangelical Academy in Tutzing organised a conference on the German question at which Brandt and the then Foreign Minister Genscher spoke, alongside Kuczynski as a representative from East Germany. While Genscher was speaking, recalled Jürgen, 'Willi Brandt whispered in my ear "the train has already left the station, unification is the only option"'.[4] Shortly beforehand Jürgen had also renewed contact with Herbert Wehner, with whom he had worked closely when both were in the Communist Party's leading theoretical discussion group in 1931/32. After the war Wehner went on to become a leading light in West Germany's Social Democratic Party (SPD) and minister for Intra-German Relations (1966–69).

Jürgen was one of the most prolific academic writers not only in the GDR but in the world – in his lifetime he wrote around 4,500 publications, including over 100 books. The range of his interests and publications was incredibly broad, covering subjects from politics to literature, on the writing of autobiographies to economics and philosophy. And throughout his life he kept up a lively correspondence with academics and leading political figures in many countries. The Kuczynski

library holds many of these letters, but unfortunately, as Thomas Kuczynski pointed out to me, Jürgen's own replies were invariably 'very
short and with little worthwhile content'.[5]

He was not only a capable writer but a popular lecturer too. He
spoke freely without extensive notes, and was always witty and erudite.
But when invited to give a lecture, he would speak and answer questions
for exactly the agreed time slot and then hold his tongue.

In his house in Berlin-Weissensee – he always lived in a rented one –
books were everywhere, from the cellar to the attic, in the corridors
and bedrooms. His library – the largest private library in all Germany –
eventually consisted of around 70,000 volumes as well as 35,000 brochures and journals. It included many first editions, some with the
authors' notes in them, and was collected over six generations of the
family. Although the Nazis stole many of its books after the family was
forced to flee, he managed to rescue some of the most precious items
beforehand and after the war was able to replace a number of the
missing volumes. In 2003 the library was purchased by the *Zentral- und
Landesbibliothek* – the Berlin City Library – and is now part of its
historical collections. This library was more than simply a collection of
books; it represents a history of the family, and is also a repository of
Western culture and civilisation.

Jürgen's marriage to Marguerite appears to have been a very happy
one with few, if any, serious disagreements, although that was probably
more down to her tolerance and patience than to his own efforts. She
was a translator and economics specialist in her own right, but largely
compromised her own academic ambitions to support him and be there
for the children. She did, however, publish a number of significant
works under her own name and collaborated with her husband on
many. The editions on the French history of science, including the
Tableau Economique (1972), which she edited together with Ronald L.
Meek are still highly valued. But she envied his productivity, and once
said to him: 'By the time I've produced a footnote you've written a
whole book!'

For Marguerite life was not so straightforward as for her husband.
Although she was recognised as one of the earliest leading German
economists, her role as Jürgen's wife and mother to their three children
meant that, like so many other talented women, she was obliged to put

FIGURE 12.2 Jürgen in his library at home in Berlin-Weissensee
Source: SLUB Dresden/Deutsche Fotothek/Günter Ackermann.

her own career on hold. Her research work became secondary and, as a result, her contribution has become overshadowed by that of her more famous husband.

From 1947 until 1960 she worked in a number of GDR economic institutions and latterly at the Institute of Marxism-Leninism, on the preparation and editing of *The Collected Works of Marx and Engels*. She retired from paid work in 1960, but then became the key figure in the rediscovery of the works of the French Physiocrasists,[6] particularly Quesnay and Turgot, who were tremendously influential on early economists.

She was throughout her life Jürgen's sounding board, reading almost all his draft manuscripts and commenting critically on them. But there is no doubt that the disruption caused by the family's enforced exile, the birth and nurturing of three children, and looking after her husband's material needs under often difficult circumstances, left her little opportunity to pursue her own academic interests to the full. She was clearly prepared, though, to place those interests or ambitions behind those of her husband. Without Marguerite he would never have been able to complete the enormous amount of work he did. Throughout his time in academia in the GDR he also had a number of personal secretaries-cum-collaborators who were invaluable in helping him with his research, editing and preparing manuscripts for publication.

Together he and Marguerite had three children. Madeleine was born in Germany before they fled the Nazis, Peter and Thomas in Britain during their parents' years of exile. Madeleine had her early schooling in London, Peter and Thomas their very early years there, but the boys would experience much of their growing up in the GDR.

Madeleine eschewed the family academic tradition to become a gardener before studying agriculture and taking a job in the Ministry of Agriculture. In the late 1950s she left that job to become a translator and interpreter.

Thomas and Peter did become academics, although Peter did so reluctantly. After taking his *Abitur* (A-levels), he sought to distance himself from the family's intellectual interests and began an apprenticeship in mechanical engineering at the Dresden-Klotzsche aircraft manufacturing works, where he learned about metals and fine manual work. He soon returned to the fold, though, taking a Ph.D. in English Literature at Potsdam, where his doctoral supervisor was Leonard Goldstein.

Interestingly, Leonard Goldstein was a post-war exile in the opposite direction to Peter's own family. He was born in the Bronx, New York, into a Jewish immigrant family from the Ukraine. He experienced the Great Depression of the 1930s in the USA as a young man, and joined the US Communist Party. After serving in the US Navy during the Second World War and surviving the assault on Iwo Jima, on the Japanese front, he returned to the USA to find himself caught up in the emerging McCarthy witch-hunts. He was blacklisted academically so decided to seek work abroad, and finally, in the early 1960s, he settled with his wife in the GDR, where he taught English literature at Potsdam University. He would become a close friend of Peter and his wife Ingrid.

Peter was for many years a lecturer in American literature and cultural studies at Martin-Luther-University Halle/Wittenberg. Both his dissertations dealt with popular utopias in the Middle Ages and the Early Modern Age. He began with Shakespeare's inverted world, went on to the Land of Cockaygne and finished with *Schlaraffenland*. He also published on American literature and politics. With the demise of the GDR and after unification, the university was restructured and, in 1992, he was told he had been too '*systemnah*' (close to the system) and had belonged to the 'GDR elite'. Because of this there was no place for him in the new academic structure; he subsequently realised that this meant he was effectively blacklisted. This enforced unemployment provided him with the stimulus to return to his youthful interests and take up wood-carving; he always had a strong, if hidden, artistic bent, and in his youth he had sketched and built models. He went on to produce exquisitely crafted utensils and complex geometric sculptures from wood, mainly for family and friends.

Peter's wife, Ingrid, is a prominent academic and literary critic in her own right and has carried out research into English working-class autobiographies and pre-twentieth-century women's writing. She taught at the Martin-Luther-University Halle/Wittenberg and, after reunification, at the University of Duisburg.

Thomas studied statistics at the Berlin School of Economics, where he wrote his thesis on economic history. Thereafter he worked for twenty years at the Institute for Economic History of the GDR Academy of Sciences, dealing especially with the application of mathematical methods in economic history. From 1988 until 1991 he was Director of the Institute. When the entire Academy was closed as a result of reunification he lost his post. Since 1992 he has worked as a freelance scholar and journalist, writing on history and economics, and carrying out research for a new text edition of Marx's *Capital* (vol. 1) to be published in 2017.

Because Jürgen always stressed his loyalty to the Communist Party and, after 1946, the SED, this has been taken by many observers to imply that he was an unthinking and blind follower. The West German-born historian Ute Frevert is no exception: 'In his published autobiographical writings', she writes:

> he continually stressed unwavering and unconditional loyalty to the Party leadership. He saw communism as a belief system that demanded faith and did not tolerate any doubts and diversions. Like Catholicism it engaged the full spirit, not just a fragment of it. In return, it offered a steady, protective home where one could develop strong feelings of belonging and a secure identity. Those feelings did not leave room for other types of identification ...[7]

Such writers make no allowance for the fact that many communists were often plagued by doubt and were not indifferent to what happened under Stalin or to how the Party in the GDR was authoritarian and invariably dogmatic, but they rarely gave public expression to such views for fear of damaging the Party or the state to which they had pledged their loyalty. Such condemnatory views also take no account of the need during the 1930s and 1940s for absolute discipline and loyalty on the left, given first the fascist threat and then under the adverse conditions imposed on East Germany in its attempt to build a socialist society. That experience formed the basis for the subsequent attitudes and behaviour of many communists, including Jürgen.

He had protested against the reversing of a tentative de-Stalinisation in the GDR during the late 1950s and was almost expelled from the Party over it. But he never considered abandoning the GDR, despite all the blows, and viewed those like Hans Mayer, the literary critic, and the philosopher Ernst Bloch, who did so, to be traitors or Judases, although his views on the actions of such individuals mellowed with time.

Although he was the eternal optimist he did suggest, in the early 1980s, that the stationing of Pershing missiles in West Germany and the increased threat of nuclear Armageddon was a real cause for pessimism about the future of humankind. The Party, once again, lambasted him for such 'defeatist' comment.

In 1982, in answer to a questionnaire posed by *Forum*, the GDR's student newspaper, he answered that his favourite maxim was 'De omnibus dubitandum' (doubt everything), which was also Marx's favourite. He did, though qualify this by excepting the methodology of dialectical and historical materialism. Such comments were anathema to many in the Party leadership who considered doubt or scepticism to be destructive and subversive. Jürgen says that only in the 1980s was he able to push through his viewpoint that research institutes were extremely useful for the development of ideas, but only if open debate were possible. But, 'open criticism from the bottom up was forbidden until 1989', he would write later. On reaching the age of 85, the *Frankfurter Allgemeine Zeitung*, in a feature, called him 'a maverick thinker and happy Marxist'. That description, he avowed, also characterised his Institute, where animated debate and open criticism was de jure. It was characterised by others in the GDR as an 'island of the blissful ones', a recognition of its privileged status.

Towards the end of his life, when Jürgen was asked by a journalist from the newspaper *Die Tageszeitung* (*TAZ*) whether he was happy with his life or whether he felt shame and sorrow about what had happened to the GDR, he responded:

> What do you mean, sorrow? One doesn't feel sad about history, one experiences it. And those who know history are so used to everything that has happened. ... You mustn't forget that I am an educated man, who has experienced the last three thousand years.

In his book, *Ein Leben in der Wissenschaft der DDR* (A Life in Academia in the GDR), published in 1993, Jürgen provided a rather self-justifying and somewhat jaundiced picture of intellectual life in the GDR. He wrote that in reality basic democracy in the country had been 'in a worse state than in the bad old days of the Federal Republic and that press freedoms were fewer than those under Frederick the Great'. He bemoaned the suppression of academic creativity, and gave the example of Leipzig University, which had occupied an esteemed position in the early years of the GDR, yet during the 1950s and 1960s a number of its leading academics like Bloch and Mayer fell out of favour because of the Party's intolerance of differing viewpoints, and had little option but to leave the country.[8]

Given that Jürgen remained loyal to the GDR to the end of his life and lent his support to the system despite any reservations he may have had, remarks such as those above could be considered a belated conversion or a post-factum confession.

He had an encyclopaedic knowledge and read the whole of Marx's *Capital* once every four years, but he was not in the first instance a genial theoretician; he wrote no significant theoretical work with lasting impact.

Some of his contemporaries have argued that his writing on such a broad range of subjects meant that he lost focus, because although he was a prodigious writer he has left posterity no school of thought based on his work. They have suggested that if he had written less, he would have had greater influence, but that was the way he was, he could not have been otherwise. Perhaps the most significant and influential book he wrote was *Geschichte des Alltags des deutschen Volkes* (A History of the Everyday Life of the German People) in five volumes.

He said of himself, 'I'd rather be seen as a piece of old iron than a modern piece of scrap-metal', and indeed, in his thinking, he was essentially conservative; his assessments and interpretation of capitalism scarcely changed over his lifetime.

He often boasted, only partly in jest, that he had written more in his lifetime than Marx and Engels together. And even on literature, art or history he wrote more than many another professor who specialised in those areas. He became involved in contemporary discussions on every topic, unless it was one he did not wish to. In his book *Dialog mit meinem Urenkel*, Jürgen asks himself whether the dabbling in so many different fields was really acceptable. He lays the question in the mouth of his great-grandchild, who asks whether this does not amount to dilettantism. He clearly felt he needed to answer such an accusation.

Jörn Janssen, a London-based but German-born historian, got to know Jürgen while completing his Ph.D. in Bremen on the subject of social housing and how industrial production influences or determines architectural design. He had read Robert Kuczynski's pioneering work in this area, which he describes as inspirational. He and Jürgen began a regular correspondence and Janssen visited him several times at his home in Berlin-Weissensee and they became friends. He describes Jürgen as always being very helpful, completely modest and not at all egotistical.[9]

So what are we are left with in terms of a Jürgen Kuczynski heritage? He was indeed a one-off, and his real merit is that he existed at all. When the problems of the GDR became insurmountable, because of his unique background, he became a carrier of hope, even at such an advanced age. Peter Beurton had this to say about his legacy:

> He remained all his life a Marxist economist, a historian and university lecturer, but also a propagandist for Marxism. He was not a noted philosopher, much more a publicist, writing for various magazines, journals and papers. He was one of the best journalists among economists and one of the best economists among journalists. In the GDR he was one of the best agitators and promoters of economic theory. For him the Marxist classics held the central truths and his goal was to publicise these works and ideas. He wanted to help everyone comprehend them, as 'something every child can understand'.

The day he died on 6 August 1997, a month before his ninety-third birthday, he left an almost completed hand-written article on his desk intended for publication in the *Junge Welt* newspaper. It was so meticulously prepared that his secretary was able to type it up for publication without the need of editing.

As David Childs said in an obituary he wrote for *The Independent*:

> Jürgen Kuczynski was a remarkable member of the remarkable Jewish Central European intelligentsia of the inter-war period. Like many of them he turned to Marxism as an answer to the ethnic and national rivalries, and economic and political chaos which followed the First World War. Many of them subsequently saw Stalin's version of Communism as the God that failed, and returned their Party cards. Kuczynski did not.[10]

At his funeral in Berlin on 22 August 1997, the journalist Klaus Hartung wrote in *Die Zeit*:

> He not only formulated his own obituary and indicated the key quotations to be used, but even the funeral was an expression of

his vigour. His organising hand was tangible: the ceremony was simple, unsentimental, non-metaphysical. Funeral guests were asked to give any contributions they wished to a fund for Cuban children and to bring only modest floral tributes ... Here, quietly and emphatically an epoch came to an end, an epoch in which he was the last figuration of the GDR. He was laid to rest in Berlin's Dorotheen Friedhof where the elite of Berlin's bourgoisie are buried. He lies between artist Herbert Sandberg and dramatist Heiner Müller and a stone's throw from his old friend Bertolt Brecht.

The concluding paragraph of Hartung's article reads:

Everything was very moving and dignified. What was missing, affects us, his contemporaries. A witness to Berlin's history, a notable figure of the century, was buried but no representative from the city council, the academies or from the new united Germany took any notice or sent a wreath. In a shameful manner, yes frankly unconsciously, the official side of the present, has admitted that German history and the city of Berlin is still divided. The funeral, a public event, was ignored by the Berlin public.

Twelve years after his death and after much lobbying by his friends and family, Jürgen Kuczynski has been honoured by the naming of a small square in Berlin-Weissensee, close to where he used to live: Jürgen-Kuczynski-Park.

Notes

1 Conversation between the author and Peter Beurton, 8 May 2016.
2 Jürgen Kuczynski, *Feunde und Bekannte*, Schwarzkopf & Schwarzkopf, 1997, p. 124.
3 http://opus.kobv.de/zlb/volltexte/2014/21721/pdf/Ausstellung_Kuczynski.pdf.
4 Ibid., p. 147.
5 Personal conversation between the author and Thomas Kuczynski, 24 November 2015.
6 Physiocracy is an economic theory developed by a group of eighteenth-century Enlightenment French economists who argued that the wealth of

nations was derived from the value of 'land agriculture' or land development. It is one of the first developed theories of economics.

7 Ute Frevert, 'Jewish Hearts and Minds? Feelings of Belonging and Political Choices among East German Intellectuals', *Leo Baeck Institute Year Book*, 2011.

8 Jürgen Kuczynski, *Ein Leben in der Wissenschaft der DDR*, Westfälisches Dampfboot, 1993, pp. 14–18.

9 Personal conversation with the author, 26 January 2016.

10 *Independent*, 13 August 1997.

13

URSULA REVEALS HER PAST

Only from the mid-1960s onwards and with the rehabilitation of the Soviet Union's top agent in Japan, Richard Sorge, did Ursula begin tentatively to talk about her own intelligence work. She had throughout her life rejected the idea that she was a hero or someone special because of what she had done. She described herself as 'merely a courier'. But that is perhaps taking modesty to an extreme. In Russia she has been called *Superwoman of the GRU* – the title of a book published in Moscow in 2002.

However, she only received permission to publish her memoirs in the 1970s. *Sonjas Rapport* (Sonya's Report) was published in the GDR in 1977 and became an immediate best-seller. It had to be agreed with Moscow and clear numerous hurdles in the GDR itself before publication, but was then translated into more than twelve languages.

Ursula was no Mata Hari or cold, calculating woman with a penchant for intrigue and subterfuge. She believed passionately in justice and felt outraged by misery and racism, and it was this that motivated her. She undertook secret work on behalf of the Soviet Union, in its struggle against fascism and against outside attempts to extirpate it because she felt it was essential at the time to take sides unequivocally.

She was very much a red-bloodied woman who was determined to live life to the full, have lovers and bear children, which she did in the most adverse of circumstances. Ironically, it was possibly the fact of her being a mother with small children at the height of her career as a secret agent that threw her potential nemeses off the scent and enabled her to complete her assignments successfully.

In her later years she revealed that her past work as a secret agent still dogged her life, and she often had nightmares in which 'the enemy is at my heels and I have no time to destroy the information'. And when she found herself in new surroundings she was 'forever discovering hiding places for illegal material'.

'When Stalin died in 1953', she wrote, 'I was in East Germany, and every communist I met considered it as I did – a great loss.' And, to put it into context, she quotes Andrei Sakharov – the leading nuclear physicist, later dissident and Nobel Peace Prize winner – who at the time of Stalin's death wrote to a friend with no trace of irony: 'I am under the influence of a great man's death, I'm thinking of his humanity.' But as Sakharov comments in his memoirs:

> very soon I would be blushing every time I recall these sentences. I can't fully explain it – after all, I knew quite enough about the horrible crimes that had been committed … but there was still a lot I did not know. Somewhere in the back of my mind, the idea existed … that suffering is inevitable during great historical upheavals … and above all, I felt myself committed to the goal which I assumed was Stalin's as well: after a devastating war to make the country strong enough to ensure peace.

Those words undoubtedly echo Ursula's own feelings and those of so many communists and sympathisers with the Soviet Union at the time. When Krushchev revealed Stalin's guilt and the enormity of his crimes at the 20th Party Congress in 1956 the Russian people and communists the world over were stunned, as Ursula was. For many on the left Stalin, as leader of the Soviet government, had been seen as the man who had turned a backward peasant country into a powerful industrialised nation, laying the foundations for a socialist state, and who was the figurehead of the anti-fascist movement, the architect of

Hitler's defeat. All that was called into question by Krushchev's revelations.

For the first half of the twentieth century there was hardly any other secret agent, whether male or female, on whichever side, who during their career was active consecutively in three hot spots of intelligence gathering – with Richard Sorge ('Ramsay') in China, with Sándor Radó and the Red Orchestra in Switzerland and then with Klaus Fuchs in England. Even Chapman Pincher acknowledges her as 'the most successful woman espionage agent of all time'.[1] During her career her cover was never blown and she was given assignments time and again, carrying them out with calm and commitment, knowing full well what could happen to her if she were caught. The subsequent hanging of Richard Sorge by the Japanese, Fuchs' long jail term and the execution of the Rosenbergs in 1953 make that abundantly clear.

What happened to Rudolf?

Ursula had lost contact with her first husband and Michael's father, Rudolf Hamburger, after they divorced in Switzerland and he returned to China alone. The conspiratorial and secretive nature of intelligence work meant that they could no longer contact each other even if they had wanted to while they were both still working as secret agents. Once the war was over, however, she must have wondered what had happened to him and why neither she nor the children had heard anything more from him. They would, though, meet up again, much later, in very unusual and unexpected circumstances.

Rudi, or Rolf as he was better known, had been only 11 years old when the First World War broke out. He was the son of a Silesian textile manufacturer who made handsome profits during that war from the state's insatiable demand for uniform materials. His was a cultivated, bourgeois Jewish family which counted the great dramatist Gerhart Hauptmann among its friends. In his youth Rolf would be very moved and influenced by seeing Hauptmann's social dramas that included *Before Sunrise* and *The Weavers*.

The family lived in a small villa near the factory in Landeshut (today Kamienna Gora in Poland). Rolf, like many other children of that period growing up in the German Reich, went to the local school where he sat alongside other pupils from very different backgrounds. One of his best friends at school was a young and bright working-class boy, who one day invited him home. What he discovered in the boy's home – the extreme poverty, the smell, the noise and roughness of family relationships – was a profound shock, as he relates in his memoirs. He had never imagined that his privileged life was anything but normal. That childhood experience would underpin his developing social conscience and help determine the course of his life. He was the artist of the family and went on to study architecture in Dresden, Munich and Berlin. It was in Berlin where he would meet his future wife, the vivacious and politically committed Ursula Kuczynski.

Rolf's brother Otto was already working as a businessman in Shanghai, as a representative for a machinery import company when the couple first arrived in China. Max, their father, would later manage to flee the Nazis, first staying with Otto in Shanghai before moving on to join his third son, Viktor, in the USA, but would spend the last two years of his life in Switzerland.

While the couple were living in China, Ursula became involved with the Soviet agent Richard Sorge and began allowing him to use their home as a place for illegal meetings; she didn't tell her husband as she knew he would not approve. But it became impossible to hide these meetings from Rolf. He was livid when she told him the truth and told her that she was placing the whole family in danger. Not only did he feel personally betrayed, but he knew it could jeopardise his own work and even plunge the whole family into needless danger. Undertaking such activities in China could result, even for foreigners, in a death sentence. When, on top of this, Ursula decided to join Sorge in working for the military wing of the Soviet Union's secret service (GRU), it effectively finished off their marriage. Rolf's anger and depression in the face of this situation was not helped by the effect world events were having on life in Shanghai and the awful news coming daily out of Germany as the fascists brutally imposed their racist ideology on the country.

The Japanese invaders were also ruthlessly pursuing their appalling colonial war in China, and even among Rolf's German compatriots Nazi ideology was gaining ground. The seeming indifference of the Western nations to Hitler's insatiable demands helped steer Rolf's hopes towards the Soviet Union as the only credible alternative to fascism. All this encouraged him to take a fateful decision – with the increasing danger of a fascist world, he felt he also had to do more to help prevent it happening, just as his wife was doing, despite being totally unsuitable for the role. His son Michael says he was simply too honest and open and found it almost impossible to dissimulate.[2] Despite having built up a reputation as a capable architect in the meantime and also enjoying his work, he felt he could no long remain on the political sidelines.

When Rolf contacted GRU offering his services, they were initially uncertain about his suitability and tried to dissuade him, but he was insistent. In the end they agreed to try him out and asked him to accompany Ursula to Poland and help give her the cover she needed. A seemingly stable family unit would arouse less suspicion than a single woman with a child. His engagement with the Soviet secret services dates from that year, 1936, although in MI5's files he is erroneously described as already working for them in 1930.

Rolf agreed to accompany Ursula to Poland probably also in the hope of rescuing their marriage, even though she was at the time pregnant with another man's child. It was there that Michael's sister Janina was born and, although not Rolf's own child, he was prepared to adopt her as his own. Michael and his sister would only learn twenty years later, in the GDR, who her real father was.

The 5-year-old Michael recalled how he loved the short time they spent in Zakopane, in the Tatra mountains during the winter, living in a fairytale wooden cottage, where he learned how to ski with his parents. His mother schooled him at home because they had to move homes so frequently and it would have been impossible to enrol him in a Polish school. With his father he learned how to build model houses and factories using building blocks, paper and cardboard.

When the family moved on to Switzerland, Rolf and Ursula went through a formal divorce – their attempt to patch up the marriage or at least reach a mutually comfortable modus vivendi had not worked. They divorced in Vevey in October 1939.

Rolf now found himself in a delicate situation. With his Jewish background, a return to Germany was impossible and his German passport was no longer valid anyway. He, like Ursula, purchased an easily available Honduran one; his was in the name of Rodolfo Alberto

Hamburger and, using it, he returned to China in 1939 to work for GRU. He settled in Chungking (today Chongqing), capital of the Chinese Nationalists at the time, but it would only be a very short time before he was exposed and arrested as a spy. He was kept in jail for a whole year, tortured and left without any communication with the outside world. He was saved by a stroke of luck. His businessman brother Otto was still living in Shanghai at the time, and had received a coded telegram from an anonymous source from which he was able to make out that his brother was in jail. Otto immediately mobilised friends, and through diplomatic channels, probably Soviet ones, managed to obtain Rolf's release.

After his release he continued operating as a Soviet secret agent and a year later was sent to Tehran, where he found work in one of the ministries. While there, both Rolf and his employers were taken by surprise when Hitler unexpectedly invaded the Soviet Union in June 1941. Immediately the 'Persian corridor' to the Soviet Union was occupied separately by US, British and Soviet troops.

Two years later, Rolf would be denounced by a treacherous collaborator and, in 1943, arrested again by the occupying forces. He spent several weeks in US and then British custody. The MI5 and FBI agents there were suspicious of his activities, particularly on the basis of his dubious Honduran passport. They searched his flat but failed to find his radio transmitter, which he had hidden in a disused chimney. They came to the conclusion that he was only a small fish and let him go with orders to leave Persia within 24 hours. That is what happened, according to his own memoirs. Only later when he disappeared off the map, did his interrogators become convinced that he had been perhaps a much more important spy than they had imagined and that he was probably now working underground elsewhere. A note in an MI5 file, though, gives a rather different story to the one he gave, and records that he was handed over to the Russians directly at their request.[3] There is even a letter, dated 15 February 1946 and addressed to Kim Philby from MI5's J. H. Marriott, referring to Hamburger as 'a Soviet Agent who was detained in Iran in May 1943 first by the Americans and then by the British, and by the latter subsequently handed back to the Soviet Authorities'. This letter asked Philby if he had any 'information on the present whereabouts of Hamburger'. There was also a request to question Ursula Kuczynski about Hamburger's whereabouts, though there is no record of this having been followed up. Also included in the file is a letter from Marriott to the US embassy referring to a connection between 'Rudi and Ursula' – Rolf had given his contact address as 129 Rue Lausanne, Switzerland, the same address at which Ursula and Len had been living. This lead also does not seem to have been followed up.

Interestingly, the former MI5 officer Peter Wright, in his book *Spycatcher*, tells yet another, rather different, story about Rolf's arrest and work as an agent, but this has not been corroborated by other sources and sounds rather far-fetched. A former MI6 agent, Robert Zaehner, who after leaving intelligence work became Professor of Ancient Persian at Oxford University, was interviewed by Wright. He wondered if Zaehner had more information concerning a spy in Persia who had been mentioned by KGB defector Konstantin Volkov. Zaehner told Wright he couldn't think who this mystery spy could have been, but suggested it might have been Hamburger. Wright says that:

> After MI6 recruited Hamburger, he was arrested by the Russians, then turned loose, before being reemployed by MI6 again. The dates tallied perfectly with the time Volkov had access to files in Moscow, and it seemed obvious that Hamburger had simply been turned in prison, and tasked to find out whatever he could about his British employers. (Rudi Hamburger was the first husband of 'Sonia' …)

Wright's allegation that Rudi was recruited by MI6 is not corroborated by any evidence in released MI5 files or by any other sources. It remains a very unlikely version of the facts.

According to Rolf's own account, after his release by the British and Americans his only real option was to go to the Soviet Union, where he was convinced he would be offered asylum and support. What happened to him there, though, is beyond anyone's worst nightmare. He managed to reach Moscow, but on his third day there he was arrested and accused of being a US agent. He faced intense daily interrogation, his interlocutors demanding that he admit to being an anti-Soviet spy. Despite lack of food, sleep and rest, he refused to be broken. After interrogation by Soviet security agents he was returned to his cell each day at the crack of dawn and threw himself on his plank-bed in despair. In his reminiscences he wrote:

> Exhausted and sleepless I lie there. That noble goal of fighting for a better life has failed, my ideals brutally destroyed. My thoughts take me back to the days when my decision was gestating, to take leave of my beloved profession, forget architecture and devote myself to something else, which at that moment was larger, it challenged us all, to prepare and take up the struggle against an inhuman destructive force. Afterwards I would build houses for the new society.
>
> And those who we look to as an example, who have already achieved a step towards the new in painful effort, and since the outbreak of war are defending it by making enormous sacrifice; they label me a potential enemy, a traitor who belongs in prison. That is more difficult to cope with than the prison cell, the hunger, the predicament of having no rights. For me, every connection with the outside world is cut off. As far as family and friends are concerned I've been buried. My request for legal assistance is refused.[4]

After regular interrogations and still strenuously denying the accusations, but without a proper trial, he is given a five-year sentence in a labour camp. Then begins a horrendous Calvary through various prison camps. This is followed by the huge blow of having his original sentence transmuted to ten years, after a bureaucrat in the Ministry of Justice decided that the original sentence was based on a mistake and it should have been longer. On top of this come the denunciations by stool pigeons in the camps, which also add more years to his sentence. He gives full details of his camp experiences in his posthumously published memoirs. In Usollag, a camp located in woodland in the Urals, where he was sent in the late 1940s, he meets other Germans who have been arrested in the Soviet Zone of Occupation, including the writer Heinrich Alexander Stoll, with whom he becomes friends; they would meet again when both manage to survive and return to the GDR.

Throughout his trials and the daily pitiless battles for existence, Rolf nevertheless strives to maintain his moral integrity, his tolerance, patience and faith in humanity. He is eventually released from internment in 1953, but is not yet free: he is sent into internal 'exile' and kept under virtual house arrest in a small town in Kazakhstan which he is not allowed to leave. As a stateless citizen, not a prisoner of war, nor a former Party member and with no one outside who knows of his existence, he is caught in a Kafkaesque limbo. But then, over a year later, purely by chance, he reads in a newspaper that a delegation of GDR architects is due to visit Moscow and among them will be his old student friend and colleague, Richard Paulick. He manages to get a message sent to him through illegal channels.

Richard Paulick and Rolf Hamburger had become close friends during their student days. Paulick was one of those responsible for the rebuilding of historic Berlin after the devastation caused by the Second World War. He was also closely involved in the rebuilding of Dresden's baroque architecture, and was director of the *Muster- und Experimental-Büro an der Deutschen Bauakademie* (Model and Experimental Office at the German Architectural Academy) in Berlin. From 1957 he was chief architect and director of the construction office in Hoyerswerda, and from 1963 the leading force behind the planning and establishment of the town of Halle-Neustadt, built from scratch for the workers of the nearby large chemical plant.

Paulick, once he had received Rolf's note, together with Ursula, set the wheels in motion for his eventual release. Ironically, that same year, 1955, West German Chancellor Konrad Adenauer managed to secure the release of the last German prisoners of war still being held in the Soviet Union, to great jubilation.

With the imminent arrival of Rolf in the GDR, Ursula decided that she had to tell Janina the truth about her real father, to which the 19-year-old responded rather primly, 'Mummy, I'm not at all happy that you had so many men.'

Rolf arrived in East Germany on an October day in 1955, aged beyond his years. The meeting with his son Michael was highly emotional as well as awkward. Michael described him as 'not a broken man, but much changed from the image his son still had of him in his head, grey-haired, slightly bowed, voice rather cracked and like someone emerging from a cellar and is dazzled by the sunlight'.

How could they reconnect after sixteen years of not seeing each other? It was not made easier by the fact that Rolf was unwilling to talk about his experiences in the Soviet Union, beyond vague mention of working on buildings and construction sites. Such attitudes were typical of many of those who emerged from Soviet labour camps. It was not to do with fear or of having committed to silence, but probably, as with many of those who returned from the front in the First World War, the conviction that it would be impossible to communicate the horror and senselessness of it all, as well as the feeling that either you would not be believed or viewed as a traitor. In addition, for those who were convinced communists, was the reluctance to provide the 'enemy' with any ammunition.

Ursula's son Peter felt that Rolf was still in love with her and would have liked to revive their married life together in the GDR, but she was still happily married to Len. Rolf was, though, very angry at her portrayal of him in her barely disguised autobiographical novel, *Ein Ungewöhnliches Mädchen*, published in 1959. When *Sonjas Rapport* came out in 1977 and described her work as a Soviet agent he was so furious that he broke off communications with her completely.

Rolf returned to Dresden in the GDR, where he picked up the threads of his life, joining the SED – out of conviction – and began work once more as an architect. He became deputy head of the building team responsible for constructing the new town of Hoyerswerda, where he was highly respected by his colleagues who marvelled at his 'imagination'. The author Brigitte Reimann in her novel *Franziska Linkerhand* based the character of the old architect Landauer on Hamburger. In recognition of his contribution to GDR architecture, he was eventually elected vice president of the country's architectural academy.

After the demise of the GDR, Eduard Kögel,[5] in his research into Hamburger's life, discovered that he had been an informant for the country's State Security organisation, but it is clear from the files that he didn't provide his handlers with much useful information. He was asked to keep his colleagues under observation, but refused to collect compromising personal information on them. In 1977, after the release in Germany of Ursula's book of reminiscences, which became a great publishing success, the German security service suggested that he might wish to write and publish his own, but he responded that he was not interested. He felt they merely wished to capitalise on his reminiscences as a secret Soviet agent. From this point on he refused any further co-operation with the State Security apparatus. During his years working in the GDR he had also become increasingly irritated and frustrated by the Party's policies, its interference and dominance of everything. He had become largely disillusioned with 'real-existing socialism'.

He may have felt, almost certainly correctly, that the story of his dreadful experiences in Soviet labour camps and the appalling way he had been treated, would not be accepted for publication by the GDR authorities. He was also very unhappy with the way Ursula had portrayed him in her book and saw it as a betrayal. He did, though, write up his reminiscences of life in the GULAG, probably during the 1970s, but kept the typescript in a drawer at home. These were based largely on notes he had made during his incarceration and smuggled out. He died on 1 December 1980 in Dresden and is buried there in the Heidefriedhof. A family member living in Britain described him laconically, but with admiration as, 'the last Victorian Communist'.

Rudolf Hamburger's memoirs of life in a Soviet prison camp, *Zehn Jahre Lager: Ein Bericht* (Ten Years in a Labour Camp: A Report), is Kafkaesque and very reminiscent of Solzhenitsyn's *One Day in the Life of Ivan Denisovich*. It was published posthumously in 2013. In it he relates his horrendous experiences in painful detail, eloquently, honestly and with unembellished veracity. It would be some consolation to believe that it was simply the exceptional story of one individual's fate, but it is in fact representative of tens of thousands who went through a similar hell.

Michael did offer his father's manuscript to a number of British and US publishers, but they rejected it on the basis that they had already published sufficient such camp experience narratives.

It is difficult to know whether Rolf's long incarceration in the Soviet Union could have been avoided or at least curtailed. Ursula lost contact with him once they had separated and he returned to China, but did she not wonder where he was, what had happened to him? Did she ask any questions? Could the GDR party leadership have done more to rescue him if they had known? These are all questions that remain unanswered.

Notes

1 Chapman Pincher, *Treachery*, p. 278.
2 Personal conversation, May 2015.
3 The file on Rudi Hamburger (The National Archives, KV/6/41), in an extract from the Middle East Security Summary of 29 May 1943 says he was arrested towards the end of April by US security authorities. They 'reported [him] to be engaged in espionage and sabotage. On two occasions he was known to have bought information on railway and military installations – principally British – in Persia. ... During interrogation he maintained that he was not working against the Allies but was merely collecting information for his "Group", the particulars of which he resolutely refused to disclose. ... The Russian Security Authorities claimed him as one of their agents. He then admitted to his interrogators that he had for long been a professional agent of the Russians and would remain one. His task, he alleged, was to collect political information about Allied intentions. He said his interest in the railway was twofold – to discover if the Allies were really doing their best to send supplies to Russia – and to study its potentialities for post-war supplies, when Russian would be rebuilding her industries. At their request, he has been handed back to the Russian authorities.'

 This clearly provides a link to Ursula re. working for the Soviets (mentioned by H. Shillitoe in a memo) but no further action seems to have been initiated with respect of Ursula.
4 Rudolf Hamburger, *Zehn Jahre Lager*, Munich, Siedler Verlag, 2013.
5 Eduard Kögel, 'Zwei Poelzigschüler in der Emigration: Rudolf Hamburger und Richard Paulick zwischen Shanghai und Ostberlin' (1930–1955), dissertation, Bauhaus University, Weimar.

14

THE SUN SETS ON A DREAM

The end of the GDR

Jürgen lived in the GDR throughout its forty years of existence and his sister Ursula moved there only a year after it was founded in 1949. Their lives in the GDR would be very different from those they had led beforehand.

Irrespective of how history finally judges the GDR, tens of thousands of its citizens at all levels of society genuinely believed that they were helping to build a new and democratic society on the ruins of Hitler's 'eternal Reich' and devoted their lives to that goal. They had to battle not only enemies without, but the dogmatists, careerists, opportunists and hangers-on in their own society. Both Ursula and Jürgen would often experience frustration and irritation in the face of such individuals in their own party and government, but were prepared to persevere.

Jürgen, Ursula and their families were visited regularly in the GDR by their sisters and families from Britain, as visits in the other direction were, until the thawing of the Cold War, impossible. That post-war period is dealt with rather fleetingly here, largely because to do it justice would involve a detailed study of the GDR's birth and development over the forty years of its existence. Throughout those years Jürgen was involved almost exclusively in running the Institute of Economic History in Berlin, carrying out research and writing daily. Ursula, after a short period working in several minor government positions, took up a successful career as a freelance writer of both novels and non-fiction. Both were members of the SED and played active political roles. After she published her book of reminiscences, which became a best-seller, Ursula was invited to address many readers' groups and to give lectures. In the eyes of a new generation she took on the mantle of a model communist. Jürgen had some influence in the ruling party because of the leading role he had played in exile. His views were listened to, if not always acted upon, and within the country as a whole he had the reputation of being a non-dogmatic and creative thinker. For a number of the dyed-in-the-wool dogmatists, he was considered a dissident. But both he and Ursula, because of their track record and their Jewish lineage, were treated in the GDR, certainly after Stalin's death, more as national assets.

It is not widely known that Stalin and the GDR leadership itself always envisaged German division as an unfortunate and temporary measure – the aim of German reunification was anchored in the GDR's first constitution – and there were early attempts made to promote that process. Ursula comments on this in her memoir:

> The Soviet Union's proposals for unification made in our name in 1952 got a hefty 'no' for an answer. Chancellor Adenauer of West Germany said in 1954: 'The best way to regain the German East is through rearmament'. And secretly West Germany was re-armed with the help of the USA.

The 'temporary' division became more entrenched with the hardening of the Cold War and led to an unsatisfactory two-state solution. Over the years, however, it became more widely accepted in both East and West that the two German states were there to stay. Once the GDR leadership realised that unification was no longer feasible or indeed desired in the short term, it actively promoted the idea of a GDR nationhood. Achievements and status were exaggerated – perhaps understandably in the face of West German arrogance and its assumption of being the sole representative of all Germans – but nevertheless it was embarrassing and painful even for many of its own citizens.

As an afterword to her reminiscences as a Soviet agent, Ursula wrote in 1991:

I worked within the possibilities open to me. Today that may seem opportunistic, and I have to ask myself how often was I dogmatic? How often did I believe in things which I now know are wrong? How often did I think of comrades as traitors, who proved to be the victims of our form of German Stalinism? ... I have to come to terms with my bitterness against the party leaders who could manipulate me and mislead me to the extent they did. Many good men and women now live in deep disappointment and have turned away from all they believed in. I cannot do that ... I still want social justice, access for everyone to a good education, and most of all I want no one to starve, and peace in the whole world. As much as ever I hate the arrogance of the rich, the power of money. I hate racism and fascism ... What I did not like in our country [the GDR] was the dogmatism within the party which increased with the years, nor the exaggeration of our achievements and the covering up of faults. And these grew worse when our economic growth came to a stop. I felt more and more sensitive to dishonesty in the reports and speeches from above, showing the isolation of the politbureau [Party leadership] from the people. It pained me and it angered me to see how we made ourselves look ridiculous in the eyes of the workers who knew the facts from their own factories ... But I still believed that a better socialism could be achieved if the old men were forced into their long-overdue retirement, and younger, able ones took over who might cure our almost chronic ailments.

These thoughts very much echo those of her brother Jürgen. With hindsight, in 1996, he asked himself the question whether he was also guilty and responsible for a social system from which people had increasingly turned away, and he tried to answer this question in a dialectical way. One should, he said:

differentiate between human failings and historical failings. When Kant asserts that good will is the decisive factor he was perhaps correct, if we wish to judge human character. But people also have a historical character. And I, like so many of my friends, failed. Not Harich and Havemann, nor me even in 1957/58, but yes me too,

> if you take the whole history of the GDR and my own activity into account. In history good will does not count, not honest endeavour, but only success. And there I completely failed. It is indeed a question of changing the world, not making it a little more bearable by setting a good example.

Jürgen defended state socialism, but criticised a thousand things in it, instead of the other way around.[1]

Increasingly, and certainly from the 1970s onwards, there was among many GDR citizens and leading intellectuals a strong sense that the country had reached an impasse and the Party leadership was incapable or unwilling to do anything about it. This is also reflected in a short comment by Markus Wolf, former head of the GDR's foreign intelligence service, who wrote in *Funksprüche an Sonja* (Radio Messages to Sonya) – a book of individual essays celebrating Ursula's work as an intelligence agent – about a conversation he had with Ursula [called Ruth in the book, as this was her pen name and the name under which most people in the GDR knew her] and her Soviet friend and fellow intelligence officer, Natasha:

> By the mid-1970s a period had come which had thrown up a number of new problems and these became the focus of our conversation. I remember a meeting lasting several hours with Natasha and Ruth [Ursula Kuczynski] at a writers' rest home on the Schwielow Lake near Werder. The worry about the situation in our country, the increasingly bad mood affecting wide circles of GDR citizens, the ever growing chasm between the situation as portrayed in the media and reality on the ground dominated our talks …

He also asks himself, 'why could no one in our countries manage to successfully promote the human values of freedom and justice which are intrinsic to that socialist idea and communism for which we fought?'[2]

At the conclusion of the last plenary conference of the GDR's governing Socialist Unity Party, on 18 October 1989, when the old leadership was swept aside and a new one elected, 150,000 members took part in a huge demonstration, many with home-made posters calling for real socialist democracy. They rallied in Berlin's Lustgarten and the gathering was addressed by a whole number of party members, including the 82-year-old Ursula. In her speech, which was often interrupted by applause, she said the following:

I was asked to speak to you by the city leadership of the Party, and the most refreshing thing is that I didn't have to submit my speech for approval beforehand, nothing in it has been censored and nothing has been prettified ... My speech is about loss of trust in the party ... My anger and my pain is also a result of the following: I ask myself: we have more than 2 million members of the party and I know from hundreds of events, from all the people I meet, I know from my own sons and my grown-up grandchildren, how long they have been genuinely concerned, but then often plunged into despair by the situation in our country. And what concerns me very much, is that if our party members, ordinary party members had been able to go onto the streets, there would have been over one and a half million of them, and they would have protested with posters saying, 'We want a clean socialism!' and 'We want real socialism, we don't want a deformed one!' but that didn't happen, because it couldn't happen because the apparatus of power wouldn't allow it. It was physically, psychologically and technically impossible.

And I've thought about that a lot. That the party that was supposed to be leading, that the comrades who all honestly believed in socialism and were worried about the way things were going, but were prevented from taking to the streets. It wasn't possible because an apparatus, a party apparatus existed which made it impossible. It wasn't that comrades were cowards; it just wasn't possible. And in any renewal of socialism, we need to reflect deeply on that; why were things that way?

I have to say to you, after the changes that are now happening, go and become part of the Party, work in it, change the future, work as clean socialists! I have courage, I am optimistic because I know that will happen, and I ask every comrade, whether in the Party apparatus or not, to work together, because it is beginning to change and it can only change if we all become involved.

Her short speech was greeted with thunderous applause. Her optimism and hopes, however, were not fulfilled, could not be fulfilled, because history in the form of the popular people's movement within the GDR itself, and the role of powerful West German forces and other Western governments, largely determined a different course. Once unification had been achieved, the hopes, the demands and aspirations of many East Germans were ignored and their interests steam-rollered. Markus Wolf wrote:

> Should we give up? My whole being resists that. Not because I, at my age, find it difficult to abandon ideas that have developed throughout my whole life, but because there has to be an alternative to a world in which money rules. My intellect tells me that.[3]

This was Ursula's attitude too, even though she was now too old to make a meaningful contribution.

FIGURE 14.1 Ursula and Len walking in the Brandenburg countryside near their home in Carwitz

Source: Peter Beurton. Photo: Barbara Köppe.

In *Funkspruche an Sonja* Wolf said of her:

> In my memory I will always see her, even in old age, as unchan-
> gingly beautiful, through her whole being, her charisma, she was a
> wonderful woman. We were both on the same wavelength – and
> that governed and determined our relationship. A real, deep friend-
> ship. Ursula – Sonya – Ruth – had many friends. With her whole
> life, she has left footprints. These will not be obliterated so easily.

Everyone said of her how friendly, modest and helpful she was. She certainly
never played or attempted to play the heroine or boast about what she had
done. It is perhaps supremely ironic and significant that two people –
Markus Wolf and Ursula Kuczynski – whose lives were devoted to
secrecy, subterfuge and iron discipline would become, in the late 1980s,
two of the most vociferous advocates of open, democratic government.

In the wake of German unification in 1990, Ursula wrote perceptively:
'Seen historically, unification was a necessity. You cannot divide a nation
forever by a wall, but much is now being destroyed in culture, science,
industry and social institutions that would have been worth keeping.'

One year later, in 1991, she was given clearance by the British government to visit the United Kingdom for the launch of her book
Sonya's Report in English. She was 84 years old, so it was no doubt
assumed that she no longer posed a danger to the state.

In today's Germany, Ursula Kuczynski/Ruth Werner is a largely
forgotten individual, from an era of history that few wish to be
reminded of; there are no streets or squares named after her, no
monuments. There is, though, a tiny *Ruth Werner Verein* (Ruth Werner
Association) in the east dedicated to her memory, and in 2015 it organised an exhibition of her life and work in the *Scheunenladen* in the
village of Carwitz in Brandenburg, where she and the family spent
many happy holidays, and where her son Peter now lives.

Peter said of her:

> Indeed, her children were her whole life – and as far as anyone can
> have several whole lives, she could. That was perhaps her most
> astonishing characteristic. And let's put it this way – there is always
> something in every biography that is unfathomable. The life of my

mother was also characterised by a lot of luck. It was the luck of a great optimist, who was always curious about the future. She was Jewish, a communist and patient humanist, a modest and taciturn woman but right to the end, despite all the disappointments and frustrations, she remained a person very much of the left.

Both she and Len remained devoted to each other since they first met. As they aged, they increasingly enjoyed spending time with their children and grandchildren and taking long walks in the Brandenburg countryside, north of Berlin. Ursula, like Jürgen, remained politically active almost until the day she died, but after the demise of the GDR she did become very depressed and this probably accelerated her own demise. In the very last years of her life, when she had become very frail, she was looked after largely by her daughter Janina. She died on 20 July 2000. Len had pre-deceased her almost three years earlier, on 29 October 1997.

FIGURE 14.2 Ursula on her ninetieth birthday with Jürgen, Brigitte, Sabine and Renate

Source: Kuczynski family archive.

Notes

1 Jürgen Kuczynski, *Fortgesetzter Dialog mit meinem Urenkel*, Berlin, 1996, p. 81.
2 Markus Wolf, *In Eigenem Auftrag*, Schneekluth, 1991, p. 326.
3 Ibid.

15

THE BRITISH KUCZYNSKIS

At the end of the war the Kuczynski family became separated after their years together in Britain. Ursula and Jürgen went back to live in Germany, but the other siblings remained in Britain, which had become their home. As they were the younger ones when the family arrived as refugees, they had settled more easily and perhaps, in the meantime, become more British than German. While Ursula and Jürgen became actively involved in the attempt to build a new democratic Germany, their sisters in Britain put all their efforts into the British Communist Party. Only Barbara and her husband remained outside, becoming members of the Labour Party. Brigitte and Barbara were already young adults when the family left Germany, while Sabine and Renate experienced their extended childhood in Britain. All five Kuczynski sisters married British men, even though Sabine's husband, Frank, had a German father. Whatever role, if any, the sisters played in Ursula's clandestine work it was probably minimal, and with the end of the war any such activities almost certainly came to an end. The MI5 files present no evidence of any of the family members actually working on behalf of the Soviet Union, apart from the minor role played by Brigitte in helping her sister Ursula recruit agents to work clandestinely in Nazi Germany.

The first general election held after the war, in July 1945, came as a shock to the Conservatives, who had been convinced that Churchill, the hero of the war, would romp home. Instead there was an overwhelming majority for a Labour government. On the first day of the new parliament, the massed ranks of Labour members sang 'The Red Flag', and the Tories were scandalised.

The victorious battle against fascism, the alliance with the Soviet Union and a determination not to return to the bad old pre-war days of poverty and unemployment had revolutionised many who clearly wanted a break with the past. The newly elected Labour government did indeed bring in a number of progressive and 'socialist' measures, including the establishment of a proper welfare state and a National Health Service, as well as the nationalisation of the coal mines and the railways, but it stopped short of introducing a full socialist system.

Despite the election of a Labour government, though, it wasn't very long before the world was thrust back into the old confrontational pattern, with the Soviet Union cast as the main enemy. After Churchill's ominous speech at Fulton, Missouri and his evocation of an 'iron curtain' descending across Europe, communists in Britain, after their brief period of acceptance as part of the mainstream, were once again stigmatised as the 'enemy within' and as quasi-Soviet agents, an accusation that was given credence by the arrest and prosecution of the atom spy Klaus Fuchs and later the revelations around the group of ex-Cambridge graduates, Burgess, Maclean and Philby, who had become Soviet agents.

Large numbers of people throughout Europe were war-weary and looked forward to rebuilding their lives in peace and in hope of a better future, and in a number of countries there was a genuine and widespread demand for revolutionary social change. Communist parties which had played key roles in the resistance to and defeat of fascism emerged with great popular support. This situation frightened the USA and conservative political forces, and they determined to roll it back. A campaign was unleashed to frighten people with stories of a Soviet threat and an impending invasion by Soviet forces, despite the fact that the country had been completely devastated and was in no position to wage war anywhere. The idea of an impending new war with the Soviet Union – this time with nuclear weapons – was rejected by many, but the short-lived co-operation that had flourished after the end of the war in many European countries between anti-fascist forces soon disintegrated in the wake of the increasingly virulent anti-Soviet rhetoric. The use of Marshall Aid as a bribe to Western European countries to bind them within the US sphere of influence was extremely effective in stimulating post-war growth, full employment and the increasing availability of consumer products. With the establishment of NATO in 1949, the emergence of two German states and the re-arming of West Germany the situation became once again extremely tense and intractable.

In the wake of the dropping of nuclear bombs on Japan at the close of the war and the clear determination of the USA, with British collusion, to continue developing such weapons despite the evidence of their horrendous destructive power, there arose a worldwide peace movement. Clement Attlee, the Labour prime minister, however, gave the green light for Britain to develop its own nuclear bomb and did so in absolute secrecy, without even informing his Cabinet colleagues.

Communists were active from the very beginning in the peace movement, as were the Kuczynski sisters in Britain, with the war still a recent memory. This movement enjoyed widespread popularity and huge conferences were held in a number of European cities demanding a peaceful world and the banning of nuclear weapons. It enjoyed the support not only of communists but of progressive church leaders, mainstream politicians, artists and intellectuals. The right-wing press, however, condemned the movement as a communist front with the goal of undermining Western governments and paving the way for a Soviet invasion. The ongoing and popular campaign to prevent the re-arming of West Germany, where former Nazis again held leading positions, was also strongly supported by the Kuczynski sisters and their husbands. The peace movement was also a key target of MI5 monitoring, as its files reveal. It was a time of fear, suspicion and witch-hunts, the most infamous of which were those carried out in Washington by the House Committee on Un-American Activities, closely associated with Senator Joseph McCarthy.

The families also became closely involved and active very early on in the Campaign for Nuclear Disarmament, despite the initial scepticism and disapproval of the Communist Party leadership, which saw the campaign as a largely middle-class movement with pacifist aims.

Despite the harshness of the Cold War, the Communist Party of Great Britain maintained a slowly declining, but relatively stable core membership, and a strong presence in the trade unions throughout the period until the late 1980s. It went through a number of crises, largely as a result of the impact of outside events on the Party, not least the Krushchev revelations about Stalin's crimes which had enormous repercussions, and were followed by the suppression of the Hungarian uprising in 1956. Despite everything and any doubts they may have had, the Kuczynski sisters, apart from Barbara who was not a member, remained loyal until the Party broke apart in 1991. Not long after the Krushchev revelations, there came the infighting over the Soviet–Chinese conflict, when a number of members who supported China formed their own party in 1965 – the Communist Party of Britain (Marxist-Leninist). The Prague Spring and its suppression by Soviet tanks in 1968 also caused deep divisions. Then in 1977 came a breakaway initiated by the Party's Surrey district secretary, Sid French, who felt the Party was becoming too Euro-communist and that it should stay loyal to the Soviet party line. He set up the New Communist Party. The Euro-communist wing of the CPGB began looking towards Italy and Spain for inspiration and away from the Soviet Union. However, the real implosion took place in 1991 and coincided with the demise of East European state socialism. The CPGB split into two main factions, Democratic Left, which followed a more Euro-communist policy and distanced itself completely from the Soviet model of socialism. The other faction went on to 're-found' the party as the Communist Party of Britain and retained control of the 'Party's paper', the *Morning Star*. These momentous changes impacted on the Kuczynskis in different ways. Brigitte and her husband first went with the Democratic Left faction, but she later joined the Labour Party. In contrast, Sabine remained a strong supporter of the *Morning Star*, which allied itself with the CPB when the Party split irrevocably. Renate had been involved in the small 'hard-line' Straight Left faction within the CPGB for some time before the split, but refused to become ghettoised, retaining links with several groups.

All the siblings remained in contact with each other, even across the Cold War divide, although relations, as in any family, had their ups and downs. Jürgen, as the eldest, was revered rather than loved by his younger siblings; he remained closest to Ursula. Barbara ploughed her own furrow and, although progressive in outlook, she did not share her siblings' commitment to the communist cause. Only Renate maintained regular contact with her, mainly by telephone. Brigitte, although close to the two younger sisters politically, maintained only loose contact with the others. Sabine and Renate, as the two youngest, were closest, and their families spent alternate Christmases with each other.

From around 1960 onwards the three sisters, Renate, Sabine and Brigitte, took it in turns to take their annual holiday with family members in East Berlin. Ann remembers the family driving – they went by car – speedily through the 'enemy camp' of West Germany to reach the territory of the GDR as quickly as possible. She felt this was rather odd, but it reflected Cold War attitudes of the time.

The Simpson family (parents and three children) would stay with Ursula in Berlin and also spend days with Ursula's family in the countryside at Carwitz where they had a holiday home or 'dacha'. While in East Berlin they also visited Jürgen but such visits were only occasional and, as Renate's daughter, Ann, relates, the children were commanded to be on their best behaviour and not talk too much. In Jürgen and Marguerite's household matters were conducted rather formally. Ann clearly felt little affinity with Jürgen's family, but on the other hand was immediately drawn to Ursula. Ursula had a profound influence on her life, she says, not politically, but as a human being. Ann was full of admiration for her and the life she had led. She was chatty, warm and uncomplicated. In her company life was so easy-going. When Ursula heard that Ann had a boyfriend (she had just met Christian, her future husband), thinking of her own life, she impressed upon her: 'make sure you have a baby before you miss the opportunity!' Ann was over thirty at the time. She also felt close to Ursula's daughter, Janina, who she says was, like her mother, warm and talkative, although not so politically involved as the rest of the family.

Renate

Renate (nickname 'Rene') was physically very similar to her elder sister Sabine. She was tall and slim with a gentle, but earnest manner. She was widely liked and admired by those who knew or worked with her.

FIGURE 15.1 Renate and Arthur Simpson with their children Ann, Ludi and
      Robert
Source: Ann and Ludi Simpson.

She made few if any enemies, being an integrating figure and tolerant
of the views of others.

She was the only member of the British branch of the family who
left reminiscences of her childhood and about her life in Britain as a
young refugee, arriving in 1934 when she was only eleven years old.
Two of her three children, Stephen (known as Ludi) and Ann, made
tape recordings of her in the late 1990s as an oral history document. In this
section I make use of those recordings and quote from them, but have
summarised where I felt appropriate.

Renate dearly loved Olga, her German nanny, called Ollo by all the
children. This is the same Olga who accompanied Ursula to Switzerland to look after the children. 'As I grew up', Renate said, 'she swore
that she would bring up my children too.' But Renate had other ideas,
and was determined to be there for her own children and not have a

nanny because, from her own experience, it was clear that the nanny became in many respects more important than the mother. She and her siblings spent a considerable amount of time with Olga, perhaps more than with their mother because both parents were often absent, particularly Robert. But in Renate's early years he was probably more at home than some fathers are today. He was, though, even then pre-occupied with his research and writing, and often travelling around the country and abroad, as he was politically very active and became a strong supporter of the growing peace movement. Towards the end of the 1920s he spent considerable time in the United States while the girls were still quite small, often six months at a time, and was sometimes joined there by his wife.

Apart from Olga and an adult friend of the family who also helped if needed, the girls were left very much to their own devices. Jürgen had already left home, so Ursula, as the eldest of the sisters, took command as long as she was still in Berlin, but the girls were able to enjoy a considerable amount of freedom, unusual for children at the time.

Renate remembers that they couldn't play noisy games in front of the house because their father had his study there and, when he was at home, didn't wish to be disturbed. Even at table he expected his children to keep quiet until they were old enough to join in the lively discussions of the adults. But he was much loved by them all, not least because he didn't have to concern himself much with disciplining them. He collected stamps with Sabine (Bine, as she was known in the family) and played chess with the older children. Their mother, on the other hand, did come in for some criticism because the role of disciplinarian fell to her, although Renate relates that she was in reality a doting mother, particularly when any of them were ill, even though Olga was always at her side.

In 1929 Renate started primary school in Berlin, but was not happy there. The strict discipline and daily, formalised instruction contrasted sharply with the idyllic freedom she had enjoyed up to then around the house and in the gardens of the big house on Schlachtensee; that loss was hard to take. In that era in Germany physical activity and fresh air were considered essential for a healthy life, so the girls were often driven out of the house by their parents or nanny to play outside, come rain or shine. Renate recalled that Sabine, though, would just sit in a dry spot and read while she pestered her to play games.

The children's idyll was rudely shattered in early March 1933 when a group of Nazis arrived on the doorstep, demanding to search the house. Renate relates:

> anyone coming to search your house is a shock and a crude intrusion into your life, whether they are the police or criminals, but these were just Nazi thugs. They invariably came first thing in the morning. I don't know who opened the door, but they just barged in anyway. We were still in bed and had to quickly make ourselves presentable and go downstairs into one room where we were made to sit while they searched. But they were not very clever so they missed a whole lot of things that could have been very incriminating for us. In retrospect one episode was very amusing, but could have been calamitous. I hadn't realised, but our nanny was a member of the Communist Party, so you can imagine what sort of a household it was – highly political – on her bedside table lay her communist party membership card and contribution stamps that were waiting to be stuck in it, but they didn't even notice it!

They were really after Robert, but he had already escaped their clutches.

The Nazis returned for him again that same evening, but of course he had made good his escape once he gathered that they were searching for him. 'They came back several times', Renate related, 'not always so early in the morning but ringing the bell like mad and asking after my father, but they couldn't get anything out of us of course.'

Robert, unlike many others of Jewish background, had no illusions about what would happen to him if he were caught. Lots of people, though, did have illusions, Renate said. They would say, 'Oh, this Nazi business, you know, it won't last long.' Many of them stayed on and ended up in concentration camps.

Renate takes up the story again:

> After my father had gone, we were still able as a family to meet up that summer in Honfleur, Normandy, France, in a house that belonged to a good friend of the family, Mary Kelsey, a US

Quaker.[1] She had, for some time, been running a summer school for young people. We were allowed to use the house when there was no school and could meet up with my father there – for my parents that was a wonderful moment.

It was there that Barbara Kuczynski met her future husband, Duncan.

After their mother returned to Germany with the girls, they stayed in the Berlin house until she eventually managed to sell it – at a much reduced price, of course, 'because that's how it was if you were not a Nazi'.

'I was quite good at primary school but at secondary school', Renate relates, 'I seemed to be doing everything wrong and got fed up, I did not feel happy at all.' She came home one day and told her mother that she didn't want to go to school anymore. This was in 1934, and as her mother knew they were about to leave Germany – although she couldn't tell the children for fear of the authorities finding out – told her daughter she didn't have to. This pleased Renate immensely, but she was left oblivious of the real reasoning behind the decision. The parents always had to be very circumspect about what they said in front of the younger children in terms of politics or about the Nazis because they might have then inadvertently said things at school which could have endangered them all:

> We followed our father, almost a year after he'd escaped. My sister Barbara had just taken her Abitur or A-level equivalent and was the first to join my father in London for about half a year to give him some semblance of home life, and then the rest of us followed.

Jürgen stayed on in Germany and became part of the resistance movement:

> so in that sense there was something you could do, but by that time my mother was just over fifty and she wouldn't have got herself involved … I mean if you were Jewish you were finished, but being Jewish and a communist was even worse.

Robert came to London in 1933, at the beginning of the university year in October, and the rest of the family followed in February 1934, joining him in the house at 25A Upper Park Road in Hampstead, northwest London.

My mother 'only learned how to cook after we moved to London, when she was fifty', Renate says, 'and although she was very messy in the kitchen, she was also quite imaginative'. Renate recalled her mother spending a lot of her time in those early years before war broke out writing letters to friends back in Germany, telling them: 'For God's sake get out.' It was her mother's way of fighting, she says. Renate looked up to and found both her parents inspirational and never resented their commitment to political and social causes, despite seeing less of them because of it.

For all those refugees fleeing the rise of fascism in Europe, the experience of exile was almost without exception traumatic, not only for the first but also for the second generation born either shortly before emigrating or afterwards. Overnight, they lost their language, culture and roots, were plunged into an alien, quite often hostile, world.

When Renate started school in England she didn't know a word of English. Her parents placed her in a small private girls' school run by four friends – Kingsley School in Belsize Park. Her mother and father could already speak English as they had spent longer periods in the USA. Robert had been to a French gymnasium in Berlin, so also spoke French from early childhood, as her mother did.

Renate enjoyed her school in London, despite having to overcome the language barrier. She was fortunate in soon making friends there with the daughter of another exile family, the Wolffs. Her parents were befriended by the Wolffs and their daughter Tanya was already going to the school. Very soon there would be a number of other German refugee children in the school too. Renate says that the first year was very hard for her, but she was aware of the real need to learn the language, and after only a relatively short time she found herself top of the class in English grammar.

In September 1939, after war had been declared, the first major state-organised evacuation scheme began. Plans were put in operation to evacuate children, pregnant mothers, the disabled and the blind from major population centres. The government was preparing for the expected mass bombardment of British cities and large-scale casualties. Many of the wealthy used their money to send their children to safe havens abroad, to rural boarding schools or moved the whole family to a country cottage. Most of the 1 million official evacuees who left the cities, though, were working-class children, as were most of their hosts, who received a small allowance towards the upkeep of their new charges. This whole process signified a serious interruption of the children's education, as well as psychological and emotional stress for all concerned.

Renate's school was evacuated to Bossiney Court, Tintagel, in Cornwall. She was then sixteen and about to take her final school examinations or 'Matric', as it was then known. She would not be given much opportunity to enjoy the bracing sea air and clifftop walks, however. Not long after they had arrived, in early 1940, all German pupils were immediately sent back to London, because as 'enemy aliens' they were considered potentially dangerous. No Germans were allowed to stay near the coast – and no distinction was made here between Nazi sympathisers and anti-fascists or Jews. The powers that be no doubt felt that Renate could perhaps use her torch to send coded signals to German U-boats lurking out in the Irish Sea. There was much concern at the time as it was felt that the country was facing the imminent threat of a German invasion.

This all happened only a fortnight before the girls were due to sit their exam, but the authorities arranged for them to take it at another school in London. Renate didn't mind being back in the capital and at home anyway, because it was almost time for her to leave school. As a result, but not out of choice, she would also experience the first Blitz on London in August 1940. In that same year she joined the UK section of the Free German Youth organisation alongside her sister Sabine who was already a member.

A gifted student, after leaving school at 16, Renate began studying economics at the LSE, where her father taught. She had hardly begun her course when the student body was evacuated to Cambridge to escape the intensified bombing on London that took place that September of 1940. This move would turn out to be serendipitous, as it was there that she would meet her future husband and life-long comrade, Arthur Simpson.

September was also the month scheduled by Hitler for an invasion of Britain, but this had to be postponed as Göring's promised domination of the skies over the island remained unfulfilled. That month, though, saw continuous air battles over southeast England between the Nazis' Messerschmitts and Heinkel bombers and the British Spitfires and Hurricanes in the so-called 'Battle of Britain'.

In Cambridge, students from the evacuated colleges were allowed to attend lectures and use the university library if they needed. There were some wonderful teachers, Renate recalled, 'really out of this world'. One of them was Harold Laski, a leading Labour Party activist, and 'just about the best lecturer you could imagine'. Laski had been one of her father's colleagues and he had told Renate about Laski, saying: 'you will find he will always wear a red tie and have a red handkerchief in his pocket and is as righteous as hell'. 'Of course he was a bit of an actor', she said, 'but he was a wonderful person, for any student, but particularly if you were specialising in politics and government. He was very caring too, he'd do anything for his students.'

In 1942, while still a full-time student, she was elected onto the National Union of Students (NUS) executive. After completing her degree in 1943, she was asked by the students' union if she would like to work for it, as they were looking for a new full-time worker. Before the war the NUS office would have had dozens of people working in it, but now had only a skeleton staff, because all the eligible young men had been drafted; there was an acute shortage of staff everywhere.

As part of her work for the NUS, she recruited students to the 'Land War' to harvest crops during college holidays, and toured Britain to recruit smaller colleges to the union, working under the guidance of its national secretary, Margot Kettle, a Communist Party member and wife of the well-known literary critic Arnold Kettle. At this time, Renate was also elected from the LSE student body as a delegate to the founding congress of the Free German Movement in Britain, which was held in London, and chaired by her father.

She also did her stint for the war effort, fire watching in Cambridge, 'which meant you had to walk around, after bombing raids, checking that there were no unexploded bombs lying around'. She recalled the night when there really was an awful raid on Cambridge – it only had one major raid – and found herself on fire watching duty that evening in the Fitzwilliam Museum. For a young woman, quite an exciting but also scary responsibility, hearing the bombs fall, seeing the fires in the distance and wondering if your building would be next.

When the Germans intensified their bombing raids on London, a popular movement sprang up to demand proper air raid shelters for the population. Many of those leading the campaign were communists. As the government continued dragging its feet, they demanded that the tube network be opened up as temporary shelter. This was strongly resisted by the authorities until local people simply took things into their own hands and went down into the tunnels anyway and spent the night there during bombing raids. Renate says:

> the tube was taken over by the people because the government had not supplied enough shelters. The underground was the safest place, and so people began using the tube stations at all sorts of hours and there were many in bunks. So when I used the tube to go somewhere, I would see all these people half asleep, propped up against the wall.

However, when Renate moved back to London in 1944 permanently she decided to sit things out above ground. That same year she joined the British Communist Party and for the rest of her life would become very much what she termed 'a political animal – someone who took the world seriously, who understood that changes were made by people working together to make decisions, good or bad'.

In 1943 Renate met Arthur, a marine biologist, while working for the NUS. They married in March 1945, before the end of the war, in Hampstead Town Hall. He was secretary of the Science Faculty Committee of the NUS and, when Renate started working there full-time, they got to know one another well because she was in charge of organising events like faculty committees and agricultural camps in which he was also involved.

Arthur was born in 1916 in Simla, India, where his father, George Simpson, a renowned meteorologist, was working for the government. He had been a member of Scott's historic Antarctic expedition in 1910, and there constructed one of the continent's first weather stations. He was left in command when Scott and his party left on their last fateful journey to the South Pole. For his pioneering work in meteorology he was given a knighthood.

After passing his 'Matric' Arthur travelled to Australia where he worked on his uncle's sheep farm, before going up to Sydney University New South Wales to study for a B.Sc. in agriculture. After graduating in 1939, he returned to Britain and war was declared while he was on his way home. Back in Britain, he went to Hull to complete a second degree in zoology under Britain's foremost marine biologist, Alister Hardy. The beginning of the war meant that fisheries research was closed down, so he began work for the National Institute of Agricultural Botany in Cambridge. After starting there he felt it was his duty to sign up for the armed forces and 'do his bit' in the war. But the Institute would not let him go because the work he was doing was deemed to be highly important.

He went on to undertake research into agricultural pests on commercial crops and became Chair of the Cambridge branch of the Association of Scientific Workers. While at the institute, in 1941, he too joined the Communist Party, but as he was working for the government he was obliged to keep a low profile. As a civil servant, he could not be an open communist or to take part in political activities. Renate would be the political activist in the family.

As a young married couple Renate and Arthur moved first to Lowestoft, where Arthur took a job with the Ministry of Agriculture, Fisheries and Food. Later, from 1958 onwards he became director of its shellfish research laboratory at Burnham-on-Crouch. Renate found work as a local authority housing officer. In 1948, their first child, Ann, was born, followed by Robert (later known as Amila) in 1950. These births prompted letters to the local press with demands for nursery schools which were totally lacking. In 1953 their third child, Stephen (known as Ludi), was born. Later that year the family moved again to Conwy in north Wales, where the two older children attended Welsh schools. Arthur had taken up a post there as director of the fisheries laboratory.

Ann told me that her parents were very liberal in the way they brought them up, but one rule was enforced while the children were still at home: everyone was expected to be present for the evening meal.

In the household, Arthur was the taciturn one, while Renate did most of the talking and would, Ann says, 'talk at them'. Although both Ann and Stephen were both very close to their mother, Ann describes her as a 'typical Jewish Momma, overpowering, hands-on and often right'. Both Ann and Stephen took on board virtually everything she said on political matters and both joined the Communist Party as young adults. Their brother Robert had strong conflicts with his parents during adolescence, but when he went to university he too was active in communist student politics and became secretary of Birmingham University NUS. However, after graduation, he threw overboard his parents' politics and adopted an alternative, hippy-like lifestyle. He went on to change his name, first to John and then to Amila, a Brazilian indigenous name, and became alienated from both his parents and his siblings over shorter or longer periods.

During the 1950s and 1960s, Renate was very active in the local Communist Party branch and began fundraising for the *Daily Worker*. Then, in 1954, she and her sister Sabine were sent to East Berlin as interpreters at the World Peace Council congress, a task she took on again when it was held in Helsinki in 1955 as well as in Colombo, Ceylon (now Sri Lanka) in 1957. In 1962 and 1963 she again attended World Peace Council congresses, this time in Moscow while still working as a German and social studies teacher at Chelmsford FE college (all these visits abroad were duly noted in MI5's files on the family).

Renate kept in close contact with Jürgen and Ursula in East Berlin and regularly exchanged family and political news. Ludi says that he remembers vividly each Christmas receiving parcels from East Berlin with gingerbread biscuits and sometimes decorated gingerbread houses, which he and his siblings looked forward to each year. Ironically, at the time, there was much talk about the sending of food parcels to Eastern Europe, but here was a British family receiving food parcels from the East.

In 1958, the family moved from Colwyn Bay to Lowestoft in East Anglia, where Renate began secretarial work supporting Lou Hitchins, the new principal of Chelmsford Further Education College. There she taught occasional classes in German and social studies, and also, in 1959, took on a part-time teaching post for history and current affairs at the Harris girls' secondary school in Lowestoft.

In Maldon, where they lived, she became CND district membership secretary and continued working for the local Communist Party branch. Much later, after retiring, Arthur also joined CND and felt able to take up political and social activities again.

Renate was active in her local parent–teachers association and, apart from Communist Party work and fundraising for the *Daily Worker*, was also involved in the campaign to keep the Maldon–Witham railway line open during the infamous Beeching railway butchery in the mid-sixties. Rural lines like those in East Anglia were particularly affected. Protests helped save some stations and lines, but the majority were closed as planned and Beeching's name remains irreversibly associated with the closures and the loss of many local services in the period that followed.

Journalist David Aaronovitch, in his reminscences, recalls his mother and other local Parliament Hill comrades like Jock Nicolson and Renate's sister Bridget campaigning on freezing mornings outside Gospel Oak station to keep the North London Line open in the face of Beeching's proposed cuts. Their particular battle was successful and, as he writes, 'Today's commuters cannot know that they should thank those chilled Commie leafleters of a generation ago.'[2]

With the expansion of higher education during the 1960s, Renate took a job, in 1964, as a research assistant to Ernest Rudd, who led the first research unit into higher education. She interviewed prospective landlords about attitudes to students in the year before Essex University's first intake in 1964, and found a niche for her own future research when she was asked to write a brief history of doctoral degrees for one of the unit's publications. In 1967, her husband Arthur was appointed senior chief scientific advisor to the government on the catastrophic *Torrey Canyon* oil spill – one of the worst of its kind off the British coast.

During this period she was also involved in translating Marx's *Theories of Surplus Value, Vol. 2* into English for the Soviet state publishing house in Moscow, where her daughter Ann would later spend a year studying at the university. Between 1969 and 1971 she pursued her own research into postgraduate education in Britain.

In 1970 Arthur was offered a post in Cuba, working for the Food and Agricultural Organization of the UN. Only eleven years after the successful revolution against the Batista dictatorship, it was an exciting time to be in Cuba. There he would assist in research and training at the Centro de Investigaciones Pesqueras (Fisheries Research Centre) in Havana. In 1971 Renate joined him there. In Cuba she continued her research into higher education, but examined the country's own system, and later published her results.

In 1975 they both moved to Manila in the Philippines; Arthur, still working for the FAO, was asked to undertake research as part of the South China Sea Fisheries Programme. Renate again followed her own interest and carried out research into the higher education system there, also publishing the results. In 1976 the couple returned again to Maldon in East Anglia and Arthur retired from paid work, while Renate continued her research into the history of postgraduate education in the UK. The results of that research were published in 1983 under the title *How the Ph.D. came to Britain*; it was later expanded into *The Development of the Ph.D. in Britain 1917–1959 and Since*, which was published in 2009, and a celebratory party was held in Coram's Fields Centre in Bloomsbury, attended by many academics and friends, including the historian Eric Hobsbawm.

In 1980, after a lifetime of travelling and living in so many different places and countries, Renate was relieved that they were able buy a studio flat in Bloomsbury. But being back in London didn't mean she would become politically inactive – far from it. She once again took up the reins of political activism, her energy and passionate commitment seemingly undiminished. She became an active member of the Camden branch of the Communist Party, London CND, Cuba Solidarity, Caribbean Labour Solidarity and the Marx Memorial Library. She campaigned ardently for the freedom of the former New Jewel Movement government leaders imprisoned in Grenada after the US invasion of the island. Alongside her friend Nicola Seyd she organised regular second-hand book sales to raise funds for the *Morning Star* and they were both founder members of the Socialist Film Society. She was also an enthusiastic member of the Royal Statistical Society, among the many other organisations and campaigning groups she belonged to.

During the late 1970s she translated her sister Ursula's autobiography, *Sonya's Report*, into English. She gave copies to her sisters, but Ursula was against publishing it in the UK at the time because she felt it might cause the British family members problems. It was eventually published in 1991, although her sister Barbara was still opposed to its publication and Brigitte, too, did not wish to be mentioned in it. Ursula came over for the launch and gave a number of interviews to the British media, who were extremely interested in her story.

Until a diagnosis of the onset of Alzheimer's disease in 2009, when she was 85, and her eventual move to a residential care home in 2011, Renate remained politically and socially active until the end. She was survived by her three children: Ann, Robert/Amila, Stephen and their children. Arthur pre-deceased her in 2002.

Renate's son Stephen, known as 'Ludi', has so far been the only one of the British side of the family to follow in the footsteps of his grandfather and uncle, becoming a statistician and demographer. After working as a research fellow, he became Professor of Population Studies at the University of Manchester, where he retains an honorary post. He is perhaps best known for his contributions to estimating those missed in the national censuses, to debates about ethnicity and segregation in Britain, and to local authority planning models. He is currently working on a variety of research projects, as well as lecturing in Latin America.

Sabine

When Sabine arrived in Britain she was 15 years old. She would be only 22 when, in 1941, she married Frank Loeffler, also the child of a German refugee. At that time he was Secretary of the Refugee Council in Britain, which was devoted to aiding anti-fascist exiles. She was tall and willowy with a gentle demeanour and always generous with her help for others; the impression she gave was very much of the middle-class lawyer's wife, rather than the feisty radical she was. They marked their wedding with a celebratory breakfast in the Isokon building in Lawn Road, cooked for them by Philip Harben.

As every adult member of the family needed to earn their keep during the early exile and war years, Sabine found paid work assembling radio parts. At the same time she joined the Camden branch of the Communist Party. After having given birth to three children she became a nursery teacher in a Montessori school. Later she went into

FIGURE 15.2 Sabine working in the *Morning Star* archive
Source: Harriet Loeffler.

journalism and during the late 1960s undertook voluntary work as a translator for the World Peace Council, as did her sister Renate, attending conferences in Helsinki and Sri Lanka before becoming the librarian at the *Daily Worker* (later renamed the *Morning Star*) for two decades before retiring from the paper in 1989 at the age of 70. But not willing to put her feet up, she then became a volunteer librarian at the Marx Memorial Library.

During the post-war period, the acute housing shortage and lack of rent controls were ongoing issues of contention throughout the country, not least in London. Whether one lived in an East End tenement or in a middle-class block of flats, there would invariably be a need for organised struggle in order to obtain or maintain decent housing conditions and affordable rents. The grandly named Parliament Hill Mansions where Frank and Sabine lived in northwest London were very much in need of renovation. This led Sabine to establish the Lissenden Gardens (Gospel Oak) Tenants Association in 1972, which would successfully campaign to have the flats transferred from private ownership to Camden Council, which then carried out the necessary modernisation. The owner had originally planned selling Parliament Hill Mansions to a property developer.

Her husband Frank was born in Oxford in 1920. His father, George, a chemist who came from Germany, took his wife Elizabeth to Canada at the outbreak of the First World War and lived there for the duration, to avoid being interned in Britain. They returned when the war ended via Germany to settle in the Channel Islands. Frank's early experiences of moving around helped shape his later interests – he would become the Chair/Secretary of the Refugee Council. He read law at Cambridge in the 1930s, when it was a hotbed of political activism and there was a very lively communist group. There he would have come across a number of the more famous or infamous alumni. It was at Cambridge where he too cemented what would be his life-long commitment to communism.

During the Second World War, he worked in an electronics factory – a protected industry – and also volunteered as an air raid warden in Hampstead, where he was then living. After the war he returned to practise law, and set up chambers in Bedford Square with the Belsize Park-based communist lawyer Jack Gaster. The firm was Gaster, Vowles, Turner, and Loeffler and became well known for its advocacy work on social justice. Frank was a long-time member of the Haldane Society, which united like-minded left-wing lawyers, and he was a keen theatre-goer, supporting the socialist drama group Unity Theatre.

Frank became a regular visitor to Franco's Spain, where he defended the rights of political prisoners in the wake of Franco's defeat of the Republican government. He worked as an advisor for the legal team on the Julian Grimau case in the early 1960s. Julian Grimau, a Spaniard, had fought in the Spanish Civil War, but returned to Spain from exile to work underground. He was arrested, tortured, and thrown out of the window of a police building, all of which he survived. Frank was at the heart of a massive global protest movement in 1963 to prevent his execution on the orders of Franco himself. Franco's Civil Guard, extraordinarily, refused the order to mount a firing squad and the regular army had to be brought in to do the job. A botched execution ensued, whereby twenty-seven bullets were fired before the officer in charge had to deliver a coup de grace.

Amongst the many cases of alleged injustice Frank handled, one of the most difficult was being asked to represent Jack Hendy (father of the left-wing lawyer John Hendy QC), one of the leaders of the Electrical Trade Union (ETU) who was accused of vote-rigging in 1960.

The ETU was one of the best organised unions in the country and it had been able to negotiate good wages and conditions for its members. For many years it had been led by communists. The employers, supported by the national press, were determined to break the union's strength, so when new national leadership elections were announced in 1960 – it was traditionally a well-run and democratically organised union – a well-orchestrated campaign of red-baiting and anti-communist hysteria was unleashed in the media. Several of the union's leaders feared that this campaign would cost them the election so, in panic, indulged in vote-rigging to ensure their re-election. Unfortunately for them, a disgruntled ex-communist and whistle blower, Frank Chapple, spilled the beans and as a consequence the leaders were put on trial.

The case became a virtual show trial, orchestrated by the employers and the government of the day. The media went into overdrive around the case, and the accused were virtually convicted before the trial had even begun, making fair process almost impossible. Although several of the union's leaders were put on trial, only two leading communists were convicted of vote-rigging. The real aim of the trial, though, was to break the Left's strength in the union and to demonstrate the deviousness and untrustworthiness of communists everywhere; this was, after all, the height of the Cold War. In that sense it was highly successful. The judge at the trial upheld the ballot-rigging allegations against only Frank Haxel and Frank Foulkes. The trial judge, Justice Winn, exonerated Jack Hendy of electoral fraud, noting that he had, in the industry, acquired the nick-name of 'Honest Jack'. Winn accepted that he was 'a man of intellectual honesty as well as intellectual power, personally honourable to the extent that he would not adopt any course of conduct which seemed to him to be unjust, unless a considerable advantage to the Communist Party left him no choice'. Jack and a number of other leading activists were expelled by the new, dominant right-wing leadership of the union and were barred from holding office for seven years, despite Winn's exoneration. Jack went on to study law at night school and became a barrister, although he never practised. Instead he taught industrial law at Ealing Technical College.

Frank Loeffler was, though, equally happy using his legal skills to assist neighbours facing problems with house repairs or with welfare issues, and offered free legal advice, wrote letters on behalf of tenants and, after his retirement, embarked on a long battle on behalf of residents in the housing block where he and Sabine also lived to ensure they were paying fair charges for building work. Following his retirement, he could often be spotted walking near his home in Lissenden Gardens with his pipe clenched firmly between his teeth. He died, aged 87, in 2007; Sabine pre-deceased him on 8 January 2005, aged 85. They had three children, Harriet, Caroline and Ian. Caroline became a painter, and worked for many years in animation. Later she trained as a yoga teacher. Harriet taught for twenty years in comprehensive schools, before training as a psychotherapist and working in private practice.

North London, particularly around Hampstead, Muswell Hill and Belsize Park, where both the Loefflers and Nicolsons lived, held a significant number of refugee families, many Jewish, and the Communist Party was quite strongly represented in the area. One of those who lived in Belsize Park for a time and was also a member of the local branch was James Klugmann. He had been a key figure in the recruitment of a whole number of Cambridge students to the Party in the 1930s, including Philby, Burgess and Maclean. He went on to become one of the Party's leading intellectuals and editor of its theoretical journal *Marxism Today*. He was, during his life, also kept under continuous surveillance by MI5.

Barbara

Barbara was the fourth born of the Kuczynski siblings, arriving in the world in 1913, one year before the outbreak of the Great War. She would be the only one of the children not to join the Communist Party. Even from an early age she appeared to be different temperamentally from the others, but whether this had anything at all to do with her later political stance is doubtful.

She came to Britain as a 20-year-old, in the spring of 1934. She had stayed on in Germany after her father left in order to complete a

FIGURE 15.3 Barbara, Duncan and their son Neil on holiday in France
Source: Neil Taylor.

secretarial course so that she would have some qualifications when she arrived in the country. In the UK she took on a number of short-term jobs before beginning work for the Ministry of Economic Warfare, which needed bilingual analysts for the material coming out of Germany. She was presumably not thought of as a threat then, despite the family already being on MI5's list of subversives, perhaps because it was felt that her access to economic and agricultural material was less sensitive than access to military matters would have been, or she may have just slipped through the net.

From her diary written at the time, she made it clear that she saw little possibility of a return to Germany, even in the long term. After she met her future husband, Duncan Burnett Macrae Taylor, at a Quaker summer school in Honfleur, Normandy in 1936, this feeling was cemented. After a whirlwind romance they married in January 1937 and the marriage would last until Duncan's death in 1982. After their marriage Barbara felt that Britain was now her home country and had no wish to return to Germany.

The couple moved to Redruth in September 1939 as the school at which Duncan was then teaching, Marylebone Grammar, had been evacuated at the start of the war. Barbara, by then pregnant with her daughter Fran, gave birth in February 1940. Duncan was called up in the summer of 1940 and Barbara returned to London with their daughter, who, they were belatedly informed by doctors, was severely mentally disabled. When Fran was hardly a year old Barbara had suspected that she was disabled in some way, but the doctors had told her that she was merely a late developer. After being a full-time carer for her daughter, she and Duncan eventually managed to find a place for her at Camphill, a Rudolf Steiner school just outside Aberdeen, in Scotland, where Fran would spend the remaining years of her life. Later, the couple had a second child, a boy, Neil.

Their connection with the Rudolf Steiner school led both parents to become very much involved in raising support and funds for the Steiner Waldorf School Fellowship, although they were not adherents of the associated philosophical outlook of anthroposophy. According to their son Neil, they were very successful in raising funds and support for an organisation that, at that time, was relatively inexperienced in those fields. The first Steiner school had been founded in Kings Langley in 1922, then several became established in other parts of the country. Because of the couple's work in fundraising and active campaigning on mental health issues, they were asked to become governors of a number of special schools, which they did. As they were not politically 'tainted' in the sense of being associated with communist politics and had expertise in the area, they were readily welcomed.[3]

After being demobbed Duncan, like Brigitte's first husband, went to work for the BBC, where he would remain for most of his adult life in the schools broadcasting section. There he was involved in producing children's programmes, particularly on historical subjects. He very much enjoyed the work and related well to children and teachers. The attention of MI5 (because of his close association with the Kuczynski family) meant that his career path would be blocked. As a deemed security risk, he was not allowed to take up more responsible positions within the organisation although he was clearly capable of doing so and was well-liked. While MI5 had no evidence of his being involved in espionage, nor of his being a member of the Communist Party – as far as is known, he was not – or a member of any other associated organisation, they nevertheless felt that, as someone married to a member of the Kuczynski family, he was not to be trusted. Duncan went on to write a number of successful children's books, possibly because such writing gave him more creative freedom than he was allowed at the BBC. Barbara also took up writing but in the form of translations of cookery books into English.

Despite Barbara's non-political stance – like Duncan she was never active in a left-wing organisation – she was still kept under observation by the British security services simply because she was a Kuczynski. Burke, in his book *The Lawn Road Flats*, asserts that Barbara's husband was 'also known to be a member of the CPGB and serving as an intelligence officer with the RAF' [during the war]. However, their son Neil confirmed to me that neither of his parents 'ever joined the Communist Party or had any inclination to do so'.

According to Neil, his parents always voted Labour, but his mother felt closer to the left of the party than his father. 'They were never involved in any political movements such as CND but were active in several charitable organisations', he told me, and recalled that:

> They worked hard, over their lifetimes, for the Camphill move-ment because of what it did for my sister. My mother was on the committee of the Council for Children's Welfare, which was founded to ban horror comics, but then took on other issues. She then joined the governing body of a school in Ongar for disturbed children run by the ILEA, and my father was for many years on the governing body of Morley College in south London.

Barbara, it seems, was invariably viewed by her siblings as 'the odd one out, not because of her lack of commitment to the communist cause, but in character she was also very different from her sisters.' However, despite such issues, they all remained on speaking terms and would often hold long telephone conversations.

Neil read history and Chinese at Cambridge, but instead of pursuing an academic career he opted for the much more exciting practical application of his studies. He went into the travel business and co-founded a travel agency in Bristol, specialising in the pioneering work of opening-up China and Albania to tourism during the 1960s and 1970s; he has been closely following the development of China now for fifty years. In recent years he has focused on lecturing and on tours for those interested in the history of Eastern Europe, and has published travel guides to Berlin and the Baltic states. Through his marriage to an Estonian, the family now owes its extension into a new European country.

Brigitte/Bridget

Brigitte, given the nickname 'Brix' by her sisters, was born on 15 July 1910, four years before the outbreak of the First World War at a time of revolutionary ferment. Although this would not have impinged on baby Brigitte, it will have had a political impact on her parents.

The Kuczynski girls were all sent to state primary schools. Brigitte did not like it when her mother took her to the school gates, she recalled, because the poorer children would taunt her about her 'posh' mother. After primary school she was then sent to a boarding school for her secondary education, before going on to university. She told her own daughters that the school was quite Spartan – a strict regime with an early rise and a naked swim in the lake before lessons in the summer months and skiing in winter. It certainly made her physically tough and sporty. Her school reports, though, were far from glowing. One of the teachers wrote cryptically to her parents that 'she was becoming too much influenced by certain other pupils'. Did they mean politically perhaps? She certainly became politicised very early on, joining the Socialist Youth movement at university, where one of her fellow members was Golo Mann (the third child of Thomas). She would join the Communist Party a short time later, in Heidelberg.

She went to university first in Berlin, where she read constitutional law and history, before going on to Heidelberg to complete her Ph.D. However, the rapid rise of the Nazis prevented her completing it there. Shortly before submitting her dissertation in 1933 she was expelled for being a communist student activist and even imprisoned for a short period. The city and university archives in Heidelberg still have a records of her time there and of her arrest.

In the city archive it is recorded that:

> Brigitte Kuczynski, born on 17 July 1910 [sic] in Berlin-Schöneberg, was in Heidelberg as a student from 30 April 1930 until 11 Aug. 1933 apart from short intervals (e.g. on 5 September she left for Vienna and returned on 5 May 1932 via Berlin).

FIGURE 15.4 Brigitte in 1968
Source: Jose Nicolson.

When she finally deregistered with the police on 11 August 1933 she gave no exact destination and the report notes only that she was 'auf Reisen' (travelling). No documentation of any arrest was noted.

There is a report from the university, dated 31 July 1938, stating that, 'In implementation of the ministerial decree, the following students have been excluded from studies' (there follows a list of 49 students including Brigitte).

There is also a document from the civilian 'Group Leader' to the head of police, dated Heidelberg, 17 July 1933:

> Re. The behaviour of the single, 23 year-old student Brigitte Kutzinski [sic], resident at Neue Schlossstrasse No. 26, here.
>
> On 17 July 1933 I have brought a criminal charge against the above named person because, on 11 July 1933 around 20.15 hrs,

on the Neue Schlossstrasse, she committed a public nuisance, in that she slapped the student Heekmann while exchanging a Hitler salute, and had therewith caused offence. Kutzinski [sic] is herewith expelled.

Signed

the Group Leader

After a week in prison she was released when the Catholic policeman guarding her, who was no friend of the Nazis, let her go and told her to get out of the country as quick as she could. Her sister Renate recalled that when she arrived to join the family, in France at the time, she was covered in bed bug bites all over her body. As a child this made a deep impression on Renate, who thought being bitten by bugs was a normal part of being in prison. Brigitte then left them to go on to Switzerland where she was able to complete her Ph.D. She stayed in Basle between 1933 and 1934, before settling in Britain in 1936.

After their father had escaped via Czechoslovakia to Britain in 1933, their mother followed shortly afterwards with the two youngest children, Renate and Sabine. Barbara was already in the country and Brigitte arrived a short time later.

A family consisting of two parents and their four children needed to find a steady source of income very quickly if they were to survive in exile. This meant that everyone had to pull their weight. Robert was the only one in employment at the time, but received only a modest salary from the LSE, so Brigitte began working as an au pair for five shillings a week plus her keep. With her first week's wages she bought a Penguin edition of *Hamlet*, only to be told by her employer that she should not be buying books but saving for her old age!

From 1936 to 1941 she worked as a research assistant at the LSE, on the history of prices and wages and colonial population statistics. Her father had been able to arrange this job and her research was carried out largely for him. She met Anthony Lewis there when she was 25 years old and he was still a 19-year-old student, and they married in 1936. Anthony became a sociologist and, to begin with, took work in advertising, before joining the BBC. A short time later the family moved into Flat 4 of the Isokon building in Lawn Road, Hampstead (see Chapter 7). Now, as Bridget Lewis, she was listed as a member of the Lawn Road Residents' Association executive committee in 1938.[4] Her uncle Hermann Deutsch, also a refugee from Nazi Germany, was already living in Flat 10 of the same building.

David Burke in his book *The Lawn Road Flats*, writes extensively about the significance of the Isokon building/Lawn Road Flats in connection with Soviet counter-intelligence operations in the UK. He writes that Alexander Foote, the former Soviet agent who later worked for MI5, was recruited by 'the Soviet agent Brigitte Kuczynski (Bridget Lewis) to the GRU in the flats in October 1938'. He offers no evidence for his allegation that Brigitte was a Soviet agent or that Foote was recruited to the GRU by her. What we do know is that Brigitte, on behalf of Ursula, vetted Foote and, after he had agreed to become involved in a clandestine mission in Nazi Germany, sent him on to Ursula in Switzerland. In any case, Foote contradicts Burke's allegation himself by saying that he had been recruited by the Soviets already in Spain. This issue is also dealt with in the section of Chapter 7 covering Ursula's work in Switzerland.

For a short time in 1941, Bridget and her husband spent time in Bristol and Weston-super-Mare, where Anthony was carrying out listener research for the BBC while she helped with the Communist Party election campaign. From late 1941 to 1942 she also worked for the BBC's Listener Research Department, but one day, not long into the job, and with no prior warning, she was unceremoniously escorted out of the building by security staff and told not to return. Clearly, MI5 had caught up with her and after checking her background were determined to keep such a 'dangerous red' out of Auntie's kitchen. A note in an MI5 file says that she first came to their attention in 1936 as a member of a thirteen-strong delegation of communists to the House of Commons to lobby their MPs in support of Republican Spain. At the time Spain was locked in a life or death struggle with Franco's fascists, amply supported by Hitler and Mussolini, while other Western countries like Britain and France imposed an arms embargo and a strict policy of 'non-intervention'.

From 1942 to 1943, Bridget worked as a manager at Collett's, well known as London's biggest left-wing bookshop, and owned by Eva Collett Reckitt, who was one of the heirs to the Reckitt & Coleman multinational food and consumer goods company. After rejecting her privileged background, Eva became a dedicated member of the Communist Party. Bridget managed the shop at a time when interest in the Soviet Union and socialism in Britain was reaching a peak.

The marriage between Anthony Lewis and Bridget broke down quite early on, and although they did not divorce until 1947, they parted and pursued their own separate lives. Anthony was a rather quiet and reclusive individual, and after their separation he continued to keep very much to himself and led a quiet life, never remarrying. Bridget herself was also rather self-effacing and reticent. Physically, she was smaller than her two younger sisters, more stocky and perhaps, outwardly, more taciturn. She was well liked by those who came in contact with her and the firmness of her politics was expressed more through an inner determination than any ostentatious militancy.

Not long after her separation from Anthony she met the communist journalist Arthur Long and had two children with him, Mark and Laura, but he left her while she was still pregnant with Laura. Mark said he had no contact with his father again until shortly before he died. In 1948, Bridget met Jock Nicolson, a Scottish communist and railway worker, at a Communist Party school in Hastings. Having two children and being ten years older than Jock appeared to be no barrier to his falling in love with her. They were married a year later, in May 1949. Jock, who was living in Scotland at the time, was understandably keen to move down to London and join Bridget there, but the impending 1950 national elections would frustrate that wish. The Party asked him to stay on in Scotland and become Willie Gallacher's election agent. It would be months before he and Bridget could begin living together as man and wife.

Jock was kept extremely busy during the campaign to get Willie Gallacher re-elected as the Communist MP for Fife West in that 1950 national election. Bridget did, though, manage to visit Jock in Scotland for two weeks towards the end of the campaign. With the entrenching of the Cold War and the vehement opposition of the powerful Catholic Church in the area, Gallacher lost the election but still managed to obtain over 9,000 votes, coming in third. Jock himself would later stand unsuccessfully as a parliamentary candidate in North St Pancras for the Communist Party on four occasions, with Bridget again helping with canvassing and organising hustings.

A year later, in 1951, the couple had a baby daughter, Josephine (known as Jose). Jose told me, that if she had been born a boy she thinks she would have been called 'Joseph' after Stalin, rather than Josephine.

In 1959/60 Bridget and Jock were closely involved in organising a big rent strike by council housing tenants in St Pancras. The newly elected Tory council had introduced large rent increases which resulted in widespread anger and indignation on the part of the largely working-class tenants. Opposition to the proposed rent rises was led by communists Don Cook and Arthur Rowe, both transport workers, who barricaded themselves into their homes and were besieged for several weeks. They were supplied with food and essential items which were placed in a bucket and hoisted by rope to the balcony. The strike lasted over ten months, accompanied by large supporting demonstrations and even strikes by local council workers and railwaymen, led by Jock Nicolson. Protected by police, both mounted and on foot, bailiffs eventually smashed their way into the barricaded flats and the two leaders were evicted. Although that battle was lost, the issue of council house rent regulation became a national issue and received widespread media coverage.

From 1952 to 1953, Bridget worked as a research assistant to Robin Page Arnot and helped him produce his classic *History of the Scottish Miners*. Then from 1952 until 1961 she went on to work as assistant to the Commercial Secretary of the Romanian Legation. While there, she was apparently approached regularly by various firms seeking to trade with the country and, in her capacity as the representative they had to deal with, was offered many 'presents'. She often came home just before Christmas with a hamper or parcels of goodies, as her daughter Jose recalls. Brigitte said, though, that any firm that tried to 'buy her off' in this way was immediately put on her blacklist. Following this job, she spent the following fifteen years, until her retirement in 1975, working for the Moscow Narodny Bank producing its press bulletins.

In this connection, while she was still employed by the bank, the flat where Bridget and Jock lived was broken into. The door had been forced and things were scattered everywhere but the only thing that was missing was a silver medal, embossed with cyrillic script, given to all employees by Moscow Narodny Bank to commemorate the 50th anniversary of the founding of its London branch. The police never did throw any light on the burglary. The suspicion was that MI5 had been involved. They were probably hoping the medal could be used as evidence of her espionage work for the Soviet Union.

All her adult life – for around thirty years – Bridget held a position of some sort in her Party branch (Adelaide) and the family flat became the hub of branch activity. She also conceived the idea of the Marx-Engels walks – taking interested parties around the locations in London where Marx and Engels had lived or been active – to raise money for the branch. She became very involved in the Belsize Housing Association as secretary/treasurer, and helped organise demonstrations and protests on behalf of residents who were battling negligent and profiteering landlords. Her son, Mark Long, says that hardly a day passed without some form of political discussion taking place in the family home, particularly around the supper table. The children also remember being taken on demonstrations, to meetings or helping out at fundraising bazaars for the *Morning Star*.

The family was never flush with money, and while they were not poor there were few luxuries. Jock was a manual worker with British Rail, so didn't earn a large wage, and Bridget's salary at the bank would not have been generous. Clearly, little of the infamous 'Moscow Gold' filtered down to the family, even though Bridget was allegedly a Soviet agent at the time.

Jose Nicolson relates an amusing example of her mother's efforts to save money. The shortest route from the station to the Moscow Narodny Bank's office where she worked took her past Harrods. One year, with a sale on there, she bought some lovely brown corduroy zip jackets for the children as they were on offer at a good discount. Later they discovered that they were part of a uniform consignment intended for Gordonstoun, the boys' public school that Prince Charles had attended, but no longer conformed to the school's new requirements, so were put on general sale.

For many years, from around 1976 until it ceased publication in 1981, Bridget was also a member of the editorial board of Palme Dutt's Marxist journal, *Labour Monthly*, and wrote theatre and book reviews for it. Her brother Jürgen had also worked for the same journal during his exile in Britain.

In her later life, Bridget became fascinated with making quilts and took local classes in patchwork and quilting, becoming very proficient in the craft. She sold many examples of her work to raise money for her Communist Party branch. Her family reckoned she must have raised around £12,000 in this and similar ways over the years.

When the Communist Party broke up in 1991, with a large tranche going on to form Democratic Left and another group forming the Communist Party of Britain, she and Jock belonged to the Democratic Left group. Subsequently, in 1995, at the age of 85, she joined the Labour Party, despite the fact that this was the time when it lurched to the right under Tony Blair and abandoned any claim to be a socialist party. Her attitude was that the Tories had to be defeated and the only way to do that was to support Labour.

The image of Bridget, as conveyed by family and friends and the obsequies at her funeral, was of a woman far removed from that of a dangerous Soviet secret agent, as she has been invariably portrayed in the espionage literature; her love of family and of books, of walking, caravanning and holidaying abroad were all emphasised. She had been very much opposed to the publication of Ursula's reminiscences (*Sonya's Report*) in English in 1991, and did not want her name mentioned, possibly fearing repercussions. 'I have got all that out of my system', she said to her children.[5]

Jose Nicolson told the author in a personal conversation in 2015: 'As you may have gathered, Bridget was quite a secretive person who did not reveal much of certain sides of herself to us.' She said that reading the MI5 files at Kew for the first time after her mother died was, in this sense, quite illuminating for her because it disclosed a side of her that she never knew. Mark confirmed this to me, saying that she 'never referred to her clandestine past', although she had told them about her childhood in Berlin and why she had been forced to flee the Nazis, he said. Jose herself was not involved in party politics, apart from taking part in socialist Sunday school and a brief stint in the YCL, though she would, she says, still define herself as a leftist, but a non-aligned one.

Brigitte's son Mark is a founder, performer and writer in the People Show, a theatre group founded in 1966. It has been creating devised performances in theatres, telephone boxes, on the streets, even on water, for over five decades. In its publicity it declares that it has been a 'radically disruptive influence and has made a major contribution to the current theatre landscape. It is committed to creating theatre in its widest sense, embracing emergent technologies whilst remaining sensitive to the human scale.'

Laura, who died in 2015, 'remained a socialist and feminist up to her dying day', her sister Jose says. She was part of the 'contraceptive train' together with the writer, broadcaster and founder of the Irish Women's Liberation Movement, Mary Kenny, and other Irish women in the seventies.

As a sort of coda to her life, Brigitte's name popped up in a *Guardian* article celebrating seventy years of the BBC's *Woman's Hour* radio programme on 10 October 2016, nineteen years after her death: 'While listener Bridget Long [her then married name], writing to the *Daily Worker* in 1946, complained: "The programme is much too patronising. What women want is a programme to compensate us for being tied to our domestic chores, to help us keep in touch with the world outside, whether it's books, films, politics or other countries."'[6] She would undoubtedly have been tickled and gratified to see that her strongly held viewpoint that women should be offered more demanding brain-food than merely domestic affairs was still worthy of being quoted.

While the lives of the Kuczynski sisters and their families who settled in Britain may not have been as colourful or adventurous as those of their two eldest siblings, they did make significant contributions to British society. Their engagement in a whole number of social and political campaigns, their work for world peace, as well as their academic and research achievements, were socially valuable. The sisters maintained their strongly held principles and world outlook throughout their lives. Brigitte, Sabine and Renate could all have enjoyed relatively affluent middle-class existences without all the demands and stresses of left-wing political activism if they had chosen to do so. Instead they held true to their strongly held principles and beliefs. Whether they and their husbands would have achieved more in terms of career progression and academic achievement if they had not been held back by the stigma of being associated with the Soviet Union and the British Communist Party and blacklisting by the security services, is a moot point, but is highly likely.

David Aaronovitch, in his book of reminiscences, *Party Animals*, refers several times to the Kuczynski family. He knew both Sabine and Frank Loeffler as well as Bridget and her husband Jock Nicolson, who lived close by in Hampstead. The families were all in the same Party branch. He remembers branch meetings in his own family's front room when, on 'Many nights their gentle burble and the smell of Frank Loeffler's pipe ushered in sleep for us children'. David's half-sister Sabrina was friends with Bridget's daughter Laura.[7]

In his book he devotes a whole chapter to the Kuczynskis. While he was looking for files among those released by MI5 on his own family in the National Archives, he serendipitously stumbled across those of the Kuczynskis and became fascinated. In his chapter 'Party Spies', he quotes from the files and cobbles together a potted version of the family's connections with intelligence work, as depicted by MI5, but the chapter contains a number of inaccuracies.[8]

Notes

1 Jürgen Kuczynski, *Memoirs*, vol. 1, p. 95.
2 David Aaronovitch, *Party Animals*, London, Jonathan Cape, 2015.
3 Personal conversation with Neil Taylor.
4 Ibid., p. 139.
5 Personal conversation with Ingrid Kuczynski.
6 *The Guardian*, 10 October 2016, 'Woman's Hour reaches 70th birthday – and no need for "light dusting of powder"'.
7 Aaronovitch, *Party Animals*, pp. 65, 71.
8 Aaronovitch, *Party Animals*, pp. 200–223.

16

CHILDREN OF THE WAR

In the context of the attempt by the German fascists to eradicate Jews entirely from Central Europe, Merilyn Moos' interviews with second generation refugees from Nazi Germany who settled in Britain are interesting in the light they cast on the psychological impact of resistance or passivity in the face of such threats. In her research she was interested in discovering what impact the whole fascist experience and the Holocaust has had on those succeeding generations who didn't experience it directly. All those she interviews in her book, *Breaking the Silence*,[1] apart from one, are from Jewish families, but those who were born into active anti-fascist families (in the main communists), she argues, appear to be less traumatised and psychologically scarred than those who were persecuted and fled because of their Jewishness alone. She argues that being active opponents of Nazism and having some understanding of the historical and political context, rather than being 'simply victims', provided a vital psychological support and there was not the same debilitating feeling of 'survivor's guilt'.

Because of the tumultuous history of the Hitler period, the impact of the Stalin revelations, and rise of anti-semitism in the Soviet Union, compounded by the tense Cold War confrontation and entrenched anti-communism in the West, the children and grandchildren of those intimately caught up in those processes were also marked, scarred even, by these additional factors. Those parents/grandparents who became communists and actively fought fascism were seen as heroes, but also, by some, as traitors or misguided believers in a seriously flawed system. These dichotomous viewpoints are epitomised in *The House of Twenty Thousand Books*, the biography of Chimen Abramsky written by his grandson Sasha Abramsky. It is a portrait of another East European Jewish émigré, from a devout Orthodox background, who settled in Britain in 1939. Although, to be more accurate, Chimen Abramsky did not choose to settle in Britain, but found himself trapped there by the outbreak of war, and then stayed. He would join the Communist Party of Great Britain, serving on its National Jewish Committee, and became a leading figure among Party historians, counting people like Eric Hobsbawm, Sam Aaronovitch, Hyman Levy and Rafael Samuel among his close friends. In his Highgate home he amassed a collection of around 20,000 books, which even if it did not quite match the size of the Kuczynski's library, was substantial and held many very valuable editions of Marxist classics as well as Jewish historical documents.

Abramsky would leave the Communist Party in the late 1950s and devote himself increasingly to a study of Jewish history. While his grandson writes movingly and evocatively about his grandfather's fascinating life and the central role his library played in it, he betrays the seeming inability of a younger generation to fully comprehend the role communism played in the struggle against fascism during the 1930s and why people like his grandfather joined and stayed in the Party for so many years. He finds it difficult to comprehend how his grandfather could ignore Stalin's crimes or how he could accept the 'strict discipline' of the Communist Party. His book does, though, provide a counterweight, of a sort, to the Kuczynski story, and another perspective on the 'Jewish exile' experience written by someone who has chosen to emphasise the Jewish ethnic aspect above the political.

Many of those second generation exiles have faced problems coming to terms with their complex family backgrounds, followed by integration into what was, at least for their parents, a foreign country. They will have experienced this as a rupture in their lives. Once arrived, many of their parents refused to continue speaking their native languages and began using English, even within the family. The

Kuczynskis were no different. That is why the children of such families often grew up without speaking their parents' native tongue. This fact also compounded the feeling of alienation, of something missing or lost from their inheritance. This second generation, growing up in completely different circumstances, was also invariably alienated from not only the political beliefs but even the Jewish background of their parents. Interestingly, in this context, all of Robert Kuczynski's six children would marry non-Jews and remain strictly secular, clearly demonstrating that any consciousness of Jewish culture or sense of a racial belonging had become secondary, if relevant at all. None of them celebrated Jewish festivities.

Harriet, Sabine's eldest daughter, in her reflections about the influence her parents had on her life, regrets that they never discussed their concerns, worries or doubts with their children about what was happening in the communist movement or the Soviet Union.

'Any doubts my parents had about the Soviet Union', she told me:

> they did not share with us children just as they would not have done with people outside the Party. Both my parents 'survived' Hungary [the 1956 uprising], which they defended, and the suppression of the 'Prague Spring' in 1968 about which they expressed sadness.
>
> When the MI6 papers were released it was a huge relief to me that both my parents at separate branch meetings were reported (presumably by a mole) to be visibly upset about these events. When I read of their tears and accusations of fascist-type behaviour in the Soviet Union I was very relieved and wished that they could have told me at the time, but they maintained the 'communist right or wrong' defense.

This attitude of refugee parents was commented on by Merilyn Moos in her book, mentioned above. Harriet felt that her parents saw things very much in black and white and compares their beliefs to a religion. 'I knew how capitalism worked and the "evils" of it from a young age', she said.

> The theory was explained by my mother to me in simple black and white terms for my young mind to absorb. Later in life I came

to think that black and white is how my mother in particular saw the world. That was not easy for me; I was as a child often confused living with parents whose beliefs seemed so different from friends' parents. I wanted to defend their beliefs but I couldn't because I didn't feel I could marshal the arguments necessary so I went quiet on the matter.

She also recalls being taken along to many demonstrations and political events because of her parents' beliefs. She adds that she is 'immensely grateful to both my parents for their guidance and help in my development of a social conscience'.

'It became, in some ways easier at secondary school', she continued:

because I got into a crowd which included a high profile girl whose parents were communists and were friendly with mine. However I remained embarrassed by their views and ashamed that our family was not like others. Then there was the Jewish strand of my upbringing that was denied – the acceptance of which has come to me only recently. I had quite a few Jewish friends at school and later in life who were keen to tell me that if my mother was Jewish then I was. I resisted the idea because it didn't make sense. This conflict simmered on and off for years. I have since then acknowledged that I am Jewish, albeit secular.

I felt I had let my parents down by not becoming a Young Communist or an adult one and not even versed in the arguments and theory. But paradoxically I am much more political now as I get older but I see things less in black and white.

Harriet also began learning German later in life and reflecting on her Jewish background, feeling she had been deprived of important aspects of her parents' heritage.

Barbara's son, Neil, also began learning German as an adult and makes regular trips to Germany, perhaps also in an attempt to recapture something he felt lacking in his upbringing. Such reflections and belated attempts to regain a lost heritage appear to be typical of a considerable number of second generation refugees.

Mark Long, the son of Brigitte and Arthur Long, has this to say about family life:

> I am without doubt the result of my upbringing. Socially, environmentally, politically and emotionally. And proud of it. The older I get the more I appreciate how exceptional our families are. I was brought up in a one hundred percent committed communist household, whose major motivation in life was their full time commitment to the cause.

His father, Arthur, left Brigitte and his son when the latter was still only one or two years old, to be replaced by Jock Nicolson, who Mark says, was 'in every sense my father'. With regard to Brigitte, he says that it was only later in life that he discovered the more precarious hinterland she trod.

His parents' waking hours, he says, were devoted to forwarding the struggle. Yet the children 'were never ignored or side-stepped. As much time was devoted to our needs as to theirs.' Every part of his subsequent adult life has been informed, Mark says, by the Kuczynski/Nicolson oeuvre, apart from one aspect. Sport, which was a complete blind spot for the parents. 'There were of course', he concludes, 'all the tensions, rows, tragedies, lies and misdemeanors that any healthy family experiences.'

Having an English father, said Ursula's son Peter Beurton, made him 'different' right from the start when the family moved to the GDR. When he reached the age of 13 he realised he had by then been living in Germany longer than in England and that saddened him. The family always spoke English at home together, but Ursula and Peter spoke German to each other. He said that he always wanted to visit England again, but that was impossible for many years. As an adult he felt completely German, but with a close English background.

His father spoke to him more about the past than his mother did. He told him many stories about Spain, how he had hidden from the bombs dropped by German aircraft, and seen his comrades killed around him. 'Spain was his baptism of fire, it meant everything to him', Peter said. Len collected memorabilia from his time there and kept it in a small, battered case. He would take things out of it every few months as if to remind himself of those days, then he would put them lovingly back again. He bequeathed that case to his son, and the items are all still in there just as he left them.

Ursula's son Michael, after giving up science to concentrate on English literature, began in the 1960s to translate Shakespeare into German and subsequently made his career in the theatre as a dramaturge at the Deutsches Theater in Berlin. Apart from his translations of some fifteen Shakespeare plays, he has also turned his hand to Sean O'Casey, Arthur Miller and Tennessee Williams. He has published extensively on playwrights and theatre and been invited to lecture tours in England and the United States. He is the co-author of two standard books in English on the German theatre.

In his political activity he diverged somewhat from the common family position, in the sense that he supported a strategy he called 'integrative subversion' to try and change the GDR into a more democratic socialist country from within. In 1989 he became one of the founders of the opposition movement Neues Forum. How far his personal aspirations were frustrated by the course of history after 1989 is another question, but he has remained active in the sphere of cultural and political debate, was elected Vice-President of the reunited German Shakespeare Society, and is a long-standing member of PEN.

Both he and his half-brother Peter clearly felt to some extent that they were 'outsiders' in the GDR, because of their early experience in Britain and their unique family context. Renate's daughter, Ann, on the other hand, told me that she never felt that her family were outsiders, but she was nevertheless aware of them being different. She was brought up without religion, so at school decided to refuse to attend religious assemblies. She and a Quaker girl were the only two not to attend, and this also made her conscious of difference.

At 11, like many of her British peers, she began learning French at school, which she enjoyed. In later life, though, she did regret that her mother had not spoken German with her, although she had begun teaching her two brothers the language. Culturally, Ann felt completely English, although at home her mother did introduce some German cultural traditions, like the celebration of Christmas on December 24th. Ann felt privileged, she said, because they celebrated it partly in the German way and partly in the English way so they enjoyed an extended celebration. Christmas for the Simpson family was invariably spent with Sabine and her family and, if they were in London, Boxing Day with Brigitte's family.

As an 18-year-old, after finishing her A-levels, she joined a work camp in the GDR. These were organised by the GDR's youth organisation, the FDJ, to introduce young people from abroad to GDR life. She and the others worked building new blocks of flats.

She was active in Birmingham University student politics during the late 1960s, and returned to take a masters in 1970 at the Centre of Russian and East European Studies at the time the Radical Students' Alliance was being set up.

She spent some time in Moscow as an exchange student, and was there in August 1968, an eventful moment, as Soviet troops invaded Czechoslovakia that same month. Later, she won a scholarship to take a full-time Russian language course at Moscow's Lomonosov University. In 1979 she went to live in the GDR for three years, as representative of Britain's National Assembly of Women at the Women's International Democratic Federation (WIDF). In East Berlin she met, and in 1981 married, Christian, who is French. She returned with him to live in France and worked there for twenty-five years for the trade union CGT, which had strong links with the French Communist Party. Today, Ann is a member of the French Socialist Party.

The parents' communist convictions certainly impacted on the way all the children developed socially and politically, with various degrees of emulation. However, the fuller revelations of the crimes committed under Stalin, the eventual demise of the East European communist states and the new realities of the contemporary world have all helped erode or modify their views. But in all cases, even if there is no longer a belief in or sense of loyalty to communist ideas, each in his or her own way retains a commitment to social justice, to humanitarian goals and political renewal.

Note

1 Merilyn Moos, *Breaking the Silence: Voices of the British Children of Refugees from Nazism*, Lanham MD, Rowman & Littlefield International, 2015.

17

THE SPYING BUSINESS AND THE ROLE OF MI5

Espionage and spying have always held a fascination for historians as well as the general public and the subject has been a great draw for authors and journalists, some making serious contributions to our historical understanding, others simply making wild assertions and cashing in on the marketability of the genre. It can be titillating, and sensational, allowing us to peek through the keyhole into a world with which few of us will have had contact.

The myriad books on espionage very largely repackage and recycle many well-worn myths and clichés. This applies very much to the handling of the Kuczynski family, particularly in connection with the case of the atom spy Klaus Fuchs and the passing of vital information about the building of an atomic bomb to the Soviet Union.

Most writers on spies and espionage, by the very nature of their subject matter, tend to exaggerate, bulk up the importance or even sensationalise the lives and activities of their individual subjects. Most also write from a perspective of the espionage business itself, either as former 'insiders' or as partisan commentators. Few attempt to place such activities in the wider political and historical context. This makes any impartial or balanced assessment of the role and motivations of those involved in espionage or intelligence-gathering more difficult.

The spy writer John le Carré, who himself was recruited to spy on left-wing gatherings and later worked for MI5, said in 2016 that the whole question of spying was 'a question that's haunted me these 45 years'. He admitted that he had 'betrayed colleagues and friends', but insisted that such actions were justified in protecting his country and defending a free society. Spying, he said 'felt like betrayal, but it had a voluptuous quality: this was a necessary sacrifice of morality and that is a very important component of what makes people spy, what attracts them'.[1] That is the point of view of a former secret agent from the other side of the Cold War divide.

In the West, the Kuczynski family is known primarily, if not exclusively, for its association with espionage, although emphasis on this aspect has served to distract from, and obscure, the family's overall achievements and its contribution to our humanistic legacy. Labelling and categorising them as 'spies' has done more to feed the insatiable industry in Soviet spy stories than it has to enrich our historical knowledge. It has also ignored the circumstances in which they became involved in intelligence work as well as their motivation for doing so.

There is hardly a book written by a US or British writer about twentieth-century espionage that does not include a member of the Kuczynski family in its index – usually Ursula (code name 'Sonya') or Jürgen, but also Brigitte. Various academic papers have also been written about the family and their involvement in the spying business. The well-known British writer on espionage, Chapman Pincher, whose writing focused mainly on espionage and defence issues, described the Kuczynskis as 'that malevolent family'. It goes without saying that a 'traitor' to one side is likely to be seen as a 'hero' by the opposing side. It is all a question of perspective.

Anyone who passed information to the Soviet Union has been viewed as a traitor in the West, and although most did so for little or no monetary gain – and they were the vast majority – it was said that they were simply ideologically blinkered believers in an abhorrent system. Rarely, in the West, have there been attempts to question the labelling, show empathy or comprehend the motivations of such agents and collaborators. Few writers about espionage in this period have looked at it in the context of the struggle against fascism and the dream of building more just societies on the ruins of both the First World War and the devastation left after the defeat of fascism in the Second.

The spy novelist Michael Hartland made an ITV documentary in the 1980s, *Sonia's Report*, on Ursula's life as a Soviet agent. The programme was built around an interview he conducted with her in Berlin. Hartland's novel, *The Third Betrayal*, published in 1986, is based on the Klaus Fuchs case and includes a sketch of the Kuczynski family, but with added fictional drama, in which Ursula's son, Peter is murdered.

So much that has been written about the family has been speculative or inaccurate. Ursula, the most high profile of the family in this respect, was always called a '*Kundschafter*' in the GDR, never a spy. The German term *Kundschafter* has the less loaded connotation of scouting, reconnaissance or reconnoitering. In her case this is certainly more appropriate, as she never undertook any actual spying activities herself, but was involved in recruiting others and in transmitting information, albeit as a clandestine and paid operative.

In his book *Spycatcher* Peter Wright places Ursula among the top Soviet operatives. Their agents were, he writes:

> controlled by the 'great illegals', men [sic] like ... Richard Sorge, Alexander Rado, 'Sonia', Leopold Trepper, the Piecks ... They were often not Russians at all, although they all held Russian citizenship. They were Trotskyist Communists who believed in international Communism and the Comintern.

The Soviet Union was highly successful during the 1930s and 1940s in recruiting people willing to pass information on to them. It invariably did this not by offering large sums of money, but by simply suggesting that they could best help advance the anti-fascist struggle and the cause of socialism by becoming Soviet agents.

Potential recruits were rarely asked to spy on their home countries in order to undermine their security, nor were they being asked to help a putative 'enemy' as the Soviet Union at that time was a potential and later actual ally. Such arguments proved persuasive in many cases.

Many individuals in Europe joined communist parties during the 1930s in order to support the struggle against fascism. Providing all help and support to the Soviet Union, particularly in the face of Western animosity, became almost an obligation. The majority of those who helped the Soviet Union by passing on information and recruiting others to the cause did not see themselves in the first instance as spies or agents and in many cases could hardly be defined as such.

Anyone in the British Communist Party who decided to become involved in clandestine work for a foreign power was told that they could no longer remain in membership or work for the Party. While there were those who ignored this unwritten stricture, most complied with it. That position has been corroborated by people like ex-Soviet agent Alexander Foote, who later defected and worked for MI5 and was no longer sympathetic to the communist cause. In his book, *Handbook for Spies*, he wrote: 'The spy will have no obvious links with the Communist Party. If he or she ever was a Communist, you will find that they dropped out some time ago – at the time of their recruitment.'[2]

The Kuczynski family was closely connected with the European communist movement and associated with the world of intelligence gathering over several decades. Its tradition of progressive social engagement and commitment to the anti-fascist struggle was firmly rooted. The family was caught up in the tumultuous historical conflicts of the twentieth century and felt compelled to take sides, whatever the cost.

Even during the 'phoney war' that began in 1939, in the period before an alliance with the Soviet Union came about, most communists, like the Kuczynskis, did not hold back from continuing their struggle against fascism. Future historians will possibly look back on that whole period of the rise and defeat of fascism, followed by the Cold War, and view the ideological conflict and the role of secret agents in a rather different light.

The released files in the MI5 archive on communists, sympathisers and left-wing individuals cover several hundred people, including the Kuczynskis. These range from files on Stalin, Trotsky, Charlie Chaplin, Paul Robeson, Sylvia Pankhurst, Morgan Phillips Price (Moscow correspondent of the *Manchester Guardian*), Sir Michael Redgrave and J. B. Priestley, through to the Germans Walter Ulbricht and Hanns Eisler, to name but a random few. The files include the names of many German anti-fascists, African leaders and other foreign nationals, as well as most leading members of the British Communist Party. It is probably one of the most comprehensive data banks of communists and sympathisers held anywhere.

The government archive of the secret services (MI5) – those of MI6 are not accessible – holds ninety-four files on the Kuczynski family. These released files have an official note on them stating that there are a number of further files on the extended Kuczynski family '*of Soviet intelligence officers and associates*' (my emphasis).

As early as 1934, MI5 recorded the closure of the *Finanzpolitische Korrespondenz* (Financial Political Correspondence), the journal Jürgen edited in Germany, and noted non-commitally that he could no longer continue as editor due to the new law forbidding non-Aryans from carrying out journalistic activities.

During the Hitler–Stalin Pact period the files record that 'MI5 began monitoring his activities more closely and on 23 November 1939 a Home Office Warrant was granted allowing MI5 to intercept mail sent to his address at 39 Upper Park Road, London, NW3. On 20 January 1940 he was interned by the Aliens Tribunal on the evidence that he was an alien and a communist ... he was released from Warner's Camp, Seaton, Devon on 25 April on the grounds that membership of the KPD was not sufficient reason for internment. On his release he moved into No. 6 Lawn Road Flats.'[3]

A file on the Kuczynskis (dated 16 March 1940) has a note attached from the Investigation Branch of the GPO in connection with the interception of post addressed to 'Dr. Jürgen and Marguerite Kuczynski at 36 Upper Park Road – a redirection notice has been received for post to be sent to 6 Lawn Road Flats. The check has been transferred accordingly.' (Jürgen and Marguerite had lived in Upper Park Road before he was interned, but Marguerite had moved into 6 Lawn Road before his release.) At this time, Brigitte was living next door at no. 4 and when Ursula came up to London she would stay with her. There is a later notification from MI5 to the GPO (dated 1950) for postal interception on 4 Lawn Road to be discontinued, although Brigitte had moved from there some time before (noted in the same file).

It will probably remain an enigma as to how this 'dangerous communist and spy' was allowed to operate in Britain without let or hindrance and go on to work for the US armed forces before the end of the war. Although MI5 were closely monitoring Jürgen and keeping tabs on him, they appeared to accept, or could do little about, his working for the US army with access to highly classified documents.

Most of the books and papers that have since been written about the Kuczynski family have taken MI5 data at face value, and then the authors have added their own speculation, compounding any inaccuracies. A prime example of such a book is Ernest Volkman's *Spies: The Secret Agents Who Changed the Course of History*. Volkman is a prize-winning correspondent, espionage 'expert' and author of numerous articles. His short chapters on Ursula Kuczynski (he calls his chapter Ruth Kuczynski – her pen name was Ruth Werner; she was never called Ruth Kuczynski) and Klaus Fuchs are littered with inaccuracies. He even concludes his chapter on Ursula by saying, 'It is unclear whether she is still alive' – she died in 2000, a good six years after he wrote that. Even in the days before Google and Wikipedia, a simple phone call could have established that simple fact. Chapman Pincher misspells Ursula's code name as 'Sonia', and in Robert Williams' book on Klaus Fuchs he includes a Kuczynski family tree with the sisters Renate, Ursula, Binchen [sic] and Sabine, leaving out Barbara and not realising that 'Bine' or 'Binchen' was Sabine's family nickname. These are just several small examples of the multiple mistakes in these books, many of which are based as much on speculation as hard fact.

Chapman Pincher's best-selling book *Treachery: Betrayals, Blunders and Cover-ups: Six Decades of Espionage* deals extensively with the Kuczynskis, particularly Ursula, Jürgen and Brigitte. His main thesis is that MI5 was particularly incompetent in its dealings with the Kuczynskis and that this 'negligence' was almost certainly due to the fact that Roger Hollis, head of MI5, was, in Pincher's estimation, a secret Soviet agent. Pincher carried out substantial research and was a good investigative journalist, but many of his allegations are based on purely circumstantial evidence. He alleged that Brigitte and Jürgen were both employed by GRU, the Soviet military counter-espionage service, and that Brigitte was part of the Red Orchestra network, but gives no concrete evidence to back up these allegations. His assertion that Roger Hollis, while he was head of MI5, visited Brigitte at her London home on several occasions in secret, while based on oral evidence by one of Brigitte's former lodgers, is hardly credible. Such visits would not only have contravened the very basic precautions every secret agent learns to take, but Pincher seems also to forget that at the time this was supposed to have taken place Brigitte was under regular surveillance by MI5, her phone was tapped and her mail opened.

He does, though, quite rightly, criticise *The Authorised History of MI5*, which surprisingly fails to cover the agency's activity in connection with 'Sonya' at all.

There are also transcriptions available in the Wilson Center Digital Archive made up of a series of eight notebooks and loose pages kept by Alexander Vassiliev, the journalist and former KGB officer, while researching in the KGB archives during the mid-1990s.[4] Here there is mention made of the Kuczynskis – Jürgen, Ursula and Renate but no mention of Brigitte, Sabine or Barbara. There is mention of Renate passing on envelopes to Ursula – something she herself corroborated, but says she could not recall by whom and that she was unaware of what was in the envelopes. The KGB entry states that:

> Since January 1946, S. [Sonya] has been inactive, and no personal contact with her is maintained. However, from time to time she keeps us informed about her situation using pre-arranged signals, which we passed on to her through her sister, Renata [sic] Simpson, in 1948.

In another entry, it is noted that the atom spy Klaus Fuchs approached Jürgen and asked him to facilitate contact with the Soviet Union. In response Jürgen passed his name on to Ursula who re-established the contact and became Fuchs' courier. The KGB entry states that, 'F. [Fuchs] was recruited for intelligence work in England in Aug. 1941 by our operative, former military attaché secretary Cde. Kremer, on a lead from Jurgen Kuczynski (brother of our illegal station chief in England, "Sonya")'.

What is surprising to discover in the MI5 files released for the period covering the early 1930s throughout the 1940s, is that you would hardly be aware that the rise of fascism in Europe was the chief threat to peace and democracy on the continent or that, from 1939 to 1945, a massive war against fascism was raging. Throughout the period covered by the files on the Kuczynski family, there appears to be a stronger emphasis on communism and its supposed threat to Britain than on fascism, even though fascist organisations were also being monitored by the security services.

The family was kept under almost continual surveillance by MI5 since its arrival in the country in the 1930s until at least well into the 1960s if not beyond. However, Robert Kuczynski does not appear to have been included in its surveillance, although there are reports on him in the files. The files on the family are included under the designation: 'Communists and suspected Communists, including Russian and Communist sympathisers'. The members of this German refugee family, of Jewish background – all very much involved in the struggle to defeat Hitler fascism – were viewed by Britain's security services as a mortal danger to the country's security.

As Charmian Brinson points out in her essay, '"Very Much a Family Affair": The Kuczynski Family and British Intelligence', 'it is perhaps surprising that while watchful of all six of his children, MI5 does not appear to have opened a file on him [Robert] ...'[5] She writes, though, that the release of his Home Office Aliens Department file indicates the relatively favourable position he held in Britain, though the Enemy Aliens Tribunal gave him a 'B' status, denoting some doubt as to his reliability. 'But immediately "quite a lot of English influential people," including Walter Adams of the London School of Economics, wrote to the judge protesting against his decision and the grading was changed to the harmless 'C' category'.[6] (Every foreign alien was given an A, B or C rating – 'A' indicated that they should be immediately arrested and interned, 'B' not immediately interned but to be placed under restrictions and 'C' those who didn't need to be interned.) His son Jürgen was not given such kid-glove treatment and, as related in an earlier chapter, was interned for a short time as a category 'A' enemy alien, i.e. a high security risk.

Unlike our usual understanding of the way a spy behaves, Jürgen never made any secret of his close relationship with the Soviet Union or his membership of the Communist Party. Even under the Nazis as well as in exile in the UK, he openly visited the Soviet embassy, met Soviet friends and regularly met and conversed with other Communist Party members. This clear political commitment did not prevent his recruitment, in 1944, as a key member of the US armed forces to help them with their strategic bombing initiatives during the Second World War. He never clandestinely 'penetrated' targeted institutions or applied for positions on the basis of whether they could offer opportunities for espionage. What he was able to pass on to his Soviet contacts was largely in the form of his own reports and items of information he picked up in the normal course of his work as a statistician and academic. He felt the information he was passing over would help speed up the defeat of fascism and also assist in the reconstruction of a socialist society after the war. The three sisters Brigitte, Sabine and Renate were also open members of the Communist Party of Great Britain and made no attempt to hide this fact. Renate said about her sister Ursula's espionage work: 'I was aware that you do not talk to her about that. But I was very proud of what she was doing. She was the first of my family to join the (German) Communist Party.'

In a recording made in 2008 for her son Ludi, Renate had the following to say about her links with Ursula: 'I had, on one occasion, perhaps more than once, been given an envelope with money to pass on to Ursel' (the family nickname for Ursula). She doesn't remember who gave it to her, she said, 'and I wouldn't have asked about it anyway but passed it on knowing that it would be helpful'.

In 2009 she told Ludi that on one occasion in the late 1930s Ursula had asked to borrow her identity papers (British naturalisation and ID documents, probably soon after she herself had been given them, so this would have been when Renate was between the ages of 16 and 21). She does not remember if she got them back, and 'was too tactful to ask what Ursel would do with them. I assume she learned how to copy them, or used them herself.'

As with most secret service files on so-called 'subversives', much of the information in MI5's files says as much about the attitudes and mindset of the investigators as it does about those being investigated. Much of its collected information is characterised by paranoia, and is often based on hearsay from various informants who may well have had their own axes to grind. The overwhelming amount of material is mundane, banal and innocuous; it is also riddled with inaccuracies. There are often quite contradictory assessments noted. For instance, in 1940 the following report was made on Jürgen:

[Jürgen] Kuczynski might be described as a Communist intellectual. H. considers that he is a sincere believer in Communism but only a fellow traveller with Moscow. His interests are too much involved in intellectual pursuits to allow him to be an active agent of his political faith. H. does not believe for a moment that Kuczynski is an Ogpu [the Soviet Union's main directorate of state security] agent. [underlined in pencil in the original document] I take this opinion of H's seriously as he knows Kuczynski personally and is, of course, a bitter opponent of Communism.

The identity of informer 'H' is not divulged.[7] Another file then characterises him as a 'dangerous' individual.

It is fascinating to realise how the secret services almost anywhere in the world, whether they be the FBI, CIA, the GDR's Stasi or indeed MI5, betray an almost visceral fear and suspicion of artists and intellectuals. This in itself demonstrates not only the type and calibre of the recruits to the service, but also the climate of Cold War paranoia and the fear of ideas. MI5's monitoring of communist intellectuals, for instance, was far more rigorous than it was of ordinary working-class members.

The journalist Lara Feigel notes such attitudes in MI5's long-term surveillance of the writer and communist Doris Lessing between 1943 and 1959, as revealed in its 'bloated files' on her. Feigel writes that the information contained in these files 'is no more enlightening than the information that Lessing was prepared to state publicly herself'. But the banality of the observations and the comic misunderstandings, often based on ignorance, are par for the course with secret service agencies. In the files, Lessing was named variously as Dorothy Lessing, Nessing and Lacy and the titles of her books were noted wrongly. One investigator spent a fruitless 'four months trying to trace "Doris Lacey an authoress". The only consistency in the files', Feigel writes, 'is Lessing's file number'. MI5's preoccupation with the Kuczynskis was very much a reflection of this mindset. with the added ingredients of them being 'foreign and Jewish'.

The security service commonly known as MI5 (Military Intelligence, Section 5) is the UK's domestic counter-intelligence and security agency and is part of the country's intelligence machinery alongside the

Secret Intelligence Service (SIS, also known as MI6) focused on foreign threats. All come under the direction of the Joint Intelligence Committee (JIC). A meaningful examination of the role played by these security services, how they operate and what they actually achieve, is made extremely difficult due to the very nature of their work.

There have been no in-depth examinations carried out on the role played by class in the work of these services, or an assessment of how far they actually do defend the interests of the nation as a whole or whether they are simply upholding establishment values. And no one, as far as I am aware, has examined the actual use value of their mammoth work in carrying out continuous surveillance and monitoring of the Communist Party, its members and those suspected of having links with it since the Communist Party was formed in 1920. What did they actually achieve in terms even of the goals they set themselves?

Any research into the workings of the secret services is, of course, not made easy by the opaque nature of such organisations and their extreme reluctance to release files, even after decades. What they do release is very selective. The released files on the Kuczynski family, though, certainly underline a strong class and establishment bias.

Kim Philby cast a rare ray of light on their class character. After his defection, he was invited by the GDR security service to address a meeting of its officers. It is very possible that Ursula Kuczynski also attended the event, but we have no direct confirmation of this. Philby told his audience that he was able to avoid being rumbled by the British security services for so long because he had been 'born into the British governing class'. This was revealed in a video recording of a speech he gave to GDR agents in 1981, and uncovered by the BBC in 2016. In the *Guardian*'s report of the discovery (4 April 2016) it stated that:

> The overall impression given by the excerpts of Philby's speech broadcast so far by the BBC is of a British intelligence service staffed by ill-disciplined and inept upper-class twits. In the video, Philby says further: 'Because I had been born into the British governing class, because I knew a lot of people of an influential standing, I knew that they would never get too tough with me. They'd never try to beat me up or knock me around, because if they had been proved wrong afterwards, I could have made a tremendous scandal'.

Stella Rimmington, the former head of MI5, in an interview with Rob Cowan on BBC Radio 3,[8] talked about her work and characterised the agency's dealing with the Soviet Union as 'with our enemies'. Quite an extraordinary characterisation when one realises that the Soviet Union was never at war with Britain (and only once was Russia, in pre-Soviet times, over the Crimea) or that the Soviet Union and the communist bloc had ever overtly threatened Britain or the West militarily, even though there was clearly an ideological polarisation and competition between the power blocs. Rimmington also revealed how she was recruited to MI5 'by a tap on the shoulder', an indication of how she, as a member of the establishment like so many of her peers in the security services, was deemed to be eminently suitable for defending class privilege, and so seeing the Soviet Union as 'the enemy' would be second nature to her.

In an interview with the Russian journalist Genrikh Borovik, Kim Philby told him:

It took me a long time to decide to work for the communists, but the most important period was my last two years at Cambridge. ... The study of Marxism and seeing the Depression in England. Books and lectures and the rise of fascism in Germany. Fascism was one of the deciding factors for me. I was becoming convinced that only the communist movement could resist it. Of course, there were doubts and unfounded expectations. But there was also dis- satisfaction with myself. I kept asking myself – why not give yourself totally to this movement? I had only one alternative: either I told myself, yes, or I give up everything, betrayed myself, and dropped politics altogether.[9]

This declaration encapsulates the doubts, dilemmas and soul-searching of many, like the Kuczynskis, who in the end decided to pass on information to the Soviet Union.

In another BBC radio broadcast about the communist historian Eric Hobsbawm – another refugee of Jewish background – who was also placed under surveillance by MI5, Cathy Massiter, a former MI5 officer revealed the lack of emphasis the secret services placed on the fascist threat. When asked by the interviewer, Frances Stonor Saunders, if right-wing individuals or organisations were also kept under surveillance by MI5, Massiter replied that they were looked after by one person![10] Although Massiter was talking about a period after the war, clearly communism was still perceived as the only real danger, at least until the focus changed to the 'war on terror' after 2011.

After the Soviet–Nazi Pact, Jürgen, following the official Comintern line, in a number of his speeches condemned the war as an imperialist one. As the leading figure among communist German exiles in Britain, he was able to bring his comrades also into line. His activities opposing the war gave MI5 the pretext for increasing their surveillance of him and the immediate family.

One of the files on Jürgen, written by an outraged, unnamed MI5 officer (29 January 1940) states that: 'Jürgen Kuczynski is sending money from England to interned German Communists in France. Cannot something be done in the UK to suppress these practices as Communism is now proscribed in France?'[11] At this time Britain was at war with the Nazis, but this official is concerned about German anti-fascists being offered financial support by another German refugee. Despite the rising threat of a fascist fifth column in the country and of an imminent invasion by Nazi Germany, MI5 was apparently more preoccupied with communists than fascists.

In another report, Jürgen is described in very negative terms: He uses 'trenchant anti-British rhetoric' and reveals his 'hatred' for the country, it says, but the reporters fail to give details or provide evidence for this accusation. Another note by Miss Bagot (Millicent Bagot was Roger Hollis' assistant and worked in Department F2B of MI5 and was a specialist on communist activity), says: 'I really do feel strongly that something ought to be done about this man … all sources I have who occasionally report on him unite in saying what a bad and anti-British character he is … we should be doing something about him.' These allegations were made during the 'phoney war' period, when Jürgen would have been accusing Britain of pursuing merely an inter-imperialist struggle with Germany.

One can only assume that the secret services interpreted any arguments against contemporary government policy (particularly the policy of appeasement, the 'phoney' war and general anti-Soviet attitudes) as de facto 'anti-British'. Particularly at that time, any attacks on the ruling classes or on governmental policy were invariably interpreted as being aimed against Britain itself rather than, as intended, at the establishment – two very different things.

The authorities argued that Jürgen's active opposition to the 'imperialist war' was reason enough to have him interned. 'This alien is a communist and/or working in sympathy with that movement', the evidence read. The Aliens Tribunal on 20 January 1940 duly ruled that he be interned. As previously noted, an appeal was immediately made to secure his release, and a well-organised campaign was launched on his behalf, led by the defence lawyer D. N. Pritt.

Even though MI5 kept tabs on many German refugees, and particularly those with communist or left-wing associations, the intensification of its surveillance of the Kuczynski family probably came about as a result of information given by Alexander Foote, who had been recruited by Ursula and worked with her as a secret agent in Switzerland. It was that information which almost led to Ursula's arrest in Oxford in 1950, and which had also implicated Brigitte. Foote apparently told MI5 that it was Brigitte in London who in 1938 had interviewed and recruited him on behalf of Ursula to carry out clandestine work in Germany.

However, MI5 had been keeping an eye on Brigitte well before Foote's revelation; for instance it advised the BBC in 1941 not to employ her on secret work since she was well known as an active communist and 'had a large circle of extremist contacts',[12] and noted that Brigitte was 'known to be a Soviet agent of long standing'. Despite this remark, she was never questioned, not even after the interrogation of Ursula and her departure for East Germany following the arrest of Klaus Fuchs. The MI5 officer J. C. Robertson announced his intention to investigate Brigitte 'owing to her past implication in Soviet espionage' and her family connections, but it never happened.[13] In fact, by October 1950 it was decided to suspend security checks on her altogether. Despite the heavy surveillance, phone tapping and interception of mail, MI5 never discovered anything about Brigitte in terms of espionage activities beyond the fact that she assisted Ursula in the recruitment of Foote.

Brigitte was described by MI5 as 'a schoolteacher of the Montessori sort' … and as having moved into Lawn Road Flats following her marriage to Anthony Gordon Lewis at Hampstead Registry Office on 4 July 1936. The agency, as the files reveal, began taking an interest in her because of the work she had been doing in support of Spain's Republican government during the Spanish Civil War. Her husband was then working for the BBC's Listener Research Station in the Home Intelligence Department of its Public Relations Division. He was also being monitored by MI5.

In MI5's files there are numerous detailed records of Brigitte's movements over several days, which involve the exact times she took her son Mark to and from Windrush Nursery, went shopping, and visited various bookshops with her daughter Laura in the pram. The agency was very good at recording times but, as the reports note, the agent was not able to get close enough to reveal what Brigitte said to the woman who lived nearby at 64 Belsize Park Gardens (though there is a detailed description of what she was wearing). When Brigitte sent someone with a parcel to the post office, they were followed for the rest of the day.

In the files, there are also transcripts of telephone conversations between Barbara and Brigitte, including one in which Barbara is fuming after the security services went to interrogate Duncan, her husband, at his office (the attention of the security services was hardly surprising, but conducting the interrogation at the office was clearly a means of intimidation). Barbara is quoted as saying 'I'm smoking' instead of 'I'm fuming' – revealing that her idiomatic English was still not perfect. The transcript concludes with the two sisters carrying on an 'interminable' discussion about colour schemes for their sister Sabine's flat.

Despite all the allegations that have been made, there is precious little hard evidence of Brigitte being a GRU agent. This is also backed up by what Ursula wrote in the original manuscript of her reminiscences as a Soviet agent, held in the GDR State Security archives. The manuscript was discovered by the journalist, historian and academic researcher Bernd-Rainer Barth, and he reveals that in it Ursula states that she asked Brigitte to help her find some former International Brigaders, but did not confide in Brigitte for what purpose she required them. Whether she wrote this merely to protect her sister or because it is in fact true, is now virtually impossible to prove conclusively.

When Robert Kuczynski contacted Barbara in September 1947 to let her know that MI5 had visited Ursula in Oxfordshire, she and her husband Duncan became quite worried. The telephone conversations between all the family members were regularly tapped, and MI5 records reveal a lengthy one at this time between Frank Loeffler, Sabine's solicitor husband, and Barbara concerning the implications of the MI5 visit and the possibility of Ursula being deported. It seems clear from this that family members were aware, to some extent at least, that Ursula was involved in clandestine work.

By October 1950, after it had been decided to suspend security checks on Brigitte, MI5 turned its attentions to Barbara – the only one of the family not to have joined the Communist Party and probably the only one not in the least implicated in intelligence work, spying or in communist activity. MI5 felt they could put pressure on her husband Duncan as he would have been keen to safeguard his job at the BBC.

Perhaps the only flimsy piece of circumstantial evidence that could have cast suspicion on Barbara is that for a time she lived at the same address in London as Otto Hamburger, the younger brother of Ursula's first husband and cousin of the refugee physicist Heinz London, who was at the time employed at the Atomic Energy Research Establishment at Harwell, as Fuchs had been. This, though, may have been pure coincidence, as we know that German communist refugees often stayed at each other's homes and showed solidarity with each other.

William Skardon interrogated Barbara at her home on 7 February 1952, but found her 'uncooperative', as she denied any knowledge of his interview with Ursula; however, MI5 knew this was untrue from the information gained by phone tapping. MI5 summarised its case against the Taylors (Barbara and Duncan) as they saw it thus: 'they subscribe completely to the Communist viewpoint ... and there is no doubt that their sympathies lie in that direction', they were after all 'readers of the *Daily Worker*', and it noted, as an additional indication of the couple's radical sympathies that Duncan, a BBC employee, 'had chosen not to wear a black tie on the occasion of King George VI's death'. Their son Neil told me that his parents never read the *Daily Worker*.

On 20 March 1952, a few weeks after interrogating Barbara, Skardon phoned her husband, saying he wished to interview him on his own. None of the other sisters – Brigitte, Sabine or Renate – were interviewed by MI5, though its interest in the family continued well into the 1950s.

It is decidedly odd that the only member of the Kuczynski clan who was not at all involved in intelligence activities turned out to be the only one, apart from Ursula, to be interviewed by MI5. Because of MI5's intervention, the sisters and their husbands, like many other known communists, all became victims of blacklisting and were in this way disqualified from a number of jobs they applied for.

What MI5 files on the Kuczynskis also reveal about the agency inter alia is an apparent underlying anti-semitic prejudice and adherence to racial stereotypes. A note concerning the arrival in exile of Robert at Surrey Docks notes: 'Passport not underlined but *had the appearance of a Jew*' (my emphasis). Two other reports on St Pancras Communist Party branch meetings that Bridget attended note that:

> The AGM of the St. Pancras branch of the Communist party of Great Britain was held at Tallents Hall, Drummond Street on 13/07/1939. Meeting lasted three hours. There were about 70 people present *of whom about 50% were Jews*. A similar report on 05/07.1940 on the St. Pancras branch meeting held on 02/06/1938 ... about 60 people present, *about 10% were Jews.*
>
> *(My emphases)*

It was noted that 'There was no disorder'. Then in an observational description of Bridget, her physical details, height, dress, hair colour, etc. are given and then, after a semi-colon, the observer writes: '*Jewess*' [my emphasis]. During the interrogation of Ursula by MI5's Jim Skardon, he reported that 'She preserved *a Slav-like indifference* [my emphasis] to the kind of arguments we made' [i.e. telling her that non-co-operation could have repercussions on her family].

It is well-known that racism and anti-semitism at the time was widespread in the country, but particularly among those belonging to the ruling establishment, and these examples appear to underline that. That such anti-semitism in the security services was probably quite widespread is also supported by the example of the novelist Graham Greene. He was a one-time MI5 operative, and in his early novels revealed a strong streak of anti-semitism, although the worst examples were 'cleaned up' in subsequent reprints.

The mistakes and prejudicial comments that were made in official documents is again revealed in a letter from the British Consul in Geneva to the Passport Office in London, in connection with Ursula's application for a British passport, in which he writes: 'Mrs. Beurton, Polish by birth [sic]', who 'was unable to get the necessary signature of a British citizen in Switzerland so had the passport application form signed by Mme Ginsberg, assistant librarian at the League of Nations, who is well known for her communist sympathies'. The Foreign Office then writes to MI5 asking if they have any files on Ursula Beurton. MI5 replies: 'We have no record of Mrs. Ursula Beurton and only one possible trace of her ex-husband *with a communist smell*' (my emphasis). It goes on: 'How about the husband – can you investigate his passport application? I do not like the whole thing but just cannot put a finger on a weak spot.'

There is a dearth of hard facts to support any allegation that other members of the Kuczynski family, apart from Ursula, actually worked for the Soviet secret service beyond providing her with limited assistance. Renate's full name is mentioned in one KGB report (agents are always given only pseudonymic code names or denoted by an initial).[14]

It would appear that Jürgen was, despite the many allegations, never a KGB or GRU agent as such. Although he was given the pseudonym of 'Karo', he is also mentioned with his full name in KGB records. In the *Yellow Notebooks*, smuggled out of the Soviet Union by Alexander Vassiliev, the KGB record notes that:

> Our agents in England as well as leaders of the German Communists in London gave K. a positive reference … starting in 1936 K. established contact with our embassy in London, and in 1941, this connection fell to us, and K. began giving various types of informational materials, surveys and reports, *although he was never formally recruited*.
> *(My emphasis)*

The KGB report goes on to list the sort of materials Jürgen handed over to them and, from this list, it would appear that they were made up of easily accessible government documents, but nothing of a top secret or highly sensitive nature. The report goes on to mention the Soviets' 'temporary suspension' of Jürgen in 1943 and notes that, '"K's" sister is in the network of the Red Army's Intelligence Directorate'.

Significantly they make no mention here of the other siblings as involved in any way.

The KGB report goes on:

> When the Berlin station was renewing ties with him in December 1945 K. categorically refused the offer to work with our organs, saying this would be a burden on him, that as a German Communist, he supposedly wanted to work only for Germany ... 'K' subsequently continued to insist on being excused from working with us and submitted written statements to that effect.

This, together with aspersions made by two of his former comrades in exile and later in the SED leadership, led the KGB to express their suspicions of him as a 'double dealer'.

What is certain is that Ursula had been recruited in 1930/31 during her stay in China by the Soviet agent Richard Sorge. She was probably the first and only member of the family to give her full commitment. It is also reasonably safe to assume that she mentioned her clandestine work to her brother Jürgen, who was looked up to and revered by his sisters. How much detail she told him is impossible to assess, but she did involve Jürgen in it to some extent and he must have been aware of what she was doing, even if not the full extent. It is also safe to assume that the other four sisters were not unaware that Ursula was 'doing something for the anti-fascist movement' which involved a lot of secrecy. After all, she was moving from country to country and appeared to be able to survive, even with small children, without holding down a 'proper job' or having a husband who could support her financially. She had been separated from her first husband Rudolf, and they divorced while she was in Switzerland. However, despite the siblings' closeness, it would be wrong to surmise that all family members were fully cognisant of what she was doing, that they were themselves agents or that they were intimately involved in her work. They clearly did give support and even acted as couriers from time to time, as Renate relates, but that in itself is hardly evidence of them being agents, although writers like David Burke assume them to be.

MI5 surveillance was even continued into the next generation. While Ursula's son Michael Hamburger was studying at Aberdeen

University he proposed the nomination of the black US singer Paul
Robeson for the honorary post of Rector. He sent a letter, in October
1951, from the Student Union office, informing the International
Union of Students in Prague of this proposal. The letter was intercepted
by MI5 and is held in its Paul Robeson file.[15]

What is still, and may well remain, a conundrum in terms of MI5's
treatment of the Kuczynski family, is how and why both Ursula and
Jürgen were allowed to leave Britain after the war without any attempt
to arrest and properly interrogate them. Ursula had already been visited
by Special Branch officers in Oxford but the matter was not pursued.
For a time MI5 appeared to refocus its attentions on Barbara and her
husband Duncan, who worked for the BBC.

Chapman Pincher was convinced that MI5 chief Roger Hollis was a
secret Soviet agent and used this allegation to support his theory of why
Ursula and Jürgen were allowed to operate without hindrance in the
country and to leave before they could be arrested. In an interview
Pincher gave to the German television channel ARD in 2000 for their
film on Ursula, called *Decknahme Sonja: Das geheime Leben der Agentin
Ruth Werner* (Codename Sonya: The secret life of the agent Ruth
Werner), he told them that he was still convinced Hollis was a double
agent because both Ursula and he had been in Shanghai at the same
time, visited the same club and were both good tennis players. Hollis
also knew Ursula's friend Agnes Smedley.

Pincher does, though, raise legitimate questions about why Ursula
and other members of her family were not properly interrogated and
why Ursula was not kept under proper surveillance while she resided in
Oxfordshire.

In summary, what we are able to establish from the released files and
KGB records, as far as the Kuczynski family is concerned, is that Ursula
was the only member of the family to be a full-time Soviet agent
working for the Military Intelligence Directorate. Jürgen was more of a
collaborator than an agent, although he was given the code name
'Karo' by Soviet intelligence. KGB records also note that he refused to
work for them as an agent. Both Ursula and Jürgen ceased working in
any capacity for the Soviet secret services after the defeat of fascism and
once they had returned to Germany. Renate Simpson is mentioned by
name once in Vassiliev's *Yellow Notebooks* of KGB records as someone

who occasionally passed on letters from Soviet intelligence officers to her sister Ursula. None of the other members of the family are mentioned. Lack of evidence can never prove anything beyond doubt, but it is a very strong indicator that the so-called 'spying and espionage' activities of the family have been in all probability exaggerated.

A serious and thorough depiction of the role of the secret services during this period and a proper assessment of what they actually achieved is overdue, but is unlikely to happen before all files are released into the public domain. Until then the released files on the Kuczynski family are all we have to go on. These hardly reveal them as dangerous Soviet agents or disclose that they did any damage to Britain's interests.

Notes

1 John Banville, Review of John le Carré's *The Biography*. *Guardian*, 16 January 2016.
2 Alexander Foote, *Handbook for Spies*, Museum Press, 1949 (p. 8).
3 Ibid., pp. 136, 137.
4 Alexander Vassiliev, *Yellow Notebook #1*. 2009, The Wilson Center Digital Archive, Washington D.C.
5 C. E. J. Brinson, '"Very Much a Family Affair": The Kuczynski Family and British Intelligence', in *Essays in Memory of Hamish Ritchie*, ed. Ian Wallace, Amsterdam, Brill Rodopi, 2015.
6 'Tactics of the German Communist Party', document passed to MI5 by Karl Otten, n.d. [c. April 1940] The National Archives. KV2/1872. 81A (Quoted in Brinson, 'Very Much a Family Affair'; see above note 5).
7 MI5 file, The National Archives, KV2/1871 (77a). A note on Jürgen written by D. G. White.
8 *Essential Classics*, BBC Radio 3. Interview with Stella Rimmington by Rob Cowan (in week 23–27 March 2015).
9 Genrikh Borovik, *The Philby Files*, ed. Philip Knightly, London, Warner Books, 1995.
10 *The Hobsbawm File*, BBC Radio 4. Presented by Frances Stonor Saunders. 13 April 2015 at 20.00.
11 MI5 file, The National Archives, KV2/1871 (74a).
12 Charmian Brinson, MI5 file, The National Archives, KV2/1567 (47c) July 1947, J. H. Marriott [B2 of MI5].
13 Ibid.
14 Vassiliev, *Yellow Notebook #1*, p. 128 (pp. 86–87 in online document).
15 MI5, Paul Robeson File, P.F. 44,990 (189B).

18

EPILOGUE

The legacy of the Kuczynski family members portrayed here will remain contentious, and open to different historical interpretation. What can hardly be denied, though, is that all of them devoted their lives to an ideal in the firm belief that they were struggling on the side of justice and progress. They remained committed to their principles despite hardship, setbacks and invariably inclement conditions.

Any assessment of the family's contribution to humanity will be made primarily on the basis of where one stands on the political spectrum, but few could argue that these family members were not motivated by genuine humanistic principles and joined the communist movement in order to fight for a better world. Evaluating their legacy is not straightforward and is obfuscated by the unavoidable historical identification of communists and communism with Stalinism and the Soviet Union, as well as unreconstructed Cold War attitudes.

One of the chief motivations for the Kuczynskis to espouse Marxism and communism was a basic belief in a rational, a scientific outlook, that life and indeed the universe can best be understood and mastered by means of science. Marxist politics was understood as akin to science, a rational approach to solving social problems. At the same time they saw science as being fundamentally on the side of progress: good science is progressive, and good progress is scientific. Ludi wrote that his mother Renate saw her brother's and father's scientific achievements (in the area of economic theory and analysis) as on a different plane, over and above any political accomplishments. She saw it, he suggests, as adding to a one-directional and timeless process rather than the minor impact that political contributions bring. Ludi himself grew up differently, he says, and came to see scientific achievements as more humdrum – anyone can manage that – whereas political achievements are a prerequisite for humans being able to make progress on a larger historical scale, and thus make full use of scientific discoveries. Such an assessment is undoubtedly open to challenge and in any case can only go some way in explaining the behaviour of individual family members, but it deserves reflection.

Robert's full-hearted engagement in campaigning on social issues and for peace while he was still living in Germany, as well as his pioneering work on demographics, set a high benchmark for his children to follow.

However, Jürgen's enormous academic output and the contribution he has made internationally to statistical and economic research has also been widely recognised. The part he played in Britain during the war, in organising and galvanising the German exile community as well as winning support from leading British figures for the anti-fascist struggle, was exemplary. He worked tirelessly and effectively to mobilise the widest possible opposition to Hitler. His subsequent role in the GDR, as a politically moderating figure and as a defender of academic principles, was significant. Whether he did enough or could have done more to promote democratic rights there is a question that will be continually debated, but few would deny that he played a generally positive role.

Ursula's main contribution – which propelled her to fame or notoriety, depending on one's perspective – was to make a significant contribution to the Soviet war effort and to the development of its atomic weapons programme. From a young age she threw herself into the anti-fascist struggle and was determined to do her utmost to prevent a fascist victory in Europe. Helping the Soviet Union as best she could, was, she felt, the best way of waging that struggle effectively. She did this while giving birth to and bringing up three children. Her courage and audacity were extraordinary.

In the years before she felt able to talk openly about her experiences as a secret agent, she did not have the high political profile or status that Jürgen had, so her ambit of influence was necessarily more restricted. Her contribution while in the GDR was made primarily in the literary field, through the books she wrote. Her courage and daring during the fascist period and her principled stand as a committed anti-fascist, expressed dramatically in her books, won her a significant readership in the GDR. Both she and Jürgen won respect and admiration for their support of the popular and peaceful demonstrations that led to the fall of the old SED regime. However, although both hoped that the country would then be given the opportunity of building a new and genuinely democratic socialism, the movers and shakers of history decided otherwise.

Their respective partners, Marguerite and Len, assumed subsidiary and largely supportive roles in their partnerships, although Marguerite was able to make significant, if small, contributions of her own to economic research. Len was one of those who had been willing to sacrifice their lives in defence of the Spanish republican government and the working people of Spain. If that battle had been successful, subsequent events in Europe and worldwide may have turned out very differently. He was lucky to return alive and relatively unscathed, but his experience in Spain did not deter him from once again risking his neck by carrying out secret surveillance work in Germany and providing information about Hitler's build-up for war.

The family's academic and research tradition has continued down the generations, passed from Robert to his son Jürgen, then through the latter's sons, Peter and Thomas, as well as Peter's partner, Ingrid, to Ursula's sons, Michael and Peter. In Britain, Renate and her partner Arthur carried out research in very different fields, but their son Ludi returned to the family tradition, becoming a leading demographer.

Ursula's son Peter studied biology and philosophy. He completed his doctorate in biology then began working at the *Akademie der Wissenschaften* (Academy of Science) on philosophical issues in biology. After reunification the Academy was closed and of the roughly 800 social scientists who worked there, most lost their jobs, but less than a handful found employment with the then newly founded Max Planck Institute for the History of Science, and Peter was one of them. Today he is officially retired but is still carrying out research in his field.

Renate's son Ludi asks rhetorically how an individual's specific actions, whether heroic or mundane and lost to history, whether in a leadership position or as minor activist, become meaningful in society. Perhaps, he suggests, the answer lies in the fact that we can all attempt to be people who bring out the potential of our times.

In that sense, the British branch of the family certainly contributed on a continuous and selfless basis to the post-war political struggles in Britain, even though on a more modest scale than their two German-based siblings. Brigitte remained a reliable foot soldier in her local Communist Party branch, supporting campaigns for better housing, for rent regulation and for the stabilisation of the post-war peace settlement, as well as joining the movements calling for the banning of nuclear weapons. She and her second husband Jock Nicolson fought for trade union rights and for a better life for all working people in the country.

Barbara was active in the promotion of support and schooling for children with disabilities, while her husband Duncan made a useful contribution to the teaching of history through his work at the BBC and as a writer of children's books.

Sabine also campaigned in her locality on housing issues and the provision of local amenities, while her husband Frank Loeffler, through his legal work, defended those in need of legal support, whether they were being persecuted by colonial or dictatorial regimes, as well as the little people fighting evictions, despotic landlordism or discrimination of any sort.

Renate, like her other British-based sisters, was active in a number of local campaigns for adequate childcare, preventing railway closures and many more, as well as in a number of international solidarity organisations. During the war, as a mature student, she played an active role helping develop the National Union of Students into a more effective organisation and mobilising for the war effort. She would later make a vital contribution to our knowledge and understanding of higher education through her comparative research in several countries and her definitive study on the development of the Ph.D. in the United Kingdom. Her husband Arthur was a diligent and capable field worker and researcher in agronomy and fisheries, working for the British government and for the Food and Agriculture Organization of the United

Nations (FAO) over many years. He was also involved in justice campaigns and, for twenty years, was active in community groups in Essex and London.

All of the sisters and their families felt themselves to be ardent democrats, not least as a result of their experience of fascism and its impact on the lives of their extended family and millions of others in Europe. They would remain adamant advocates of democratic rights and social justice. How far such aims and aspirations were commensurate with being loyal members of the Communist Party for most of their lives (apart from Barbara and Duncan) can only be judged by history. Few, though, would deny that they were genuinely committed to the aims of social justice, peace and democracy in all that they did and said. They were also widely liked and respected by those who knew them, irrespective of their political persuasions.

The numerous MI5 files on them in connection with alleged spying and espionage activities categorise them as enemies or putative enemies of the United Kingdom. There is little doubt that they would have vehemently disputed this characterisation and seen it as an offensive smear. As refugees from German fascism they were not only extremely grateful to find a welcome in Britain, but they felt completely integrated and were proud to call themselves British citizens. They felt that their activities were very much part of the historical struggle that was ongoing, to strengthen democracy and human rights.

The struggle between the Soviet Union, together with the communist movement on one side, and the industrialised capitalist West on the other, has been widely interpreted as one between 'democracy and communist totalitarianism'. It could, though, and just as easily and perhaps more coherently, be viewed as a struggle between the ruling establishments of the capitalist world, determined to hang on to their power and privilege, and the aspirations of those committed to a world of social justice. That is undoubtedly the way the Kuczynskis saw it.

The overwhelming number of communists throughout the world formed their beliefs and convictions largely on the basis of the situation in their own, individual countries. They threw themselves into what they saw as the struggles for justice and equality and against an exploitive economic system. Some, Ursula among them, were prepared to become full-time agents, putting their lives on the line to serve the interests of the Soviet Union, which they saw as leading that struggle. Her parents and siblings did not go that far, but were still willing to provide what support they could to the Soviet Union, not in order to betray their adopted country, but simply to promote what they saw as progress in the world and the success of socialism.

The foremost role the Soviet Union played in confronting fascism and defeating Hitler clearly clouded many communists' ability to separate that achievement from Stalin's abuse of power and the crimes he and the Soviet government committed. Many were also unwilling and unprepared to renounce their earlier beliefs and change their loyalties; they clung desperately to the conviction that things would change for the better and that, given a breathing space, the Soviet-dominated world would loosen up and become increasingly more democratic, particularly once the advantages of a socialist system could be demonstrated convincingly. That was the dream.

Markus Wolf, the GDR's legendary chief of counter-intelligence and a friend of Ursula Kuczynski, in his reflective memoirs *In eigenem Auftrag* (1991), recognises the role he played and the responsibility he feels he must take for the state system that employed him. He wonders how the dream of a democratic socialist society went wrong. He, like the Kuczynskis and many others, was motivated in his work by primarily humanistic and egalitarian ideals. He wrote:

> Undoubtedly and justifiably, I am increasingly confronted with the question of whether that which I did, which I thought and began to do, was too tentative, too tame, too late [he refers here to his belated opposition to the ossification of the GDR state]. I ask myself the question what we – our generation and that of our parents – missed or did wrongly, despite honest effort, in our attempt to realise the good and noble ideals of our world outlook in those countries where many people, like us, believed in the coming of socialism ... Perhaps the recognition, that I have given support and must take responsibility for the whole system that was swept away by the people in a few weeks, lies particularly heavy on me for having remained in my post for such a long time. What use is the justification that one stood up in the last hour, while others still stayed silent.[1]

The Kuczynski family was unique in that a whole generation was involved and committed to the communist project. It could be argued that some of them were sucked into clandestine activities as a consequence of their unequivocal anti-fascist stance and belief in a socialist society, rather than as a deliberate and conscious aim from the outset. While many of those who were involved in espionage on both sides of the ideological divide will perhaps at some stage in their lives question the morality of what they did, as well as ask themselves how useful their work really was in terms of its positive impact on the historical process.

Although it has been largely overshadowed by the espionage discussion, the contribution that members of the family have made in the intellectual and political spheres should be remembered and celebrated. Succeeding generations of Kuczynskis, dispersed throughout the world, are continuing the family's political and intellectual tradition but in very different ways, outside the perimeter of what is left of the communist movement and of a Marxist view of the world, and certainly far from any involvement with clandestine activities. They live in and face a very different reality, but remain, overwhelmingly, socially progressive, engaged and humanist in outlook.

Those members of the Kuczynski family portrayed here – Robert and Berta and their children – are no longer alive, and the historical era in which they lived has come to an end, as has the confrontation between communism and capitalism and the bitter struggles against fascism in Europe. Arguing the end of that era is not to deny that there are still important struggles to be waged today, but the context has changed. They lived through a period in which those of a Jewish heritage played key roles in the communist movement, not only in Europe but in the USA, Latin America and South Africa. They were on the side of the victors in the battle against fascism, but on the side of the losers in the larger ideological struggle against capitalism and the attempt to build a better, socialist society; but that fact should not deter us from looking dispassionately at their contributions.

Note

1 Markus Wolf, *In eigenem Auftrag*, Schneekluth, 1991, p. 6.

BIBLIOGRAPHY

Aaronovitch, David, *Party Animals: My Family and Other Communists*, London, Cape, 2015.

Abendstern, Edelgard, *Frauen die Gefährlich Leben*, Knesebeck Verlag, 2010.

Andrew, C. and V. Mitrokhin, *The Mitrokhin Archive*, Penguin, 1999.

Blankenfeld, Janina, *Die Tochter bin Ich*, Berlin, Kinderbuchverlag, 1985.

Brinson, C. E., 'The creation of a free, independent and democratic Germany: The Free German movement in Britain, 1943–1945', in *Europe After Hitler: Exile Vision and Post-war Reality, Yearbook of the Research Centre for German and Austrian Exile Studies*, vol. 15, 2014, pp. 1–22.

Brinson, C. E. J., '"Very much a family affair": The Kuczynski family and British Intelligence', in Ian Wallace (ed.), *Voices from Exile: Essays in Honour of Hamish Ritchie*, Amsterdam, Brill Rodopi, 2015, pp. 1–19.

Brinson, Charmian and Richard Dove, *A Matter of Intelligence*, Manchester University Press, 2014.

Brockmann, Agnieszka, *Der Kuczynski-Nachlass in der Zentral- und Landesbibliothek Berlin*, Zentral- und Landesbibliothek Berlin, 2011.

Burke, David, *The Lawn Road Flats: Spies, Writers and Artists* (History of British Intelligence), London, Boydell Press, 2009.

Burke, David, *The Spy Who Came in from the Co-op: Melita Norwood and the Ending of Cold War Espionage* (History of British Intelligence), 2013.

CIA Library, 'The OSS and the London "Free Germans"', in Jonathan S. Gould, *Strange Bedfellows*. www.cia.gov/library/center-for-the-study-of-intelligence/csi-publications/csi-studies/studies/vol46no1/article03.html

Dorpalen, Renate, 'Your Faithfull Mürt' (unpublished manuscript), 2011.

Ehrenburg, Ilya, *Memoirs: 1921–1941*, World, 1964.

Fisher, Benjamin J., 'Farewell to Sonia, the spy who haunted Britain', *International Journal of Intelligence and Counterintellligence*, vol. 15, issue 1, 2002.

Foote, Alexander, *Handbook for Spies*, Coachwhip Publications, 2011.

Gorodetsky, Gabriel (ed.), *The Maisky Diaries*, Yale University Press, 2015.

Grimm, Thomas, *Freunde und Gute Bekannte: Gespraeche mit Thomas Grimm*, Schwarzkopf & Schwarzkopf, 1997.

Hamburger, Rudolf, *Zehn Jahre Lager*, Munich, Siedler Verlag, 2013.

Hartland, Michael, *The Third Betrayal*, London, Hodder & Stoughton, 1986.

Hartland, Michael, 'Sonia, the spy who haunted Britain', *Sunday Times*, 15 July 2000.

Hennessey, Thomas, *Spooks: The Unofficial History of MI5 From the First Atom Spy to 7/7: 1945–2009*. Amberley Publishing, 2009.

Hobsbawm, Eric, *Interesting Times: A Twentieth Century Life*, London, Pantheon Books, 2003.

Jeffreys-Jones, Rhodri, *In Spies we Trust: The Story of Western Intelligence*, Oxford University Press, 2013.

Joseph, Detlef, *Die DDR und die Juden: Eine kritische Untersuchung*, Verlag Das Neue Leben, 2010.

Kalinowski, Burga, 'Bericht über Peter Beurton und seine Eltern' [Report on Peter Beurton and his parents], *Freitag* (Deutschland Radio), 17 August 2007.

Kant, Hermann, 'Gestern mit Ruth und Len: Erinnerungen an die Kundschafterin und Schriftstellerin Ruth Werner', in Rudolf Hempel (ed.), *Funksprüche an Sonja. Die Geschichte der Ruth Werner*, Berlin, Verlag Neues Leben, 2007.

Klein, Caroline and Eduard Kögel, *Made in China*, Deutsche Verlags-Anstalt, 2005.

Klemperer, Victor, *I Shall Bear Witness: The Diaries of Victor Klemperer 1933–41*, London, Weidenfeld & Nicolson, 1998.

Klemperer, Victor, *To the Bitter End: The Diaries of Victor Klemperer 1942–45*, London, Orion, 2000.

Knightly, Phillip, *The Second Oldest Profession: Spies and Spying in the Twentieth Century*, London, Pimlico, 2003.

Kögel, Eduard, *Die letzten 100 Jahre. Architektur in China*. In Gregor Jansen (ed.), *Totalstadt. Beijing case. High-speed Urbanisierung in China*, Cologne, 2006.

Kögel, Eduard, 'Zwei Poelzigschüler in der Emigration: Rudolf Hamburger und Richard Paulick zwischen Shanghai und Ost-Berlin (1930–1955)', Dissertation, Bauhaus-Universität Weimar, 2007.

Krockow, Graf von, *Die Deutschen in Ihrem Jahrhundert 1890–1990*, Rowohlt, 1990.

Kuczynski, Ingrid (ed.), *Löffel, Gabeln, Schleifen and Oloide: Schnitzarbeited von Peter Kuczynski*, self-published, Berlin, 2008.

Kuczynski, J., *Memoiren*, 4 vols, Berlin, Aufbau Verlag, 1981, 1998, 1994, 1999.

Kuczynski, J., *Die Erziehung des J.K. zum Kommunisten und Wissenschaftler: Memoiren vol. 1 (1907–45)*, Berlin, Aufbau Verlag, 1981.

Kuczynski, J., *Ein Linientreuer Dissident: Memoiren vol. 2 (1945–89)*, Berlin, Aufbau Verlag, 1999.

Kuczynski, Jürgen, *Ein Leben in der Wissenschaft der DDR*, Westfälisches Dampfboot, 1993.

Kuczynski, J., *Ein hoffnungsloser Fall von Optimismus? Memoiren vol. 3 (1989–94)* Berlin, Aufbau Verlag, 1994.

Kuczynski, J., *Geschichte des Alltags des deutschen Volkes* (5 vols), Papyrossa Verlag, 2000.

Kuczynski, J. and M. Kuczynski, *Der Fabrikarbeit in der amerikanischen Wirtshaft*, Leipzig, Hirschfeld, 1930.

Kuczynski, J. and M. Kuczynski, *Die Lage des deutschen Industrie-Arbeiters 1913/14 und 1924 bis 1930*, Berlin, Internationale Arbeiter-Verlag, 1931. (Also in *Zeitschrift für Nationalökonomie/Journal of Economics*, Springer, 1933.)

Kuczynski, Marguerite, *Bergarbeiterlohneinkommen im Ruhrgebiet*, Leipzig, Hirschfeld, 1930.

Kuczynski, M., 'German women against the Swastika', in *Women under the Swastika*, Free German League of Culture in Great Britain, 1942.

Kuczynski, Robert, *Arbeitslohn und Arbeitszeit in Europa und Amerika, 1870–1909*, Verlag von Julius Springer, 1913.

Kuczynski, Robert, *American Loans to Germany*, New York, Macmillan, 1927.

Kuczynski, Robert, *Fertility and Reproduction: Methods of Measuring the Balance of Births and Deaths*, New York, Falcon Press, 1932.

Kuczynski, Thomas, 'René Kuczynski: Radical, democrat, demographer', *Radical Statistics*, issue 112, 2015, pp. 70–75.

Lampalzer, Ute, *Marguerite Kuczynski (1904–1998)*, Zentral- und Landesbibliothek Berlin, 2013.

Lembke, Hans, *Die Schwarzen Schafe bei den Gradenwitz un Kuczynski: Zwei Berliner Familien im 19. und 20. Jahrhundert*. Berlin, Trafo Verlagsgruppe, 2008.

Linehan, Thomas, *British Fascism, 1918–39: Parties, Ideology and Culture*, Manchester Studies in Modern History, Manchester University Press, 2001.

Lownie, Andrew, *The Lives of Guy Burgess*, Hodder & Stoughton, 2015.

Moos, Merilyn, *Breaking the Silence: Voices of the British Children of Refugees from Nazism*, Lanham MD, Rowman and Littlefield, 2015.

Nicolson, Jock, *A Turbulent Life*, Glasgow, Praxis Press, 2009.

Nicolson, Jock, *Bridget and Me*, Unpublished commemorative biography, 1997.

Panitz, Eberhardt, *Geheimtreff Banbury: Wie die Atombombe zu den Russen kam*, Das Neue Berlin, 2003.

Persico, Joseph E., *Piercing the Reich*, New York, Viking Press, 1979.

Petersen, Jan, *Unsere Straße. Eine Chronik. Geschrieben im Herzen des faschistischen Deutschlands 1933/34*. [Our Street: A Chronicle. Writings from the Heart of Fascist Germany, 1933/34]. 1st edn, Dietz Verlag, Berlin, 1947. Previously published in the *Berner Tagwacht*, Bern, Switzerland, 1936.

Pincher, Chapman, *Treachery: Betrayals, Blunders and Cover-Ups: Six Decades of Espionage*, Mainstream Publishing, 2011.

Power, Mike, *Die Mauer ist Weg, Berlin ist Berlin*, Globtik Books, 2014.

Radó, Sándor, *Codename Dora*, New York, Time Life Education, 1990.

Roewer, Helmut, Stefan Schäfer and Matthias Uhl: *Lexikon der Geheimdienste im 20. Jahrhundert*, Munich, Herbig, 2003.

Rosa Luxemburg Foundation, *Creative Utopias*. www.rosaluxemburgstiftung.de/fileadmin/rls_uploads/pdfs/Utopie_kreativ/171/171_Kessler.pdf

Rossiter, Mike, *The Spy Who Changed the World*, Headline, 2014.

Rubenstein, Joshua, *The Last Days of Stalin*, Yale University Press, 2016.

Die Sammlung Kuczynski [The Kuczynski Collection]. Dir. Thomas Grimm (47 mins), Zeitzeugen TV GmbH/DEFA Stiftung/Zentral- und Landesbibliothek Berlin, 2005. This DVD provides an excellent introduction to the Kuczynski library by Jürgen Kuczynski himself, in the form of an interview he gave about his life.

Sheldon, Michael, *Graham Greene: The Man Within*, Heinemann, 1994.

Shenk, Timothy, *Maurice Dobb: Political Economist*, Palgrave Macmillan, 2013.

Simpson, Ludi, Simpson, Ann and Simpson, Amila, Unpublished commemorative booklets on Renate and Arthur Simpson's lives, as well as other family reminiscences. n.d.

Stibbe, Matthew, 'Jürgen Kuczynski and the search for a (non-existent) Western spy ring in the East German Communist Party in 1953', *Contemporary European History*, vol. 20, issue 1, 2011, pp. 61–79.

Stibbe, Matthew and Kevin McDermott (eds), *The 1989 Revolution in Central and Eastern Europe: From Communism to Pluralism*, Manchester University Press, 2013.

Tarrant, V. E., *The Red Orchestra: The Soviet Spy Network Inside Nazi Europe*, Cassell, 1995.

Trahair, R. C. S., *Encyclopedia of Cold War Espionage, Spies, and Secret Operations*, Enigma Books, 2012.

Vassiliev, Alexander, *Yellow Notebooks*, 1995. http://digitalarchive.wilsoncenter.org/collection/86/vassiliev-notebooks

Volkman, Ernest, *Spies: The Secret Agents Who Changed the Course of History*, New York, Wiley, 1994.

Werner, Ruth, *Ein Ungewöhnliches Mädchen*, Berlin, Verlag Neues Leben, 1959.

Werner, Ruth, *Sonya's Report*, London, Chatto & Windus, 1991.

Werner, Ruth, *Sonjas Rapport*, Berlin, Verlag Neues Leben (Eulenspiegel Verlagsgruppe), 2006. New, complete edition. (First published 1977).

Werner, Ruth, *Funksprüche an Sonja. Die Geschichte der Ruth Werner*, ed. Rudolf Hempel, Berlin, Verlag Neues Leben, 2007.

Williams, Robert Chadwell, *Klaus Fuchs, Atom Spy*, Cambridge MA, Harvard University Press, 1987.

Wilson, Ray and Ian Adams, *Special Branch, a History: 1883–2006*. Biteback Publishing, 2015.

Wolf, Markus, *In eigenem Auftrag*, Schneekluth, 1991.

Wright, Peter, *Spycatcher: The Candid Autobiography of a Senior Intelligence Officer*, Viking Penguin, 1987.

INDEX